7.95

12.264

STRATEGIC
MARKETING
FOR
EDUCATIONAL
INSTITUTIONS

STRATEGIC MARKETING FOR EDUCATIONAL INSTITUTIONS

PHILIP KOTLER
Northwestern University

KAREN F.A. FOX
The University of Santa Clara

PRENTICE-HALL, INC., Englewood Cliffs, New Jersey 07632

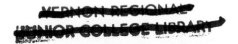

Library of Congress Cataloging in Publication Data

KOTLER, PHILIP.
  Strategic marketing for educational institutions.

  Includes bibliographies and index.
  1. Education—Marketing. 2. Public relations—
Schools. 3. Educational fund raising. 4. Educational
planning. I. Fox, Karen F. A. II. Title.
LB2806.K67 1985   370'.68'8   84-24766
ISBN 0-13-851403-8

Editorial/production supervision
  and interior design: Sonia Meyer
Cover design: Lundgren Graphics, Ltd.
Manufacturing buyer: Ed O'Dougherty

The following material is drawn from Philip Kotler,
Marketing for Nonprofit Organizations, 2nd edition
(Englewood Cliffs, N. J.: Prentice-Hall, 1982): Figures
2-3, 4-3, 6-2, 7-1, 8-1, 9-6, and 11-1; Tables 9-1 and
15-2; and portions of pages 34–44, 149–155, 198–203,
205–212, 220–221, 227–38, 248, 283–89, 297–303, 306–
7, 338–42, 358–62, 364–71.

Printed in the United States of America

10 9 8 7 6 5 4 3 2

ISBN 0-13-851403-8 01

Prentice-Hall International, Inc., *London*
Prentice-Hall of Australia Pty. Limited, *Sydney*
Editora Prentice-Hall do Brasil, Ltda., *Rio de Janeiro*
Prentice-Hall Canada Inc., *Toronto*
Prentice-Hall Hispanoamericana, S.A., *Mexico*
Prentice-Hall of India Private Limited, *New Delhi*
Prentice-Hall of Japan, Inc., *Tokyo*
Prentice-Hall of Southeast Asia Pte. Ltd., *Singapore*
Whitehall Books Limited, *Wellington, New Zealand*

THIS BOOK IS DEDICATED

To Milton and Neil Kotler,
who were my first students,
later my teachers,
and now my colleagues.

P. K.

To Sylvia and Karl Fox,
My parents and first teachers,
and to Bob Moffat.

K. F.

CONTENTS

PREFACE / xiii

part I
Understanding Marketing   1

chapter 1
EDUCATION AND MARKETING / 1

Problems facing educational institutions   What is marketing?
How are educational institutions using marketing today?   What is
a marketing orientation?   What benefits can marketing provide?
What concerns do educators have about marketing?   The plan of
this book   Summary   Notes

chapter 2
THE ELEMENTS OF MARKETING / 17

The core concepts of marketing   The marketing arena
The responsive institution   The institution's image
Summary   Notes

chapter 3
IDENTIFYING AND RESEARCHING MARKETING PROBLEMS / 47

Identifying marketing problems   The internal records system
The marketing intelligence system   The marketing research
system   The analytical marketing system   Summary   Notes

part II
Planning Marketing   70

chapter 4
THE MARKETING PLANNING PROCESS / 70

Strategic marketing planning   Steps in strategic planning
The format of a marketing plan   Marketing planning systems
Marketing control   Summary   Notes

chapter 5
ANALYZING THE ENVIRONMENT / 95

Institution/environment adaptation   Techniques for
environmental forecasting   Preparing an analysis of the
macroenvironment   Summary   Notes

chapter 6
DEFINING INSTITUTIONAL RESOURCES AND DIRECTION / 114

Assessing institutional resources   The goal-formulation process
Summary   Notes

chapter 7
FORMULATING MARKETING STRATEGY / 131

Evaluating current offerings   Identifying opportunities
Analyzing competition   Positioning   An example of strategy
formulation   Summary   Notes

part III
Understanding Markets 156

chapter 8
MARKET MEASUREMENT AND FORECASTING / 156

Defining the market   Measuring current market demand
Forecasting future market demand   Summary   Notes

chapter 9
SEGMENTING AND SELECTING MARKETS / 174

Market segmentation   Target marketing   Summary   Notes

chapter 10
UNDERSTANDING CONSUMERS / 195

Individual consumer behavior   Organization buyer behavior
Summary   Notes

part IV
Establishing the Marketing Mix 219

chapter 11
DESIGNING EDUCATIONAL PROGRAMS / 219

Product-mix decisions   Product-item decisions   New-program
development   The product life cycle   Summary   Notes

chapter 12
PRICING EDUCATIONAL PROGRAMS / 240

How consumers perceive price   Setting the pricing objectives
Choosing a pricing strategy   Setting the price   Effects of price
changes   Summary   Notes

chapter 13
MAKING EDUCATION AVAILABLE / 259

How have educational facilities been located?   How are
educational programs and services made available?   Decision
problems in distribution   Summary   Notes

chapter 14
COMMUNICATING WITH PUBLICS / 276

Planning effective communications   Public relations
The public relations process   Public relations tools
The effective communications program   Summary   Notes

chapter 15
ADVERTISING EDUCATIONAL PROGRAMS / 294

Set advertising objectives   Determine advertising budget
Decide on message   Select media   Evaluate advertising
Summary   Notes

part V
Applying Marketing   317

chapter 16
ATTRACTING AND RETAINING STUDENTS / 317

The student-recruitment process   Improving retention
Summary   Notes

chapter 17
ATTRACTING FINANCIAL SUPPORT / 351

Laying the groundwork for fund raising   Setting fund-raising
goals   Organizing for fund raising   Researching and
approaching donor markets   Coordinating fund-raising activities
Evaluating fund-raising effectiveness   Summary   Notes

part VI
Evaluating Marketing   378

chapter 18
EVALUATING MARKETING PERFORMANCE / 378

Marketing-effectiveness rating review   The marketing audit
Summary   Notes

INDEX / 391

PREFACE

In recent years, marketing has attracted the attention of college presidents, school principals, trustees, admissions and development officers, educational planners, public relations directors, faculty, and other educators. Many are interested in how marketing ideas might be relevant to the issues they face—such issues as attracting more and better students, increasing student satisfaction with the institution, designing excellent programs which carry out the institution's mission, and enlisting the financial support and enthusiasm of alumni and others.

This book addresses these and other marketing-related issues of educational institutions. As used in this book, marketing is the effective management by an institution of its exchange relations with its various markets and publics. All organizations operate in an environment of one or more markets and publics. A university operates in a student market, faculty market, donor market, and a public opinion market. Each market is made up of significant subgroups called market segments with particular needs, perceptions, and preferences. The institution has goals with respect to each significant market or market segment.

Through decades of working in business markets, marketers have formulated a conceptual system that yields systematic insights into the structure and dynamics of market exchanges. Concepts such as market segmentation, positioning, and marketing mix, among others, serve to organize the analysis of any marketing problem. The translation and application of these concepts to the problems of nonprofit organizations has already proven its value in a relatively short period of time.

The purpose of this book is to lay out the elements of marketing as they relate to educational institutions, and to demonstrate their application to educational settings. We want to acquaint educational administrators and other interested educators with the central ideas of marketing and with ways to apply them. Each chapter begins with an appropriate story that sets the theme of the chapter. All the examples we offer are drawn from educational institutions. Most chapters include exhibits of interesting developments and applications of marketing to education.

The book is divided into six parts. Part I, *Understanding Marketing*, explains the nature and relevance of marketing, and shows how marketing is involved in the institution's relationships with its constituencies. Part II, *Planning Marketing*, introduces the process by which institutions can develop strategic and operational plans, and illustrates each step, from environmental analysis to strategy formulation and implementation. Part III, *Understanding Markets*, presents ways to understand the institution's constituencies as a basis for serving them better. Part IV, *Establishing the Marketing Mix*, presents the steps in planning programs and services and in pricing, locating, scheduling, and communicating about them. Part V, *Applying Marketing*, illustrates how marketing applies to two core institutional tasks—attracting students and providing satisfaction so they remain, and attracting support from donors. Part VI, *Evaluating Marketing*, presents guidelines for evaluating the institution's marketing performance to assure that the institution continues to offer a valued educational service.

In writing this book we have benefited from the insights, encouragement, and assistance of many people:

At the University of Santa Clara: Daniel Saracino, Eugene Gerwe, Doris Herrick, James Kouzes, and Barbara Dabler. At Northwestern University: William I. Ihlanfeldt. At other institutions: Eugene Fram (Rochester Institute of Technology), Leslie A. Goldgehn (California State University, Hayward), Dennis Johnson (Johnson and Associates), John Kirkwood (Chicago Lung Association), Philip R. McDonald (Northeastern University), and John Vaccaro (The College Board).

We are also indebted to the following colleagues who reviewed the manuscript and provided suggestions: Richard Burke, National Catholic Education Association; Thomas Huddleston, Bradley University; John McGuire, Boston College; Joe Anne Adler, Lesley College; and Brent Knight, Triton College.

Nancy Allen provided invaluable assistance in locating information and checking the many details involved in drafting the manuscript. Her research skills and resourcefulness contributed to the process as well as to the final result. Donna Hunting ably coordinated the final steps of manuscript submission.

We are grateful to the fine staff at Prentice-Hall who made our manuscript into a finished book. We thank our editor, Elizabeth Classon, who directed this endeavor; Sonia Meyer, college production editor; and Rita DeVries, copy editor. We also thank John Connolly, formerly of Prentice-Hall, who first proposed this book and our collaboration on it.

We take special pleasure in presenting a book which addresses the key tasks of educational institutions. We have attended a number of schools and universities, served on the faculty of others, and consulted with educational institutions. We support the importance of their educational mission and we value the contribution they make to improving individual lives and society as a whole. We hope that this book will make a contribution to furthering the aims of education.

STRATEGIC MARKETING FOR EDUCATIONAL INSTITUTIONS

part I
Understanding Marketing

chapter 1
EDUCATION AND MARKETING

America's colleges and universities, once the passive processors of whatever applications came their way, have been forced by a shrinking pool of traditional students to turn to more active recruitment. The switch in tactics has led to a variety of new approaches to attracting students:

• Boston College has turned a relatively humble networking program into a pyramid of 3,000 alumni who contact virtually every candidate in the applicant pool, 600 students who visit their former high schools on vacation, and 100 faculty members who attend parent-student receptions organized by 90 separate councils around the country—all topped off by an enlarged staff of 28 admissions specialists. The new marketing strategy is responsible "in large measure" for effectively doubling the number of applications per year to Boston College over the past ten years.

• Business at one educational consulting firm has increased dramatically. The company's president estimates that 60 to 70 percent of colleges and universities are now involved in some type of marketing, up from roughly 25 percent five years ago—and up from virtually no such activity a decade ago. "The whole admissions profession has changed from that of gatekeeper to market analyst, enrollment specialist, and planner," says Joseph A. Merante, director of admissions and student aid at the University of Pittsburgh.

Historically, only after a student applied to a college did the wheels of the admissions office begin to turn. But the applicant process is no longer the first step. Now institutions are researching first, identifying the students they want, and then communicating with them—often on a one-to-one basis.

The reason for the interest in marketing is the decline in the number of college-age young people. The same number of colleges chasing fewer potential students has meant schools have had to scramble to maintain enrollment levels—or, in the case of some prestigious schools, to avoid lowering their high standards. Smith College chose to pare its freshman class by 10 percent in anticipation of the enrollment crunch. Officials at the school plan to keep total enrollment at previous levels by expanding exchange programs and increasing the number of older, nontraditional students.

In addition to marketing consultants, a number of schools are hiring new admissions and financial aid personnel with marketing backgrounds. Others are training admissions officers in marketing.

Many schools that have adopted marketing have experienced a marked improvement in their recruiting effectiveness. By targeting specific groups of students, for example, the University of Pittsburgh has increased its applications by 30 percent over the last five years—and the quality of students has risen also. An equally important outgrowth of the interest in marketing is that it forces a school to clarify just what it is trying to do as an institution and whom it wants to serve.

> **SOURCE:** Based on Craig Savoye, "Student Shortage Makes Colleges the Pursuers Instead of the Pursued," *The Christian Science Monitor*, August 29, 1983, p. 15. Reprinted by permission of *The Christian Science Monitor* © 1983. The Christian Science Publishing Society. All rights reserved.

As time passes, schools, colleges, universities, and other educational institutions increasingly recognize that they face marketing problems. Declines in prospective students, enrollment, donations, and other resources in the face of mounting costs remind them of their dependence on the marketplace they serve. Here are examples of problems facing seven types of educational institutions.

PROBLEMS FACING EDUCATIONAL INSTITUTIONS

Less Selective Four-Year Private Colleges

These colleges are typically small, tuition-dependent liberal arts colleges, with moderately selective or unselective admissions policies, limited state and federal support, and often strong church affiliations. This description fits approximately one-third of all the four-year colleges in the United States, about 500 institutions enrolling half a million students. These colleges provide less able and less well-prepared students with individual attention and opportunities for active participation in a cohesive atmosphere that most large insitutions cannot.

Many of the less selective four-year private colleges are concerned less with increasing admissions standards than with simply attracting enough students to keep operating. Their prospective students are often dependent on financial aid. When aid is in short supply, they enroll in public institutions. Between 70 and 90 percent of all faculty in such institutions are tenured, and this often limits responses to declining enrollment and slows needed curriculum change.[1] The increasingly urban minority population may be less interested in attending church-affiliated colleges in rural or small-town locations, preferring large metropolitan public institutions.

Selective Private Colleges and Universities

Selective private institutions are also affected by demographic and economic changes. Even the most prestigious private colleges have intensified their efforts to attract the best students, some by offering "no-need" scholarships to woo their top candidates. High costs have pushed up the annual tuition at some institutions to the price of a new car, with financial aid budgets straining to keep pace with student needs. Facing competition for students from lower-cost public institutions, private colleges and universities need to determine how they can create more value for students to warrant their selecting a private institution.

Research-oriented private universities face a dilemma in balancing an emphasis on research with students' expectations of strong teaching. Research at the expense of teaching risks losing students to smaller, student-centered institutions, whereas teaching at the expense of research may significantly alter the university's character and scholarly contribution.

State Colleges and Universities

Many state colleges and universities charge low or no tuition and get about half their budgets from state government. In times of recession, when state tax receipts drop and welfare rolls grow, state educational institutions suffer doubly. Students who might otherwise attend private institutions flock to lower-cost state schools, increasing enrollment just when legislatures are ordering budget cutbacks.

State institutions have responded to cutbacks by setting or raising tuition (as in California), merging state institutions to achieve some economies (as in Massachusetts), reducing faculty size (Michigan State), and raising admissions standards to reduce enrollment (the University of Tennessee at Knoxville). In some states, as many as one-third of the branches of the state higher-education system will be surplus in the next few years.[2] Many state institutions are emphasizing fund raising and corporate grantsmanship to reduce dependence on legislative appropriations.

Community Colleges

Established to determine and meet the educational needs of their communities, community colleges offer free or low-cost degree programs, vocational training, leisure courses, and other educational services. Although most are flourishing, some were built in the 1960s to accommodate population growth that never happened; these may be closed. Even community colleges with high demand are caught by budget squeezes and are raising fees to cover shortfalls. Some community colleges with "open-enrollment" policies are establishing admissions standards for the first time and suspending students who continue to fail courses.

Several trends are favorable for community colleges. More women are seeking higher education and many want to prepare for skilled jobs without a four-year college degree. Economic downturns tend to push students away from residential colleges and toward community colleges and the vocational programs they offer. The elderly, displaced workers or those needing retraining, and liberal-arts graduates seeking career training also look to the community college.

Private Grade and High Schools

Despite a dramatic drop in the number of school-age children, many private schools have flourished as the fortunes of public schools have declined. Parents critical of public school discipline and academic standards are fueling a resurgence of schools with religious sponsorship. In 1984, U.S. Catholic grade and high schools enrolled close to 3 million students. In the early 1980s, more than 7,000 Protestant fundamentalist schools were in operation, with new ones appearing at an estimated rate of three a day.[3] Total enrollment was estimated at 700,000, and many fundamentalist schools have waiting lists. These private schools are fortunate, but they should plan now to ensure their future performance: Some once-successful private schools face problems like those of private colleges—enrollment declines, financial pressure, and uncertain futures.

Public Schools

Many public school districts must deal with enrollment shifts and with pressures imposed by heightened public attention. Districts that closed elementary schools in the 1970s were closing high schools in the early 1980s. Widespread criticism of public schools—for low standards, weak curricula, and lax discipline—led to national studies calling for educational reform. This attention has influenced public attitudes: The 1984 Gallup Education Poll found that 42 percent of parents gave their community public schools a grade of "A" or "B," up from 31 percent a year earlier.[4] Another national poll found that three-quarters of parents rated their children's teachers excellent or good.[5] Yet teachers are abandoning the profession, complaining of low salaries, budget cuts, declining community respect, and unwilling pupils.

In this climate of criticism and lowered funding, the public schools must cope with rising costs, as teachers with seniority (and higher salaries) stay on, and with mandates to serve the educational needs of physically and emotionally handicapped, refugee, and bilingual children. Many districts have established differentiated curricula and schools, such as "basic schools" emphasizing the three Rs, to meet parental demands. Reduced tax support has forced school districts to drop curricular offerings—often advanced foreign language classes, art, music, and sports—and summer-school programs. In response, public school districts in several states have established nonprofit educational foundations that solicit donations to support public school programs.[6]

Other Organizations with an Educational Mission

Many religious, cultural, and health organizations also have education as one of their purposes. Many churches and synagogues offer extensive educational programs for members, from general-interest community programs to specialized religious education. Hospitals are launching fitness and stress-management programs for employees and local residents. These and other groups are seeking more participants and the funding necessary to carry out their programs.

From these examples we can see that a variety of educational institutions face marketing problems. Many face changing student needs and societal expectations, increasing competition for scarce client and funding resources, and unabating financial pressures. Board members, legislators, and community groups are putting tough questions to educational administrators about their institutions' mission, opportunities, and strategies. One result is that educators are often forced to take a hard look at marketing to see what this discipline might offer to keep their institutions viable and relevant.

At the same time, many educators are approaching marketing with caution. Although educational administrators have readily adopted such business functions as finance, accounting, planning, and public relations, they have been more skeptical about marketing. Marketing has the image of being primarily a function for profit-making enterprises. Educational administrators worry that marketing is manipulative and expensive, and that their boards will feel uncomfortable. Some administrators approach marketing with a "show-me" attitude. The burden of proof of the relevance of marketing falls to the marketer.

In this chapter, we address the following questions that educational administrators ask about marketing:

1. What is marketing?
2. How are educational institutions using marketing today?
3. What is a marketing orientation?
4. What benefits does marketing provide?
5. What concerns do educators have about marketing?

We conclude the chapter with an overview of the book.

WHAT IS MARKETING?

What does the term *marketing* mean? This question was recently put to 300 educational administrators whose colleges were facing declining enrollments, spiraling costs, and rising tuition.[7] Sixty-one percent said they viewed marketing as a combination of *selling*, *advertising*, and *public relations*. Another 28 percent said that it was only one of these three activities. Only a few percent knew that marketing had something to do with *needs assessment*, *marketing research*, *product development*, *pricing*, and *distribution*.

Most people think marketing is synonymous with selling and promotion. No wonder, since Americans are bombarded with television and radio commercials, "junk" mail, newspaper ads, and sales calls. Someone is always trying to sell something. Therefore, most administrators are surprised to learn that selling is not the most important part of marketing! When an institution offers appropriate products and services and prices, distributes and promotes them effectively, the products and services sell easily. "Hard selling" will be unnecessary. Peter Drucker, a leading management theorist, wrote, "The aim of marketing is to make selling superfluous."[8]

Marketing is a central activity of modern institutions, growing out of their quest to effectively serve some area of human need. To survive and succeed, institutions must know their markets; attract sufficient resources; convert these resources into appropriate programs, services, and ideas; and effectively distribute them to various consuming publics. These tasks are carried on in a framework of voluntary action by all the parties. The modern institution relies mainly on offering and exchanging values with different parties to elicit their cooperation and thus to achieve the institution's goals.

The concept of exchange is central to marketing. Through exchanges, social units—individuals, small groups, institutions, whole nations—attain the inputs they need. By offering something attractive, they acquire what they need in return. Since both parties agree to the exchange, both see themselves as better off after the exchange.

A professional marketer is skilled at *understanding, planning, and managing exchanges.* The marketer knows how to research and understand the needs of the other party; to design a valued offering to meet these needs; to communicate the offer effectively; and to present it at the right time and place. Here is our definition of *marketing*:

> Marketing is the analysis, planning, implementation, and control of carefully formulated programs designed to bring about voluntary exchanges of values with target markets to achieve institutional objectives. Marketing involves designing the institution's offerings to meet the target markets' needs and desires, and using effective pricing, communication, and distribution to inform, motivate, and service the markets.

Several things should be noted about this definition of marketing. First, marketing is defined as a managerial process involving analysis, planning, implementation, and control. This definition emphasizes the role of marketing in helping administrators face very practical marketing problems.

Second, marketing manifests itself in carefully formulated programs, not just random actions. Effective marketing activity depends upon thorough advance planning.

Third, marketing seeks to bring about voluntary exchanges of values. Marketers seek a response from another party by formulating a bundle of benefits sufficiently attractive to the target market to produce a voluntary exchange. Thus, a college that is seeking students will offer a strong academic program, financial aid, jobs, and other benefits to those who choose to attend.

Fourth, marketing means the selection of target markets rather than an attempt to be all things to all people. Marketers routinely distinguish among possible market segments and decide which ones to serve on the basis of market potential, mission, or some other consideration.

Fifth, marketing helps institutions survive and prosper through serving their markets more effectively. Effective marketing planning requires that an institution be very specific about its objectives.

Sixth, marketing relies on designing the institution's offering in terms of the target market's needs and desires. Efforts to impose a program, service, or idea that is not matched to the market's needs or wants will fail. Effective marketing is client-oriented, not seller-oriented.

Seventh, marketing utilizes and blends a set of tools called the marketing mix—program design, pricing, communications, and distribution. Too often the public equates marketing with only one of its tools, such as advertising. But effective marketing requires an understanding of all the factors influencing buyer behavior. For example, a school may do no advertising and yet attract a large following because of its location or its reputation for effective teaching.

HOW ARE EDUCATIONAL INSTITUTIONS USING MARKETING TODAY?

Educational institutions vary in their use of modern marketing ideas. Some colleges and universities are beginning to actively apply marketing ideas, whereas many private schools are just becoming aware of what marketing has to offer. Public schools have generally not shown any interest in marketing, but they would like more public support nonetheless.

The point at which an educational institution turns toward marketing generally depends on the depth of its marketing problems. Institutions that enjoy a sellers' market, with an abundance of customers, tend to ignore or avoid marketing. Thus, colleges in the 1960s had their pick of students and were oblivious to marketing.

Institutions typically become aware of marketing when their market undergoes a change. When students, members, funds, or other needed resources get scarce or harder to attract, the institution gets concerned. If enrollment or donations decline or become volatile, or new competitors appear, or new consumer needs emerge, these institutions become receptive to possible solutions such as marketing. This began to happen to educational institutions in the 1970s.

Colleges—particularly four-year private colleges—have been particularly hard hit by population and economic trends. The annual number of high school graduates peaked at 3.2 million in 1977 and declined to 2.8 million in 1983, a decline that will continue through the 1980s. A decline in the proportion of high school seniors who choose to attend college could reduce the pool of potential students still further. Operating costs are rising, and potential students are increasingly resistant to high tuition at private institutions.

By their responses to these trends, college administrators can be divided into three groups. The first group is doing little or nothing. Either enrollment has not slipped, or, if it has, the administrators believe the decline is temporary or easily reversible. Many believe that marketing methods would be "unprofessional," and some believe that marketing would lower the stature and quality of higher education.

A second group has responded by increasing the budget of the admissions office, the college's "sales department." The admissions office hires more recruiters, issues more elaborate catalogs, and places ads in selected media. Some admissions offices have experimented with novel methods to increase their application and enrollment rates:

- The admissions staff of one college passed out promotional Frisbees to high-school students vacationing on the beaches of Fort Lauderdale during the annual Easter break.
- St. Joseph's College in Rensselaer, Indiana, increased freshman admissions 40 percent through advertising in *Seventeen* and on several Chicago and Indianapolis rock radio stations. The admissions office also planned to introduce tuition rebates for students who recruited new students, but this was canceled.
- Milligan College has offered a $50 rebate each semester to each student who recruits another student for the college. Both students must stay enrolled, and a student's total bonus cannot exceed his or her tuition.
- Brown Mackie College, a for-profit business college in Salina, Kansas, offered a "money-back guarantee"—a full tuition refund to any graduate who doesn't get a job offer within 120 days of graduation.

Colleges that rely on stepped-up promotion may create new problems. Aggressive promotion may anger the college's publics, especially faculty and alumni. Such promotional activities may turn off as many prospective students and their families as they turn on. Aggressive promotion can attract the wrong students to the college—students who drop out when the college does not match expectations. Finally, this approach can create the illusion that the college has undertaken a sufficient response to declining enrollment—an illusion that may slow down the needed work on "product improvement," the basis of all good marketing.

Marketing goes beyond attracting more applicants. Colleges may assume that if they only had enough students, their problems would go away. Yet they may also need to attract the goodwill and financial support of alumni, foundations, and other donors, a task that cannot be accomplished by promotion alone.

The third group of administrators works in a small but growing number of colleges that have undertaken a genuine marketing response. These institutions analyze their environment, markets, and competition; assess their existing strengths and weaknesses; and develop a clear sense of mission, target markets, and market positioning. By doing this, they hope to develop the capability to attract the students and other resources they want from their target markets. Few educational institutions fully embody the marketing approach. We draw our examples from a variety of schools, colleges, and other educational programs that have at least selected and implemented elements that help them respond more successfully to their markets.

WHAT IS A MARKETING ORIENTATION?

Many people think adding a marketing function means that the institution has adopted a marketing orientation. This could not be further from the truth. Most educational institutions have admissions offices, fund-raising programs, and alumni offices, and they may even include advertising and public-relations experts on their staffs. They are using some marketing tools, but they are not necessarily marketing-oriented. What distinguishes an institution with a marketing orientation?

Meeting Customers' Wants and Needs

A *marketing orientation* holds that the main task of the institution is to determine the needs and wants of target markets and to satisfy them through the design, communication, pricing, and delivery of appropriate and competitively viable programs and services.

An institution with a marketing orientation concentrates on satisfying the needs of its constituencies. These institutions recognize that efficiency and good programs and services are all means or results of satisfying target markets. Without satisfied target markets, institutions would soon find themselves "customerless" and tailspin into oblivion. The employees in a marketing-oriented institution work as a team to meet the needs of their specific target markets.

Satisfying target markets does not, however, mean that an educational institution ignores its mission and its distinctive competencies to provide whatever educational programs happen to be "hot" at the moment. Rather, the institution seeks out consumers who are or could be interested in its offerings and then adapts these offerings to make them as attractive as possible.

Serving the Long-Term Interests of Consumers and Society

Is meeting consumers' perceived needs and wants too narrow an objective for an educational institution? Probably so. First, students often have long-range needs that they do not yet perceive. Although students may say that they prefer to "take it easy," their longer-range interest may require not only a diploma but also real mastery of information and skills that the diploma stands for. The school or college must set the curriculum and standards that will ensure this. Education also serves the larger needs of society by preparing people to be productive and carry out their civic responsibilities.

Second, most educational institutions have multiple objectives. Students may view the school as a retail store whose function is to sell them what they want to purchase, but the school's mission is usually much broader. The mission statement of a church-supported college may emphasize academic excellence, educating the whole person, and deepening religious commitment; some students may prefer easy courses, multiple-choice exams, and sleeping in on Sunday morning. An educational institution must weigh the needs and preferences of students while preserving the institution's academic reputation and other institutional goals and commitments.

A growing number of marketers see their responsibility to take four factors into account in their marketing decison making: consumer needs, consumer wants, consumers' long-term interests, and the interests of society. This orientation can be called a *societal marketing orientation*:

> A *societal marketing orientation* holds that the main task of the institution is to determine the needs, wants, and interests of its consumers and to adapt the institution to deliver satisfactions that preserve or enhance the consumer's and society's well-being and long-term interests.

What a Marketing Orientation Is Not

Even though most educational institutions want to be responsive to the needs of their students and other constituencies, they often get sidetracked by their traditions and institutional culture. Instead of a *marketing* (or *societal marketing*) *orientation*, they may reflect a preoccupation with their product (a *product orientation*), with efficiency (a *production orientation*), or with pushing consumers to select the institution's current programs (a *selling orientation*). Here we shall describe each of these alternative orientations.

Product Orientation. Many schools strenuously resist modifying their offerings even (or particularly) when the purpose is to increase their appeal. Other institutions keep adding new courses and majors because faculty or administrators like them. In either case, such institutions show little concern for examining how the course content and teaching approaches are regarded by current students, employers, and others. This *product orientation* presumes that the school's major task is to offer programs that it believes are "good for" its clients. Although educational institutions should hold high standards of quality, they should periodically test their assumptions about the suitability and attractiveness of their programs.

Production Orientation. Research-oriented university faculty who have been insulated from dealing with students may balk at teaching needed remedial freshman courses. Administrators may prefer to maintain the same curriculum and course schedules year after year because the system is easy to run. They may focus their attention on "running a tight ship," even if human needs must be bent to meet the requirements of the production process. Administrators in some large universities act as though they are processing objects instead of serving people, showing little concern for the educational experiences of individual students. Marketers describe this as a *production orientation*, one based on the belief that the major task of an institution is to produce and distribute its programs and services as efficiently as possible. Striving to be efficient is worthwhile, but efficiency at the expense of failing to serve customers' wants and needs is misguided.

Selling Orientation. Some institutions believe that they can increase their market by increasing their selling effort. Rather than developing more attractive programs, they increase the budget for advertising, personal selling, sales promotion, and other demand-stimulating activities. A *selling orientation* assumes that the main task of an institution is to stimulate the interest of potential consumers in the institution's existing programs and services. Although these sales-oriented steps will usually produce more interest in the short run, selling effort alone will prove ineffective if more basic problems are ignored. Increasing the selling effort in no way implies that the school has adopted a marketing orientation that will generate more interest in the school in the long run.

Educational administrators may find elements of all five of these possible orientations in their institutions—marketing, societal marketing, product, production, and selling orientations. Each orientation has its place, but to implement a marketing (or societal marketing) orientation, an administrator must clearly differentiate the marketing orientation from those that emphasize only part of the task—production, product, and selling.

WHAT BENEFITS CAN MARKETING PROVIDE?

Institutions that understand marketing principles often achieve their objectives more effectively. In a free society, institutions depend upon voluntary exchanges to accomplish their objectives. They must attract resources, motivate employees, and find customers. Proper incentives can help stimulate these exchanges. Marketing is the applied science most concerned with managing exchanges effectively and efficiently, and it is relevant to educational institutions as well as to profit-making firms.

Marketing is designed to produce four principal benefits:

1. *Greater success in fulfilling the institution's mission.* Marketing provides tools for comparing what the institution is actually doing with its stated mission and goals. Careful analysis prepares the groundwork for programs to address the real problems. For example, analysis may indicate that few people are attracted to a school because its mission and resulting programs are too narrow. Knowing this, the administrators may decide either to increase public interest in the school's specific mission, or to continue to serve the smaller number of students who find its present mission and programs appealing. Marketing helps identify problems and plan responses that will help the institution fulfill its mission.

2. *Improved satisfaction of the institution's publics.* To succeed, institutions must somehow satisfy consumer needs. If the institution fails to develop satisfactory programs for its customers—students, donors, and others—the resulting bad word of mouth and client turnover will ultimately hurt it. Institutions that are insensitive to clients' needs and desires may find more apathy and lower morale. Such institutions ultimately find it difficult to attract new students and adequate alumni support. Marketing, in stressing the importance of measuring and satisfying consumer needs, tends to produce an improved level of client services and satisfaction.

3. *Improved attraction of marketing resources.* In striving to satisfy their customers, institutions must attract various resources, including students, employees, volunteers, donations, grants, and other support. Marketing provides a disciplined approach to improving the attraction of these needed resources.

4. *Improved efficiency in marketing activities.* Marketing emphasizes the rational management and coordination of program development, pricing, communication, and distribution. Many educational institutions make these decisions without considering their interrelationship, resulting in more cost for the given result. Even worse, uncoordinated marketing activities may completely miss the mark or turn away the very groups they were designed to attract. Since few educational institutions can afford to waste their resources, the administrator must achieve the maximum efficiency and effectiveness in marketing activities. An understanding of marketing can help in this task.

WHAT CONCERNS DO EDUCATORS HAVE ABOUT MARKETING?

For many people, modern marketing carries negative connotations dating back to Plato, Aristotle, Aquinas, and other early philosophers who considered merchants unproductive and acquisitive. In modern times, marketers are accused of getting people to buy things they do not want or need, even things they cannot afford. Customers are seen as victims of high-pressure and sometimes deceptive selling. Educational administrators, unfamiliar with marketing, sometimes question marketing's usefulness and appropriateness for education.

Criticisms of Marketing

Some educators abhor the idea of marketing; others are interested but feel that marketing must be introduced cautiously. Two main criticisms may arise:

1. *Marketing is incompatible with the educational mission.* Some administrators, trustees, faculty, and alumni believe that marketing is for profit-making businesses, and that educational institutions should be "above" marketing. They feel that educational values and techniques are direct opposites of the values and techniques of business and that the two worlds cannot and should not be brought closer together. In their view, the purpose of education is to impart knowledge, analytical skills, and habits of reflection and rationality, whereas the purpose of marketing—and of business in general—is simply to make money. They view marketing as "hard selling" and believe it cheapens education and the educational institutions that use it.

Ironically, most educational institutions engage in marketing whether they realize it or not. Consider a typical private college. The college has an *admissions office* whose staff visits high schools and seeks to attract the best students. The college's *development office* assiduously cultivates wealthy alumni in a search for the large gift. The college's *public relations* people busy themselves with editors and community organizations to disseminate favorable news and impressions about the college. The *dean of students* directs academic and personal counseling programs and runs extracurricular activities to increase students' satisfaction with the college. The *alumni office* maintains contacts with graduates and provides activities and information to enlist their support. These and other administrators, faculty, and staff have the responsibility of sensing, serving, and satisfying different markets, although if asked, they may deny that they are engaged in marketing.

2. *Marketing should not be needed.* Even when administrators of educational institutions accept the usefulness of marketing, they may believe that marketing should be unnecessary. Administrators, board members, and others often feel that people should want the educational experiences and services the school has to offer. After all, they reason, people "know what is good for them," and education is good for people.

Administrators of publicly supported schools are shocked when legislatures cut their budgets and voters turn down school bond issues. They may wonder why parents are pulling their children out of public schools and willingly paying to send them to private schools. Private-school administrators may wonder why alumni aren't more active in school affairs and why donations have dropped off.

An institution that understands its markets realizes that people's attitudes and preferences change. Rather than presuming that it will always hold the pride of place once afforded to it, the institution carries out marketing research in order to continue to satisfy its markets.

THE PLAN OF THIS BOOK

This book presents marketing concepts and tools that are directly relevant to applying marketing in schools, colleges, universities, and other educational institutions. Although some terminology may be new, all the examples are from educational institutions. The aim is to illustrate each marketing concept and tool and to demonstrate how each can be used.

The book is divided into six parts. The topics are carefully sequenced to provide the reader with a cumulative understanding of marketing and an ability to apply these ideas directly to educational institutions. Most readers will be best served by reading the chapters in the sequence presented.

Part I, Understanding Marketing, presents the basic marketing concepts—exchange, needs, and wants—and shows how these apply to the institution's relationships with its publics and markets and to the images they hold of the institution. We present frameworks for identifying marketing problems and for conducting research to understand the dimensions of these problems.

Part II, Planning Marketing, introduces the process by which the institution develops strategic and operational plans. To plan successfully, the institution needs to understand its internal and external environments, assess its tangible and intangible resources, and formulate its mission, goals, and objectives. These steps precede strategy formulation, determining where the institution should focus its efforts and what organizational changes will be needed to support the strategic plan.

Part III, Understanding Markets, describes the ways marketers determine the actual and potential market size, segment the total possible market into market segments, and select those markets that the institution can best serve. After selecting target markets, the institution will seek to understand how consumers decide what programs and services they want.

Part IV, Establishing the Marketing Mix, presents the steps in planning programs and services and in pricing, locating, scheduling, and communicating about them.

Part V, Applying Marketing, illustrates how marketing applies to the two core institutional issues—attracting students and providing satisfaction so they remain, and attracting support from donors.

Part VI, Evaluating Marketing, presents guidelines for evaluating the institution's marketing effectiveness to ensure that the institution remains responsive and relevant in the future.

SUMMARY

Marketing is of growing interest to schools, colleges, universities, and other educational institutions that face declining enrollment, rising costs, and an uncertain future. They realize their dependence on the marketplace and wonder how they can be more successful in attracting and serving their publics. Marketing is a management function that offers a framework and tools for doing this.

What is marketing? Marketing is more than the use of selling, advertising, and promotion to create or maintain demand. Marketing is the skill of planning and managing the institution's exchange relations with its various publics. Our definition is this: Marketing is the analysis, planning, implementation, and control of carefully formulated programs designed to bring about voluntary exchanges of values with target markets for the purpose of achieving institutional objectives. Marketing involves the institution in studying the target market's needs, designing appropriate programs and services, and using effective pricing, communication, and distribution to inform, motivate, and serve the market.

Marketing has its critics as well as its advocates. Some educators feel that marketing is incompatible with the educational mission and cheapens education and the institutions that use it. Even if marketing could be useful, they feel, it would be unnecessary if people only recognized that education was "good for them." Its advocates say that marketing actually helps the institution to carry out its educational mission by increasing the satisfaction it offers its target markets. Marketing helps the institution to develop viable programs and to price, communicate, and deliver them effectively.

NOTES

[1] Charles E.P. Simmons, "Private Colleges to the Barricades," *Liberal Education*, December 1975, p. 447.

[2] Ian R. Stewart and Donald G. Dickason, "Hard Times Ahead," *American Demographics*, June 1979, p. 20.

[3] *Newsweek*, April 20, 1981, p. 68.

[4] George H. Gallup, "Gallup Poll of the Public's Attitudes toward the Public Schools," *Phi Delta Kappan*, September 1984, p. 25.

[5] *Newsweek*, April 27, 1981, p. 79.

[6] Patricia Clarke, "Beyond the Bake Sale: Saving Public Schools from Bankruptcy," *California Living Magazine, San Francisco Sunday Examiner and Chronicle*, December 12, 1982, p. 10.

[7] Patrick E. Murphy and Richard A. McGarrity, "Marketing Universities: A Survey of Student Recruiting Activities," *College and University*, Spring 1978, pp. 249–61.

[8] Peter F. Drucker, *Management: Tasks, Responsibilities, Practices* (New York: Harper & Row, 1973), pp. 64–65.

chapter 2

THE ELEMENTS
OF MARKETING

Dealing with a college's many publics is a large part of the president's job. Foundations are particularly important, since they have the resources to make substantial grants. A dozen new presidents of historically black colleges recently met with a like number of foundation executives to discuss how to foster a relationship that would benefit both parties.

"We came to the realization that a high number of black college presidents are new," said Henry Halsted, vice president of the Johnson Foundation, which helped sponsor the conference. "This is a new generation and there is a special situation here. The presidents are at institutions with limited resources, so it helps to be more knowledgeable and sophisticated about grant making."

"On the other side," he added, "the foundation world has a lot to learn about this particular constituency. Race relations is a principal area of interest for foundations, and they have to look at places that make a difference. They have to open opportunities and open channels."

Black colleges also want to convey an up-to-date public image, emphasizing their traditions and their contributions to society:

• A two-page ad in *Business Week* shows four women dressed in 1880s styles, standing in front of a bank of modern computer tape drives. The caption says, "Spelman College has changed a lot since 1881. And it hasn't changed at all." Although the curriculum has changed over a century, Spelman still has the purpose it had in 1881—"to prepare black women for useful lives in the world." The ad includes the names of the 29 top corporate executives who form the Spelman College National Corporate Committee.

• The United Negro College Fund uses ads emphasizing the contribution of black colleges in training future doctors, teachers, and the other skilled graduates that America needs.

By establishing responsive relationships with their publics, these black colleges help ensure their continued success.

> **SOURCE:** Based on Charles S. Farrell, "Black Colleges and Foundations Try 'Hand-Holding,' " *The Chronicle of Higher Education,* January 18, 1984, p 3; and other sources.

To succeed, an educational institution must deal effectively with its many publics and generate a high level of satisfaction. The top administration of the institution usually carries particular responsibility for these areas. Clark Kerr, former president of the University of California at Berkeley, described the position this way:

> The university president in the United States is expected to be a friend of the students, a colleague of the faculty, a good fellow with the alumni, a sound administrator with the trustees, a good speaker with the public, an astute bargainer with the foundations and the federal agencies, a politician with the state legislature, . . . a persuasive diplomat with donors, (and) a champion of education generally. . . .[1]

Every college president wants to create a positive image for the institution, attract able students and provide a good education, hire well-qualified faculty and administrators, and enjoy the support of foundations, alumni, and other donors. In addition to top administrators, every person associated with the institution has a role in creating and maintaining positive relations with its publics.

Managing responsive relations is no small task, but the institution that does so reaps tremendous benefits. People who come in contact with the institution report high personal satisfaction:

- "My college was terrific—the faculty really cared about students and taught well."
- "This adult education class is the best I've ever taken."
- "Our local high school offers a quality program for both college prep and vocational students. Students get a good education here."

These publics become the best advertisements for the institution. Their goodwill and favorable word of mouth reaches others and makes it easy to attract and serve more people. Alumni take pride in the institution and are glad to contribute to its future success. The institution receives favorable attention from the news media, further spreading its story.

Unfortunately, some educational institutions are not very responsive to their students and publics. In some instances, the administration would like to be more responsive but lacks the resources or influence over employees. The budget may be insufficient to hire, train, and motivate good faculty and staff. Or administrators may lack the power to require employees to give good service, as when the employees are unionized or under civil service and cannot be disciplined or fired for being insensitive to students and others. One inner-city high school principal complained that his problem was not poor students but poor teachers, many of whom were "burned out" and uncooperative but could not be removed.

Other institutions are unresponsive simply because they are more concerned with other things than customer satisfaction. Some universities focus on research and treat undergraduate students as disturbances. As long as institutions exist by mandate (such as government agencies) or are without competition, they often behave bureaucratically toward their publics.

By contrast, responsive institutions realize that to attract students and other needed resources, they must offer programs and other benefits that their publics desire in exchange. The responsive institution takes steps to understand its publics and to improve the satisfaction it offers them. This satisfaction is ultimately reflected in the institution's public image.

In this chapter, we lay the groundwork for an understanding of marketing. The following topics are presented:

1. The concepts of wants, needs, demands, and exchange
2. The publics of an educational institution
3. The characteristics of a responsive institution and the nature of satisfaction
4. The institution's public image and how it is formed, measured, and modified

THE CORE CONCEPTS OF MARKETING

Marketing is a basic human activity by which people obtain what they need and want through creating and exchanging products, services, and other things of value with others. The underlying core concepts of marketing include *needs*, *wants*, and *demands*; and *exchange*. We will consider each in turn.

Needs, Wants, and Demands

The starting point for the discipline of marketing lies in human wants and needs. People need food, air, water, clothing, and shelter to survive. Beyond this, they have a strong desire for recreation, education, and other services. Given a choice, people have strong preferences for particular versions of basic goods and services.

A useful distinction can be drawn between *needs*, *wants*, and *demands*. *A human need is a state of felt deprivation of some basic satisfaction.* People require food, clothing, shelter, safety, belonging, esteem, and a few other things for survival. These needs are not created by their society or by marketers; they exist in the very texture of human biology and the human condition.

Human wants are desires for specific satisfiers of these deeper needs. A young American who wants to study medicine will start by enrolling in a college or university, rather than becoming an apprentice to a doctor. Within the same culture, individual wants will vary because of differences in life experience and tastes. One person may feel well educated and successful upon completing high school, whereas another strongly desires a Ph.D. from a prestige university.

As a society becomes more complex, the wants of its members expand. They are exposed to more objects, activities, and services, some of which arouse curiosity, interest, and desire. Producers strive to build desire for the things they produce. The surest way is to form a connection between a given object (or activity or service) and a person's preexisting needs, by presenting the object as satisfying one or more particular needs. Note that the marketer does not create the need but can shape the want. For example, formal education has been promoted as a way to get a good job, to develop competencies, and to broaden interests and become more mature. Human wants are continually being shaped and reshaped by social forces, technological innovation, and the desire for novelty and change.

Demands are wants for specific products or services that are backed up by an ability and willingness to buy them. Wants become demands when backed up by access to purchasing power. A person who wants to attend a private college must have or borrow the money, obtain a scholarship, or work to pay tuition. A school sponsoring a $200-a-plate dinner as a fund raiser must make sure that there are enough school supporters who want to attend and can make such a large donation.

Educational institutions sometimes confuse wants and needs. A vocational school may think the student needs a course in welding when the student really needs a job. That is, a school may get caught up in what it has to offer and miss the consumer's real concern. A school may offer students less (or more) than what they expect because the school doesn't understand their wants and needs. The student who finds another school that provides a better program will have a new want but the same need.

Institutions that focus on their existing programs and fail to understand underlying needs suffer from "marketing myopia."[2] They are so enamored of these programs that they lose sight of what their students, donors, and other publics need or will need in the future. Educational institutions that hold tightly to traditional programs often act as though students' needs and wants should never change. Or the alumni office may continue offering pregame barbecues when alumni want continuing education. Such institutions forget that what they have to offer must solve a consumer problem.

Exchange

The fact that people have needs and wants lays the groundwork for marketing. *Marketing exists when people decide to satisfy their needs and wants through exchange.*

Educational institutions are resource-dependent. Most schools and colleges depend on donations, tuition, and grants for financial support; students and other clients as recipients of the institution's services; and administrators, faculty, and staff as providers of the educational and other services for which the institution was founded. Without the ability to attract students, money, staff, faculty, facilities, and equipment, the institution would cease to exist. Dozens of private educational institutions have done so in the past few years alone.

Most educational institutions obtain the resources they need through exchange. *Exchange is the act of obtaining a desired product or benefit from someone by offering something in return.* The institution offers satisfactions—goods, services, or benefits—to its markets. In return, it receives needed resources—goods, services, students, volunteers, money, time, and energy. This exchange is shown in Figure 2-1. Each party to an exchange generally expects to be better off as a result of the exchange.

FIGURE 2-1   Institutional survival through exchange

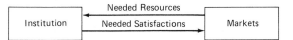

Analyzing Exchange Flows

A marketer interested in actualizing an exchange will make a careful analysis of what the other party wants and what the marketer might offer. Here is an example:

Suppose a college wants to encourage particularly able students to attend. The director of admissions collects the names of several hundred prospects. The director and the admissions staff screen the prospects according to pre-determined criteria of what the college wants.

The college is looking for students who scored above 1200 on the SAT, who seek a small liberal arts college and are likely to stay through graduation (not transfer), and who can pay all or most of their college expenses. The college may consider some of these wants more important than others and weight them accordingly.

To continue our example, we will focus on the case of one prospective student who is highly attractive on these criteria and who has contacted the college for information. A member of the admissions staff contacts the student to discuss what the college has to offer and, of equal importance, what the student wants in a college. The admissions representative finds out that the student wants an attractive campus where students are friendly and live on campus, he wants a strong mathematics department, and he wants to complete his bachelor's degree without piling up debts. Ideally, the admissions representative would try to determine the importance the student places on each of these wants.

The college needs to face the question, Can we make a good case to attract this student? If the college is an urban commuter campus, there may be little or no *exchange potential*. The college would have to offer the student much more of the other wants to try to compensate for its deficiencies.

On the other hand, suppose the college's characteristics match the student's wants and that there is a basis for a transaction. The college may extend the student an invitation to visit the campus for a tour and an interview with the director of admissions. The student tour guide may talk about how friendly the students are and show off the comfortable new dormitories. The director of admissions will emphasize the quality of the mathematics faculty and courses, and point to the career success of mathematics graduates. If the director is also impressed by the student's ability and motivation, the director will recommend acceptance and extend the student an offer of admission to the college, placement in the freshman honors math sequence, and a partial scholarship.

The prospective student might like the offer but ask for financial assistance to cover room and board. In turn, the director of admissions might be able to arrange a campus job to pay for room and board. This process of trying to find mutually agreeable terms is called *negotiation*. Negotiation can lead either to mutually acceptable terms of exchange or to a decision not to transact.

We have analyzed the exchange process from the perspective of two people, but others will usually be involved before the agreement is reached. The director of admissions will need to work with the financial aid office to approve offering a scholarship. The prospective student probably needs parental approval to attend the college.

Since actual decision situations often include more than two parties, the marketer needs to consider how other participants affect the exchange process. In this case, the parents want their son to attend a college that will be within 300 miles of home and where he could join a fraternity. At the same time, the parents want to feel proud to tell friends and associates that their son is attending a prestigious college. The college wants the parents to support their son's choice and to think well of the college. The prospective student wants his parents to feel he has made a good choice and to be willing to help him financially. The college must consider these various wants in designing an offer to attract the student.

This example illustrates exchange analysis in the context of attracting one honors student. Of course, the admissions office's task is to attract and enroll a whole class, not just one student. Attracting students is discussed at length in Chapter 16.

THE MARKETING ARENA

So far in this chapter, we have emphasized two points: Exchange provides a way for individuals and groups to meet their needs and wants, and analyzing exchanges helps us understand how to encourage transactions. In this section, we look at the arena in which educational institutions carry out exchanges. Figure 2-2 depicts the institution's:

- *Internal environment*, consisting of its internal publics; specifically, the board of trustees, administration, faculty, staff, and volunteers

FIGURE 2-2   Major components of an institution's marketing arena

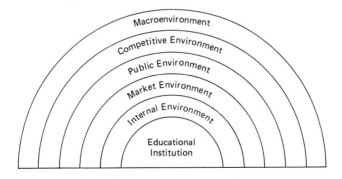

- *Market environment*, including students, donors, suppliers, and marketing intermediaries
- *Public environment*, consisting of local publics, activist publics, the general public, media publics, and accreditation and other regulatory groups
- *Competitive environment*, those groups and organizations that compete for the attention, participation, and loyalty of the institution's markets and publics
- *Macroenvironment*, the demographic, economic, ecological, technological, political, and social forces that affect the institution and its work

In this section, we will present the first three levels of the institution's marketing arena. (The competitive environment and the macroenvironment are discussed in later chapters.)

The Institution's Publics

Every educational institution has several publics, and the institution has to manage responsive relations with most or all of them. We define a *public* as follows:

> A public is a distinct group of people and/or organizations that has an actual or potential interest in and/or effect on an institution.

Figure 2-3 shows sixteen major publics, individuals, and groups that have an actual or potential interest in and/or effect on a university. We will discuss the most important ones here, beginning with the university's internal publics.

Administrators. The administration is responsible for running the institution. Reporting to the president are high-level administrators organized by function, product, market, and/or geographical area. Thus, reporting to a college president are administrators taking care of functions (such as the vice president for business), programs (such as the dean of the engineering school), and markets (such as the dean of students).

Board of Trustees. The president and other administrators are usually responsible to a board of trustees. The board's job is to oversee the institution and to make sure it is operating efficiently to realize its objectives.[3] Among the board's more important responsibilities are the following:

1. Selects or approves the chief officer of the institution.
2. Participates in setting or approving long-range strategy for the institution.
3. Develops or approves policies for the conduct of institutional affairs.
4. Develops or approves compensation levels and salaries of higher management.
5. Participates in fund raising.
6. Considers major issues that have come before the institution.
7. Adds members who are influential and can provide further contacts with other influentials.

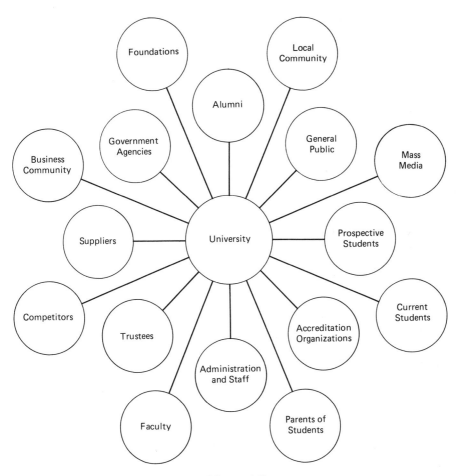

FIGURE 2-3   The university and its publics

8. Legitimizes the institution in the eyes of others.
9. Provides such specialized skills and advice as would come from lawyers and businesspeople.

Clearly, the board is an important part of the institution. Board members must be carefully selected. Most institutions seek "high-prestige" members, some seek "ordinary citizen" members, and others go after a mixture. Some boards are so involved in the institution that they are a major force in driving the institution to its best performance. They make demands on the administration to produce plans and results. They are a "whip" to the administration. Other boards are a drag on the institution. They are too conservative and reluctant to change. They remember the school as working a certain way and do not let it change with the times. Here is where administrators must market change to the board, get them "out of the dark ages," and this may require a marketing plan.

Faculty. The faculty consists of the skilled practitioners—professors, teachers, and other instructors—who deliver the institution's educational services to its consumers. At some schools, faculty members clearly understand and are fully committed to the institution's mission. In others, faculty may be at odds with the trustees and administration over the institutional mission and other issues. A school where professors are student-oriented is much more likely to attract and retain students than one where professors are cold and indifferent, all other things being equal. The school's trustees and administration need to work to enhance faculty commitment to the institution and its students.

Staff. The staff consists of the various nonfaculty employees who work on a paid basis. This could include middle management, secretaries, security officers, telephone operators, and so on.

The administration faces the normal problems of building an effective staff: defining job positions and responsibilities, recruiting qualifed people, training them, motivating them, compensating them, and evaluating them. Those employees who come in contact with consumers must be trained in a "customer-service" orientation.

Motivating the staff takes careful planning. The staff wants several things from the institution: adequate salaries, fair treatment, respect, recognition, and the feeling of working for a worthwhile enterprise. Managers must create these benefits if they expect to get in return solid work, high morale, and continuous support.

Volunteers. Volunteers are unpaid participants in the institution's work, often in fund raising and recruiting. In some educational institutions, volunteers also serve as tutors, instructors, or assistants to staff.

Volunteers often have a special commitment to the institution and its success. They may be alumni or parents of current students. They want to see others enjoy the benefits the institution offers. When the quality and reputation grow, alumni are proud and their commitment increases.

The competent volunteer staff manager will be skilled in identifying, attracting, and motivating good volunteers. Understanding the volunteer's needs, the manager will meet them in a way that draws their support and hard work. The institution will sponsor social functions for volunteers, confer awards for many years of service, and arrange other ways to recognize their contributions.

We turn now to two publics in the market environment.

Consumers. Educational institutions often have several sets of consumers and must distinguish these consumer groups and their relative importance. Consider the issue in relation to a state college. Who is the state college's primary consumer? Is it the students, because they consume the product? Is it the students' parents, who expect the college to transmit knowledge and ambition to their sons and daughters? Is it employers, who expect the college to produce people with marketable skills? Is it taxpayers, who expect the college to produce educated people? Or is it the college's alumni, who expect their alma mater to do notable things to make them proud?

Donors. Donors are those individuals and organizations that make gifts of money and other assets to the institution. Thus, a university's donors include alumni, friends of the university, foundations, corporations, and government agencies. The university development office has a professional fund-raising staff that develops a philosophy of fund raising and specific proposals that might excite potential donors. The staff tries to match the university's financial needs with appropriate donor groups. The university tries to build value in the eyes of its donors so that they can enjoy pride and other satisfactions from their relationship with the institution.

Educational institutions also attract the attention and interest of publics beyond the campus.

Local Publics. Every institution is physically located in one or more areas and comes in contact with local publics such as neighborhood residents and community organizations. These groups may take an active or passive interest in the school's activities. Thus, the residents surrounding a high school may be concerned about potential vandalism, parking congestion, and other things that may go with a large concentration of teenagers in the neighborhood. An educational institution often has a community-relations officer responsible for building cooperative relations with the community before potential conflict issues emerge.

Activist Publics. Educational institutions are increasingly being petitioned by consumer groups, environmental groups, minority organizations, and other interest groups for certain concessions or support. Some private universities have faced demands from environmental groups to limit construction of new facilities, from citizens' groups to be better community citizens, and from minority organizations to admit more minority students.

Attacking or ignoring demands of activist publics is shortsighted. Instead, the institution should intensify its efforts to stay in touch with those groups and to communicate its goals, activities, and intentions more effectively.

General Public. Members of the general public carry around images of the institution that affect their patronage and legislative support. The institution needs to monitor how it is seen by the public and to take concrete steps to improve its public image where it is weak.

Media Publics. Media publics include media companies that carry news, features, and editorial opinion—specifically, newspapers, magazines, and radio and television stations. Getting more and better coverage calls for an understanding of what the press is really interested in. The effective press-relations manager knows most of the editors in the major media and systematically cultivates a mutually beneficial relationship with them. The manager offers interesting news items, informational material, and quick access to top administration. In return, the media are likely to give the institution more and better coverage.

Clearly, an educational institution should take the interests of all its publics into account. Balancing the needs and demands of each group, however, is a demanding task. At times, the college will aim to increase its service to one group more than another. If the students complain about poor lectures and unavailable professors, then the administration will have to focus its energy on improving service to the students. This may require putting pressure on the professors to be more responsive to students. At other times, professors may complain that teaching loads are too heavy to get any research done, and the administration may seek additional money from alumni to finance lighter teaching loads. Most of the time, the administration is busy balancing and reconciling the interests of diverse groups rather than favoring one group all the time at the expense of the other groups.

So far, we have used the term *public* to describe each of the important groups that have an actual or potential interest in or effect on the institution. What, then, is the relationship between a public and a market? A public becomes a market when the institution decides it wishes to attract certain resources (participation, tuition, donations, and the like) from that public through offering a set of benefits in exchange. To be successful, the institution will strive to learn more about that public and to design an offer that will prompt the public-turned-market to engage in exchange.

THE RESPONSIVE INSTITUTION

Marketing calls for satisfying consumers by responding to their needs and wants. A *responsive educational institution* makes every effort to sense, serve, and satisfy the needs and wants of its consumers and publics within the constraints of its mission and its budget. Each institution should determine how responsive it can and wants to be and then implement programs to create this level of satisfaction.

Levels of Institutional Responsiveness

Educational institutions vary considerably in their level of responsiveness. Here we distinguish three levels, shown in Table 2-1 and described in the following paragraphs.

The Unresponsive Institution. Unresponsive institutions usually reflect a bureaucratic mentality. Bureaucracy is the tendency of institutions to routinize their operations, replace personal judgment with impersonal policies, specialize the job of every employee, create a rigid hierarchy of command, and convert

TABLE 2-1   Three levels of consumer-responsive institutions

	UNRESPONSIVE	CASUALLY RESPONSIVE	HIGHLY RESPONSIVE
Complaint system	No	Yes	Yes
Surveys of satisfaction	No	Yes	Yes
Surveys of needs and preferences	No	No	Yes
Customer-oriented personnel	No	No	Yes

the institution into an efficient machine.[4] Bureaucrats are not concerned with innovation, with problems outside their specific authority, with qualifying human factors. They will serve people as long as the people's problems fall within the limits of their jurisdiction. People's problems are defined in terms of how the bureaucratic institution is set up rather than having the institution set up to respond to people's problems.

This kind of educational institution often assumes that it knows what people need. Such overconfidence has been eroded by the realization that students now have many educational choices. The unresponsive educational institution is probably already out of business or on the way. Even public schools, which have little or no competition, are sensitive to the need for community support for bond issues and other funding.

The Casually Responsive Institution.   When American universities began to experience a decline in student applications in the early 1970s, they began to pay more attention to their students and publics. College administrators who had focused on the problems of hiring faculty, scheduling classes, and running efficient administrative services now began to listen more to the students. They left their doors open, made occasional surprise appearances in the student union, encouraged suggestions from students, and added student members to university committees. These steps moved the university into being casually responsive.

The result is a better feeling among the institution's consumers, building a partnership between the served and the serving. Whether or not the increased consumer satisfaction continues depends on whether the institution makes a show of listening or actually does something about what it hears. The institution may merely offer a semblance of openness and interest without intending to use the results in any way. If so, consumers will resent the institution and may try to force it into greater responsiveness.

The Highly Responsive Institution.   A highly responsive institution differs from a casually responsive institution in two additional ways: It not only surveys current consumer satisfaction but also researches unmet consumer needs and preferences to discover ways to improve its service. And it selects and trains its people to be consumer-minded.

Many educational institutions fall short of being highly responsive. Most rarely take formal surveys of their students' real needs and desires, nor do they encourage and train their faculty to be student-minded. Recently, a small liberal-arts college recognized this failing, and it developed the following philosophy to guide its professors. It said that the students are:

* The most important people on the campus; without them, there would be no need for the institution.
* Not cold enrollment statistics, but flesh-and-blood human beings with feelings and emotions like our own.
* Not dependent on us; rather, we are dependent on them.
* Not an interruption of our work, but the purpose of it; we are not doing them a favor by serving them—they are doing us a favor by giving us the opportunity to do so.

If this philosophy can be successfully implemented, the college will have moved a long way toward being highly responsive.

Creating a Market-Oriented Institution

A non-marketing-oriented institution cannot be transformed into a highly responsive market-oriented institution overnight. Installing the marketing concept calls for major commitments and changes in the institution. As noted by Edward S. McKay, a long-time marketing consultant:

> It may require drastic and upsetting changes in organization. It usually demands new approaches to planning. It may set in motion a series of appraisals that will disclose surprising weaknesses in performance, distressing needs for modification of operating practices, and unexpected gaps, conflicts, or obsolescence in basic policies. Without doubt, it will call for reorientation of business philosophy and for the reversal of some long-established attitudes. These changes will not be easy to implement. Objectives, obstacles, resistance, and deep-rooted habits will have to be overcome. Frequently, even difficult and painful restaffing programs are necessary before any real progress can be made in implementing the concept.[5]

Many educational institutions start by seeking marketing advice and expertise from outside advisors or from administrators or staff with marketing backgrounds. When the institution decides to become more market-oriented, it needs to develop a plan for institutional change. Achieving a marketing orientation calls for several measures, the sum of which will, it is hoped, produce a market-oriented institution within three to five years. These measures are described below.

Top Administration Support. An institution is not likely to develop a strong marketing orientation until its president believes in it, understands it, wants it, and wins the support of other high-level administrators for building this function. The president is the institution's highest "marketing executive" and has to create the climate for marketing. A university president, for example, must remind the faculty, registrar, housing director, and others of the importance of serving the students. By setting the tone that the institution must be service-minded and responsive, the president prepares the groundwork for introducing further changes later. Exhibit 2-1 presents one college president's memo on establishing a marketing orientation.

EXHIBIT 2-1   Memo from a college president on the need for a consumer orientation

As surely as there are "Fifty Ways to Leave Your Lover," as the popular song says, there are fifty ways and fifty reasons for a student to end his love affair with his college. Short-term campaigns to accommodate students meet the urgency of the moment, but do not build long-term goodwill. Some research indicates that students leave colleges not for big reasons, but for accumulations of little reasons that erode their justifications of college choice.

The problem is how to inculcate responsiveness, or "marketing consciousness," within the entire collegiate community, making everyone connected with the institution aware that (1) no one *has* to attend your college; (2) no one has to *remain* at your college; and (3) everyone wants to be treated with respect, and to be appreciated. In modern society, no service- or people-oriented establishment can prosper without a sense of responsiveness, a may-I-help-you approach on the part of all.

An educational institution has a responsibility to set a high example in valuing humankind. A surly clerk in the registrar's office, a defensive custodian, an irritable residence director, an abrasive secretary can easily undo in moments the goodwill created by the warm friendship of a professor or the congeniality of a dean. How may we heighten the marketing consciousness of the whole institution? How do we assure the student consumer that he is entitled to as much courtesy and kindness at his or her school as at the bank, airlines, clothing shop, grocery, and so on?

At the heart of a consumerist approach in any *service* industry is an adaptation of an old rule: Perform your service as if you were on the *receiving* point rather than the delivery point of the transaction. If teachers would teach as they would like to be taught, custodians cleaned as they would like their houses cleaned, questions were answered as we would want our own questions answered, the world would be happier, and the college would be a better place. In truth, marketing consciousness will have to be promoted (perhaps "marketed") within the college community.

   1. The president, as chief executive, will have to strike the official posture with an initial memo or position paper in which he makes it clear that: (a) students and all publics are due the utmost courtesy, consideration, and thoughtfulness; (b) temper tantrums, "telling people off," deviousness have no part in the academic

EXHIBIT 2-1 (continued)

setting; (c) this is not just a passive policy, but everyone should be constantly asking, How can I be of help? The clientele is the key to institutional good fortune, personal prosperity, and a clear conscience toward consumers and the society.

2. Since most institutions now use some sort of evaluative process, included among performance standards for personnel judgments could be the matter of marketing consciousness. How does the individual reflect the institution's commitment to a consumeristic approach? That standard then feeds into salary decisions just as do job skill, productivity, professional growth, and so on.

3. Short seminars and workshops for different classes of employees can point up the priority the college gives to marketing consciousness. The airlines and telephone companies have been very good at instilling this approach—I have never been treated with anything but the utmost courtesy and kindness by telephone operators and airline personnel. It would be worthwhile to assemble the custodians to say: Be responsive to student needs and requests; be looking for helpful things you can accomplish that may not be in your job desciption; see to it that leaky faucets get fixed, light bulbs replaced, trash bins emptied, spills cleaned. Offer short courses to secretaries and clerks in telephone manners and good reception techniques. Chances are there are resource persons on every campus who could provide such instruction.

4. Put a statement in the catalog declaring the college's intent. You may want to note that constraints of purpose, law, finances, propriety will not permit the institution to say "yes" to everything. But it is institutional intent to be responsive, consumeristic, courteous, and conscientious in all matters.

5. Place statements in the faculty handbook and in personnel policy manuals concerning the college's commitment to a high level of marketing consciousness.

6. Place squawk boxes in a few prominent places so that anyone who feels he's been dealt less than the minimum of human kindness may report the incident. A follow-up by the worker's supervisor will impress the point that the institution is serious about its commitment.

7. Encourage supervisory personnel to make a special effort to reward and compliment those who consistently go the extra mile, and who exhibit a heightened concern for the welfare of the clientele. Let the president write thank yous for exceptional courtesy and responsiveness. Word will spread.

8. If the institution publishes an internal newsletter, each issue could highlight a particular example of consumer concern: a faculty member's visit to the hospital bedside of a student recovering from an accident; a student providing a spontaneous campus tour in response to the request of a "walk-on" visiting alumnus; a secretary's detailed explanation of a complicated Bureau of Immigration form for the benefit of a befuddled international student.

Human kindness ought to be in generous supply among the humane personnel of the learning community. Such will also prove to reduce attrition and to be good for the institution.

SOURCE: Written by Thomas E. Corts, President, Samford University, Birmingham, Alabama, and included with his permission.

TABLE 2-2   Job description for a university director of marketing services

Position Title: Director of Marketing Services
Reports to: Vice President, University Relations
Scope: University-wide
Position Concept: The Director of Marketing Services is responsible for providing marketing guidance and services to university officers, school deans, department chairpersons, and other agents of the university.

Functions: The Director of Marketing Services will:

1. Contribute a marketing perspective to the deliberations of the top administration in their planning of the university's future
2. Prepare data that might be needed by any officer of the university on a particular market's size, segments, trends, and behavioral dynamics
3. Conduct studies of the needs, perceptions, preferences, and satisfactions of particular markets
4. Assist in the planning, promotion, and launching of new programs
5. Assist in the development of communication and promotion campaigns and materials
6. Analyze and advise on pricing questions
7. Appraise the workability of new academic proposals from a marketing point of view
8. Advise on new student recruitment
9. Advise on current student satisfaction
10. Advise on university fund raising

Responsibilities: The Director of Marketing Services will:

1. Contact individual officers and small groups at the university to explain services and to solicit problems
2. Prioritize the various requests for services according to their long-run effect, cost-saving potential, time requirements, ease of accomplishment, cost, and urgency
3. Select projects of high priority and set accomplishment goals for the year
4. Prepare a budget request to support the anticipated work
5. Prepare an annual report on the main accomplishments of the office

Major Liaisons: The Director of Marketing Services will:

1. Relate most closely with the president's office, admissions office, development office, planning office, and public relations department
2. Relate secondarily with the deans of various schools and chairpersons of various departments

Effective Organization Design. The president cannot do the whole marketing job. Eventually, a marketing manager must be added, either a marketing director or a marketing vice president. A marketing director essentially operates as a resource manager who takes responsibility for building and coordinating marketing resources and activities. Table 2-2 shows a job description for a university director of marketing services. In contrast, a marketing vice president participates in policy and strategy formulation at the highest levels, where he or she can influence other top administrators to take a market-oriented view of the institution's students and other publics.

Internal Marketing Training. The new marketing manager needs to make a series of presentations to introduce marketing to various groups in the institution. The first presentation should be for top administrators and trustees, since their understanding and support are essential if marketing is to "take" in the institution. Further presentations should be made to admissions, development, alumni-relations, and student-services personnel.

Marketing-Oriented Hiring Practices. Training can go only so far in inculcating the right attitudes in administrators, faculty, and other employees. If some of the faculty strongly prefer concentrating on research and dislike students and teaching, it may be hard to change their attitudes and behavior. The college can start to hire faculty who are more teaching- and student-oriented. The first principle in developing a caring faculty is to hire caring people. Some people are more naturally service-minded than others, and this can be a criterion for hiring. Periodic workshops on listening skills, advising, classroom presentation skills, and techniques for evaluating student learning can help faculty feel more confident in working with students.

New employees should go through a training program that emphasizes the importance of creating consumer satisfaction. They can be taught how to handle complaints and problems in a calm, helpful manner. Skills in listening and problem-solving would be part of the training.

Rewarding Market-Oriented Employees. One way to convince everyone of the importance of a market orientation is to cite those who have done an outstanding job of serving consumers. By the calling of attention to examples of commendable consumer-oriented performance, other employees may be motivated to emulate this behavior.

The Nature of Satisfaction

Responsive educational institutions aim to create satisfaction:

Satisfaction is a state a person experiences when a performance or outcome has fulfilled his or her expectations.

Thus, satisfaction is a function of the relative levels of expectation and perceived performance.

What determines whether the consumer is highly satisfied, somewhat satisfied, somewhat unsatisfied, or highly unsatisfied with a purchase, such as the decision to attend a particular school or college? There are two major theories.

Expectations-performance theory holds that a consumer's satisfaction is a function of the consumer's product expectations and the product's perceived performance.[6] If the product matches expectations, the consumer is *satisfied*; if it exceeds them, he or she is *highly satisfied*; if it falls short, he or she is *dissatisfied*. If a college fails to perform as the student was led to expect, the student will revise his or her attitude toward the college and may drop out, transfer, or bad-mouth the college. On the other hand, if the college meets expectations, the student will tend to be satisfied.

The other theory, *cognitive dissonance theory*, holds that almost every purchase leads to some postpurchase discomfort, and the issues are how much discomfort results and what the consumer will do about it. As stated by Festinger:

> When a person chooses between two or more alternatives, discomfort or dissonance will almost inevitably arise because of the person's knowledge that while the decision he has made has certain advantages, it also has some disadvantages. Dissonance arises after almost every decision, and further, the individual will invariably take steps to reduce this dissonance.[7]

Under this theory, we can expect a student to feel some postpurchase dissonance about a college choice. Problems with professors, other students, or housing are likely to stir doubts in the student's mind as to whether the right choice was made.

The dissonant consumer will seek ways to reduce the dissonance because of a drive in the human organism "to establish internal harmony, consistency, or congruity among his opinions, knowledge, and values."[8] Dissonant consumers will resort to one of two courses of action. They may try to reduce the dissonance by abandoning or returning the product (dropping out), or they may try to reduce the dissonance by seeking information that might confirm its high value (or by avoiding information that might disconfirm its high value).

The amount of dissatisfaction depends upon the person's method of handling the gap between expectations and performance. Some try to minimize the felt dissonance by seeing more performance than there really is or thinking that they set their expectations too high. A dissatisfied person will exaggerate the perceived performance gap. For example, consider two students enrolled in the same class, where the instructor always lectures, never allows time for questions, and is rarely available outside of class. One student may reduce the gap between expectations and performance by concluding (correctly or not) that the instructor is a very knowledgeable and busy person and that students should consider themselves lucky just to be able to take that class. The second student, in contrast, may be highly critical and may find fault with the instructor's performance in other ways as well. The second student will be more prone to drop the class or, if his or her response to other aspects of the school is also negative, to leave the school.

The school that overclaims is likely to create subsequent dissatisfaction. If a school underclaims, it may create high satisfaction among students and other publics; but by downplaying the benefits it offers, the school may discourage applications from those who would in fact be quite satisfied with the institution. The safest course is for the school to plan for and to deliver a certain level of performance and to communicate this level to its students and other publics.

Measuring Satisfaction

Satisfaction can be measured in several ways, including image studies, surveys, and panels, as well as indirect measures such as retention and continuing donations. Ways to assess the institution's image are presented in this chapter. Marketing-research techniques are discussed in Chapter 3, and ways to assess student satisfaction in Chapter 16. Here we will consider an additional measure of satisfaction, complaint, and suggestion systems.

A responsive institution will make it easy for its consumers and publics to complain if they are disappointed in some way with the service they have received. The administration will want complaints to surface for three reasons: First, a responsive institution will want to know when its students or other publics are dissatisfied; they are often the best—and the only—observers of certain aspects of the institution's performance. Second, the institution may need to make significant changes, and complaints and suggestions can help identify the most important areas for attention. To ignore or fail to ask for complaints or suggestions leaves the institution without this potentially valuable information. Third, some people will take the initiative and complain when they are dissatisfied, but others will simply bad-mouth the school, drop out, or stop donating if they feel the school is not interested in hearing about its failings.

How can complaints and suggestions be facilitated? The school can make it easy for dissatisfied (or satisfied) people to express their feelings. For example, it could place suggestion boxes in the corridors. It could survey students or other publics (discussed in more detail later). Once complaints are received, the school must have procedures for handling them speedily and equitably. The institution might establish an ombudsman system to hear serious grievances and seek remedies. In addition to satisfying individual complaints, the school should try to identify the major categories of complaints. For example, it might count the number of complaints about quality of instruction, dorm facilities, food, and other areas, and then rate the seriousness and remediability of complaints in each area. The school should focus its corrective actions on those categories showing a high frequency, high seriousness, and high remediability.

A good complaint-management system will provide much valuable information for improving the institution's performance. At the same time, a complaint system may not uncover the amount of real student dissatisfaction, since:

1. Many people who are disappointed may not complain, because they either feel too angry or believe that complaining would do no good. One study found that only 34 percent of a group of dissatisfied people said they would complain.
2. Some people overcomplain (the chronic complainers), and this introduces a bias into the data.

Some critics have argued that complaint systems do more harm than good. If people get an opportunity—indeed, an invitation—to complain, they are more likely to feel dissatisfied. Instead of having their disappointment ignored, they are asked to spell it out and are led to expect redress. If redress is not forthcoming, they will be more dissatisfied. Although this might happen, we believe that the value of the information gathered by soliciting complaints far exceeds the cost of possibly overstimulating dissatisfaction.

Balancing Consumer Satisfaction and Other Goals

The responsive institution strives to create a high level of satisfaction, although not necessarily the maximum level. Here are our reasons.

First, satisfaction can always be increased by accepting additional monetary or nonmonetary costs. Thus, a college might hire better-qualified faculty, build better facilities, and lower the tuition to increase student satisfaction. But obviously the college must operate within a budget and can provide only the satisfaction level it can afford, not necessarily the maximum level desired.

Second, the institution has to satisfy many publics. Increasing the satisfaction of one group might reduce the satisfaction of another. For example, a college needs to pay faculty acceptable salaries while holding tuition at a level students and their parents are willing and able to pay. The college must balance the needs and expectations of each group, providing acceptable levels of satisfaction within the constraints of the institution's total resources. Systematically measuring satisfaction provides a basis for assessing what each group expects and what level of satisfaction each is currently experiencing.

THE INSTITUTION'S IMAGE

A responsive institution has a strong interest in how its publics see the school and its programs and services, since people often respond to the institution's image, not necessarily its reality. Publics holding a negative image of a school will avoid or disparage it, even if the institution is of high quality, and those holding a positive image will be drawn to it. The same school will be viewed as responsive by some groups and unresponsive by other groups. People tend to form images of schools based on often limited and even inaccurate information, images that affect their likelihood of attending, recommending the school to a relative, donating, or joining the faculty or staff.

Every educational institution has a vital interest in learning about its "images" in the marketplace and making sure that these images accurately and favorably reflect the institution. Garvin summarizes the importance of reputation like this:

> An institution's actual quality is often less important than its prestige, or reputation for quality, because it is the university's perceived excellence which, in fact, guides the decisions of prospective students and scholars considering offers of employment, and federal agencies awarding grants.[9]

An institution's present image is usually based on its past record. Therefore, an institution cannot change its image through a quick change in public relations strategy. Its image is a function of its deeds and its communications. A strong favorable image comes about when the school performs well and generates real satisfaction, then lets others know about its success.

Educational administrators want to know the following things about image: (1) what image is; (2) how image is measured; (3) what factors contribute to image formation; (4) how image can be changed; and (5) the relationship between image and a person's behavior toward the object. These are discussed in the following sections.

Definition of Image

The term *image* came into popular use in the 1950s and is currently used in a variety of contexts: institutional image, corporate image, national image, brand image, public image, self-image, and so on. Its wide use has tended to blur its meanings. Our definition of *image* is as follows:

> An image is the sum of beliefs, ideas, and impressions that a person has of an object.

This definition enables us to distinguish an image from similar-sounding concepts such as *beliefs, attitudes,* and *stereotypes.*

An image is more than a simple belief. The belief that it is difficult to get admitted to Harvard University would be only one element in a large image that might be held about Harvard University. An image is a whole set of beliefs about an object.

On the other hand, people's images of an object do not necessarily reveal their attitudes toward that object. Two persons may hold the same image of Harvard and yet have different attitudes toward it. An attitude is a disposition toward an object that includes cognitive, affective, and behavioral components.

How does an image differ from a stereotype? A stereotype suggests a widely held image that is highly distorted and simplistic and that carries a favorable or unfavorable attitude toward the object. An image, on the other hand, is a more personal perception of an object that can vary greatly from person to person.

Image Measurement

Many methods have been proposed for measuring images. We will describe a two-step approach: first, measuring how familiar and favorable the institution's image is, and second, measuring the location of the institution's image along major relevant dimensions (called the semantic differential).

Familiarity–Favorability Measurement. The first step is to establish, for each public being studied, how familiar it is with the institution and how favorable it feels toward it. To establish familiarity, respondents are asked to check one of the following:

Never heard of	Heard of	Know a little bit	Know a fair amount	Know very well

The results indicate the public's awareness of the institution. If most of the respondents place it in the first two or three categories, then the institution has an awareness problem.

Those respondents who have some familiarity with the institution are then asked to describe how favorable they feel toward it by checking one of the following:

Very unfavorable	Somewhat unfavorable	Indifferent	Somewhat favorable	Very favorable

If most of the respondents check the first two or three categories, then the institution has a serious image problem.

To illustrate these scales, suppose that parents are asked to rate four local schools—A, B, C, and D. Their responses are averaged, and the results are displayed in Figure 2-4. School A has the strongest image: Most people know it and like it. School B is less familiar to most people, but those who know it like it. School C is negatively viewed by the people who know it, but fortunately, not too many people know it. School D is in the weakest position: It is seen as a weak school, and everyone knows it.

Clearly, each school faces a different task. School A must work at maintaining its good reputation and high community awareness. School B must bring itself to the attention of more parents, since those who know it find it to

FIGURE 2-4   Familiarity–favorability analysis

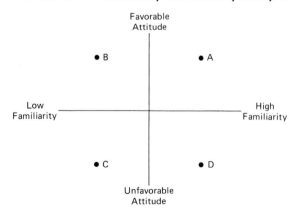

be a good school. School C needs to find out why people dislike it and take steps to improve, while keeping a low profile. School D would be well advised to lower its profile (avoid news), mend its ways, and, when it is a better school, start seeking public attention again.

Semantic Differential. Each school needs to go further and research the content of its image. One of the most popular tools for this is the *semantic differential*.[10] It involves the following steps:

1. *Developing a set of relevant dimensions.* The research first identifies the dimensions that people normally use to reflect the object. People could be asked, "What things do you think of when you consider a school?" If someone suggests "well-trained teachers," this would be turned into a bipolar adjective scale—say, "inferior teachers" at one end and "superior teachers" at the other. This could be rendered as a five- or seven-point scale. A set of relevant dimensions for a school is shown in Figure 2-5.

2. *Reducing the set of relevant dimensions.* The number of dimensions should be kept small so as to avoid respondent fatigue in having to rate *n* institutions on *m* scales. Osgood and his co-workers feel that there are essentially three types of scales:

- Evaluation scales (good–bad qualities)
- Potency scales (strong–weak qualities)
- Activity scales (active–passive qualities)

Using these scales as a guide, or performing a factor analysis, the researcher can remove scales that fail to add much information.

FIGURE 2-5   Images of three schools (semantic differentials)

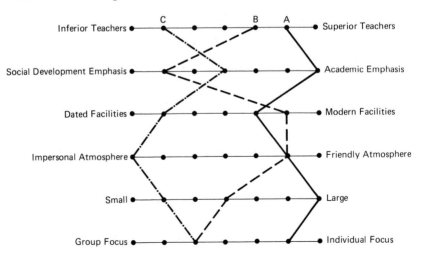

3. *Administering the instrument to a sample of respondents.* The respondents are asked to rate one institution at a time. The bipolar adjectives should be arranged so as not to load all the poor adjectives on one side.

4. *Averaging the results.* Figure 2-5 shows the results of averaging the respondents' pictures of schools A, B, and C. Each school's image is represented by a vertical "line of means" that summarizes how the average respondent sees that institution. Thus, school A is seen as a large, modern, friendly, and superior school; school C, on the other hand, is seen as small, impersonal, and inferior.

5. *Checking on the image variance.* Since each image profile is a line of means, it does not reveal how variable the image actually is. If there were 100 respondents, did they all see school B, for example, exactly as shown, or was there considerable variation? In the first case, we would say that the image is highly *specific*, and in the second case that the image is highly *diffused*. An institution may or may not want a very specific image. Some institutions prefer a diffused image so that different groups can project their needs into this institution. The institution will want to analyze whether a variable image is really the result of different subgroups rating it, with each subgroup having a different but highly specific image.

The semantic differential is a flexible image-measuring tool that can provide the following useful information:

1. *The institution can discover how a particular public views it and its major competitors.* It can learn its image strengths and weaknesses along with those of its competitors and take remedial steps that may be warranted.

2. *The institution can discover how different publics and market segments view it.* Suppose the image profiles in Figure 2-5 represented the images of one school held by three different publics (rather than three different schools evaluated by one public). The school would then consider taking steps to improve its image among those publics who view it most unfavorably or among those publics whose image is likely to have the most influence on the school's effectiveness.

3. *The institution can monitor changes in its image over time.* By repeating the image study periodically, the institution can detect any significant image slippage or improvement. Image slippage signals that the institution is doing something wrong. Image improvement, on the other hand, verifies that it is performing better as a result of some steps it has taken.

Image Causation

What determines the image that a person holds of an object? A theory of image determinants would help the institution to understand the factors that have caused its present image and to understand how to produce a change.

There are two opposite theories of image formation. One holds that image is largely *object-determined*—that is, people are simply perceiving the reality of the object. If a school is located next to a lake and surrounded by beautiful trees, then it is going to strike people as a beautiful school. A few people might describe it as ugly, but this would be dismissed as the peculiarity of certain individuals or their lack of real experience with the object. The object-determined view of images assumes that (1) people tend to have firsthand experience with objects; (2) people get reliable sensory data from the object; and (3) people tend to process the sensory data in a similar way in spite of having different backgrounds and personalities. These assumptions in turn imply that institutions cannot easily create false images of themselves.

The other theory holds that images are largely *person-determined*. Those holding this view argue that (1) people have different degrees of contact with the object; (2) people placed in front of the object will selectively perceive different aspects of the object; (3) people have individual ways of processing sensory data leading to selective distortion. For these reasons, it is held that people are likely to hold quite different images of the object—that is, that there is a weak relation between the image and the actual object.

The truth lies somewhere in between. In other words, an image is influenced by both the objective characteristics of the object and the subjective characteristics of the perceiver. We might expect people to hold rather similar images of a given object mainly under the following conditions: when the object is simple rather than complex; when it is frequently and directly experienced; and when it is fairly stable in its real characteristics over time. Conversely, people may hold quite different images of an object if it is complex, infrequently experienced, and changing through time.

Image Modification

The administrators of an educational institution are often surprised and disturbed by the measured image. Thus, the principal of school C (see Figure 2-5) might be upset that the public sees the school as dated, impersonal, and of low quality. The administrator's immediate reaction is to disbelieve the results by complaining that the sample is too small or unrepresentative. But if the results can be defended as reliable, the administrator must consider what ought to be done about this image problem.

The first step is for the school's administrators and board to develop a picture of a *desired image* that they want to have in the general public's mind, in contrast to the *current image*. Suppose school C would like the public to have a more favorable view of the quality of its teachers, facilities, friendliness, and so on (shown in Figure 2-6 as the desired image). It is not aiming for perfection, because the school recognizes its limitations. The desired image must be feasible in terms of the school's present reality and resources.

The second step is for the school to decide which image gaps it wants to work on initially. Is it more desirable to improve the school's image of friend-

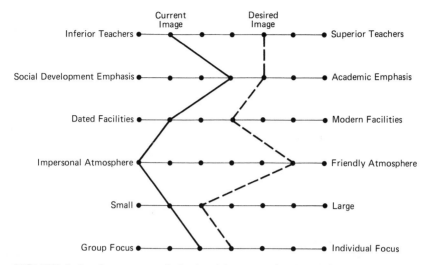

FIGURE 2-6   Current and desired image of school C

liness (through programs for parents, staff training, and so on) or the look of its facilities (through renovation)? Each image dimension should be separately reviewed in terms of the following questions:

1. What contribution to the school's overall favorable image would be made by closing that particular image gap to the extent shown?
2. What strategy (combination of real changes and communication changes) would be used to close the particular image gap?
3. What would be the cost of closing that image gap?
4. How long would it take to close that image gap?

For example, management might decide that it would be more effective and less costly to improve the school's image of friendliness than to improve its physical facilities. An overall image-modification plan would involve planning the sequence of steps through which the school would go to transform its current image into its desired image.

An institution seeking to change its image must have great patience. Images tend to be "sticky" and last long after the reality of the institution has changed. Thus, the quality of teachers might have deteriorated at a well-known school, and yet it continues to be highly regarded in the public mind. Image persistence is explained by the fact that once people have a certain image of an object, they tend to be selective perceivers of further data. Their perceptions are oriented toward seeing what they expect to see. It will take highly disconfirming stimuli to raise doubts and open them to new information. An image can enjoy a life of its own for a while, especially when people are not likely to have new firsthand experiences with the changed object.

The Relation Between Image and Behavior

Institutions are interested in image measurement and modification because they assume that there is a close relationship between the public's image of the institution and the public's behavior toward it. The institution feels that it can obtain better public response by acquiring a better image.

Unfortunately, the connection between image and behavior is not as close as many schools and colleges believe. Images are only one component of attitudes. Two people may view a school as small and yet have opposite attitudes toward a small school. Furthermore, the connection between attitudes and behavior is also tenuous. Parents might prefer a small school to a large one and yet end up enrolling their child in the large one because it is closer to their home or neighbors recommended it.

Nevertheless, one should not dismiss image measurement and planning simply because images are hard to change and their effects on behavior are unclear. Quite the contrary. Measuring an object's image is a very useful step in understanding what is happening to the object and to point to some possible desirable changes in its image. Furthermore, although the connection between image and behavior is not strong, it does exist. The connection should be neither overrated nor underrated. The institution should attempt to make an investment in developing the best image it can for the advantages this might bring.

SUMMARY

The marketing effectiveness of an educational institution depends upon satisfying the needs and wants of its markets and publics within the constraints of its mission and resources. The institution must engage in voluntary exchange to attract the resources it needs. Exchanges take place when both parties expect to be better off after a transaction. By analyzing what each party wants and can offer, the marketer can better understand how to plan an exchange.

The marketing arena of an educational institution includes numerous publics. A public is a distinct group of people and/or organizations that has an actual or potential interest in and/or effect on the institution. When the institution seeks some response from a public, we call it a market. A market is a distinct group of people and/or organizations that has resources they want to exchange, or might conceivably be willing to exchange, for distinct benefits.

Educational institutions vary in their responsiveness to their publics. Some are unresponsive and bureaucratic, but to the extent that consumers have alternatives, such institutions are vulnerable. Many schools and colleges are taking steps to become more responsive, conducting studies of consumer satisfaction and of consumers' needs and preferences, and responding to complaints and suggestions. Responsive institutions recognize the importance of satisfied consumers and publics.

Educational institutions have a strong interest in how they are perceived by their publics and markets. The "image" an institution possesses can be more influential than its reality. Ideally, the image accurately and favorably reflects the institution.

An image is the sum of beliefs, ideas, and impressions that a person has of an object. The educational marketer will want to measure how familiar and favorable the institution's image is and how various groups evaluate the institution on relevant attributes. Once the institution has determined how it is perceived, the administration must decide whether the image is accurate. If it is and yet it is unfavorable, the institution will want to undertake changes to improve itself and to communicate about these changes.

NOTES

[1] Clark Kerr, *The Uses of the University* (Cambridge, Mass.: Harvard University Press, 1964), p. 29.

[2] Theodore Levitt, "Marketing Myopia," *Harvard Business Review*, July–August 1960, pp. 45–56.

[3] See Richard T. Ingram and Associates, *Handbook of College and University Trusteeship: A Practical Guide for Trustees, Chief Executives, and Other Leaders Responsible for Developing Effective Governing Boards* (San Francisco: Jossey-Bass, 1980), for a comprehensive discussion of the responsibilities of trusteeship.

[4] See Anthony Downs, *Inside Bureaucracy* (Boston: Little, Brown, 1967).

[5] Edward S. McKay, *The Marketing Mystique* (New York: American Management Association, 1972), p. 22.

[6] Ralph E. Anderson, "Consumer Dissatisfaction: The Effect of Disconfirmed Expectancy on Perceived Product Performance," *Journal of Marketing Research*, February 1973, pp. 38–44.

[7] Leon Festinger and Dana Bramel, "The Reactions of Humans to Cognitive Dissonance," in Arthur J. Bachrach, ed., *Experimental Foundations of Clinical Psychology* (New York: Basic Books, 1962), pp. 251–62.

[8] Leon Festinger, *A Theory of Cognitive Dissonance* (Stanford, Cal.: Stanford University Press, 1957), p. 260.

[9] David Garvin, "Models of University Behavior," Working Paper 82-27, Division of Research, Graduate School of Business Adminstration, Harvard University, 1982. The same point is also developed in David Garvin, *Economics of University Behavior* (New York: Academic Press, 1980).

[10] C.E. Osgood, G.J. Suci, and P.H. Tannenbaum, *The Measurement of Meaning* (Urbana: University of Illinois Press, 1957). Other image-measuring tools exist, such as object-sorting (see W.A. Scott, "A Structure of Natural Cognitions," *Journal of Personality and Social Psychology*, Vol. 12, No. 4 (1969), pp. 261–78), and multidimensional scaling [(see Paul E. Green and Vithala R. Rao, *Applied Multidimensional Scaling* (New York: Holt, Rinehart and Winston, Inc., 1972)].

chapter 3

IDENTIFYING
AND RESEARCHING
MARKETING PROBLEMS

For over 125 years, the California Province of the Sisters of Notre Dame de Namur staffed eleven secondary schools in the dioceses of Seattle, Sacramento, San Francisco, Oakland, Monterey, Los Angeles, and Honolulu. Then, within a single decade, the Sisters closed or withdrew from six of the eleven schools owing to increasing educational costs and a decreasing number of teaching sisters.

At least, those appeared to be the problems. But the remaining five schools were also in trouble. Enrollment at Notre Dame High School in San Jose dropped 40 percent, from 512 in 1970 to 317 five years later. When the school responded by easing admissions standards, enrollment surged to

421 over the next four years, then sagged again as strict enforcement of academic and behavior standards led to dismissals.

In 1979, the Sisters began a thorough study of the remaining high schools, including San Jose. They compiled data on teaching-staff requirements, student demographic trends, and values that affected the schools' philosophy and curriculum. And they brought in a business and marketing consultant with extensive experience working with Catholic schools. After visiting schools, meeting with school administrators, and reviewing data, the consultant concluded that the underlying problems were not the shortage of funds and teaching sisters. Instead, the schools were victims of neglect—poorly managed, without long-range planning.

Based on the consultant's analysis, the Sisters made decisions on three of the five remaining schools. They concluded that Notre Dame High School, San Francisco, should be closed. The province did not have enough Sisters to staff all its schools, and they concluded that other Catholic high schools in San Francisco were adequately meeting the need.

Having made this decision, the Sisters went to work developing long-range plans, enrollment marketing programs, and more effective management structures for two other schools, including Notre Dame High School in San Jose. This school, in addition to the steep enrollment decline, had run a deficit for eight years. The consultant helped the principal to indentify the school's specific problems and encouraged her to get additional information on the school's image, the satisfaction of current students and their parents, and the school's market position.

The principal hired a team of marketing professors to conduct an image study of the school and to examine the sources of its students over the previous five years. With this information, the principal and the school's board of trustees could better understand the school's position in relation to other schools. They could then set realistic enrollment goals and plan long-range recruiting strategy.

SOURCE: Information provided by the Sisters of Notre Dame de Namur, California Province.

Administrators need appropriate, accessible information in order to make decisions about current and future programs, as well as to anticipate marketing-related problems. Some administrators find that the most basic information was never collected or never recorded. In other cases, the information was sloppily kept or even destroyed. Some educational institutions have collected lots of information but don't know how that information might be usefully organized and interpreted to aid in decision making.

This chapter considers how an institution can identify its marketing problems and how the marketing information system can be structured to provide the information required for resolving marketing problems and building on opportunities. We use the term *marketing information system* to describe the institution's system for gathering, analyzing, storing, and disseminating market-relevant information.

The role and major subsystems of a marketing information system are illustrated in Figure 3-1. At the left is the marketing environment that administrators must monitor—specifically, target markets, marketing channels, competitors, publics, and macroenvironmental forces. Developments and trends in the marketing environment are picked up through one of four subsystems— the *internal records system*, the *marketing intelligence system*, the *marketing research system*, and the *analytical marketing system*. The information obtained through one or more of these subsystems then flows to the appropriate administrators to help them in marketing planning, implementation, and control. The resulting decisions and communications then flow back to the marketing environment.

Many educational institutions fail to see that internal records and marketing intelligence systems can play an important part in helping identify and resolve marketing problems. Formal marketing research projects ideally build on a base of existing data and marketing intelligence, rather than starting from zero.

FIGURE 3-1   The marketing information system

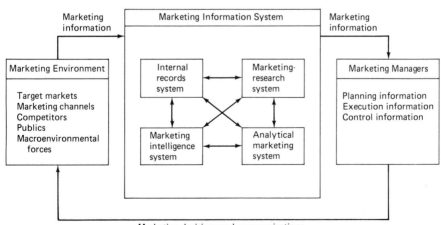

Marketing decisions and communications

This chapter presents an overview of the following topics:

1. Identifying marketing problems
2. The internal records system
3. The marketing intelligence system
4. The marketing research system
5. The analytical marketing system

These topics will be exemplified in later chapters in the book as we discuss specific marketing problems and approaches.

IDENTIFYING MARKETING PROBLEMS

Each educational institution needs to identify the specific marketing-related problems it faces. Correct problem identification is essential, since marketing planning and action can address only identified problems.

Suppose the Sisters of Notre Dame had decided to close Notre Dame High School, San Jose, because of "increasing educational costs," when the real problem was unrealistically low tuition. And suppose the Sisters never realized that the low tuition fee was interpreted as a signal that Notre Dame wasn't as good as other Catholic girls' high schools in San Jose. The Sisters might have made a serious and irreversible decision without an adequate understanding of the school's actual strengths and weaknesses.

Once problem areas have been identified, the institution can study the important ones in detail and develop marketing plans to address them.

An educational institution can systematically identify marketing problems in three ways. First, administrators can list observed problems in a *marketing problem inventory* and can ask others to do the same. Second, they can consider the demand for various programs and services and *determine the demand patterns* that present problems for the institution. Third, the institution can undertake a comprehensive *marketing audit* to determine the status of its current marketing activities. A marketing audit replaces the need for the first two approaches, because an audit considers each potential problem area and demand state. We will look at each approach in turn.

The Marketing Problem Inventory

A *marketing problem inventory* is a list of the marketing problems the institution has identified. The inventory should include those situations that might suggest present or future difficulties with the school's markets and publics. No two people or groups within the institution will see precisely the same problems. The director of an admissions office may identify "difficulty meeting the announced May 1 decision notification date" as a problem, whereas applicants are more concerned about getting a thorough review. Those compiling the marketing problem inventory may want to include lists from others as well.

Figure 3-2 shows a marketing problem matrix to compare the problems facing the college as a whole and each separate department.

An institution carrying out a marketing problem inventory may be surprised at the number of problems it identifies and the extent to which some problems emerge that were overlooked or never examined from a marketing perspective. Private schools with religious sponsorship tend to cite financial problems, such as increasing salaries and benefits to attract able teachers and providing for capital improvements and repairs on aging facilities. Notre Dame High School shares both these concerns, but it also identified the following specific problems:

1. Applications were down.
2. Downtown urban renewal had pushed drunks and prostitutes into the area, including the sidewalk in front of the school.
3. As the percentage of minority students grew, those parents (including minority parents) who selected the school for its elite image grew less satisfied.
4. A nearby Catholic girls' high school was attracting away applicants by promoting its beautiful suburban campus, varied extracurricular activities, and exclusivity.

FIGURE 3-2 Marketing problem matrix for a college

	College	Dept. 1	Dept. 2	Dept. 3	. . . . .	. . . . .	. . . . . *N*
Declining Overall Enrollment/ Credit Hours							
Declining Enrollment in Selected Disciplines							
Insufficient Attraction of High-Quality Students							
Poor Image							
Low Retention/ Student Satisfaction							
Low Faculty Satisfaction							
Insufficient Attraction of Funds							

5. Students completing eighth grade at the nearby Catholic grammar school tended to apply to the other high school, since the counselor who had favored Notre Dame had left for another position.
6. Some of the best students transferred after their sophomore or junior year to schools with more extracurricular activities.
7. Parents donated less time and money to the school as mothers went to work to meet family needs.
8. The school's tuition was significantly lower than that of other area Catholic high schools, causing financial and image problems for Notre Dame.

Some of these problems are more important than others, and the school will need to rank them and determine the factors that contribute to them.

Determining Demand States

An educational institution usually has some idea of what level of demand it seeks. A residential college in a rural area may be constrained by available dormitory facilities to enroll no more than 800 students but must enroll at least 725 in order to meet its financial commitments. A Sunday school may seek to enroll as many children as can be encouraged to attend, whereas a public-school program for physically handicapped children wants to serve only those children who need special services.

Marketing arises when an institution forms an idea of a *desired level of transactions* that it wants with a target market. At any one time, the actual demand level may be below, equal to, or above the desired demand level. The task of marketing management is to influence the level, timing, and character of demand in a way that will help the institution achieve its objectives. By comparing the actual demand state and the desired state, the institution can identify problem areas.

The Marketing Audit

Although the marketing problem inventory and the analysis of demand states will assist in identifying problems areas, most educational institutions will benefit from undertaking a *marketing audit*. The person or team carrying out the marketing audit gathers information critical to evaluating the institution's marketing performance. The auditor examines existing information, such as application and enrollment trends, fund-raising results, and other institutional reports, and also interviews administrators, faculty, staff, students, and others.

The marketing audit is not a marketing plan but an independent appraisal by a competent consultant of the main problems and opportunities facing the institution, and what it can do about them. The auditor will produce some short-run and long-run recommendations of actions the institution could take to improve its performance. The administration has to weigh these recommendations and implement those it feels would contribute to improved marketing performance. Since many educational institutions would benefit from conducting a marketing audit, we provide a separate chapter on the methods, components, and outcomes of a marketing audit in Chapter 18.

Next, we turn to the four subsystems of the marketing information system.

THE INTERNAL RECORDS SYSTEM

The most basic information system used by administrators is the *internal records system*. Every institution accumulates information in the regular course of its operations.

A college will keep records on its students, including names, addresses, ages, courses taken, grades received, major fields, test scores, payments, financial-aid awards, and so on. From academic transcripts, student files, and applications, the college can develop statistics on the number of applications received, the acceptance rate, the average high-school grade-point average and admissions test scores of students who enroll, the frequency distribution of majors, and other useful statistics. The college will also have records on faculty, administrators, staff, costs, billings, assets, and liabilities, all of which are indispensable for making management decisions. The college's placement office will keep records on students who use its services and can determine graduates' job-hunting success, fields selected, and typical salary offers. The placement office may also have reports from employers on graduates hired, their promotions, and intended job areas for future recruiting.

The development office will keep track of alumni and other donors, their addresses, past contributions, and other data. Its campaign progress file will show the amount raised to date from each major source, such as individuals, foundations, corporations, and government grants. Its cost file will show how much has been spent on direct mail, advertising, brochures, salaries, consulting fees, and so on.

Every internal records system can be improved in its speed, comprehensiveness, accuracy, and accessibility. Periodically, an institution should survey its administrators for possible improvements in the internal records system. Table 3–1 shows the major questions that can be put to them. Once their opinions are gathered, the information-system designers can design an internal records system that reconciles (1) what decision makers think they need, (2) what decision makers really need, and (3) what is economically feasible.

Most internal records systems were devised to *record* data, not to make it useful. Some educational institutions have taken great strides in making data easily accessible via desktop terminals to administrators who need it, but at other institutions the time lag between request and reply is so great that administrators stop asking and instead make decisions on information already in hand.

TABLE 3-1   Questionnaire for determining marketing information needs of decision makers

---

1. What types of decisions are you regularly called upon to make?
2. What types of information do you need to make these decisions?
3. What types of information do you regularly get?
4. What types of special studies do you periodically request?
5. What types of information would you like to get that you are not now getting?
6. What information would you want daily? weekly? monthly? yearly?
7. What magazines and reports would you like to see routed to you on a regular basis?
8. What specific topics would you like to be kept informed of?
9. What types of data-analysis programs would you like to see made available?
10. What do you think would be the four most helpful improvements that could be made in the present marketing information system?

THE MARKETING INTELLIGENCE SYSTEM

Whereas the internal records system supplies administrators with information on the past, the *marketing intelligence system* supplies them with information on current happenings. Here is our definition:

> The marketing intelligence system is the set of sources and procedures by which managers obtain their everyday information about developments in the external environment.

Educational administrators gather marketing intelligence mostly on their own, by reading newspapers and other publications and talking to people inside and outside the institution. This informal approach can spot important developments, but administrators may learn too late of some other important developments, such as a potential donor or pending legislation affecting the school's activities.

An institution can improve the quality of marketing intelligence. First, the institution must convince administrators, faculty, and staff of the importance of gathering marketing intelligence and passing it on to others in the institution. Administrators should be aware of the kind of information that would be useful to others in the institution.

Second, the institution should encourage outside parties with whom it deals—professional associations, lawyers, accountants—to pass on any useful bits of information. For example, a college's attorney may inform the development office of clients who might be interested in making bequests to the college.

Third, the institution could hire or delegate people to carry on specialized intelligence-gathering activity. For example, a "mystery shopper" might contact the admissions offices of several colleges and report back on how well they deal with inquiries. Quite probably, the "shopper" will report receiving widely different receptions, some of which may be "turnoffs" and others highly effective. Specialized intelligence gathering can also reveal whether the institution's own staff is really practicing a customer orientation and suggest the need for additional training.

Fourth, the institution can establish an office specifically responsible for gathering and disseminating marketing intelligence. The staff would scan major publications, abstract the relevant news, and disseminate the news to appropriate administrators. The office would install suggestion and complaint systems so that students and others would have an opportunity to express their attitudes toward the institution. It would develop a master index so that all the past and current information could be easily retrieved. The staff would assist administrators to evaluate the reliability of different pieces of information. These and other services would greatly enhance the quality of the information available for making marketing-related decisions.

THE MARKETING RESEARCH SYSTEM

The third major subsystem is the marketing research system. Here is our definition of *marketing research*:

> Marketing research is the systematic design, collection, analysis, and reporting of data and findings relevant to a specific marketing situation or problem facing an institution.

From time to time, administrators need marketing research studies to make specific decisions. Educational institutions often seek answers to such questions as these:

- What are the demographic characteristics of residents of this community college district?
- How many high school seniors might be interested in attending this college?
- What proportion of graduates of regional high schools select this college?
- Would a job-skills course for re-entry women be well received? How many students might enroll?
- How much should the college charge for the computer-skills course? How much would/could potential students pay?

Who conducts these studies for educational institutions? A large university will typically have a research director (with the title of Director of Institutional Research, Vice President for Planning, or the like) who coordinates other professionals. The institutional research office selects problems or clarifies problems posed by others in the institution, designs studies, and either carries them out or contracts with outside marketing research companies. A smaller instituion may hire a marketing consultant or research firm to design and carry out the

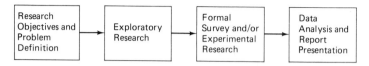

FIGURE 3-3   The marketing-research process

research, or the project may be carried out by administrators or faculty members trained in research techniques. Finally, the institution might contact local business schools about assistance from marketing faculty or students.

Administrators who need marketing research results need to know enough about its potential and limitations to get the right information at a reasonable cost and to use it intelligently. One protection is to work with experienced and credible researchers. In addition, administrators should know enough about marketing research procedures to review the plan and to evaluate the interpretation of results.[1]

Figure 3–3 describes the four basic steps in sound marketing research. We will illustrate these steps in connection with Notre Dame High School.

Notre Dame High School's enrollment had dropped to about 70 percent of capacity. The principal was concerned that students who once would have selected Notre Dame were going elsewhere. Not knowing the causes, the principal was not sure what marketing actions, if any, could halt and reverse the enrollment decline. Since the school's budget did not permit a large-scale study, the principal hired a team of marketing professors with educational marketing experience. The research team agreed to design and implement a study that would provide useful findings and recommendations. To keep the costs low, parent volunteers and school staff assisted in compiling and charting some of the data.

Research Objectives and Problem Definition

The first step in research is to define the research objectives. The overall objective may be to learn about a market, to determine the most attractive program to offer, or to measure the effect of a communications program. In any case, the problem guiding the research must be clearly specified. If the problem statement is vague, if the wrong problem is defined, or if the uses of the research are unclear, the research results may be useless or even misleading.

The marketing researchers working on the Notre Dame High School study defined the overall research objective as that of discovering how current students and their parents evaluated Notre Dame in relation to competing schools. To accomplish this objective, the researchers identified the following main elements as influencing school choice:

1. The demographic characteristics and educational aspirations of students and parents
2. The images students and parents hold of Notre Dame and of likely competing schools
3. The location of the school in relation to students' homes

Exploratory Research

At the exploratory research stage, before carrying out a formal (and therefore more expensive) research study, researchers often review existing data, do observational research, and interview individuals and groups informally to arrive at an understanding of the current situation.

Analysis of Secondary Data. Marketing researchers typically begin by gathering and reviewing secondary data, if any exists. *Secondary data* are relevant data that already exist somewhere, having been collected for another purpose. Secondary data are normally quicker and less expensive to obtain and provide the researcher with a start on the problem. Afterward, the researcher can gather *primary data*—namely, original data collected to address the problem at hand.

In looking for secondary data, the researchers for Notre Dame High School could consult the following major sources of secondary data:

1. *Internal records.* The researchers checked Notre Dame High School files for data on enrollment, transfers, and other data that might be relevant. The residences of current students were marked on a wall map of the greater metropolitan area, along with "feeder" elementary schools and competing high schools, to determine the role of location on high-school choice.

2. *Government.* The federal government publishes more marketing data than does any other source in the country. The U.S. Bureau of the Census issues the *Census of Population* and *Census of Housing.* The National Center for Education Statistics is another source of data. The researchers for Notre Dame High School could use local census data to determine trends in the number of children approaching high-school age.

3. *Educational associations.* Notre Dame High School is one of six Catholic high schools in the archdiocese. The archiocesan education office could provide information on school enrollment and capacity. The researchers could ascertain whether Notre Dame's enrollment decline was in line with a normal decline in its area or was exceptional.

4. *Competitors and other private organizations.* The researchers could see whether any useful secondary data could be obtained directly from other schools in the area. They could also get data from area Catholic grade schools on the high schools attended by their graduates for the past several years.

Secondary data from these and other sources can be useful as long as researchers are careful to check them for relevance, impartiality, validity, and reliability. The researchers are also likely to find many unanswered questions for which they will have to collect primary data, through either observation or interviewing.

Observational Research. One major way to collect primary data is through observation. The researchers could visit the school and observe the students' reactions to the curriculum, teachers, and each other. Observation could suggest factors affecting enrollment that could be measured later.

Qualitative Interviewing. In addition to observation, researchers often need to conduct some interviews during the exploratory stage of a marketing research project. Interviewing can suggest factors that play a role in the marketing problem. In the exploratory stage, interviewing should emphasize uncovering new qualitative information rather than obtaining quantifiable results. Therefore, exploratory interviews are open-ended. People were asked leading questions as a means of stimulating them to share their thoughts and feelings regarding Catholic high schools or other relevant topics.

Qualitative research can be used to (1) probe deeply into consumers' underlying needs, perceptions, preferences, and satisfaction; (2) gain greater familiarity with and understanding of marketing problems whose causes are not known; and (3) develop ideas that can be further investigated through quantitative research. Quantitative research, on the other hand, seeks to produce statistically reliable estimates of particular market or consumer characteristics. Quantitative research usually entails interviewing or surveying a much larger number of people than does qualitative research, and it assumes that the interviewer knows in advance what specific questions to ask.

Qualitative research is not only a desirable first step, it is sometimes the only step permitted by limited school budgets. For Notre Dame High School, the researchers decided to interview the school's administrators about what parents and students sought in a Catholic high school. In addition, they talked with parents whose children attend Catholic grade schools about their perceptions.

Two methods could be used: individual interviewing and group interviewing. *Individual interviewing* consists of interviewing one person at a time, either in person or over the telephone. *Group interviewing* consists of inviting from six to ten people to gather for a few hours with a trained interviewer to discuss a program, service, or institution. The interviewer needs good qualifications, including objectivity, knowledge of the subject matter, and some understanding of group dynamics and consumer behavior; otherwise, the results can be worthless or misleading.

The meeting is typically held in pleasant surroundings—a home, for example—and refreshments are served to increase the informality. The group interviewer starts with a broad question, such as, "What experiences do you feel will make the greatest contribution to your child's future success?" Questions would then move to the subject of educational experiences, then to schooling, and then to Notre Dame High School compared with others. The interviewer encourages free and easy discussion among the participants, hoping that the group dynamic will bring out real feelings and thoughts. At the same time, the interviewer "focuses" the discussion, and hence the name *focus group interviewing*. The comments are recorded through note taking or tape recording and subsequently studied to understand the consumers' attitudes and buying process. Focus group interviewing is becoming one of the major marketing-research tools for gaining insight into consumer thoughts and feelings.[2] In many cases, the results of focus group interviews guide the subsequent development of survey instruments or of marketing experiments, which we turn to next.

Formal Research

After defining the problem and doing exploratory research, the researchers may wish to carry out more formal research to measure magnitudes or to test hypotheses.

The researchers for Notre Dame High School learned that administrators felt school morale was low and that, in fact, graduates of nearby Catholic elementary schools were more frequently selecting other Catholic high schools. Notre Dame's administrators also wanted to know what parents and students felt were the schools' strengths, as a basis for improving recruiting efforts. The principal and the researchers agreed on the desirability of quantifying these factors.

At this point, the marketing researchers can design a formal survey or a marketing experiment. Each is described below.

Survey Research. Many administrators take an oversimplistic view of survey work. They think it consists of writing a few obvious questions and finding an adequate number of people in the target market to answer them. Designing a reliable survey requires training and experience. Here we will describe the main considerations in developing the research instrument, selecting the sample, and collecting the data.[3]

Designing the research instrument. The main survey research instrument is the questionnaire. Constructing good questionnaires calls for considerable skill. The questionnaire should be pretested with a small sample before being used on a large scale.

A common error occurs in the *types of questions asked*: the inclusion of questions that cannot be answered, or would not be answered, or need not be answered, and the omission of other questions that should be answered. Each question should be checked to determine how it serves the research objectives. Questions should be dropped that are merely interesting (except for one or two to start the interview), because they lengthen the time required and try the respondent's patience.

The *form of questions* can affect the response. An *open-ended question* is one to which the respondent is free to answer in his or her own words; for example, "What is your opinion of Notre Dame High School?" A *closed-ended question* is one to which the possible answers are supplied. Types of questions are described and illustrated in Exhibit 3–1.

EXHIBIT 3-1   Types of questions

A. CLOSED-ENDED QUESTIONS		
NAME	**DESCRIPTION**	**EXAMPLE**
Dichotomous	A question offering two answer choices.	"In selecting this school, did you visit the campus?" Yes ☐ No ☐
Multiple choice	A question offering three or more answer choices.	"With whom did you discuss your college decisions?" No one ☐ Parents ☐ School counselor ☐ Friends at school ☐ Other ☐
Likert scale	A statement with which the respondent shows the amount of agreement/ disagreement.	"Smaller colleges generally provide a better education than larger colleges." Strongly disagree 1 ☐ Disagree 2 ☐ Neither agree nor disagree 3 ☐ Agree 4 ☐ Strongly agree 5 ☐
Semantic differential	A scale is inscribed between two bipolar words, and the respondent selects the point that represents the direction and intensity of his or her feelings.	*East Ridge College* Large __:__:__:__:__:__ Small Difficult__:__:__:__:__:__ Easy Modern __:__:__:__:__:__ Old- fashioned
Importance scale	A scale calling for rating the importance of some attribute from "not at all important" to "extremely important."	"For me, attending a college close to my home is": Extremely important 1 __ Very important 2 __ Somewhat important 3 __ Not very important 4 __ Not at all important 5 __
Rating scale	A scale calling for rating some attribute from "poor" to "excellent."	"East Ridge College's dormitory facilities are": Excellent 1 __ Very good 2 __ Good 3 __ Fair 4 __ Poor 5 __

B. OPEN-ENDED QUESTIONS

NAME	DESCRIPTION	EXAMPLE
Completely unstructured	A question that respondents can answer in an almost unlimited number of ways.	"What is your opinion of East Ridge College?"
Word association	Words are presented, one at a time, and respondents mention the first word that comes to mind.	"What is the first word that comes to your mind when you hear the following?" College _____ East Ridge _____ Study _____
Sentence completion	Incomplete sentences are presented, one at a time, and respondents complete the sentence.	"In selecting a college, the most important consideration in my decision is _____
Story completion	An incomplete story is presented and respondents are asked to complete it.	"Jane was trying to decide what college to attend. She visited several colleges, including East Ridge. As she walked across the East Ridge campus, she noticed the students walking toward the library. This aroused in her the following thoughts and feelings. *Now complete the story.*"
Picture completion	A picture of two characters is presented, with one making a statement. Respondents are asked to identify with the other and fill in the empty balloon.	
Thematic Apperception Test (TAT)	A picture is presented and respondents are asked to make up a story about what they think is happening or may happen in the picture.	

The *choice of words* also calls for considerable care. The research should strive for simple, direct, unambiguous, and unbiased wording. The *sequencing of questions* in the questionnaire is also important. The lead questions should create interest, if possible. Open-ended questions are usually better here. Difficult or personal questions should be introduced toward the end in order not to create an emotional reaction that may affect subsequent answers or cause the respondent to break off the interview. The questions should be asked in as logical an order as possible in order to avoid confusing the respondent.

Questions about the respondent (age, income, educational level, and so forth) are usually asked last, because they tend to be more personal and less interesting to the respondent.

In the case of Notre Dame High School, the researchers constructed a questionnaire calling for an evaluation of Notre Dame, two other Catholic high schools (one a girls' high school, the other coed), and the respondent's local public high school on 25 attributes. Respondents were also asked to rate the importance of each attribute. Separate versions were prepared for students and parents, modifying the wording of each attribute. Exhibit 3–2 shows an excerpt of the student version of the questionnaire.

Selecting the sample. The marketing researchers must identify respondents who can supply information relevant to the research objective. Three decisions are required.

EXHIBIT 3-2 Excerpts from Notre Dame High School questionnaire (student version)

YOUR RATING OF *NOTRE DAME HIGH SCHOOL*

	Strongly disagree	Disagree	Neither agree nor disagree	Agree	Strongly agree
1. It is convenient to get to Notre Dame High School from my home.	[ ]	[ ]	[ ]	[ ]	[ ]
2. The school buildings and grounds are attractive and pleasant.	[ ]	[ ]	[ ]	[ ]	[ ]
3. The teachers are well qualified.	[ ]	[ ]	[ ]	[ ]	[ ]
4. The students at Notre Dame come from similar family backgrounds.	[ ]	[ ]	[ ]	[ ]	[ ]
5. Only the best students are admitted to Notre Dame.	[ ]	[ ]	[ ]	[ ]	[ ]
6. The cost of tuition at Notre Dame is very high.	[ ]	[ ]	[ ]	[ ]	[ ]
7. Scholarship assistance is available for students who need it.	[ ]	[ ]	[ ]	[ ]	[ ]
8. Notre Dame High School has a good record for getting its graduates into college.	[ ]	[ ]	[ ]	[ ]	[ ]
9. I can get to Notre Dame High School by public transportation.	[ ]	[ ]	[ ]	[ ]	[ ]
10. Parents' concerns are given a lot of consideration at Notre Dame.	[ ]	[ ]	[ ]	[ ]	[ ]

We would like to know how *important* the following school characteristics are to you in selecting a school for yourself. Please be sure to tell us *how important they are to you.*

HOW IMPORTANT IS HAVING A SCHOOL:

	Of no importance	Moderately important	Important	Very important	Extremely important
1. Which is convenient to get to from your home?	[ ]	[ ]	[ ]	[ ]	[ ]
2. Which has pleasant and attractive buildings and grounds?	[ ]	[ ]	[ ]	[ ]	[ ]
3. Which has well-qualified teachers?	[ ]	[ ]	[ ]	[ ]	[ ]
4. Where students come from similar backgrounds?	[ ]	[ ]	[ ]	[ ]	[ ]
5. Where only the best students are admitted?	[ ]	[ ]	[ ]	[ ]	[ ]
6. Which is inexpensive?	[ ]	[ ]	[ ]	[ ]	[ ]
7. Which has scholarship assistance available for students who need it?	[ ]	[ ]	[ ]	[ ]	[ ]
8. Which has a good record for getting its graduates into college?	[ ]	[ ]	[ ]	[ ]	[ ]
9. Which can be reached by public transportation?	[ ]	[ ]	[ ]	[ ]	[ ]
10. Which gives consideration to parents' concerns?	[ ]	[ ]	[ ]	[ ]	[ ]

1. *Sampling unit.* This answers the question, *Who is to be surveyed?* The proper sampling unit is not always obvious from the nature of the information sought. In the Notre Dame High School survey, should the sampling unit be the father, mother, student, or all three? Who is the usual initiator, influencer, decider, user, and/or purchaser?

2. *Sample size.* This answers the question, *How many people should be surveyed?* Large samples obviously give more reliable results than small samples do. However, it is not necessary to sample the entire target market or even a substantial part of it to achieve satisfactory precision. Carefully chosen samples, although small, can often provide good reliability.

3. *Sampling procedure.* This answers the question, *How should the respondents be chosen?* Table 3–2 shows types of samples. To draw valid and reliable inferences about the target market, a random probability sample of the

TABLE 3-2   Types of probability and nonprobability samples

A. *Probability sample:*

Simple random sample	Every member of the population has a known and equal chance of selection.
Stratified random sample	The population is divided into mutually exclusive groups (such as age groups), and random samples are drawn from each group.
Cluster (area) sample	The population is divided into mutually exclusive groups (such as city blocks), and the researcher draws a sample of the groups to interview.

B. *Nonprobability sample:*

Convenience sample	The researcher selects the easiest, most available members of the population from whom to obtain information.
Judgment sample	The researcher uses his/her judgment to select population members who are good prospects for relevant information.
Quota sample	The researcher finds and interviews a prescribed number of people in each of several categories (e.g., age, sex, education level).

relevant population should be drawn. Random sampling allows the calculation of confidence limits for sampling error. But random sampling is almost always more costly than nonrandom sampling. Some marketing researchers feel that the extra expenditure for probability sampling could be put to better use. Specifically, more of the money of a fixed research budget could be spent in designing better questionnaires and hiring better interviewers to reduce response and nonsampling errors, which can be just as fatal as sampling errors. This is an issue that marketing researchers and administrators must carefully weigh. In the case of Notre Dame High School, the researchers surveyed half the current students and all the parents, since the additional cost was small and it simplified the sampling task.

Contacting the respondents. Respondents are typically surveyed by telephone, mail, or personal interviews. *Telephone interviewing* stands out as the best method for gathering information quickly. It also permits the interviewer to clarify questions if they are not understood. The three main drawbacks of telephone interviewing are that (1) only people with telephones can be interviewed, (2) only short, not too personal, interviews can be carried out, and (3) experienced interviewers are needed, so the cost is higher than mail. The *mail questionnaire* may be the best way to reach people who would not give personal interviews or who might be biased by interviewers. On the other hand, mail questionnaires require simple and clearly worded questions, and the return rate is usually low and/or slow. *Personal interviewing* is the most versatile of the three methods. The interviewer can ask more questions and can supplement notes on the interviewee's comments with personal observations. Personal interviewing is the most expensive method, since it requires skilled interviewers and more technical and administrative planning and supervision.

Experimental Research. We have talked about formal research in its most common form, the survey. Marketing researchers are often eager to go beyond measuring the perceptions, preferences, and intentions of a target market and seek to measure actual cause-and-effect relationships. For example, the Notre Dame researchers might like answers to such questions as these:

- Would a brochure emphasizing the extracurricular and social benefits of attending the school attract more inquiries than the current brochure, which describes the academic program but says very little about other benefits?
- Would the number of referrals increase if the school conducted a special program and luncheon for eighth-grade counselors from nearby Catholic schools?
- Would neighborhood coffees hosted by mothers of current students yield more inquiries, applications, and enrollments than would result from similar households where mothers were not invited to a coffee?

Each of these questions might be addressed by surveying people and asking them for their reactions. However, survey answers don't always reveal people's true opinions or what they would actually do. In contrast, experimental research creates situations where the target market's actual behavior can be observed and its causes identified.

Let us apply the experimental method to the third question. The school would contact mothers of current students and ask each about her willingness to hold a coffee in her home and invite mothers of prospective students. Suppose the school found 20 mothers willing to do so. In order to compare the effectiveness of the coffees with the usual recruiting efforts, the school would ask ten of these mothers to each hold a neighborhood coffee at which Notre Dame's principal or admissions director could talk about the school. Each hostess would provide the school with the names and addresses of those mothers who attend. The other ten mothers would be asked to provide the school with the names and addresses of the neighborhood mothers they would otherwise have invited to a coffee. The school would send information packets to those mothers who attended a coffee and to those mothers who were named but did not attend a coffee.

As inquiries and applications are received, the director of admissions can check them against the two lists of names and record the response received from each household. At the end of admissions season, the director of admissions can compare the numbers of inquiries, applications, and enrollments received from each list. If households where the mother attended a coffee were more likely to follow up with an inquiry, application, and enrollment than were similar households where the mother was not invited to a coffee, the director of admissions could suspect that the coffees made a difference, and would want to determine if the difference in results was statistically significant (not just a chance occurrence). If so, and if there seems to be no other factor to explain the difference in results, the director would conclude that the coffees were an effective addition to the school's recruiting effort. The director would then invite other mothers to hold neighborhood coffees. The director of admissions should continue to monitor the effectiveness of neighborhood coffees, rather than assume that they will always be an effective approach.

The experimental method is often worth the additional effort and expense because the results are usually more conclusive and reliable. The method requires selecting equivalent groups of subjects, giving them different treatments, controlling extraneous variables, and determining whether observed differences are statistically significant. To the extent that the design and execution of the experiment eliminates alternative hypotheses that might explain the same results, the researcher and the institution can have confidence in the conclusions.[4]

Data Analysis and Report Presentation

The final step in the marketing research process is to develop meaningful information and findings to present to the administrator who requested the study. The researcher will tabulate the data and develop one-way and two-way frequency distributions. Averages and measures of dispersion will be computed for the major variables. The researcher might attempt to apply some advanced statistical techniques and decision models in the hope of discovering additional findings. The researcher's purpose is not to overwhelm management with numbers and fancy statistical procedures, but rather to present major findings that will help the administrator make better marketing decisions.

A marketing research report should clearly describe the following:

1. The objective or principal question the research was designed to answer
2. The research questionnaire or experimental procedure
3. The characteristics of the sample
4. The qualitative and/or quantitative results
5. Clear statements of the research findings
6. The implications of the research findings
7. Recommendations for action

In addition to preparing a written report, the researcher should meet with the administrator who requested the study, to go over the major findings of the research and to explain the recommendations. This meeting is an opportunity to make sure the results are clearly understood before any action plans are implemented.

THE ANALYTICAL MARKETING SYSTEM

The marketing information system contains a fourth subsystem called the *analytical marketing system*. The analytical marketing system consists of a set of advanced techniques for analyzing marketing data and marketing problems. These systems are able to produce more detailed findings and conclusions than can be gained by only commonsense manipulation of the data. Although some large educational institutions make extensive use of analytical marketing systems, in smaller institutions administrators have often resisted these approaches as too technical or expensive. The advent of small computers and convenient terminal access is rapidly overcoming this reluctance.

An analytical marketing system includes *advanced statistical procedures* for learning more about relationships within a set of data and their statistical reliability. It allows management to go beyond the frequency distribution, means, and standard deviations in the data, to answer such questions as these:

- What are the best predictors of persons who are likely to apply to this school versus competing institutions?
- What are the best variables for segmenting the market, and how many segments will be created?

Researchers can turn to statistical packages such as SPSS (Statistical Package for the Social Sciences) for many of these statistical procedures. Other applications specific to marketing are described in marketing journals and other sources.

An analytical system may also include *quantitative models* to help make better marketing decisions. Each model consists of a set of interrelated variables that represent some real system, process, or outcome. These models can help answer "what if?" and "which is best?" questions. Several large universities

FIGURE 3-4 The analytical marketing system

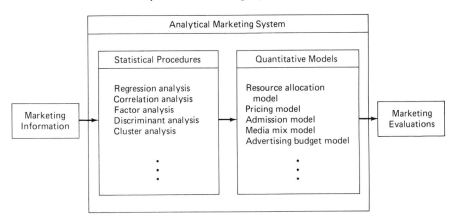

have developed quantitative models to use in allocating resources among programs and departments.[5] Some universities now use models of the admissions process to predict the relationship between inquiries, applications, acceptances, and enrollment. Others have developed models to predict the comparative academic success of applicants for admission based on prior academic record and other variables. These and other models will be more widely developed and used as educational institutions strive to refine their marketing strategies.

SUMMARY

Each educational institution needs to understand its specific marketing problems, so that marketing plans can be developed to address them. The institution must (1) identify its marketing problems, and (2) gather marketing information to clarify the nature of its problems and guide marketing activities.

Problems can be systematically identified in three ways. First, the school can prepare a marketing problem inventory. A marketing problem inventory includes problems and situtations that might suggest present or future difficulties with the school's markets and publics. Second, the school can compare the actual demand state it is experiencing with its desired state to determine where discrepancies—and therefore problems—exist. Third, the school can carry out a marketing audit to examine its marketing environment, objectives, strategies, and activities. Once the problems are identified, the school needs marketing information to clarify the problem areas and to guide planning to solve them.

Four systems make up the marketing information system. The first, the internal records system, consists of all the information that the institution gathers in the regular course of its operations. It includes information on students, programs, and finances. Many research questions can be answered by analyzing the information in the internal records system.

The second, the marketing intelligence system, describes the set of sources and procedures by which administrators obtain their everyday information about developments in the marketplace. An institution can improve the quality of its marketing intelligence by motivating its managers to scan the environment and report useful information, and by hiring intelligence specialists to find and disseminate information within the institution.

The third, the marketing research system, consists of the systematic design, collection, analysis, and reporting of data and findings relevant to a specific marketing situation or problem facing an institution. The marketing research process consists of four steps: developing the research objectives and problem definition; exploratory research; formal survey and/or experimental research; and data analysis and report presentation.

The fourth, the analytical marketing system, consists of advanced statistical procedures for analyzing the relationships within a set of data and their statistical reliability, and quantitative models that help make better marketing decisions.

NOTES

1 Current books on marketing research include Larry H. Litten, Daniel Sullivan, and David L. Brodigan, *Applying Market Research in College Admissions* (New York: College Entrance Examination Board, 1983); David Aaker and George S. Day, *Marketing Research*, 2nd ed. (New York: John Wiley & Sons, 1983); Harper W. Boyd, Jr., Ralph L. Westfall, and Stanley F. Stasch, *Marketing Research*, 5th ed. (Homewood, Ill.: Richard D. Irwin, 1981); and David J. Luck, Hugh G. Wales, Donald A. Taylor, and Ronald S. Rubin, *Marketing Research*, 6th ed. (Englewood Cliffs, N. J.: Prentice-Hall, 1982). For a useful brief guide to interpreting research reports, see Karlene H. Roberts, *Understanding Research: Some Thoughts on Evaluating Completed Educational Projects*, ERIC ED032759.

2 See Keith K. Cox et al., "Applications of Focus Group Interviews in Marketing," *Journal of Marketing*, January 1976, pp. 77–80; and Bobby J. Calder, "Focus Groups and the Nature of Qualitative Marketing Research," *Journal of Marketing Research*, August 1977, pp. 353–64. An excellent guide is James B. Higginbotham and Keith K. Cox, *Focus Group Interviews: A Reader* (Chicago: American Marketing Association, 1979).

3 A useful guide to conducting survey research is Earl R. Babbie, *Survey Research Methods* (Belmont, Cal.: Wadsworth, 1973).

4 For more reading on experimental research, see Seymour Banks, *Experimentation in Marketing* (New York: McGraw-Hill, 1965); and Frederick N. Kerlinger, *Foundations of Behavioral Research* (New York: Holt Rinehart, 1973).

5 See David S.P. Hopkins and William F. Massy, *Planning Models for Colleges and Universities* (Stanford, Cal.: Stanford University Press, 1981).

part II
Planning Marketing

chapter 4

THE MARKETING PLANNING PROCESS

Heights University (name disguised), with an enrollment of 6,000, half undergraduate, is a tuition-dependent private university eager to improve its academic stature and its financial condition. Like many other institutions of its rank, the university is struggling to maintain enrollment while increasing selectivity. While some of its graduate programs are well respected, undergraduate admissions standards are modest—a high school grade average of C will open the door.

For several consecutive years the university experienced operating deficits of up to $1 million a year. Tuition was increased steeply every year to cover the short-fall, resulting in further decreases in student enrollment, a painful trend for a university dependent on tuition for most of its operating income. Unrestricted annual giving for the operating budget averaged half a million dollars a year, and the budget for undergraduate scholarships was little more than $2 million.

The trustees supported stiff budget cuts to stabilize the university's situation. The president and trustees then began formal planning meetings to determine how best to move toward a solid financial situation and enhanced academic quality.

Most educational institutions first acknowledge the value of formal planning when they encounter serious enrollment and revenue declines or find that their admissions or fund-raising programs have been poorly managed and unsuccessful. At first, administrators may hope the situation is an aberration that will right itself in time without concerted action. When they realize the magnitude of the situation, they begin to investigate ways to monitor problems and develop plans to address them.

Recognizing the need for planning is only the first step. Marketing planning relies on skills that may be somewhat new to those administrators who have specialized in successfully managing day-to-day operations and have not been involved in planning. Many institutions have hired planning specialists to direct the planning process and to assist administrators in planning.

In this chapter, we lay out and illustrate the steps in the marketing planning process at both the strategic and tactical levels. By *strategic marketing planning*, we mean planning of the overall direction of the institution to respond to its markets and opportunities. By *tactical marketing planning*, we mean planning of the specific action steps needed to take advantage of the marketing opportunities identified through strategic planning.

The marketing planning process consists of six components, each of which is discussed in depth in a subsequent chapter. In this chapter, we address the following five questions:

1. How is marketing planning used?
2. What are the steps in strategic planning?
3. What are the components of a tactical marketing plan?
4. What can formal planning systems contribute to institutional effectiveness?
5. How can marketing control systems assist in assessing marketing success?

STRATEGIC MARKETING PLANNING

The general notion of planning is not new to education. Three levels of planning are used. The first level encompasses the budgeting and scheduling process. All schools must plan at this level, and many are turning to linear programming and optimization models to improve the process. A second level is short-range tactical planning—recruiting of students, physical-plant decisions, development efforts, and program and curriculum changes. Most colleges, universities, and private schools are engaged to some degree in short-range planning. In fact, some institutions are compounding their problems by relying on many short-range plans, each addressing one problem or symptom, when they should be proceeding to the third level, strategically oriented long-range planning, to focus their short-range plans. Strategic planning involves clarifying the institution's mission, assessing its resources, and examining the environment to determine what the institution's priorities and strategies should be.

We believe that educational institutions should be carrying out formal planning of two types, strategic planning and tactical planning. Strategic planning answers the question, "How can this institution best operate, given its goals and resources and its changing opportunities?" The second type, tactical marketing planning, grows out of the strategic plan and guides the execution of the strategy.

Consider the case of Heights University. The president and the board of trustees were determined to improve the university's stature. They hired a team of consultants to work with a high-level planning committee of trustees, vice-chancellors, deans, and others. The consultants talked with or surveyed key informants in the institution. The consultants then guided the planning committee in analyzing environmental trends and the school's mission, strengths, and weaknesses. In the financial category, for example, the university had a balanced budget and little debt. Its financial weaknesses included a small endowment and rising fixed-cost overhead.

Heights University's trustees decided on a strategy of improving the institution's academic quality and thus enhancing its national reputation. The trustees' plan called for the university to achieve several specific objectives, including to increase enrollment to specified levels, to be ranked within *Barron's* "very competitive" category, to qualify for the Association of Research Libraries, and to move toward Association of American Universities status.

The tactical plan followed and was based on the strategic planning process. The tactical plan included objectives and an action plan for each area—enrollment, finances, and so on. In each area, the planning committee considered the threats that might affect the plan and, where possible, set up contingency plans to deal with them. The tactical plan can be updated each year as new information becomes available.

STEPS IN STRATEGIC PLANNING

Strategic planning is new to most educational institutions. We define *strategic planning* as follows:

> Strategic planning is the process of developing and maintaining a strategic fit between the institution's goals and capabilities and its changing marketing opportunities. It relies on developing a clear institutional mission, supporting goals and objectives, a sound strategy, and appropriate implementation.

The definition suggests the appropriate steps an educational institution can take to improve its effectiveness. This chapter presents an overview of the strategic planning process (Figure 4-1), and subsequent chapters give details on each step.

First, the institution must analyze its present and future environment (Chapter 5). Second, it reviews its major resources to suggest what it can accomplish, and, third, the institution establishes its overall goals and its specific objectives (Chapter 6). Fourth, the institution selects the most cost-effective strategy for reaching these goals and objectives (Chapter 7). Finally, implementing the strategy usually requires changes in the institution's structure and systems of information, planning, and control (Chapter 3 and the final section of this chapter). When these components are aligned, they promise improved performance.

The strategic planning process should be completed at each major institutional level, because each level or component has somewhat different goals, resources, and marketing opportunities. In the case of a university, the president and vice presidents should undertake strategic planning as it affects the university as a whole and state institutional assumptions and goals to guide planning at other levels. Then each dean (for instance, engineering school, business school, music school) should formulate strategic plans for that school. In turn, each department chairperson, in consultation with faculty, can carry out strategic planning for the department. If a university operates branches in

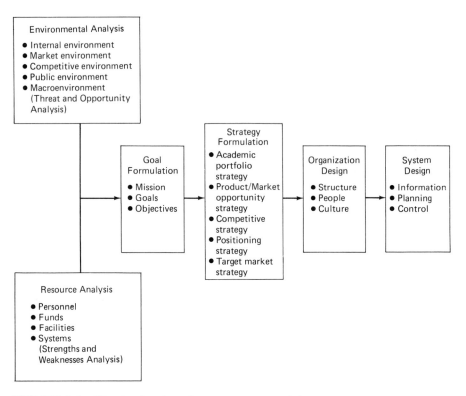

FIGURE 4-1 Strategic planning process model

different locations, each branch will need to do strategic planning, since each will have different threats and opportunities. All these plans would be sent up to top administration for review and perhaps further development with the original planners. The final plan is often presented to the university board of trustees for approval. In a smaller educational institution, the strategic planning process will be simpler and involve fewer levels, but the elements remain the same.

   Strategic planning often involves faculty as well as administrators. The faculty senate or other faculty representatives have a crucial role to play in planning, and their support is essential. Therefore, educational administrators do not simply select the most cost-effective strategy, as business managers do, because they must consider a wider variety of institutional constraints.

   We will illustrate the stages in the strategic planning process with the case of Beloit College.[1]

Beloit is a 900-student liberal arts college in southern Wisconsin. In the mid-1970s, enrollment dropped. Beloit administrators responded by instituting major changes to help ensure the school's long-term viability.

Environmental Analysis

The first step in strategic planning is to analyze the environment, because changes in the environment usually call for new institutional strategies. An *environmental audit* answers the questions, (1) What are the major trends in the environment? (2) What are the implications of these trends for the institution? and (3) What are the most significant opportunities and threats? These questions must be examined for each of the institution's major environments: its internal environment, its markets, its publics, its competition, and the larger environmental trends that may have an effect on the school. The aim of environmental analysis is to produce a documented picture of the most significant environmental developments the institution must consider in formulating its future goals, strategies, structures, and systems. Methods for carrying out environmental analysis are presented in Chapter 5.

From the environmental audit, the planners should draw out several major threats and opportunities for further examination. An *environmental threat* is a trend or potential event that will harm the institution or one of its programs unless the institution takes action.

Beloit College detected the following threats in the environmental audit:

1. In the market environment, they found that most of their students came from northern and eastern states, where the college-age population is projected to decline most.

2. In the public environment, they determined that the local community was rather apathetic toward the college and might not continue to employ students or cooperate with class projects.

3. In the competitive environment, Beloit officials hoped to compete with such prestigious private colleges as Carleton, Grinnell, and Oberlin. Beloit expected these institutions to become more aggressive in competing for students.

4. In the macroenvironment, Beloit is a private school with high tuition costs. Changes in the economic environment pose a threat to it.

The most serious threats—those that Beloit must monitor and be prepared to respond to—are those with a *potentially severe impact* and *high probability of occurrence*. It can ignore threats that are low in both severity and probability. Beloit should monitor, but need not prepare contingency plans for, threats such as competition from other colleges. By identifying and classifying threats, this college can determine which environmental threats to monitor, plan for, or ignore.

Opportunity analysis can be potentially more important than threat analysis. By managing its threats successfully, an institution can stay intact but does not grow. But by managing its opportunities successfully, the school can make great strides forward. A *marketing opportunity* is one in which the institution is likely to enjoy superior competitive advantages.

Beloit College officials identified several marketing opportunities:

1. In the market environment, Beloit surveyed employers and found that the demand for liberal arts graduates with some emphasis in applied areas was strong.

2. In the public environment, they detected that legislators and government officials would continue to support public scholarship aid for small colleges. (Subsequent changes in the economy and in federal government policy challenged this expectation.)

3. In the competitive environment, Beloit noted that its location was reasonably close to a major metropolitan area (Chicago) and was perceived to be not too far from eastern cities.

These opportunities, then, can be evaluated on the bases of attractiveness and probability of success.

Resource Analysis

Following the environmental analysis, the institution should identify the major resources it has (its strengths) and lacks (its weaknesses). Beloit carried out a resource audit (discussed in Chapter 6) focusing on people, money, and facilities. The audit determined that teaching quality was good but that the college was overstaffed. Faculty positions were cut by one-third. Beloit's financial situation was neither a clear strength nor a clear weakness. The college's small size and pleasant campus seemed to be strengths, but the location in the Snowbelt was perceived to be a weakness. Of course, Beloit must prepare a much more extensive list of intangible as well as tangible strengths and weaknesses. In particular, the school should look for its *distinctive competencies*, those resources and abilities in which it is particularly strong, and for those strengths that give it a differential advantage over its competition.

Goal Formulation

The environmental and resource analyses provide the background and stimulus for administrative thinking about the institution's basic *goals* and *objectives*. As the environment changes, top administration and the board should review and reassess the basic mission, goals, and objectives. At some schools, a review will convince participants in the planning process that the current goal structure is still clear, relevant, and effective. Other institutions will find their goals clear but of diminishing appropriateness to the new environment and resource situation, and some will discover that their goals are no longer clear and that the institution is drifting.

The *goal-formulation process* involves establishing, first, the mission of the institution; second, the long- and short-run goals; and third, what the specific current objectives will be.

Mission. An educational institution exists to accomplish some purpose. A useful way to examine the school's *mission* is to answer the following questions:[2] What is our business? Who is the consumer? What is our value to the consumer? What will our business be? What should our business be?

Beloit has to define a particular concept or brand of education if it is to stand out. Consider these possibilities: Is Beloit in the *intellectual training business*, so that its students are highly knowledgeable and perceptive about the world they live in? Is Beloit in the *personal-growth business*, aiming to help students develop their total personhood, intellectually, emotionally, and socially? Is Beloit in the *college fun and games business*, providing students "the best time of their lives" before becoming adults? Each definition implies a different consumer and a different way of rendering value to the consumer.

Beloit altered its mission statement to include career preparation as well as intellectual training: "An awareness of the available career options, together with the skills to perceive those options."

Goals. The institution's *goals* are the variables it will emphasize. Each institution has a potential set of relevant goals from which to select. For example, a college might be interested in increasing its national reputation, attracting better students, improving teaching, building a larger endowment, and so on. A college cannot successfully pursue all these goals simultaneously and must choose to emphasize certain ones. For example, if Beloit's enrollment were to fall, it would probably make increased enrollment a paramount goal.

Objectives. Next, the institution's goals for the coming years should be stated in operational and measurable form, called *objectives*. The goal "increased enrollment" must be turned into an objective such as "increasing enrollment of the next academic-year class by 15 percent." Typically, the institution will evaluate a large set of potential objectives for consistency and priority before adopting a final set of objectives.

Strategy Formulation and Implementation

Strategic planning culminates in an overall strategy for the institution or planning unit (department, program, and so on). An *institutional strategy* includes decisions about its current programs (whether to maintain, build, or drop them), and about future new programs and market opportunities. Heights University decided to take steps to enhance the quality and stature of the whole institution. Beloit College decided to retain its commitment to the liberal arts while helping students acquire career-related skills. The institution also needs to develop strategies for selecting target markets, for positioning the institution, and for addressing competition.

Strategies are not simply inspirations or "bright ideas." Nor is strategy formulation the same thing as goal formulation. Strategies grow out of and reflect the environmental analysis, resource analysis, and goal-formulation steps. Unless the institution has goals it wishes to accomplish, there is no need for strategy formulation. According to an old adage, "If you don't know where you're going, any road will take you there." Only when the environmental analysis, resource analysis, and goal-formulation steps have been carefully done can the institution's administrators and other planning participants feel confident that they have the necessary background for reviewing current programs and markets and considering changes.

Several analytical tools help educational planners to carry out this review. Two are particularly appropriate for education: *academic portfolio strategy,* which involves reviewing existing programs for market attractiveness, program quality, and centrality to the institution's mission; and *product/market opportunity strategy* to identify potential program changes and markets. These and other tools are presented in Chapter 7, which considers marketing strategy and competition in depth.

Organizational Design. The institution must have the *structure, people,* and *culture* to carry out its strategies. For example, to offer a more integrated undergraduate program, the University of Santa Clara merged its College of Science and College of Arts and Humanities. Bradley University combined admissions, financial aid, orientation, career development, placement, retention, and advisory services into an Office of Student Planning to provide the comprehensive services prospective students valued. Bradley later combined Student Planning and Student Services into a Division of Student Affairs. The new division employs a marketing framework in planning its activities. Other institutions have changed the top administrative structure or combined academic departments to carry out a strategy.

Carrying out the strategy may require not only changes in organizational structure but also the retraining or replacing of personnel in key positions. For example, if an institution changes its fund-raising strategy from reliance on wealthy donors to foundations, the vice president for development who is expert in "old-boy-network" fund raising may need retraining in corporate grantsmanship or may have to be replaced with a foundation-oriented person. If a college wants to attract adult students, admissions personnel must be prepared to counsel them effectively.

In adopting a new strategic posture, the school may also have to develop a plan for changing the "culture" of the institution. Every institution has a culture; that is, its people share a way of looking at things. The academic culture is often an outspoken critic of the "business culture" (profit as a worthwhile end) and of the "marketing culture" (that institutions have to serve and satisfy their markets). College presidents who attempt to persuade faculty to improve their teaching, spend more time with students, develop new courses for nontraditional markets, and so on, often encounter tremendous resistance. For institutions seeking to attract students, the challenge is to develop a marketing orientation in which faculty members see their job as serving and satisfying markets. Accomplishing this change can be a major task, but essential if the institution is to be successful.

Finally, the institution must design or upgrade systems needed to support the new strategies. The three principal systems are the marketing information system (discussed in Chapter 3), the marketing planning system, and the marketing control system. The latter two are discussed in this chapter.

THE FORMAT OF A MARKETING PLAN

Tactical marketing planning should follow strategic planning. Strategic planning indicates the particular programs and markets the institution should emphasize. For each selected program or market, the institution must develop a marketing strategy. The formal marketing plan summarizes the information and analysis underlying a proposed strategy and spells out the details of how the strategy will be carried out.

A marketing plan should contain the following major sections: *executive summary, situation analysis, goals and objectives, marketing strategy, action programs, budgets,* and *controls* (see Figure 4-2). These sections will be discussed in the context of a hypothetical university.

The board of trustees and the admissions office have agreed on an increase in undergraduate enrollment from 5,000 to 5,500 over the next three years.

FIGURE 4-2   Contents of a marketing plan

The director of admissions has been asked to develop a plan for accomplishing this goal.

Executive Summary

The planning document should open with a summary of the main objectives and recommendations presented in the plan. Here is an abbreviated example:

- The admissions marketing plan for the 1986–87 academic year calls for increasing new student enrollment for fall 1986 by 200 over fall 1985. Assuming an average tuition cost of $6,000 per additional student, this step, if successful, will add $1.2 million to university revenue. (Some of this additional revenue will be allocated for financial aid.) Assuming that 150 decide to live in university residence halls, the university would receive $3,000 per student, or a total of $450,000, while using otherwise underutilized facilities.

- To accomplish this, the plan calls for a marketing expenditure of $90,000. Of this, $15,000 will be spent on marketing research to measure the present image of the university held by high school and community college students in the region; $20,000 will be spent to buy appropriate mailing lists; $50,000 will be spent to develop awareness of the university's undergraduate program in community colleges and area firms with employee tuition-reimbursement plans; and $5,000 will be spent to produce new brochures on the undergraduate experience at the university.

The purpose of the executive summary is to permit higher-level administrators to preview the major direction of the plan before reading the document for supporting data and analysis. To guide the reader who wants to focus on certain aspects of the document, a table of contents typically follows the executive summary.

Situation Analysis

The first major section of the plan is the *situation analysis*. Here the administrator describes the major features of the situation affecting his or her operation. Whereas the strategic planning process revealed the situation facing the university, the director of admissions must examine those factors that affect the admissions operation in the specified time frame, the first year of a three-year plan. The situation analysis consists of four subsections—background, normal forecast, opportunities and threats, and strengths and weaknesses.

Background. This section starts with a summary of performance over the last few years. An abbreviated hypothetical example is shown in Table 4-1 for the undergraduate admissions office.

TABLE 4-1   Background data

	FALL 1982–83	FALL 1983–84	FALL 1984–85	FALL 1985–86
Number of applications received for fall	3,000	3,000	3,300	3,500
Number of applicants accepted for fall	2,700	2,700	2,800	2,900
Number of new undergraduate students enrolled	2,000	1,900	1,800	1,800
Academic year full-time tuition	$4,500	$5,000	$5,500	$6,000
Total tuition revenue from new students for academic year	$9 million	$9.5 million	$9.9 million	$10.8 million

The number of new students enrolling each year has declined slightly over the past three years. (We are not even considering the institution's retention rate—the percentage of new students who continue to attend after the first term.) These data should be followed by a description of major developments that would bear on the admissions office's strategy—macroenvironmental trends (such as population growth in the region) and changes in competing institutions, for example.

Normal Forecast. The background information should be followed by a forecast of the number of new students enrolling in fall 1986–87 under "normal" conditions—that is, assuming no major changes in the *marketing environment* or *marketing strategies.* The director of admissions could ask, "How many new students are likely to enroll next fall if our admissions operation continues the way it has in the past?" The forecast could be derived by assuming that present trends will continue. In this example, the director might forecast that if no marketing changes are made, about 1,800 new students will enroll. (Institutions with other backgrounds might forecast a stable level or an increase.) Or the director might use statistical curve fitting or survey a sample of applicants about intentions to enroll to make the normal forecast. The normal forecast must then be adjusted if the director expects significant changes in the macroenvironment or in the institution's strategies.

Opportunities and Threats. In this section, the director identifies the main opportunities and threats facing the undergraduate admissions office (see Table 4-2, A). Although the director may already have these in mind, they

TABLE 4-2   An example of opportunities, threats, strengths, and weaknesses

A. Opportunities and Threats Facing the Admissions Office

OPPORTUNITIES

1. The population of the region is growing rapidly, increasing the population base we can attract and serve.
2. Large employers in the metropolitan area are adopting tuition-reimbursement plans for their employees. We could attract some of these employees to our evening courses.
3. Graduates of area community colleges tend to remain here and might be attracted to transfer to the university to complete bachelor's degrees.

THREATS

1. A downturn in the economy may discourage students from applying to private universities.
2. The increasing cost of tuition may discourage applicants.
3. Community colleges offer low-cost vocational training to prepare for well-paying technical jobs in local industry, and may attract students who would otherwise attend a four-year institution.

B. Strengths and Weaknesses of the Admissions Office

STRENGTHS

1. The undergraduate students attracted in the past five years have been of higher quality than before.
2. The admissions staff is well-trained and client-oriented. Even applicants who decide to go elsewhere report favorably on the admissions staff.
3. The applicant pool has grown slowly but surely over the past six years.

WEAKNESSES

1. The admissions office is open weekdays only from 9 to 5, so potential applicants who work, or who live or attend college at a distance cannot get an appointment to see an admissions counselor.
2. Mailing lists are out of date, making the office dependent on applicant inquiries.
3. The admissions counselors have little experience working with adult applicants.

should be put in writing. Top administration can review the list and raise questions about threats and opportunities that are listed or missing. They may also ask the director to rate the opportunities and threats on their potential effects and probability, to indicate which deserve the most planning attention. Also, the director and other administrators can later see how many opportunities were acted on and what threats actually occurred.

Strengths and Weaknesses. The director should next list the main internal strengths and weaknesses of the undergraduate admissions office (see Table 4-2, B). Of course, the ultimate success of the admissions office depends in large measure on other parts of the university—such as the quality of instruction and residence facilities or the availability of certain majors—but in the short term, the admissions office cannot significantly influence changes in these.

Goals and Objectives

The situation-analysis section describes where the institution stands and what its likely future will be if no changes are made. Now the director must propose where the undergraduate admissions office should head. Specific goals and objectives need to be set.

The director of admissions starts with the enrollment objective stated by the board of trustees—to increase undergraduate enrollment from 5,000 to 5,500 over the next three years. The director then must develop specific objectives for the undergraduate admissions office to achieve this overall objective. The director decides on the following specific objectives: (1) to increase new student enrollment for the following fall term by 200 (that is, from 1,800 to 2,000), and (2) to spend $90,000 to accomplish this. Other supporting objectives would also be listed in this section—for example, quality levels based on high school grade-point average and test scores.

Marketing Strategy

The director then outlines a marketing strategy for attaining the specified goals and objectives—the steps admissions office personnel will carry out to achieve the increase in new students. Marketing strategy consists of a coordinated set of decisions on (1) *target markets*, (2) *marketing mix*, and (3) *marketing expenditure level*.

Target Markets. The director should develop a list of criteria to identify the most attractive potential student markets. Criteria might include age, sex, income, place of residence, and other variables. The director, along with appropriate admissions staff, should rate each market on these criteria to select the most promising potential student markets, those from which the university can attract a reasonable number of students who meet its admissions criteria. The director might conclude that area community college students are likely to be a more promising pool of students for the university than, for example, high school seniors who live more than 500 miles away.

Marketing Mix. The director should plan a *strategic marketing mix* that answers such basic questions as whether to emphasize personal or mail contacts with community college counselors or to rely upon direct mail or mass media to contact community college students individually. The director should then develop a *tactical marketing mix*. For the community college market in the metropolitan area, the director may decide to hire or designate a staff person to make personal visits but rely on an informational mailing to community college counselors elsewhere. To increase applications from high school students, the director would need to select a different marketing mix.

Marketing Expenditure Level. Marketing strategy also requires deciding on the marketing expenditure level. When an admissions office takes on a marketing approach to prospective students, it will usually need to increase its budget. The increased expenditure is generally warranted to the extent that it results in more enrolled students; however, if competition exists, the institution may find over time that it must spend more money per enrolled student. In this example, the total admissions office budget will be far more than the $90,000 allocated for attracting additional students.

Action Program

Each strategy element must be translated into appropriate actions. For example, the strategy element "attract more community college students" could lead to the following actions: "Hire a community college liaison person to visit community college campuses"; "hold a conference for community college counselors on helping community college students make the transfer decision" (not specific to this university); and "send a letter and brochure on the university to second-year community college students." The most cost-effective actions should then be assigned to specific individuals with specified completion times.

The overall action plan can be charted, with the twelve months (or 52 weeks) of the year serving as columns and the various marketing activities serving as rows. Dates entered will show when various activities or expenditures will be started, reviewed, and completed. This action plan can be revised as new problems and opportunities arise.

Budgets

The objectives, strategies, and planned actions form the basis for preparing the budget. For institutions and programs that must match revenues and expenditures, the budget is essentially a projected profit-and-loss statement. On the revenue side, it shows the forecasted unit enrollment and the expected net realized revenue. On the expense side, it shows the costs of providing the service as well as marketing and administration. The difference is the projected profit or loss. The administration reviews the budget and either approves or modifies it. Once approved, the budget guides marketing operations, financial planning, and personnel recruitment.

The undergraduate admissions office performs a service to the university, but it is not a profit-making operation. The budget will reflect the director's appraisal of how much money will be required to carry out the required tasks and top administration's willingness to support it, rather than be an evaluation of profit and loss.

Controls

The last section of the plan describes the controls that will be used to monitor the plan's progress. The objectives and budgets can be spelled out for each month or quarter; then top administration can review the results each period. Where objectives are not being met or budgets are being exceeded, the administrator can request plans for corrective action.

This completes the description of the contents of a marketing plan. We now turn to formal planning systems.

MARKETING PLANNING SYSTEMS

We have described strategic marketing planning and the tactical marketing plans that guide action. Some institutions prepare such plans from time to time but shun adopting formal planning systems. They see the value of "having a plan" but reject formal procedures as unnecessary or too demanding. For example, a university president offered the following justification:

1. The department heads (deans and chairpersons) do not have the time to write formal plans, nor does the top administration have the time to read them.

2. Most department heads would not be able to plan even if they were asked. They head their departments because they are scholars or leaders in the fields, not because they are managers. They might refuse to plan, or plan poorly, and this would be tolerated as long as they were performing well in other respects.

3. The department heads would not use their plans. The plans would be mere window dressing, prepared and then filed away. The plans might even be obsolete the day they were written, given the rapid changes in the academic world.

4. The administration has plans that are best kept secret from the department heads, since they might feel threatened. The department heads should not be encouraged to come up with unrealistic expectations that the president would have to reject.

5. Installing a formal planning system and making it work would cost too much in money and time.

Although we grant some validity to these arguments, the experience of a growing number of schools and colleges demonstrates that formal planning and control systems are usually beneficial and improve institutional performance. Formal planning also helps the institution communicate with its publics and maintain their support. Consider the following case:

In December 1975, All Hallows School, an eight-room parochial elementary school in a rural Connecticut community, faced closing at the end of the term. The school's enrollment had declined from 260 to 177 students in five years.

Persistent rumors of closing brought further declines. In addition, the parish carried a long-term debt on which nothing had been paid for five years. All Hallows' financial problems grew as enrollment and tuition revenue declined.

A marketing consultant worked with school administrators, parents, and parishioners to develop a formal, written long-range plan. With a clear grasp of its resources, problems, and opportunities, the school remained open and soon achieved capacity enrollment. The parish debt is being repaid. Most important, rumors of closing have ceased and parents can anticipate the school's performance from year to year.[3]

In this case, formal planning helped guide the institution and meet the needs of the school's markets and publics as well. The planning process gave the school a sense of increased confidence, and reports on the plan promoted stability by counteracting rumors.

The relationship between marketing planning and control is shown in Figure 4-3. The planning step calls upon the institution to identify attractive marketing opportunities, develop effective marketing strategies, and develop detailed action programs. The second step involves executing the action programs in the marketing plan. The third step calls for marketing control activity to ensure that the objectives are being achieved. Marketing control involves measuring results, analyzing the causes of poor results, and taking corrective actions—adjustments in the plan, its execution, or both.

Educational institutions move toward strategic planning when the administration realizes that annual plans make sense only in the context of a *long-range plan*. In fact, the long-range plan should come first, with the annual plan being a detailed version of the first year of the long-range plan. The long-range plan is based on assumptions about how the institution and its environment will change over time. Therefore, a long-range plan cannot be static and must be reworked each year (called *rolling planning*).

At this stage, the various plans begin to take on a more *strategic character.*

FIGURE 4-3 The marketing planning and control system

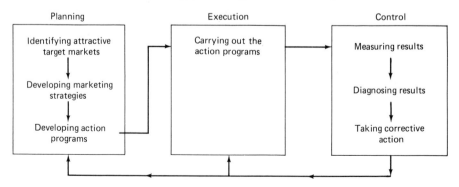

An institution beginning long-range planning often assumes that the future will be a continuation of the present and that present strategies, institutional structure, and procedures will remain appropriate. Eventually, the administration sees that the environment is full of probabilities, not certainties, and that broader strategic thinking is required. The planning format is then redesigned to stimulate administrators to contemplate and evaluate alternative strategies that will improve the institution's performance.

Administrators are then asked to develop contingency plans showing how they would respond to specific major threats and opportunities. The institution needs to take these contingencies seriously and be prepared to take action if the marketing control system signals a problem.[4] Heights University has experienced some setbacks in its enrollment and fund-raising efforts and will need to adapt its plans to changed circumstances. The development of *contingency plans* to help the institution respond and adapt to its environment marks the emergence of a true strategic-planning culture in the institution.

As the institution gains experience with planning, plan formats are often standardized to permit more meaningful comparisons among similar units. As the planning culture takes hold in the institution, further improvements are introduced. Administrators receive training in financial analysis and are required to justify their recommendations not only in terms of enrollment, donations, and so on, but also in terms of financial measures such as cost–benefit or cost-effectiveness of an activity. Where clear financial measures don't exist, educational administrators can develop substitute measures, including "shadow prices," to guide them in allocating the institution's resources.[5]

Computer-based planning models can be developed to help administrators examine the results of alternative marketing plans and environments.[6] Some institutions have developed sophisticated computer models. Stanford University's TRADES model can be used to consider alternative courses of action and evaluate tradeoffs among various policies within user-specified constraints on resources and options. Some general-purpose models have also been developed, but adapting the models to a particular institution can be exceedingly complicated, since each model is based on a particular set of assumptions.[7] To be useful, a model must reflect the institution's policies and practices—its institutional theory—in its set of assumptions.[8]

Designing the Marketing Planning Process

A planning system doesn't just happen. The institution needs to adopt or design a system that is acceptable to administrators and that serves the institution's needs. The following criteria, although proposed by Miller specifically for small colleges, are useful reminders:

- There must be support from the top. The board of trustees and president must determine if they want a formal planning process and, if so, how they will show evidence of their support.

- There must be involvement of representatives from appropriate constituencies. Faculty, administration, staff, students, trustees, alumni, and community representatives should have opportunity for input.
- The objectives of the process must be set and agreed upon.
- The process must be defined in specific, discrete steps that produce results that are used in subsequent tasks.
- The process must not be dominated by one person or committee.
- The process must not be allowed to become isolated—functionally, politically, or geographically.
- The process must include periodic needs assessments.
- The process must include feedback to involved constituencies after each stage of their involvement.
- Evaluation criteria and techniques must be identified before implementation.[9]

Usually, the initial planning system is established by top administration, often with the advice of a committee and/or an outside consultant with broad experience in designing management planning systems. The outside consultant can provide valuable perspectives on planning as well as specific procedures and forms. Some institutions then hire or designate a director of planning to take responsibility for designing the final system and to manage the planning process.

The planning director's job is not to write the plans but to educate and assist administrators in writing their plans. Planning should be done by those who must carry out the plans. In this way, they are stimulated to think out their goals and strategies and are motivated to achieve their objectives.

Since planning is a continuous process, the institution needs to develop a calendar of the planning process. The normal calendar steps for a director of planning are these:

1. Develop a set of relevant environmental facts and trends to distribute to administrators as part of their planning.
2. Work with top administration to develop overall institutional objectives for the coming year as a basis for subsequent planning.
3. Work with individual administrators to complete their marketing plans by a certain date.
4. Work with top administration to review, approve, or modify the various plans.
5. Develop a consolidated official plan for the institution for the coming period.

This calendar sequence underscores the critical role of marketing planning in the overall planning process. Individual administrators examine environmental trends and institutional objectives. They then set marketing objectives (for enrollment, donations, and so forth) for their programs for the coming period, along with proposed strategies and marketing budgets. Once these are approved by top administration, decisions can be made on needed personnel, supplies, and funds to implement them.

TABLE 4-3   Types of marketing control

TYPE OF CONTROL	PRIME RESPONSIBILITY	PURPOSE OF CONTROL	APPROACHES
I. Annual-plan control	Top administration Middle management	To examine whether the planned results are being achieved	Performance analysis Market-share analysis Marketing-expense-to-performance ratios Market-attitude tracking
II. Revenue/cost control	Marketing controller	To examine where the organization is making and losing money	Profitability by: Program or service Location Market segment
III. Strategic control	Top administration Marketing auditor	To examine whether the institution is pursuing its best opportunities.	Marketing audit

MARKETING CONTROL

Marketing control is an early warning system. When a marketing plan is implemented, many surprises are possible—a change in federal government funding, an earthquake, staff departures, and so on. The marketing control system includes techniques for determining when plan goals are being met and for making adjustments when they are not.

Table 4-3 shows three types of marketing control. Each type has its place in an educational institution. *Annual-plan control* refers to the steps taken during the year to monitor and correct performance deviations from the plan. *Profitability control* consists of efforts to determine the actual profit or loss of different programs, services, market segments, or locations. *Strategic control* consists of a systematic evaluation of the institution's marketing performance in relation to its market opportunities. We describe each form of marketing control in the following section.

Annual-Plan Control

Annual-plan control is designed to monitor the effects of carrying out the annual plan. The four steps are shown in Figure 4-4. First, the various administrators—deans, department chairpersons, director of admissions, and so on—set well-defined objectives for each month, quarter, academic year, or other period during the plan year. Second, monitoring techniques and checkpoints are established to track achievement of the objectives. Third, administrators seek to diagnose the causes of serious deviations in performance.

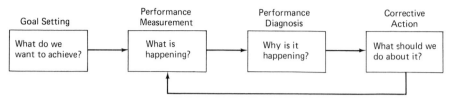

FIGURE 4-4 The control process

Fourth, the administrators choose corrective actions that they hope will close the gap between objectives and performance. This system is an example of management by objectives.

Four main control tools are commonly used: performance analysis, market-share analysis, marketing-expense-to-performance analysis, and market-attitude tracking.

Performance Analysis. *Performance analysis* is the measurement and evaluation of actual performance—measured by enrollment, tuition revenues, and/or donations in relation to performance objectives. Thus, the director of admissions would compare the actual number of new students enrolled to the expected number, and the director of development could compare the number and amount of donations received with fund-raising goals by donor type (alumnus, parent, and the like), gift size, and so on. If too few alumni are donating, if certain categories of alumni are underrepresented, or if the average gift size in certain categories is down from previous years, the causes should be carefully researched and corrective action taken.

Market Share. Institutions should periodically review whether they are gaining or losing ground relative to their competition. For example, a private school may see its applications grow 5 percent per year while competitors' applications have been increasing by 15 percent. Market share is a much better indicator of marketing effectiveness than is total sales, but market share must be used cautiously. The institution must correctly identify its real competitors. Beloit College, for example, should not measure its enrollment performance against the large state universities or the elite private universities. Instead, it should compare its enrollment performance with other colleges to which Beloit applicants also apply. A "perfect competitor" would be another college that students applying to Beloit see as equally desirable. Likewise, a Jewish Sunday school would compare its enrollment performance with other Jewish Sunday schools, not with all Sunday schools.

Marketing Expense-to-Performance Analysis. Annual-plan control also requires evaluating various marketing expenses as a ratio to performance (typically measured by revenue) to ensure that the institution is not overspending to achieve its objectives. An educational institution may want to track the ratio between enrollment marketing (admissions) *expenditures and enrollment*, and the ratio between *fund-raising expenditures and gifts received.* In addition to tracking expenses, the institution should keep track of other ratios that compare effort and results. For example, an experienced development director may periodically check the following ratios: revenue per fund raiser, number of contacts per fund raiser per period, percentage of potential contributors contacted, and percentage of donors.

Market-Attitude Tracking. Institutions should periodically check client attitudes toward the institution. The erosion of attitudes can contribute to later declines in enrollment and donations. Students may drop out or discourage potential applicants, donors may reduce the size or frequency of their gifts or quit giving, and certain academic programs may be abandoned by disgruntled majors. Knowing of these attitude shifts early can lead to precautionary changes. Market attitudes can be measured through complaint and suggestion boxes, consumer panels, and consumer-satisfaction surveys.

Revenue/Cost Control

Besides annual-plan control, institutions may periodically determine the actual profit or loss for their various programs, consumer groups, territories, or locations. *Revenue/cost analysis* requires identifying all revenues generated by a particular unit (department, program, office) or service and all the costs associated with it, then comparing revenues and costs to determine the financial status of the unit. For small educational institutions with only one or two programs, this task is reasonably straightforward. For a nursery school or other small school, it would be relatively easy, but isolating the revenues and costs of a college career placement center would be very difficult, since a highly effective placement office may attract more and better students to the college. Furthermore, the assigning of administrative overhead costs to programs is often somewhat arbitrary.

Revenue/cost analysis can be used to provide information on the relative profitability of various programs, services, branches, and other marketing entities. But it does not imply that "unprofitable" marketing entities should be dropped, nor does it measure the likely profit improvement if marginal units are dropped. The institution needs to consider whether each entity should be expected to match revenues and costs. The president of a respected graduate college of education reportedly protested the recommendation that each unit of the college be economically self-sufficient: "The library doesn't pay its own way, but we must have a library!" A business school may justify conducting continuing-education courses for area businesspeople on the grounds that it encourages donations, improves job prospects for the school's graduates, or provides a service to the community, even if revenue from such courses doesn't contribute much toward overhead.

Most educational institutions have some programs that are expected to pay their own way—or even return a surplus. For private institutions, continuing education is usually intended as a profitmaker. Academic departments, on the other hand, are often viewed as part of a portfolio: The classics department may break even or lose money, whereas the business school will generate a profit. Regardless of whether the entity is expected to make a profit, the comparison of revenues and costs can encourage thinking about possible ways of improving the revenue or reducing the costs of the entity, while preserving or enhancing its quality and functioning.

Strategic Control

From time to time, institutions should critically examine their overall marketing performance. Marketing is one of the major areas where rapid obsolescence of objectives, policies, strategies, and programs is a constant possibility. The marketing audit is a major diagnostic tool to assess the institution's marketing opportunities and operations. The marketing audit will be presented in Chapter 18.

SUMMARY

Marketing planning and control guide the institution's operations in the marketplace. Educational institutions have planning systems of various degrees of sophistication, from simple budgeting systems to formal long-range planning systems. Although educators often resist formal planning, sophisticated formal planning systems can contribute to institutional effectiveness.

Educational institutions should carry out strategic planning and tactical marketing planning. Strategic planning consists of several steps that may be carried out for institutional units as well as for the institution as a whole. The first is environmental analysis, in which the institution examines its internal environment, markets, publics, competitors, and macroenvironment. Implied threats and opportunities are identified so that the institution can prepare contingency plans and monitor changes. The institution then examines its major strengths and weaknesses in personnel, funds, facilities, systems, and other resources. In the goal-formulation step, the institution formulates its basic mission, its major goals, and its specific quantifiable objectives.

Strategy formulation requires analyzing the institution's current portfolio of programs to determine which it should build, maintain, or drop. The resulting strategy includes decisions about the institution's current and future programs and markets, and about needed changes in the institution's structure, people, and culture. Finally, the institution examines its systems of information, planning, and control to be sure they are adequate to carry out the strategy successfully.

Tactical marketing planning is the process of developing the specific plans that will implement the overall strategy. The tactical marketing plan contains the following sections: executive summary, situation analysis, goals and objectives, marketing strategy, action program, budgets, and controls. The marketing-strategy section of the plan defines the target markets, marketing mix, and marketing expenditures that will be used to achieve the marketing objectives.

Marketing control is an intrinsic part of marketing planning. Institutions can exercise three types of marketing control. Annual-plan control consists of monitoring current marketing performance to ensure that annual goals are being achieved. The main tools are performance analysis, market-share analysis, marketing expense-to-performance analysis, and market-attitude analysis. If underperformance is detected, the institution can take corrective action. Revenue/cost control consists of determining the profit or loss for various programs, customer groups, territories, or locations. Revenue/cost analysis does not indicate whether an entity should be bolstered or phased out. Strategic control consists of ensuring that the institution's marketing objectives, strategies, and systems are optimally adapted to the current and anticipated marketing environment.

NOTES

[1] This section is partly based on an article by Philip Kotler and Patrick E. Murphy, "Strategic Planning for Higher Education," *Journal of Higher Education*, September–October 1981, pp. 470–89.

[2] Peter Drucker, *Management: Tasks, Responsibilities, Practices* (New York: Harper & Row, 1973), Chap. 7.

[3] Richard J. Burke, "Can Formal Long-Range Planning Solve Your School's Problems?" *Momentum*, May 1978, pp. 38–41.

[4] Andrew H. Lupton, "Nine Ways Toward Better Management," *Educational Record*, Summer 1980, pp. 19–23.

[5] Karl A. Fox, ed. *Economic Analysis for Educational Planning: Resource Allocation in Nonmarket Systems* (Baltimore: The Johns Hopkins University Press, 1972).

[6] David S.P. Hopkins and William F. Massy, *Planning Models for Colleges and Universities* (Stanford, Cal.: Stanford University Press, 1981).

[7] Randall Porter, Robert Zemsky, and Penny Oedel, "Adaptive Planning: The Role of Institution-Specific Models," *Journal of Higher Education*, September–October 1979, pp. 586–601.

[8] See Charles Wiseman, "New Foundations for Planning Models," *Journal of Higher Education*, November–December 1979, pp. 726–44.

[9] John Edgar Miller, "Planning in Small Colleges," *Planning for Higher Education*, November 1980, pp. 25–26.

chapter 5

ANALYZING
THE ENVIRONMENT

Wayne State University, like other public educational institutions, has been strongly affected by the economic and political environment. In 1970, Michigan ranked among the top ten states in per capita expenditure for higher education; by 1982, it was in the bottom ten. Appropriations declined almost 5 percent in 1981, with further cuts in 1982. Growing unemployment brought lower receipts from income and other taxes and increased demands on welfare funds and services, putting more pressure on state funds just when the economic situation was most dire.

The effect on Wayne State was traumatic. Tuition was raised several times, each time increasing the likelihood that some students would have to drop out. A hiring freeze left 100 nonacademic vacancies unfilled, scores of nontenured faculty received termination notices, and a "brain drain" of the university's leading scholars began. Highly paid campus administrators took salary cuts of 5 to 10 percent.

In 1981, Wayne State's president, Thomas N. Bonner, declared, "We must prepare now for a diminished university by 1985." He said the need was for an institution "that focuses on our strengths and central purposes, that is better administered and more creative in its use of resources, that is less dependent on public appropriations, and that seeks always to do more with less."

Fortunately for Wayne State and Michigan's system of public higher education, an upturn in the economy in 1983 increased state tax receipts and permitted increased appropriations for higher education. But the 1983–84 appropriations still placed Michigan in 34th place in per capita expenditures for higher education, a comedown from its former stature.

Wayne State's administrators and faculty recognized that most of the institution's problems were not of its own making. The university's financial plight stemmed from problems in the automobile industry, in its worst slump since the Great Depression, and the state's almost 14 percent unemployment rate, the highest in the country. The automobile industry's problems in turn dated back to strategic decisions made years ago, as well as intense Japanese competition, the rapid multiplication of fuel costs in the 1970s, and national economic policies to counter inflation. But acknowledging that the underlying problems were beyond the school's control only reminded Wayne State University administrators of its vulnerability to outside forces and of the need to anticipate and respond to such forces.

SOURCE: Based on information from Robert L. Jacobson, "Administrators, Professors at Wayne State Argue over Depth of University's Troubles," *The Chronicle of Higher Education*, February 17, 1981, pp. 5–6; Jack Magarrell, "Serious Financial Problems Facing States Portend a Lean Year for Public Campuses," *The Chronicle of Higher Education*, February 17, 1981, pp. 4ff.; Jack Magarrell, "States Play 'Catch Up' with College Funds," *The Chronicle of Higher Education*, September 7, 1983, pp. 1 & 12; and "State Appropriations for Higher Education in 1983–84 and Changes Over 2 Years," *The Chronicle of Higher Education*, October 26, 1983, pp. 14–15.

To succeed, Wayne State University and other institutions must make timely and appropriate adaptations to a complex and ever-changing environment. This chapter will examine the macroenvironment affecting educational institutions. We will address the following questions:

1. How can institutions better align themselves with their environments?
2. How can institutions identify and evaluate environmental trends and resulting threats and opportunities?
3. What environmental forecasting techniques are useful for educational institutions?

We conclude the chapter with instructions on preparing a macroenvironmental analysis.

INSTITUTION/ENVIRONMENT ADAPTATION

The *macroenvironment* consists of large-scale fundamental forces that shape opportunities for and pose threats to the institution—*demographic, economic, ecological, technological, political,* and *cultural forces.*

Two attributes of the macroenvironment are particularly important. First, the macroenvironment is *constantly changing.* The decade of the 1970s, for example, was marked in different periods by shortages, runaway inflation, and high unemployment, as well as by various movements such as consumerism, environmentalism, and the women's movement.

Second, macroenvironmental forces are *largely outside the control and influence of educational institutions* or any other organization or group of organizations. This does not mean that educational institutions make no contribution, but only that their effect is almost always long-term rather than short-term. (One notable exception was the university-based research that led to the birth-control pill—a technological change that led to major and rapid changes in other aspects of the macroenvironment, including school enrollments!)

Educational institutions must understand and adapt to macroenvironmental trends, since few are so buffered that they can ignore the changing times. An institution's performance depends on the degree of alignment between its environmental opportunities, objectives, marketing strategy, organizational structure, and management systems. In the ideal case:

Environment→Objectives→Strategy→Structure→Systems

This says that the institution first studies the environment in which it is operating, and specifically the opportunities and threats in this environment. It then develops a set of objectives describing what it wants to achieve in this environment. Then it formulates an institutional strategy that promises to achieve these objectives. After that, it builds an organizational structure capable of carrying out the strategy. Finally, it designs various systems of analysis, planning, and control to support the effective implementation of the strategy.

In practice, this optimal alignment is hard to realize, because the various components alter at different rates. A typical situation is:

Environment	Objectives	Strategy	Structure	Systems
1985	1980	1976	1973	1970

This says that the institution is operating in a 1985 environment but with objectives that were set in 1980 for the environment at that time. Its strategy lags even more, since it is the strategy that was successful in 1976. Its organizational structure is not even geared to supporting its 1976 strategy, having been designed earlier in a quite different environment. Finally, its systems are even older and have not been adjusted to the new conditions.

Too often, in fact, institutions are run in a reverse (and perverse) way of thinking:

Structure and Systems→Objectives and Strategy→Environment

The institution believes that its structure and systems are sound because they worked during its most successful years. Using these, it chooses objectives and strategies that are manageable under the present systems and structure. Then it scans the environment to find the opportunities that are best suited to its objectives and strategy.

An example would be a hospital nursing school that provides R.N. training. Its organization, staffing, and systems are maximally adapted to providing training for would-be nurses. Furthermore, the hospital desperately needs the services the nurses in training provide. As a result, the nursing school sets its objectives in terms of attracting a certain number of students and its strategy as one of appealing to academically able students who are not interested in spending four years in college. Then it searches the environment broadly for this type of student. But the irony is that there are fewer such candidates around, since many states are beginning to require a baccalaureate degree for a registered nurse, and the most able students are selecting collegiate schools of nursing.

The main problem is that the environment is the fastest-changing element in the picture. Educational institutions traditionally do not change rapidly. Even when they can spot coming trends, they tend to move slowly to respond to them. With increasingly rapid change, some institutions continue to wait until events are upon them before mobilizing. In the 1960s, many school-district superintendents and boards of education were preoccupied with constructing school buildings and expanding programs. At that time, the decline in the number of pupils was already predictable (the children were already born), and the effects were felt in the elementary schools in the early 1970s. Only then did elementary schools begin to consider how to cope with this change in demand.

The optimal approach is to attempt to forecast what the marketing environment will be like in, say, five years. Given this environmental forecast, the institution's leaders will set objectives that will describe where they want to be then. Then they will formulate a strategy that will deliver those objectives in five years. They will begin to alter the institution and its systems so that these will support the new strategy rather than act as a drag on its fulfillment. This forward-looking thinking is depicted below:

$$\text{Environment} \rightarrow \text{Objectives} \rightarrow \text{Strategy} \rightarrow \text{Structure} \rightarrow \text{Systems}$$
$$\quad 1990 \qquad\qquad 1990 \qquad\quad 1990 \qquad\quad 1990 \qquad\quad 1990$$

Environmental Change

The character of an institution's environment may determine its survival as much as the quality of its programs or leadership. We can distinguish between the degrees of stability of an environment. The first is a *stable environment*, in which the major forces of demographics, economics, ecology, technology, law, and culture remain stable from year to year. The second is a *slowly evolving environment*, in which smooth and fairly predictable changes take place. The individual institution survives in this type of environment to the extent that it foresees change and takes intelligent steps to adapt. For example, declines in school enrollment could be predicted far in advance and planned for. The third is a *turbulent environment*, in which major and unpredictable changes occur often.

More and more educational institutions find themselves operating in turbulent environments. In *Future Shock*, Toffler documents how key technological, economic, and social forces show an "accelerative thrust," with the rate of change increasing.[1] The institution operating in a turbulent environment has three tasks: (1) systematically scanning its environment, (2) identifying environmental threats and opportunities, and (3) making intelligent adaptations to the changing environment.

Environmental Scanning

Most educational institutions engage in *environmental scanning* in an informal manner. For example, the president and other administrators of a college will read local newspapers, national magazines, journals, and publications such as *The Chronicle of Higher Education*. Exhibit 5-1 draws on an article in the *Journal of Higher Education*. Administrators may note a development in other parts of the country and consider the likely effect if it happened in their area. Some of the ideas sparked by reading or talking with counterparts at other colleges may be carefully scrutinized and incorporated into the college's

EXHIBIT 5-1. Possible macroenvironmental trends affecting higher education

Many analysts of the higher education scene have pointed to trends that they believe will have a profound effect on colleges and universities. According to Lyman Glenny, here are some probable trends:

The downturn in the number of college-age youth will have immediate and by 1988 fairly substantial, if not drastic, effects on most of the higher education institutions in the nation.

- The college-going rate has declined and then leveled off, and nothing on the immediate horizon suggests a reversal of this trend, although women will, in the short run, continue to enroll at greater rates than men.
- The increasing proportion of minority youth will be pragmatic and take job-oriented programs, primarily, as in the recent past, in the community colleges.

• • •

Adults entering college will not make up for the loss in the 18- to 24-year-old age group.

- The videodisc and videocassette will take their toll of adults in the 25- to 35-year-old age group because of their familiarity with television and habit of watching it—for learning as well as entertainment purposes.
- Adults will be less and less inclined to take credit courses leading to a degree, because the economic value of the college degree has diminished in relation to the high school diploma and because so many people now hold and will hold more degrees than required by the labor force.

• • •

- Adults will continue to become lifelong learners and will enroll in many noncollegiate types of courses and activities of both short and long duration. Colleges and universities, except for community colleges, probably cannot successfully compete in this broad, open field of educational opportunities.

• • •

Those institutions of higher education that do survive until 1995 will have stronger programs, more distinguished faculties, and better senses of mission and goals.

SOURCE: Quoted (with minor changes) from Lyman A. Glenny, "Demographic and Related Issues for Higher Education in the 1980s," *Journal of Higher Education*, 51, July–August 1980, pp. 374–78.

planning. But many ideas either will not appear in print or may be missed, or their relevance may be unclear. The result of such informal environmental scanning may be that a threat or opportunity may materialize before the college recognizes it and too late to plan a response.

In contrast, a university engaged in formal environmental scanning will have a high interest in monitoring legislative thinking, among other things. The university may hire—or join with other universities to hire—one or more intelligence officers, locate them in a Washington office, and give them a budget for initiating and maintaining contacts with knowledgeable people in Congress and relevant government agencies. These officers will assemble information on possible shifts in research funding, financial assistance programs, interest rates, and Congressional attitudes toward higher education and relay this information to university administrators for action.

Among the large amount of information flowing into the institution, administrators must be able to spot the environmental forces with the greatest import for future strategy. These forces can be classified as either threats or opportunities facing the institution. We briefly described these in Chapter 4 with reference to Beloit College. We define an *environmental threat* as follows:

> An environmental threat is a challenge posed by an unfavorable trend or specific disturbance in the environment that would lead, in the absence of purposeful marketing action, to the stagnation or demise of the institution or one of its programs.

A major threat is one that (1) would cause substantial damage to the institution's ability to function, and (2) has a moderate to high probability of occurring. No institution is free of such threats, and every administrator should be able to identify them.

The president of a private college in the Northeast would readily identify the following threats: (1) a major recession that would cut enrollment and donations, (2) a population shift toward warmer areas of the country, and (3) declining demand for liberal arts studies.

An institution facing several major environmental threats is highly vulnerable. Its administration should prepare contingency plans and consider new opportunities.

We define an *institutional marketing opportunity* as follows:

> An institutional marketing opportunity is an attractive area of relevant marketing action in which a particular institution is likely to enjoy a competitive advantage.

A major institutional marketing opportunity is one that (1) has strong potential for contributing to the institution's financial strength and reputation, and (2) carries a moderate-to-high probability that the institution would have success with it.

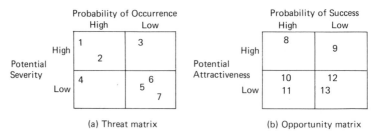

FIGURE 5-1   Threat and opportunity matrices

Among the major marketing opportunities facing a private college are (1) developing an unusually strong, high-demand program, (2) attracting one or more very large donations, and (3) hiring an outstanding scholar to join the faculty. To the extent that there are strong opportunities facing that institution, we simply say that the institution faces high opportunity.

An important exercise for administrators and other managers of an educational institution is to periodically identify the major threats and opportunities facing the institution and each of its units (schools or colleges, departments, branches, and so on). This should be done as part of preparing annual and long-range plans. Each threat and opportunity is assigned a number and then evaluated according to its probable level of effect and occurrence. The threats and opportunities can then be plotted in the *threat and opportunity matrices* shown in Figure 5-1.

The *threat matrix* shows seven identifiable threats. Management should give the greatest attention to threats 1 and 2, because they would have a strong effect on the institution and have a high probability of occurrence. Threat 3 can also hurt the institution substantially, but it has a low probability of occurrence, and threat 4 would not hurt much but is highly likely to occur. Management can safely ignore minor threats 5, 6, and 7.

The *opportunity matrix* shows six identifiable opportunities. The best is opportunity 8, which would have a high positive effect if the institution is successful at developing it, and the institution is highly likely to be successful. Opportunity 9 is attractive, but the institution may not have the resources or competence to succeed in this opportunity. Opportunities 10 and 11 are minor in their effect although easy to carry off successfully. Opportunities 12 and 13 can be ignored.

Four outcomes are possible with this analysis, shown in the opportunity–threat matrix in Figure 5-2. An *ideal position* is one that is high in major opportunities and low in or devoid of major threats. A *speculative position* is high in both major opportunities and threats. A *mature position* is low in major opportunities and threats. Finally, a *troubled position* is low in opportunities and high in threats.

Each institution should seek to move toward its major opportunities and away from its major threats. The institution must carefully appraise the nature of its opportunities. Levitt cautions:

> There can be a need, but no market; or a market, but no customer; or a customer, but no salesman. For instance, there is a great need for massive pollution control, but not really a market at present. And there is a market for new technology in education, but no customer really large enough to buy the products. Market forecasters who fail to understand these concepts have made spectacular miscalculations about the apparent opportunities in these and other fields.[2]

Even in pursuing a marketing opportunity, the institution can control its level of risk. The institution may make a token investment in researching the opportunity, without changing its current direction. Or it might make a moderate investment in the hope of being one of the first educational institutions to pursue this opportunity. Or it might make a substantial investment in the hope of becoming the leader, although this might involve great risk to its current activities.

In facing a major threat, the institution can respond in four ways:

1. *Denial.* The institution can ignore or deny that a real change is occurring. Some administrators still refuse to recognize the shrinking pool of students and how it will affect them. They believe that other, "weaker" schools will close, not theirs, and therefore they are not yet considering new strategies.

2. *Opposition.* The institution can try to fight, restrain, or reverse the unfavorable development. Opposition may be used to "buy" the time needed to make more fundamental adjustments.

3. *Modification.* The institution can try to improve its environmental fit through modifying its structure and/or programs. In the 1960s and 1970s, many small, single-sex colleges became coed.

4. *Relocation.* The institution can try to stay the same but shift its services to a more compatible environment. A school may try to attract a new market, offer classes in other locations, or even relocate its entire campus to a more advantageous location.

FIGURE 5-2   Opportunity–threat matrix

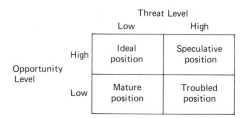

In a turbulent environment, the institution must spend more time and resources to keep abreast of significant environmental changes. It must not insist on sticking to the tried and true after this has become dysfunctional. Instead, the institution must be prepared to adapt creatively to the changing environment.

TECHNIQUES FOR ENVIRONMENTAL FORECASTING

Decisions about expansion, programs, and recruitment depend on strategic judgments about the future environment. Making these decisions would be far simpler if the institution could correctly anticipate the character of that environment. To assist in this task, a growing number of large companies are turning to formal *environmental forecasting*, an area that holds promise for educational institutions as well.

No one disputes that environmental forecasting is still more art than science. Even though there has been some progress in the methodologies for forecasting economic and technological developments, forecasting political and cultural developments remains difficult, because they interact so much with economics and technology. Some people question the value of environmental forecasting, yet the risks of missing a major threat or opportunity can be so great that many companies continue to invest in it. Our position is that long-range forecasing can contribute greatly to the identification of opportunities and assessment of risks, and that educational institutions should engage in environmental forecasting insofar as they can.

Educational institutions usually wait for events or trends to emerge before incorporating them in their planning. They feel hard-pressed to scan the present environment for threats and opportunities and respond to them, let alone to try to imagine what the future may bring. They may also conclude that environmental forecasting techniques are too difficult to implement and that they cannot afford professional forecasting services.

Institutions that cannot afford elaborate forecasting procedures should not forego forecasting altogether. Ascher reviewed dozens of forecasts of population, economic, energy, transportation, and technology trends and concluded that the accuracy of a given forecast depended primarily on the underlying core assumptions, "which represent the forecaster's basic outlook on the context within which the specific forecasted trend develops."[3] When the core assumptions are valid, the sophistication of the specific forecasting method used is often of secondary importance. Conversely, if the core assumptions are faulty, the most sophisticated methodology will not produce a useful forecast.

Of the various forecasting methods in use, the following three types are the most useful for educational institutions: *trend extrapolation, consensus methods*, and *cross-impact matrix methods*.[4] We will consider each in turn.

Trend Extrapolation

Forecasting by *trend extrapolation* assumes that trends established in recent history will continue. The underlying assumption is that the forces that created the trend will continue in the future. Consider the trend in the number of high school graduates in California from 1975 to 1981—steady for the first few years, followed by three years of straight decline (Figure 5-3). Extrapolating this downward trend very far into the future would be plausible, but probably erroneous. Projections by the Population Research Unit for California indicate that the number graduating from high school each year will increase between 1985 and 1988, then decline below the previous 1985 low before trending upward again.

The immense California state system of higher education, local community colleges, and private institutions draw most of their students from this group, so accurate projections are important. Rather than relying on simple trend extrapolation, the Population Research Unit would take into account such underlying factors as birthrate, migration trends, and rates of high school completion in the past.

FIGURE 5-3   Graduates of California public and private high schools, actual (1975-1983) and projected (1984-1994)

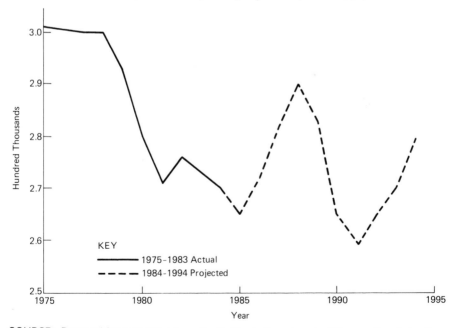

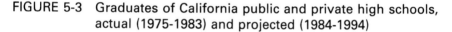

SOURCE: Prepared from statistics from the California Department of Finance, Population Research Unit, 1984 Series, Table 9, "Graduates of California Public and Private High Schools."

Trend extrapolation has several limitations. First, the shorter the time period of the forecast, the better it works. Over a relatively short period of time, past forces are more likely to continue to shape events as before. Second, the accuracy of trend-extrapolation forecasts is greater for systems that change slowly. For example, the organization of schools into age-graded classes has been a very persistent feature of education and is unlikely to change rapidly. On the other hand, the most popular fields of study at the college level may change dramatically over a decade. Third, trend extrapolation can produce unreliable forecasts if events in the recent past are assumed to be indicators of a trend when in fact they are merely brief deviations from an underlying trend. Fourth, trend extrapolation is useless for forecasting single events, since there is no causal continuum underlying such events. Thus, trend extrapolation may be useful in predicting enrollment, but not in predicting a major catastrophe that would destroy a portion of the institution's facilities. Fifth, trends can be reversed. The fact that total college enrollment increased during the 1960s and 1970s does not mean the trend will continue.

The overriding advantage is that trend extrapolation calls on the institution to organize existing data on important trends (applications, enrollment, dropouts, donations, costs, and so on) and to examine them thoroughly and thoughtfully. As administrators consider alternative future trends (increase, stable, decrease), they can identify threats and opportunities for further study.

Consensus Methods

Several forecasting techniques rely on determining a consensus of opinion about likely future events. *Consensus methods* assume that combining the opinions of several experts will result in a more accurate and therefore more reliable forecast than will a forecast by a single expert.

The *Delphi method* is a structured method for obtaining and combining opinions without the potential bias of putting experts in face-to-face contact to come to a consensus. According to Olaf Helmer, its developer:

> Delphi . . . operates on the principle that several heads are better than one in making subjective conjectures about the future, and that experts . . . will make conjectures based upon rational judgment and shared information rather than merely guessing, and will separate hope from likelihood in the process.[5]

In a typical Delphi exercise, participants receive questions by mail and return their answers to the coordinator. The questions may concern the likelihood of a future event or when a future event is likely to take place. The coordinator summarizes the opinions and sends them to all participants for further comment, particularly on opinions that differed significantly from the group median. In the third "round," the participants are invited to reassess their positions in the light of the opinions expressed by others.

The Delphi method offers four advantages. First, a Delphi exercise usually yields a "band" of opinion, which, although not a complete consensus, narrows the range. This narrowing results from the anonymous "debate" that takes place over the several rounds of the exercise, providing each participant with grounds that might warrant shifting an opinion. Second, the Delphi technique clarifies areas where opinions differ substantially. Third, participants in a Delphi exercise do not know the identities of other participants. Therefore, Delphi results can be assumed to be unbiased by personalities, reputations, or debating talents. Fourth, the Delphi process is easy to administer and relatively inexpensive compared to group meetings.

The major limitation of the Delphi method, and other consensus methods, is that they represent *opinions* about what might happen, not *statements* about what will happen. For an educational institution, Delphi methods can suggest plausible futures worthy of consideration, but the futures may not materialize.

Cross-Impact Matrix Methods

Cross-impact matrix methods go beyond trend-extrapolation and consensus methods by asking how future events or trends may be interrelated. If a particular event happens, it may prevent another from taking place or may reduce or increase its effect. For example, an economic depression may affect government financial aid policies and the rate of college attendance. To look at the rate of college attendance, financial aid policies, and economic conditions independently masks their interrelationship and gives a misleading picture of future events.

The analysis of cross-impacts includes judging the probability of one event or trend in view of the probability of interrelated events or trends. We speak of a cross-impact effect if the probability of one event's occurring varies positively or negatively as other events occur or don't occur. Several computer simulation models (such as KSIM and DYSIM)[6] have been developed to analyze the expert judgments and determine the matrix values, but such models are not essential.

As in other forecasting methods that depend on judgment, the usefulness of cross-impact analysis depends upon thoughtful identification of trends and events and the evaluation of likely effects on the selected situation or issue. The list of trends and events may be generated by an individual, although more often it is done by a group using the Delphi method (described above), the Nominal Group Technique,[7] brainstorming, or some other procedure. Group members then individually estimate the likelihood of each trend or event, giving a probability between 0 and 1, and the probabilities are averaged. Group members are then asked to consider the events in pairs and indicate whether the cross-impact would be positive, neutral, or negative.[8]

Regardless of the approach used, each educational institution should develop a consistent way to track environmental trends. Often the entire responsibility falls on the president or head of the institution or unit. Biographies of college presidents often refer to them as men and women of "vision," who sensed their institutions' potential and how the institution could make a contribution within its environment. Successful institutions encourage administrators to think through trends and possible threats and opportunities and devise plans to address or to take advantage of them.

PREPARING AN ANALYSIS OF THE MACROENVIRONMENT

Environmental scanning and environmental forecasting provide the basis for (1) producing a list of developing trends and possible events that could affect the institution, and (2) determining plausible threats and opportunities, their likelihood of occurrence, and their potential severity. The major forces of the macroenvironment can be classified under the headings of demography, economy, natural resources, technology, politics, and culture. What these environmental forces have in common is that they are external to the institution and that they have a greater influence on the institution than the institution has on them. Because the institution cannot affect these forces, at least in the short term, it must recognize them and develop plans to cope with or respond to them.

A written macroenvironmental analysis would include the six categories above (or a subset of them, if some are inappropriate). Under each category would be listed the *significant trends and possible events* that are relevant to the institution's continued operation and success, followed by *specific implications for the institution.*

Preparing an analysis is much more than a writing task. Each step involves making decisions. For example, some person or group within the institution must decide which environmental forces are potentially important. At this step, the preparers may overlook some important forces. A private elementary school may list "population size" but ignore changes in the age and family structures of the community. It might overlook the possibility of legislation forbidding landlords to discriminate in renting to families with children.

Once the relevant factors are listed, the preparers must specify the trends as carefully as possible. The preparers will probably need to turn to census and other government documents to get data on changes over time. From the data on trends, they must draw the implications for the institution. The draft should then be circulated to others within the institution for comment before the final version is prepared. The "final" version will, however, need to be updated annually or more often as new trends emerge.

Table 5-1 presents a marcoenvironmental analysis. A university was interested in the forces that would affect adult women's decisons to enroll in undergraduate degree programs. The macroenvironmental analysis takes five forces and presents factors under each that might have an influence. For each factor, relevant trends are noted, along with implications for the university.[9]

Data on the various trends came from the U.S. Census Bureau publications and other published sources. Note that this macroenvironmental analysis, prepared in 1979, would need to be updated, since subsequent events have altered some of the trends and implications noted here.

TABLE 5-1   Macroenvironmental analysis

FACTORS	TRENDS	IMPLICATIONS
I. Demographic		
A. Birthrate	Turned down in the 1960s, now at 15.3 per 1,000 population.	By 1990, 25% fewer 18-year-olds, cutting college enrollments of this age group. "Baby-boom" generation will fill work positions, blocking the upward mobility of younger workers, who may eschew college as not contributing to career success.
B. Life expectancy	Increasing slowly. Women born in 1950 can expect to live to 71.5, men to 65.6.	More justification for undertaking college study, even in middle age, because of remaining years of satisfaction and application of new knowledge and skills.
C. Marital status	Sharply increasing rate of divorce (ratio of divorces to marriages has increased 79% from 1970 to 1977, compared with 34% for the preceding decade). Increase in the number of children living with mother only.	Social and demographic changes increase the likelihood that many women will need to support themselves and their dependents. Many will view college education as a personal and academic transition toward self-support after divorce or widowhood.
D. Median age at first marriage	Ranged between 20 and 21 for three decades, now 21.0.	Many women continue to marry before the traditional age of completing college.
E. Population density	70% of U.S. population lives in metropolitan areas.	Easier for institutions to define and serve a community student market.
II. Economic		
A. Inflation	9% per year and rising. Cost of living increasing faster than wages.	Families will select less expensive institutions for their children; older women may likewise select less expensive public, over private, institutions.
B. Wage levels	Salaries paid to women continue to trail those of men, but some evidence that gap is narrowing.	Families will increasingly need two incomes to maintain current lifestyles. Thus more women will plan to work and will get college degrees.

TABLE 5-1 Macroenvironmental analysis (continued)

FACTORS	TRENDS	IMPLICATIONS
C. Productivity	Not keeping pace with salary/ wage increases.	People in dead-end jobs will seek college to upgrade qualifications and skills. Firms may hire more workers with specialized technical training but not college. Or firms may seek more highly educated (college) workers, but salaries will stay relatively low.
III. Technological A. Mechanization	Steadily increasing. Many jobs require coordination, some use of discretion. Demand for technically trained workers will grow.	Despite demand for technical skills, a college degree will often be viewed as basic entry-level qualification in many fields. Will encourage more adults to complete college.
B. Modes of instruction	Closed-circuit TV and other educational delivery systems for information and instructions are alternatives to traditional modes.	Traditional college classroom instruction may decline in favor as more effective and efficient delivery systems are developed.
IV. Political/Legal A. Equal access and B. Age discrimination/ retirement legislation	Federal guidelines and court decisions are moving in direction of making education and work opportunities more accessible for women and older people.	Universities that have acted on earlier civil rights and Equal Opportunity/Affirmative Action regulations will be pressed to eliminate age discrimination. Older women will see more value in returning to college as more higher-level jobs open to them.
V. Sociocultural A. Leisure time	Education will grow in popularity as a leisure activity.	Colleges will find more older students seeking stimulation and expecting "adult treatment."
B. Educational level	Increase in percent of population over 25 that has completed four years or more of college. In 1977, 19.2% of men and 12% of women had college degrees.	Desire to conform to backgrounds of neighbors/friends will encourage people to complete college.

SOURCE: Karen F.A. Fox, *Attracting a New Market to Northwestern's Undergraduate Programs: Older Women Living on the North Shore* (Evanston, Ill.: Northwestern University Program on Women, 1979).

Starting with the completed macroenvironmental analysis, the institution lists its perceived threats and opportunities and prepares threat and opportunity matrices. The macroenvironmental analyses and the matrices become part of the strategic planning process. Together with the resource analysis, they provide the institution with the basis for formulating its mission, goals, and objectives. These topics are presented in the following chapter.

SUMMARY

Educational institutions operate within a complex and rapidly changing marketing environment, which each institution must continuously monitor and adapt to if it is to survive and prosper. The marketing environment has five components: the internal environment, the market environment, the public environment, the competitive environment, and the macroenvironment. In this chapter, we are concerned with the macroenvironment. The alert institution will set up formal systems for identifying, appraising, and responding to the opportunities and threats posed by the macroenvironment.

The marketing macroenvironment includes demographic, economic, ecological, technological, political, and cultural forces. These environmental forces affect the institution far more than the institution affects them. Therefore, the institution ignores these forces at its peril. In fact, it should not only scan the environment to determine present opportunities and threats; it should also engage in environmental forecasting to predict what the future will be like, in order to set appropriate objectives and develop a strategy to achieve them, supported by an effective institutional structure and systems. Achieving this alignment is difficult, because the environment changes rapidly, and educational institutions often wait until events are upon them before taking action.

Environmental scanning calls for identifying the major environmental areas of interest to the institution, assigning responsibility for each area, and developing efficient systems for collecting and disseminating the information. Although many educational institutions leave this task to top administration (who in turn may depend on informal channels of information), a more formal system can help ensure that important information is not overlooked. Environmental scanning helps identify threats and opportunities that may call for a response from the institution. Threats and opportunities are then rated on likelihood of occurrence and extent of effect on the institution.

Environmental forecasting aims to correctly anticipate the character of the institution's future environment. Even though environmental forecasting is still more art than science, many companies routinely carry out or commission forecasts. We expect that educational institutions will try to adapt forecasting techniques to improve their planning. Three types of forecasting methods appear to be most useful: trend extrapolation, consensus methods, and cross-impact matrix methods. These methods help the institution identify probable trends and events as a basis for preparing an analysis of the macroenvironment.

The macroenvironmental analysis categorizes the significant trends and events facing the institution under the headings of demography, economy, natural resources, technology, politics, and culture. Each trend or event is followed by specific implications for the institution. From the macroenvironmental analysis, the institution can identify and assess threats and opportunities.

NOTES

[1] Alvin Toffler, *Future Shock* (New York: Bantam Books, 1970).

[2] Theodore Levitt, "The New Markets—Think Before You Leap," *Harvard Business Review*, May–June 1969, pp. 53–67, especially pp. 53–54.

[3] See William Ascher, *Forecasting: An Appraisal for Policy-Makers and Planners* (Baltimore: The Johns Hopkins University Press, 1978), p. 199. This book compares the results of a large number of forecasts on population, the economy, energy, transportation, and technology, and analyzes the factors that contribute to forecast accuracy.

[4] For a description of forecasting and specific forecasting methodologies applied to education, see Stephen P. Hencley and James R. Yates, *Futurism in Education: Methodologies* (Berkeley, Cal.: McCutchan, 1974).

[5] Olaf Helmer, *Analysis of the Future: The Delphi Method* (Santa Monica, Cal.: Rand Corporation, March 1967). For a report of a study using the Delphi method, see Denny R. Vincent and Kenneth W. Brooks, "A Delphi Projection: Implications for Declining Enrollment," *Planning and Change*, Spring 1982, pp. 24–30.

[6] For an explanation of these two simulation models, see "The Use of DYSIM in Technology Forecasting," Institute for the Future, Menlo Park, Cal., March 1982.

[7] For step-by-step instructions on using the Nominal Group Technique and the Delphi method, see André L. Delbecq, Andrew H. Van de Ven, and David H.

Gustafson, *Group Techniques for Program Planning: A Guide to Nominal Group and Delphi Processes* (Glenview, Ill.: Scott, Foresman, 1975).

[8] For a detailed example of cross-impact analysis, see F. Friedrich Neubauer and Norman B. Solomon, "A Managerial Approach to Environmental Assessment," *Long Range Planning*, April 1977, pp. 1–8.

[9] For another example of a macroenvironmental analysis related to education, see "Policy Choices in Vocational Education," Institute for the Future, Menlo Park, Cal., December 1979.

chapter 6

DEFINING INSTITUTIONAL RESOURCES AND DIRECTION

Eisenhower College opened in 1968 at the crest of the college enrollment boom and closed fourteen years later. The college's local founders knew little about higher education but knew that a college could help preserve Seneca Falls as a picturesque small town with little industry. Unfortunately, the college began with little planning and no clear mission and objectives.

The boosters of the proposed college did attract a dedicated, talented faculty, who developed a unique interdisciplinary world studies program. Less thought was given to attracting able students and establishing a solid financial base. Financial pressures to open the college in 1968 (rather than 1969, as proposed) meant that the admissions director spent the summer of 1968 seeking students for September. Most of the students were marginal; half were out or on probation by December.

Dwight Eisenhower, for whom the college was named, was a popular president, and the college's founders counted on the Eisenhower name to attract financial support, particularly important in the early years when the school would have no alumni base. But fund raising was difficult. By 1974, the college was in debt and enrollment was still 800 compared with a projected 1,100. To stay open, the college appealed for funds. Congress took the unprecedented step of awarding the college a $9 million share in the profits from the sale of Eisenhower commemorative silver dollars.

Although it yielded some much-needed financial support, the appeal backfired. As the public became aware of the college's precarious financial situation, enrollment dropped 50 percent over the next three years. In 1979, the college was acquired by Rochester Institute of Technology (RIT), which took over its debts and ran it as an RIT unit.

But further financial losses close to $6 million and no sign of reversal convinced RIT to sell the college. In 1982, the campus was put up for sale. Faculty began seeking jobs, students other colleges to attend, and townspeople a way to make ends meet with less income.

> **SOURCE:** Based on Anne Mackay-Smith, "The Death of a College Underscores the Plight of Private Institutions," *The Wall Street Journal*, December 14, 1982, p. 1; and Ira M. Berger, letter to the editor, *The Chronicle of High Education*, July 27, 1983, p. 23.

Given the same macroenvironmental trends and forces, one institution will succeed and another will fail and close its doors. What is the explanation for such different outcomes? Educational institutions are diverse in their histories, founders, missions, resources, and programs, and no two are affected in the same way by the events around them. An institution that understands its own character, resources, and mission is in a better position to respond by setting goals and objectives and developing an appropriate marketing program.

In this chapter, we consider two steps in the strategic planning process: *resource analysis* and *goal formulation*. We will present ways to define the internal character and identify the strengths and weaknesses of an educational institution. Once the environmental-analysis (discussed in Chapter 5), resource-analysis, and goal-formulation steps are completed, the institution has the necessary framework for developing a marketing strategy.

ASSESSING INSTITUTIONAL RESOURCES

Institutions have two kinds of resources: *intangible resources,* such as a good reputation, a long history, and traditions; and *tangible resources,* such as facilities, staff, and money. Both kinds of resources shape an institution's future success in the marketplace.

An institution engaged in marketing planning needs to consider four resource issues:

1. Its institutional environment and character
2. Its stage in the institutional life cycle
3. Its potential for adaptation
4. Its tangible resources and marketing assets

We will discuss each issue in turn.

Institutional Environment

Every educational institution has an *environment* or *character* that began to evolve in its earliest days. Educational institutions were often founded to accomplish some societal or religious purpose deeply felt by their founders. Despite many changes over subsequent decades, elements of the founders' direction remain. Institutional character derives not only from founders and early history, but also from the institution's geographical location, local climate, and size; the success of the founding organization (in the case of church-related colleges); and the match between the institution's offering and its markets.

An educational institution can often learn a great deal by reviewing its history. What were the educational, economic, social, and other forces that inspired the founding of this institution? that have maintained this institution in the past? Have these forces changed? What has been the institution's distinctive character? Has this changed? for the better? Has something been lost that would be worth reintroducing? These questions may at first appear far removed from the marketing task, but they are not. The institution that knows and reflects the best of its character and values is one that will attract participants and supporters.

The institution also needs to determine how it is perceived by students and other constituencies, because this information can reveal the extent to which the institution reflects its intended environment. The institution can look for aspects of its internal environment that are no longer well matched to its markets and the larger environment.

The College and University Environment Scales (CUES) provide a systematic way to determine the environmental characteristics of institutions of higher education. Students respond to 150 statements about college life: ". . . features and facilities of the campus, rules and regulations, faculty, curricula, instruction and examinations, student life, extracurricular organizations, and other aspects . . . which help to define the intellectual-social-cultural climate of a college as students perceive it."[1] Students respond "true" or "false" to such items as:

- It is fairly easy to pass most courses without hard work.
- Most courses are a real intellectual challenge.
- There is very little studying here over weekends.

Combining the judgments of a sample of students provides a measure of the institution's environment on five dimensions:

1. Practicality: the degree to which personal status and practical benefit are emphasized in the college environment
2. Community: the degree to which the campus is friendly, cohesive, and group-oriented
3. Awareness: the degree to which there is a concern with self-understanding, reflectiveness, and the search for personal meaning
4. Propriety: the degree to which politeness, protocol, and consideration are emphasized
5. Scholarship: the degree to which serious interest in scholarship and competition for academic achievement are evidenced[2]

A college or university can use the CUES instrument, American College Testing's ESS-Campus Climate Review, the Student Outcomes Inventory Study provided by the College Board, or other published instruments, or it may instead prepare its own instrument.[3]

Institutional Life Cycle

Education is a permanent human activity, but individual educational institutions may come and go. Although an adaptive institution increases its chances for survival, it will not necessarily enjoy continuous stability or growth. Institutions tend to pass through *life-cycle stages*. In examining its intangible resources, an educational institution should consider its life-cycle stage and its potential for continued adaptation, since adaptability may help to prolong each stage or produce new life cycles.

Figure 6-1 shows the four main stages in the life cycle of a typical institution. The institution is founded at some point and grows slowly (*introduction stage*). If it is successful, a period of growth follows (*growth stage*). The growth eventually slows down, and the institution enters maturity (*maturity stage*). If it fails to adapt to new conditions, it will enter a period of decline (*decline stage*) unless and until it finds a new mission and resources to redirect its activities.

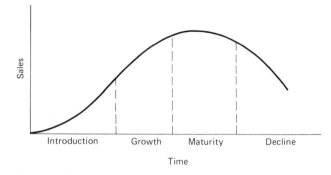

FIGURE 6-1   Typical S-shaped life-cycle curve

The duration of the complete life cycle may be relatively short, as the case of Eisenhower College illustrates. In the case of one private elementary school, the elapsed time was only three years.

The school opened with an individualized system of learning contracts and attracted 50 students. The school's teachers grew dissatisfied with the leadership of the board of directors. Two teachers took control of the school program, the board of directors resigned, and several children were withdrawn from the school. After a year, one of the two directing teachers left to establish her own school, taking half of the 40 remaining students. The original school kept on functioning with two teachers, one aide, and 20 students. The directing teacher hoped to expand to 75 students, but the school's governance structure did not conform to its nonprofit charter, and there was no budget or system of accounts and no past student records as a basis for marketing research. Tuition was paid monthly, so the director could not anticipate revenues. The school was not covering its relatively modest expenses and faced closure. The school had moved directly from introduction to decline.

When considering institutional life cycles, one must be cautious and recognize possible exceptions. For example, the elementary school described above might be flourishing today had the director kept adequate financial and student records, sought participation from key publics, defined the school's market, and so on. In fact, some institutions enjoy a second life cycle as a result of new leadership, a major benefactor, a revamped curriculum, or some other development. There is nothing inevitable about maturity leading into decline. Many educational institutions currently enjoy a comfortable and respected maturity.

One of the major contributions of marketing analysis is to identify new opportunities by which an institution can return to a period of healthy growth or enjoy an extended maturity. For example, consider how Aquinas College in Grand Rapids, Michigan, has changed:

The college began as a novitiate normal school where the Grand Rapids Dominican Sisters trained their young members for teaching in the parochial schools of Michigan. Then the Sisters invited young laywomen to enroll. In 1931 the school moved to a downtown campus and began to admit men, making Aquinas the first coeducational Catholic liberal arts college in the country. Eventually Aquinas expanded from a junior college into a senior college just before World War II, becoming the first Catholic four-year institution serving Michigan west of Detroit. In the 1970s the college conducted a self-study and implemented several new programs to better align the college with the unmet educational needs of the community.[4]

Had the college held narrowly to its original mission and ignored its new opportunities, it would have closed decades ago and would not be making a contribution today.

Not all colleges adapt so successfully. Many educational institutions are faced with contracting resources and enrollment. Some accept decline as their fate and may even close; others eventually turn to new ways in which to serve a valid educational purpose.

Potential for Institutional Change

The reason most institutions pass through maturity and go into decline is that they are unable to adapt to changing circumstances. If an educational institution cannot identify a market and serve it well enough to attract the necessary resources, it will probably close and other institutions will take its place.

Some educational institutions resist change of any kind. For some, this resistance spells doom. Students go elsewhere, faculty members leave or "retire in place," and alumni lose interest in the school. For others, the maintenance of traditions has helped assure their special place. For example, many evangelical colleges are flourishing with required religion classes and chapel, dress codes, and single-sex dormitories. In general, however, the institution that simply keeps doing the same things year after year may find itself serving a declining market.

We define an *adaptive institution* as follows:

> An adaptive institution is one that operates systems for monitoring and interpreting important environmental changes and shows a readiness to revise its mission, goals, strategies, organization, and systems to be maximally aligned with its opportunities.

What factors help explain why some institutions adapt more easily to change than others? Large institutions tend to change more slowly than small ones, because they have more complex management procedures. Well-financed institutions can adapt more readily than poorer ones, since change costs money, although poorer ones may experience more pressure to innovate. Finally, the more regulations and other constraints the institution must deal with, the more slowly it will change.

Regardless of the presence or absence of specific characteristics, all educational institutions must be prepared to respond to changing circumstances. The ability to do so is an important component of the institution's intangible resources.

Preparing a Resource Analysis

The purpose of a *resource analysis* is to identify the strengths and weaknesses of the institution. An institution should pursue goals, opportunities, and strategies that are suggested by, or are congruent with, its strengths and avoid those where its resources are too weak.

Figure 6-2 shows a form that the institution can use, with appropriate modifications, to conduct a resource analysis. The major resources listed are people, money, facilities, systems, and market assets. Each area should be thoroughly reviewed. Based on this review, the institution indicates whether its position with respect to each resource constitutes a strength (high, medium, low), is neutral, or constitutes a weakness (low, medium, high). The institution then lists the reasons for each evaluation as part of the resource analysis.

For example, suppose the checks in Figure 6-2 reflect a college's evaluation of its resources. The administrators believe that the college has an adequate number of skilled personnel, who, unfortunately, are not very enthusiastic, loyal, or service-minded. As for money, the college has enough for its operations, but most funds are committed, so it does not have the flexibility to take on new projects. The college's facilities are adequate, flexible, and well located. Its management systems for information, planning, and control are quite weak. Finally, it enjoys a strong position with students, alumni, and donors, an excellent faculty, and a good general reputation.

With the results of the resource analysis, the college can consider what opportunities its resources might support. The institution should generally avoid opportunities for which necessary resources are weak or inadequate. If the college is considering establishing a nursing program but its science faculty is weak, it should probably drop the idea, since a good science faculty is important for a successful nursing program. The college lacks a *critical success requirement* for launching a nursing program. On the other hand, a weakness need not be fatal if the institution can acquire the resources it needs. If the college has the funds to hire or build a good science faculty, it might consider going ahead with the nursing program.

As a clue to its best opportunities, the institution should pay attention to its distinctive competencies. *Distinctive competencies* are those *resources and abilities in which the institution is especially strong.* If a college has a strong

(H - high; M - medium; L - low; N - neutral)
(Checks ✔ are illustrative)

RESOURCE	STRENGTH			N	WEAKNESS		
	H	M	L	N	L	M	H
People							
1. Adequate number?	✔						
2. Skilled?	✔						
3. Enthusiastic?						✔	
4. Loyal?							✔
5. Service-minded?						✔	
Money (Income and endowment)							
1. Adequate?			✔				
2. Flexible?				✔			
Facilities							
1. Adequate?	✔						
2. Flexible?	✔						
3. Location quality?	✔						
Systems							
1. Information system quality?				✔			
2. Planning system quality?						✔	
3. Control system quality?						✔	
Market assets							
1. Student base?		✔					
2. Alumni and other donors?		✔					
3. Faculty quality?	✔						
4. General reputation?		✔					

FIGURE 6-2   Institutional resource analysis

foreign language department, it might consider such opportunities as starting an area studies program or an evening noncredit language program. Institutions often find it easier to work from their strengths than to build up their weaker areas to some average level of strength. At the same time, a distinctive competence may not be enough if the institution's major competitors possess the same distinctive competence. The institution should pay special attention to those strengths in which it possesses a *differential advantage*—that is, it can outperform competitors on that dimension. For example, Georgetown University not only has a distinctive competence in international studies, but its location in Washington, D.C., gives it a differential advantage in pursuing preeminence in that field.

In evaluating its strengths and weaknesses, the institution must not rely solely on its own perceptions. It must go out and do an *image study* of how it is perceived by its key publics (presented in Chapter 2). For example, the administration may think that the college has a fine reputation in the hard sciences, but an image study might reveal that high school counselors see the college's main strength as the humanities. The administration should study how different key markets and publics—students, parents, business firms, and so on—see its strengths and weaknesses. The findings might indicate certain strengths and weaknesses that the college is not aware of, and others that it exaggerated. Bradley University contacted 1,200 high school college counselors in Illinois and surrounding states to determine their perceptions of Bradley and similar universities, as well as their perceptions of the effectiveness of school college advising programs and how Bradley and other universities could assist them in counseling high school students.

THE GOAL-FORMULATION PROCESS

Goal formulation involves the institution in determining appropriate mission, goals, and objectives for the current or anticipated environment. The three terms are distinguished thus:

- *Mission*: the basic purpose of an institution; that is, what it is trying to accomplish
- *Goal*: a major variable that the institution will emphasize, such as profitability, enrollment, reputation, market share
- *Objective*: a goal of the institution that is made specific with respect to magnitude, time, and who is responsible[5]

We introduced these terms in Chapter 3 and will discuss them in greater detail here.

Mission

Every organization starts with a mission. In fact, an organization can be defined as a human collectivity that is structured to perform a specific mission through the use of largely rational means. Its specific mission is usually clear at the beginning. Harvard College was founded to prepare young men for the ministry and held to this primary mission for more than 150 years. As the nation industrialized, the traditional classical curriculum was broadened. Harvard established professional schools and added other programs and services that further expanded its mission scope.

From time to time, each institution should reexamine its mission by asking and answering the question, "What is our business?" Educational institutions sometimes get sidetracked by listing the courses or programs they offer, thinking that this is the same as a mission statement. Instead, an educational institution should identify the underlying need it is trying to serve. A school may be in the preparation-for-college business. Or it might be in the child-sitting business, keeping track of children while their parents work. It might be in the business of preparing learning-disabled children to return to "regular" school. Ultimately, the school will benefit by deciding what its mission (at least its primary mission) will be. Otherwise, it will lose sight of its mission and confuse it with the many intermediate goals (meet the payroll, add a French teacher, and so on) it might adopt and services it might provide.

A helpful approach to defining mission is establishment of the institution's *scope* along three dimensions. The first is *consumer groups*—namely, who is to be served and satisfied. The second is *consumer needs*—namely, what is to be satisfied. The third is *technologies*—namely, how consumer needs are to be satisfied. For example, consider a traditional junior college for young women. The college's mission scope is represented by the small cube in Figure 6-3, A. Now consider the mission scope of a comprehensive public community college, shown in Figure 6-3, B. This community college serves almost all age groups (with day-care programs and special events for children) and meets at least seven strong needs. It provides credit and noncredit classes, study trips, film and lecture series, and educational and career counseling. Still other colleges will have different mission scopes.

Often, educational institutions are eager to broaden their scope to include specialized programs and graduate professional schools, even when such offerings duplicate those available elsewhere. Multicampus state university systems have frequently set limits on the missions that are appropriate for each campus. For example, the University of Wisconsin–Madison offers Ph.D. work and professional schools, whereas the second doctoral institution, the University of Wisconsin–Milwaukee, offers only Ph.D. programs that match the needs of its urban area. The other eleven four-year campuses award bachelor's, master's, and specialist's degrees only.[6] This "mission differentiation" is designed to better serve Wisconsin's educational needs at a reasonable cost.

The mission of the institution must take into account five key elements. The first is the *history* of the institution. Every institution has a history of aims, policies, and accomplishments. In reaching for a new or expanded mission, the institution must honor the salient characteristics of its past history. Most of the students at Alice Lloyd College come from poor areas of Appalachia; all participate in campus work assignments to meet their expenses. Unless circumstances change dramatically, a decision to become an elite, selective university would violate a founding principle of the college.

The second consideration is the current preferences of the institution's *constituencies*—trustees, administrators, faculty, alumni, students, and others. Some Catholic schools that took the lead in implementing new religious services

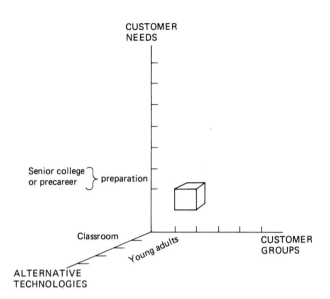

A. A highly focused junior college

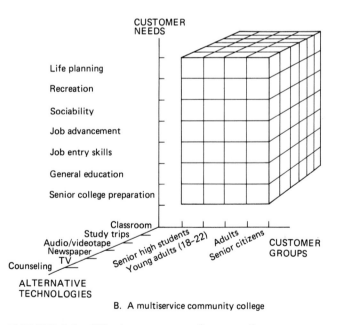

B. A multiservice community college

FIGURE 6-3 Mission scopes of two colleges

and adopting strong positions on social issues have found they have left some alumni supporters behind.

Third, the institution must be prepared to adapt its mission in response to its *environment*. For example, birth and immigration rates indicate that urban-oriented colleges and universities will increasingly serve minority students, many of whom will need vocational training and remedial programs as well as more traditional college programs.

Fourth, the institution's *resources* make certain missions possible and others not. A small private college is unlikely to become the center of high-technology graduate training and research in the United States.

Finally, the institution should base its choice of purpose on its *distinctive competencies*. Although it may be able to accomplish many things, it should aim for what it can do best. A vocational school could probably hire more faculty and become a liberal arts college, but that would not be making use of its main competence—providing vocational skills to recent high school graduates who want to enter the work force as rapidly as possible.

The institution's mission affects everything else. The mission implies a particular type of consumer and calls for a particular way of rendering value to the consumer. A college whose mission is education in the liberal arts would appeal to students who value the life of the mind. The college would invest in intellectually stimulating professors, a large library, small classes, intellectual events on campus, and so on. This mission would put the college in direct competition with many other colleges. It must believe that the intellectual market is large enough and that it has the resources and potential reputation to compete effectively for a reasonable share of those students seeking intellectual training.

On the other hand, if the college chooses to emphasize the applied liberal arts, it would promote itself to those students who place high value on career preparation. It would select careers to specialize in—law, medicine, business, engineering—and build educational programs to include solid classroom work plus field experience and visiting practitioners. It would build a major network of contacts with businesses and the professions to help place students. Thus, developing a clear definition of its mission will lead the college—and any other institution—to emphasize certain things and deemphasize others.

An institution should strive for a mission that is *feasible, motivating*, and *distinctive*, and avoid a "mission impossible." The president of a community college might like to add a medical school, but should realize that this is infeasible. An institution should reach high, but not so high as to produce incredulity in its publics.

The mission should motivate those who work for or receive services from the institution to feel they are part of a worthwhile institution. A school dedicated to academic excellence and service to society will inspire more support than one whose mission is to help relieve the boredom of the overprivileged.

The mission should be something that is perceived as significantly enriching people's lives.

A mission works better when it is distinctive. If all educational institutions resembled each other, there would be little basis for pride in and identification with one's particular institution. People take pride in working for, donating to, or attending a school that "does it differently" or "does it better." By cultivating a distinctive mission and personality, a school stands out more and attracts more loyalty.

A growing number of educational institutions have prepared or revised their formal written *mission statements* to gain the needed clarity. A well-worked-out mission statement provides everyone in the institution with a shared sense of purpose, direction, significance, and achievement. The mission statement acts as a guide to the institution's activities.

Writing a mission statement is hard work. A high-level committee will have to hold many meetings and survey many people before it can prepare a meaningful mission statement. But the time is not wasted. In the process, the administration and faculty will discover a lot about the institution and its best opportunities. Furthermore, the mission statement should serve for many years. The mission should not be changed abruptly every few years. The institution should, however, review its mission from time to time and reconsider it if it no longer works or if it does not define an optimal course for the institution to follow.[7]

Goals

An institution's mission describes what the institution stands for and whom it will serve. To guide its efforts, each institution also needs to develop major goals and objectives separate from but consistent with its mission statement.

For every type of educational institution, there is a potential set of relevant *goals*. The institution's task is to choose among them. For example, the goals of interest to a college may be increased national reputation, improved classroom teaching, higher enrollment, better-qualified applicants, increased efficiency, larger endowment, improved student social life, improved residence facilities, lower operating deficit, and so on. The college cannot successfully pursue all these goals simultaneously, because its budget is limited and because some of the goals may be incompatible.

Formulating institutional goals consists of two steps: determining what the current goals are, and determining what they should be. A review of current goals may reveal that they are inconsistent and even incompatible. For example, a college president may see the primary admissions goal as upgrading the quality of the student body; the director of admissions may see the primary goal as increasing the size of the student body; and the vice president for finance may see the primary goal as increasing the number of nonscholarship students in relation to scholarship students. The faculty may pursue the goal of a reduced teaching load to permit more time for research, whereas the administration may adopt the goal of increasing teaching loads to hold down costs.

How does an educational institution determine what its goals are and what they should be? A widely used approach is the Institutional Goals Inventory (IGI), designed by ETS to assist institutions of higher education to define their educational goals, establish priorities among those goals, and give direction to their present and future planning.[8] The IGI consists of 90 statements of possible goals (with space for up to 20 locally prepared goal statements), which respondents rate on a five-point scale from "Of No Importance" to "Of Extremely High Importance," both in terms of the institution's current situation ("Is") and how respondents would like it to be ("Should Be"). Special versions of the IGI have been prepared for community colleges and for small, independent liberal arts colleges.

Institutions are encouraged to obtain responses from several subgroups—faculty, students, administrators, trustees, community leaders, and alumni, for example. Comparing responses of the various subgroups can contribute valuable perspectives. Figure 6-4 shows sample plots of the mean "Is" and "Should Be" ratings for twelve goals statements. Ratings by four subgroups are shown. It is interesting to note that for this institution, the trustees' ratings of "Is" and "Should Be" are virtually identical, whereas ratings by the other three groups indicate room for improvement for virtually every goal area.

Determining what the goals of an institution should be is a difficult task.[9] In principle, the president and/or the board of trustees can unilaterally set goals for the college. Increasingly, however, top administration has found it essential to involve faculty, alumni, and other publics in the process of goal formulation.

Objectives

The institution may select goals based on respondents' overall ratings and/or those with the largest discrepancy between the current situation and the desired state. The chosen goals must be restated in an operational and measurable form called *objectives*. The goal "increased enrollment" must be turned into an objective such as "a 15 percent enrollment increase in next year's freshman class." A stated objective permits the institution to think about the planning, programming, and control activities required to achieve that goal. Such questions as these arise: Is a 15 percent enrollment increase feasible? What strategy should be used? What resources would it take? What activities would have to be carried out? Who would be responsible and accountable? All these critical questions must be answered when deciding whether to adopt a proposed objective.

Typically, the institution will be evaluating a large set of potential objectives at the same time and examining their consistency. The institution will probably discover that it cannot simultaneously achieve "a 15 percent enroll-

	Faculty	Student	Administrators	Trustees

Assistance for Faculty and Staff   1 2 3 4 5   1 2 3 4 5   1 2 3 4 5   1 2 3 4 5

43. Conduct basic or applied research in academic disciplines.

46. Opportunities for the continuing professional development of faculty and staff.

49. Allow faculty and staff to attend scholarly or professional meetings.

53. Provide opportunities for development off-campus.

Continuing Education   1 2 3 4 5   1 2 3 4 5   1 2 3 4 5   1 2 3 4 5

54. Help non-college-age adults continue their education.

57. Make available educational, social, and occupational development opportunities for alumni.

60. Admit qualified adults, regardless of age, to regular college programs.

63. Cooperate with local employers in providing in-service training opportunities for employees.

Democratic Governance and Freedom   1 2 3 4 5   1 2 3 4 5   1 2 3 4 5   1 2 3 4 5

55. Students, faculty, and staff can be involved significantly in campus governance.

58. Assure that everyone may participate or be represented in making decisions affecting them.

61. Protect the right of faculty and students to present unpopular or controversial ideas in the classroom.

64. To respect individual freedom in matters of personal behavior.

Campus Community   1 2 3 4 5   1 2 3 4 5   1 2 3 4 5   1 2 3 4 5

56. Maintain a climate of faculty commitment to the goals and well-being of the institution.

59. Maintain a climate of mutual trust, respect, and concern among students, faculty, and staff.

62. Maintain climate in which differences of opinion can be aired openly and amicably.

65. A climate in which communication throughout the organizational structure is open and candid.

Key:

———— Mean rating on Is

– – – – Mean rating on Should Be

1 = of no importance/not applicable
2 = of low importance
3 = of medium importance
4 = of high importance
5 = of extremely high importance

ment increase," "a 20-point increase in median SAT Verbal scores," and "a 12 percent tuition increase." In this case, those responsible for formulating objectives must make adjustments in the target levels or target dates, or drop certain objectives altogether in order to arrive at an important and achievable set of objectives. Once the objectives are agreed upon in the goal-formulation stage, the institution is ready to move on to the detailed work of strategy formulation.

SUMMARY

Educational institutions require tangible and intangible resources to survive and carry out their missions. Three important intangibles are the institution's environment or character, its stage in the institutional life cycle, and its potential for adaptation.

A resource audit describes the institution's strengths and weaknesses in five areas: people, money, facilities, systems, and market assets. To determine its best opportunities, the institution should strive to identify its distinctive competencies, the resources and abilities it is especially strong in, and its differential advantage—areas in which it can outperform competitors.

Every institution starts with a mission that answers these questions: What is our business? Who is the consumer? What is the value to the consumer? What will our business be? What should our business be? A helpful approach to defining mission is to identify which consumer groups will be served, which of their needs will be addressed, and which technologies will be used to satisfy these needs. A mission works best when it is feasible, motivating, and distinctive. Once the institution has developed or refined its mission statement, it formulates its major goals and its specific objectives. By defining its resources and direction, the institution is better prepared to determine its strategy.

FIGURE 6-4   Sample plotting of discrepancies among 4 subgroups for 16 selected goals

SOURCE: *Goals and Climate: A Manual for Using the Small College Goal Inventory* (Washington, D.C.: Council for the Advancement of Small Colleges, 1979), p. 40.

NOTES

[1] C. Robert Pace, *CUES: College and University Environment Scales, Preliminary Technical Manual* (Princeton, N.J.: Educational Testing Service, 1962), p. 3.

[2] Pace, *CUES*, pp. 3–4.

[3] Rudolf H. Moos, *Evaluating Educational Environments* (San Francisco: Jossey-Bass, 1979).

[4] Norbert J. Hruby, *A Survival Kit for Invisible Colleges*, 2nd ed. (Boulder, Colo.: National Center for Higher Education Management Systems, 1980).

[5] Throughout this book, we use the term *goal* to refer to the broad aim or area of concern, and the word *objective* to refer to the statement of specific outcomes, including when and how the outcome will be determined. Our choice of terminology is based on its greater familiarity to educators. Marketers, on the other hand, tend to reverse the terms, using *objective* to refer to the general area and *goal* to refer to the statement of specific outcomes.

[6] Douglas F. Lamont, "Multicampus Systems of Higher Education: A New Organizational Strategy for Knowledge Work," University of Wisconsin, Madison, n.d.

[7] For an expanded discussion of analyzing institutional mission, see J. Kent Caruthers and Gary B. Lott, *Mission Review: Foundation for Strategic Planning* (Boulder, Colo.: National Center for Higher Education Management Systems, 1981).

[8] Richard E. Peterson and Norman P. Uhl, *Formulating College and University Goals: A Guide for Using the IGI* (Princeton, N.J.: Educational Testing Service, 1975).

[9] For an advanced example of goal setting in a university, see David P. Hopkins, Jean-Claude Larreche, and William F. Massy, "Constrained Optimization of a University Administrator's Preference Function," *Management Science*, December 1977, pp. 365–77.

chapter 7

FORMULATING
MARKETING
STRATEGY

Metropolis University [name disguised] is a private institution in a region plagued by persistent economic recession. The university's evening M.B.A. enrollment has fallen off, since employing companies have cut back on employee tuition-assistance programs, which support half of Metropolis's M.B.A. students.

Metropolis's share of the M.B.A. student market is also eroding, owing to competition from other schools. In one year alone, three new part-time evening M.B.A. programs were founded in the city, bringing to six the number of these programs. Only the programs at Metropolis University and State University enjoy the sought-after recognition of American Assembly of Collegiate Schools of Business (AACSB) accreditation. Fifty miles to the south, outside the immediate market area but within commuting distance of Metropolis, are two AACSB-accredited part-time evening/weekend M.B.A. programs.

Here are the Metropolis University M.B.A. program director's comments on competitive positioning:

"As far as the Metropolis area is concerned, we have attempted to position our M.B.A. program as the premier AACSB-accredited part-time evening curriculum. We are the only institution in Metropolis other than State University with a full-time tenure-track graduate business school faculty, and, of course, we view this as one of our major strengths. Almost all of our 500 part-time M.B.A. students are full-time working professionals, more than half with engineering and high-technology backgrounds. Our curriculum is more quantitative than our competitors', owing to our clientele. Thus, we have been able to differentiate our program from our competitors' in terms of the highly quantitative nature of our curriculum, our full-time tenure-track faculty, and our AACSB accreditation. In addition, we emphasize that we have a fine research library and up-to-date computer equipment to support our program, plus all the traditional student services. In contrast, many of our competitors are located in leased office space and offer very little in the way of library and computer support for their programs."

Metropolis University has substantial strengths but is buffeted by heavy competition for M.B.A. students. The institution is examining its strategy, seeking ways to strengthen its competitive position.

Strategy formulation calls for the institution to develop a strategy for achieving its objectives, discussed in the preceding chapter. For example, Metropolis University may discover that it cannot find a feasible strategy to slow its M.B.A. enrollment slide. If this is so, it may have to revise its enrollment objective. Objectives and strategies interact closely, and planners may have to move back and forth in determining a final set of objectives and strategies.

A marketing strategy embodies the ways in which an institution will take advantage of a program/market opportunity. We define marketing strategy as follows:

Marketing strategy is the selection of a target market, the choice of a competitive position, and the development of an effective marketing mix to reach and serve the chosen market.

Formulation of an institutional marketing strategy includes decisions about:

1. The institution's current programs and markets—whether to maintain, build, or drop them
2. Future new program and market opportunities
3. Analysis of competitors
4. Positioning of the institution in relation to competitors
5. Selection of target markets and designing of the marketing mix

This chapter discusses each of these decisions in the strategy-formulation process.

EVALUATING CURRENT OFFERINGS

Educational institutions often find they have many programs and desires but limited resources. Since they can't support everything, they must choose which programs will receive emphasis and which may need to be scaled down or dropped.

Making decisions about current major programs constitutes an *academic portfolio strategy*. Just as investors review their investment portfolios, so must a college or other educational institution evaluate its programs from time to time. During decades of expansion, many institutions added courses and programs. When the financial crunch hit in the 1970s, many faced the choice of making cuts across the board or of identifying the stronger programs for full support while drawing funds away from weaker programs. This can be an exceedingly painful process, but economic realities suggest that each institution focus its financial and other resources on programs that further its mission, build on institutional strengths, and meet the needs of identifiable target markets.

The academic portfolio tool shown in Figure 7-1 incorporates each of these three dimensions. In this example, selected academic departments are evaluated on *centrality to the school's mission,* on the *quality* of the program, and on *market viability* (in parentheses). Programs are ranked high, medium, or low on each dimension.

Centrality to the school's mission means the extent to which the program is directly related to the current mission that the institution has adopted. For example, clinical training would be central to a hospital school of nursing's program, but art history probably is not.

Quality is a measure of the academic depth and rigor of the program and the quality of the faculty. Quality may be measured in terms of national rankings of academic departments, but such ratings are not useful for small, unranked institutions. They must make their own judgments, probably in comparison with other institutions they perceive as competitors. They might turn to accreditation reports and outside consultants for opinions on relative quality.

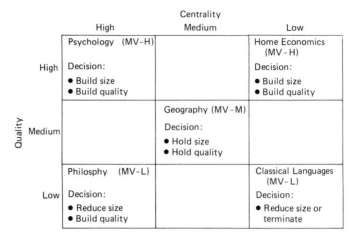

FIGURE 7-1   Academic portfolio model

Market viability is the extent to which there is present and future demand for study in this program area. A program may be of high quality and central to a college's mission, but if there is little or no student interest in that area, the program will not survive unless the institution is willing to divert money from other programs to sustain it. Determining market viability may involve examining past experience (enrollment levels, for example) and trends revealed in the environmental analyses, or may require some additional marketing research.

The school shown in Figure 7-1 has a strong liberal arts tradition. Psychology and philosophy are judged high on centrality, but philosophy is low in quality and market viability. The philosophy department should probably be reduced in size and its quality built. Although low on centrality, the home economics department scores high on quality and market viability. A plausible strategy would be to hold quality and build size. (The school should also consider whether its students are as committed to liberal arts as the school is; perhaps the school should be adding more applied courses and programs.) Classical languages rank low on all scales. Unless the school will commit the necessary resources to help make this an attractive program, the school should probably terminate the department, perhaps retaining certain courses as part of another program.

The University of Michigan uses the following criteria for eliminating programs:

- Quality: Is the program of quality and scope appropriate to the school or college mission?

- Resources needed: Is the program under consideration too costly in relation to other educational and program needs of the school or college?
- Availability: Is a comparable program offered at another institution in the state of Michigan?
- Cost savings: Can the program be made less costly or combined with other units to bring it more in line with the role and mission of the school or college? Or can it be relocated?
- Service: Does the program have a significant service value to other units within the University?[1]

Northwestern University uses four criteria (shown in Exhibit 7-1) to determine which departments will receive enhanced support: centrality, visibility, potential, and present status.

The Boston Consulting Group (BCG), a leading management consulting firm, recommends that companies appraise each of their main product lines on the basis of market growth rate (annual growth rate of the market in which the product is sold) and the company's share of the current market relative to its largest competitor. Each product line is then placed in the corresponding quadrant of the BCG matrix, shown in Figure 7-2.

This portfolio approach can be adapted for use by educational institutions.[2] For example, each academic area or program can be rated high or low on two criteria: (1) market growth rate, the growth in FTE students in that field over the past five years; and (2) market-share dominance, the ratio of FTE students of the largest competing university to FTE students of University X in that field.

Newbould defines the four quadrants as follows:

- *Stars* are programs in high-growth fields in which the institution has market-share dominance in terms of relative numbers of students. Star programs are growing rapidly and typically require heavy investment of resources—to add faculty, expand related library collections, acquire equipment, and so on. If the necessary investment is made and the area proves of enduring interest, the star program will turn into a cash cow and generate cash in excess of expenses in the future.
- *Cash cows* are programs in low-growth fields that attract a high share of the market for such programs. They produce revenues that can be used to support high-growth programs or to underwrite those with problems.
- *Question marks* are programs in high-growth fields but in which the institution has a low market share. The institution faces the decision of whether to increase its investment in the program, hoping to increase its market share and make the program a star, or to reduce or terminate its investment on the grounds that the resources could be better used elsewhere.
- *Dogs* are those programs that have a small market share in slow-growth or declining fields. Dogs usually make little money or lose money for the institution. The institution may decide to drop or shrink dogs. Unless dogs must be offered for other reasons, maintaining them may come at the expense of other opportunities for increasing excellence.[3]

EXHIBIT 7-1 Northwestern University's criteria for investing in a department

I. Centrality to the Purpose of a Distinguished University

   A. The field must be important to the intellectual life of the University.

   B. Strengthening the field should contribute directly to strengthening the achievement and academic reputations of at least some other field in the University.

   C. The cutting edge of the field should be identifiable so that the investment can be targeted appropriately and so that the risks associated with an investment are well understood.

   D. The field must have an important teaching role at the undergraduate and/or the graduate level.

II. Visibility

   A. The field must be broadly visible to academics.

   B. There should be a substantial external constituency for the research and scholarly output of the field.

   C. The field should be a principal field in almost all distinguished universities so that distinction at Northwestern will be recognized broadly by the universities that Northwestern aspires to join.

III. Potential

   A. The potential for intellectual development and vitality must be substantial; if it is a growth area, that is even better.

   B. The potential for external funding is important but should not be a necessary condition for selection.

   C. There should be potential for important research achievements that will benefit other fields within the University.

IV. Present Status

   A. Northwestern's present activities in the field must be sufficiently strong so that an investment can cause Northwestern to be clearly recognized as one of the top ten in its field and, it is hoped, one of the top five.

SOURCE: *Strategies for Excellence*, A Report of the Faculty Planning Committee, Northwestern University, May 1980, pp. 58–59.

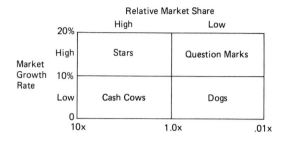

FIGURE 7-2   The BCG matrix

Figure 7-3 presents a BCG-type matrix of the master's-degree programs offered by a midwestern state university.

We have presented two portfolio methods, the academic portfolio method and an adaptation of the BCG product portfolio matrix, as well as the criteria used at the University of Michigan and at Northwestern. Using a portfolio approach offers a major advantage over simply assessing each program individually. Portfolio methods emphasize an institution's academic programs as an interrelated set. Decisions about increasing or reducing investment in particular programs are based on the institution's resources and the relative needs and contributions of each program area. Correct assessment of program strengths and weaknesses lays the groundwork for strategy formulation.

FIGURE 7-3   BCG-type matrix for all master's programs at a midwestern university

Market Share

		High		Low	
		Stars		Question Marks	
High		Art	Physical education	Business	
		Music	Speech; audiology	Chemistry	
		Geology	Languages	Home economics	
		Architecture	Geography		
		Cash Cows		Dogs	
Low		Education	Public administration	Engineering	Biology
		English	Journalism	History	Physics
		Philosophy	Library	Political science	Economics
		Sociology		Psychology	Mathematics

Market Growth Rate

SOURCE: Based on Gerald D. Newbould, "Product Portfolio Diagnosis for U.S. Universities," *Akron Business and Economic Review*, Spring 1980, p. 44.

IDENTIFYING OPPORTUNITIES

After examining its current portfolio of programs, the institution may discover that it does not have enough stars or cash cows and that it should enhance its offerings or search for new programs and markets. Needed is a systematic approach to *opportunity identification*. The *program/market opportunity matrix* is a useful device. Figure 7-4 shows a program/market opportunity matrix for a college interested in expanding enrollment. (The same matrix format may also be used to identify new donor markets and fund-raising programs.) Starting with a blank nine-cell matrix, the planning group considers existing prospects and "brainstorms" additional ideas that would fit in each cell. The matrix encourages planners to think in terms of both programs and markets.

Each cell in Figure 7-4 has a name. Potential opportunities—in this case, for a college—are listed in small letters. The administration should first consider cell 1, *market penetration*. This cell raises the question of whether the college can maintain or expand its enrollment by deepening its penetration into its existing markets with its existing programs. This strategy is effective only if the current market is not already saturated. A community college may be able to attract more adults to its leisure/fitness courses by increasing advertising and promotion, whereas many liberal arts colleges seeking to attract more 18-year-old freshmen are apt to be disappointed.

FIGURE 7-4 Program/market opportunity matrix

		PRODUCTS	
	Existing	Modified	New
Existing	1. Market Penetration	4. Product Modification – Improve facilities – Upgrade instruction and placement	7. Program Innovation – New courses – New departments – New programs
Geographical	2. Geographical Expansion – New areas of city – New cities – Foreign	5. Modification for Dispersed Markets – Programs offered on military bases or at U.S.-based firms abroad	8. Geographic Innovation
New	3. New Markets A. Individual – senior citizens – homemakers – ethnic minorities B. Institutional – business firms – social agencies	6. Modification for New Markets A. Individual – senior citizens – homemakers – full-time workers B. Institutional – business – government	10. Total Innovation – New courses – New departments – New schools For new markets

MARKETS (vertical axis label)

Cell 2 raises the question of whether the college should consider expanding into *new geographical markets with its existing programs*. The college could open a branch in another part of the city, or in a new city, or even start a campus in another country. For example, Southern Methodist University in Dallas offers M.B.A. courses in Houston, and Antioch operates campuses abroad.

The planners then move to cell 3 and consider possibly offering *existing programs to new* individual and institutional *markets*. Some colleges and universities are successfully attracting such nontraditional student markets as senior citizens, homemakers, and full-time employees of local companies.

Next, the planners can consider whether the college should *modify* its *current programs to attract* more of the *existing market* (cell 4). A school may find that interest and enrollment go up when it improves its residential facilities, upgrades the quality and reputation of its placement service, or adopts a more attractive schedule of courses. Standard courses can be shortened, or offered in the evening or on weekends. For example, Alverno College, a private women's school in Milwaukee, instituted a weekend college that drew large numbers of homemakers and working women.

Cell 5 is labeled *modification for dispersed markets*. Colleges such as the University of Maryland offer courses and programs for members of the armed forces in the United States and overseas. Business firms with large overseas operations may represent an untapped market.

Program modification for new markets (cell 6) may be a more realistic growth opportunity for most educational institutions. For example, a college may decide to serve retired people by providing special courses or schedules for them. Iowa State University instituted "Eldercollege," a series of short courses, and more than 600 colleges host Elderhostel programs each summer. Mission College in San Jose, California, offers special job-entry courses in typing for the elderly.

Program innovation (cell 7) means developing new courses, departments, or programs. Few institutions outside the Sunbelt will be expanding over the next decade, but many will need to add new courses and programs or overhaul existing ones to maintain current size and to attract more consumers. For example, Stanford's Mechanical Engineering Design Division has added a master's degree program in product design.

Geographic innovation (cell 8) involves finding new ways to serve new geographical areas. For example, with an electronic blackboard, a professor can write something in one location and have the notes transmitted over telephone lines to a distant city. Home computers, interactive television, and other new media technologies, as well as existing television and radio instruction, will increase the range and format of courses.

The final category, *total innovation* (cell 9), refers to offering new programs to new markets. Various "universities without walls" have been established in the past decade. Empire State College, part of the New York State system, is one of the newest. Some institutions are growing by developing more continuing education programs or starting evening college-degree-completion programs. Most traditional educational institutions cannot use this strategy.

The program/market opportunity matrix can help administrators imagine new options in a systematic way. The identified opportunities must be evaluated for their centrality, market viability, cost, and other features; the better ones can then be pursued. The results of the program/market opportunity analysis and the preceding portfolio analysis provide the basis for the institution's formulation of its strategic plans.

ANALYZING COMPETITION

Virtually every educational institution faces competition, yet for decades, few administrators talked openly about it. Educators generally believed that most schools, colleges, and universities were worthy and had something to contribute. They preferred to focus on their own institutions and to believe that they did not compete for students, faculty, and donors. Competition sounded like a concern for business, not for education.

Administrators are now aware that even strong schools cannot afford to ignore competition:

- For students: Academically prestigious institutions compete with each other for the most qualified students, as do less-selective institutions.
- For faculty: In some academic areas, there are six or more job openings for each new Ph.D. graduate, and colleges and universities must compete with business and industry for this talent.
- For donors: Educational institutions receive over $9 billion in donations and foundation grants each year, but each must make a case to prospective donors to arouse their interest and obtain their support.

Competition for students, faculty, and donations is a fact of life, with advantages for prospective students, faculty, and donors. The existence of many educational alternatives encourages institutions to offer attractive programs of the best possible quality and, in some cases, to specialize to take advantage of unique strengths and circumstances. Schools and colleges cannot afford to be smug about their faults when other institutions can offer similar or better programs or other features that attract students. Some of Metropolis University's competitors have priced their M.B.A. programs significantly lower, a step they can afford, since they do not have Metropolis's fixed overhead costs for physical plant, equipment, and a full-time faculty.

In their competition for resources, educational institutions can use the following marketing assets, among others: program quality, program uniqueness, price, convenience, reputation, and well-qualified students and faculty (who attract others like themselves).

In the sections that follow, we present ways to analyze competitors, and we examine the competitive roles an institution may play and how they relate to institutional survival and growth.

Analyzing Competitors

Here we will illustrate competitive analysis with the case of competition for students. An educational institution may be interested in knowing the following things about its competition:

- Which institutions do we compete with for students, and how successful are we?

Then, for each competitor:

- What programs does it offer, and how good are they?
- What is its financial situation?
- What are its admissions criteria?
- What is its enrollment? enrollment trends?
- What are the threats and opportunities facing the institution?
- What are the institution's strengths and weaknesses?
- What competitive strategy is the institution using?

The institution's competitors are anything that might receive the attention of a potential student (faculty member, donor) as an alternative to the institution's offer. Consider the case of Owen, a computer sales representative, whose thought process is shown in Figure 7-5. Owen has spent some time thinking about his goals, which now include running in the Boston Marathon, traveling in Europe, and getting ahead at work. Of these three desires, his practical nature suggests he should focus on getting ahead at work. He decides

FIGURE 7-5 Types of competitors facing an M.B.A. program

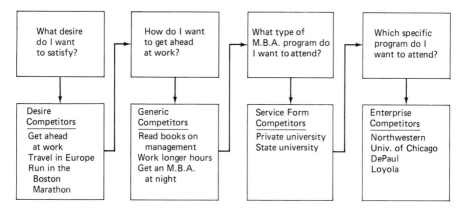

that getting an M.B.A. at night would help him most, and since his company will pay all his educational expenses, he decides to attend a private-university M.B.A. program. This example shows that in Owen's mind, there were numerous competitors to getting an M.B.A. at a particular university.

To answer the question, Which institutions do we compete with for students, and how successful are we? there are two approaches.

First, colleges that require the Scholastic Aptitude Test of the College Board can refer to Table 19 of the Summary Report prepared for each participating college. Table 19 ranks the 35 other institutions to which a given college's applicants, admitted students, and matriculants most often send their SAT scores. (A hypothetical example appears in Table 7-1.) This information, although very useful as an indicator of competition and easy to obtain, does not allow an assessment of how individual students chose one institution over others.

Second, educational institutions can assess application overlap by comparing totals of shared applications.[4] A study conducted at Boston College illustrates the approach. A questionnaire was sent to more than 2,500 accepted applicants, asking them to list all the schools to which they applied. For each school listed, students indicated whether or not they were accepted. Students who decided against attending Boston College were asked the name of the school they planned to attend. The researchers focused on college choices of students who were accepted at both Boston College and a competitor and who thus had a real choice.

The draw rate was computed for each competing institution by taking the ratio of the number of joint applicants who chose the competitor after having been accepted by both. The top 15 competitors were then categorized by draw rate. Schools in the High category accepted 70 percent of the students Boston College accepted, whereas competitors in the Low (highly selective) category accepted 30 percent or less. The Middle category of colleges and universities included six institutions: Holy Cross, Tufts, Georgetown, the University of New Hampshire, Notre Dame, and the University of Vermont. These are Boston College's closest competitors, and where possible, Boston College should strive to improve in areas where competitors are deemed more attractive.

Both approaches can identify the college's competitors, but neither tells on what attributes students evaluate the institutions and with what results. We address this issue later in this chapter when we discuss positioning.

The other questions on competitive analysis can often be answered using available data. For example, a competitor's catalog provides information on programs, faculty, and enrollment and may also specify admissions criteria. Faculty quality can be judged by where advanced degrees were obtained, and by consulting faculty elsewhere in the same disciplines. If the competitor is of national stature, its academic programs may be ranked in one of several national polls. Faculty turnover can be assessed by comparing catalogs for several consecutive years. The institution can probably construct a good approximation of

TABLE 7-1 Excerpt from a hypothetical Table 19 of the College Board Summary Report

SAMPLE COLLEGE

TABLE 19: Shared Prospective Applicants: Institutions Most Frequently Receiving Other ATP Reports

COLLEGE	STATE	TYPE AND CONTROL	NUMBER	%	% MALE/ FEMALE	SAT VERBAL MEAN	SAT MATH MEAN	MEAN %ILE H.S. RANK	MEAN ESTIM. PARENT CONTRIB.	% MIN-OR-ITY	BROAD AREA OF STUDY				
											% ART AND HUM.	% BIO. SCI.	% BUS.	% PHY. SCI.	% SOC. SCI.
A State University	A	4-Yr. Publ	4,535	26	50/50	469	502	77	$2,380	12	8	28	22	9	29
B University	A	4-Yr. Priv	2,932	17	51/49	443	483	74	$1,700	11	4	30	24	13	25
University of C	A	4-Yr. Publ	2,793	16	51/49	470	511	77	$2,290	7	8	25	23	10	29
D County Community College	A	2-Yr. Publ	2,512	14	60/40	503	538	81	$3,190	3	7	23	21	9	33
E University	A	4-Yr. Priv	2,013	11	52/48	506	548	83	$2,810	12	7	39	10	13	25
F University	M	4-Yr. Priv	1,940	11	53/47	528	548	82	$4,120	7	8	21	21	4	43
...	...	...	...	...	...	...	...	...	...	...	...	...	...	...	...
CC State College	C	4-Yr. Publ	716	4	62/38	541	576	87	$3,170	13	9	25	15	10	34
DD University	A	4-Yr. Publ	711	4	55/45	446	500	76	$1,450	4	5	33	17	19	20
EE University	A	4-Yr. Publ	653	4	38/62	440	488	76	$1,760	7	5	40	18	11	19
FF University	D	4-Yr. Priv	634	4	65/35	546	586	87	$3,720	11	8	22	14	13	36
GG State College	E	4-Yr. Publ	616	3	57/43	482	518	78	$3,210	8	9	22	28	11	25
HH University	A	4-Yr. Publ	611	3	19/81	437	472	75	$1,640	3	2	53	13	5	23
II College	A	4-Yr. Priv	599	3	51/49	452	473	75	$1,360	7	4	11	25	4	51
Colleges not listed			46,309	—	48/52	481	514	77	$3,140	9	9	24	22	9	31
No other college			91	1	46/54	450	488	72	$4,040	11	6	30	17	4	31
Sample College			17,747	100	50/50	475	509	77	$2,760	9	8	24	23	9	30

SOURCE: *College Guide to the ATP Summary Reports*, Admissions Testing Program of the College Board, 1982, p. 47. Reprinted with permission, copyright © 1982 by the College Entrance Examination Board, New York.

143

the threats, opportunities, strengths, and weaknesses of the competitor. Non-profit educational institutions must file financial statements, which are available to the public. From these and other sources—news stories, competitors' annual reports and other publications—the institution can develop a clear picture of each competing institution.

We now turn to the competitive roles educational institutions may play.

Competitive Roles

An analysis of competing institutions or specific programs within competing institutions often reveals the following competitive roles: the *leader*, the *challenger*, the *follower*, and the *nicher*. The selection of a particular role will depend on the institution's/program's size, stature, and resources, as well as those of its competitors.

The *leader* is the acknowledged dominant institution or program in a particular geographical, disciplinary, or other market. Although leadership could reflect size and/or quality, the leader usually strives to maintain its premier position by increasing the applicant pool to raise the quality of admitted students, and by hiring distinguished faculty. The leader may also take advantage of its strength to increase program or institution size. For example, a large private midwestern university with a nationally ranked law school has 15 applicants for each place, and the quality of applicants has improved each year. The law school could increase revenue without lowering student quality by admitting a certain number of additional law students each year. With this additional revenue, it can hire additional distinguished faculty who will further enhance the law school's reputation, attracting more and better applicants in the future.

The *challengers* are the runner-up institutions or programs that aspire to match or surpass the leader. They may strive to enhance their reputations by establishing more prestige programs or by adding faculty and other resources to improve on existing ones. The institution may compete by introducing innovative programs, by expanding the number of sites where programs are offered, and by advertising its programs more intensively.

The *followers* strive to hold on to their present markets and to be as much as possible like the market leader. Market followers may refine existing programs to meet the needs of their target markets, but typically they are not very innovative.

The *nichers* are those institutions and programs that aim to find and fill one or more niches that are not well served by other educational institutions. Nichers may specialize by serving one type of market (adults over 65), by offering a unique program (M.B.A. in Telecommunications), by offering a customized program (quality control seminars for a single corporation), by providing unique program features (an early-morning engineering degree program), or by providing a unique delivery system (TV-transmitted classes). To be successful, nichers should look for niches that are of sufficient size and growth potential to be attractive, that are not well served by other institutions, and that the institution can serve effectively.

Nicher institutions may find that once they have succeeded in a particular niche, they will attract other institutions as competitors. Consider an institution offering a unique program. When other schools see that the program is drawing substantial interest, they may want to set up similar programs. The nicher that initiated the program can often maintain a dominant role as a supplier of that program if it has distinctive competence and differential advantage over competitors, if it controls resources that are in short supply (such as a top expert in the field on the faculty), and if it has marketing advantages—such as a strong institutional and program reputation, good public relations, and satisfied participants and graduates. Even though an institution does not need all these advantages to succeed, the more it has, the better its chances of continuing success.

Educational institutions that understand their markets, analyze their competition, and engage in strategic planning can usually maintain their current strengths and build on them better than can institutions that do not. In the next section, we take up positioning strategy.

POSITIONING

Every educational institution holds a position in the minds of those who have contact with or know about the institution. A *position* describes how a person or group perceives the institution in relation to other institutions. People often describe schools and colleges in such comparative terms as these: "the Big Ten school with the best football team," "the Harvard of the West" (Stanford), "the best law school if you want to work on Wall Street," and so forth. A position may also describe the institution or program on some dimension that could be used to compare institutions, such as "the M.B.A. program for quant jocks."

The school or college may or may not be satisfied with its current position. Instead of holding a desirable and distinctive position, it may be considered weak, unfriendly, large and impersonal, "too academic," or "too social" in comparison with other institutions. It may not know what its current position is, or it may be striving to maintain a position that is at odds with the school's reality and performance. The institution may want to adopt a new position more in line with recent changes in its direction and programs, and more attractive to students, donors, and others.

Developing a *positioning strategy* consists of the following steps: (1) assessing the institution's current position in the relevant market, (2) selecting the desired position, (3) planning a strategy to achieve the desired position, and (4) implementing the strategy. Figure 7-6 shows these four steps, which are discussed below.

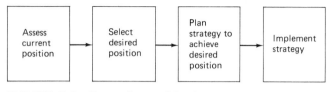

FIGURE 7-6   Steps in positioning strategy
development

Assess Current Position

To find out its current position with respect to its competitors, the institution must survey relevant groups that can make such a comparison. And although knowing comparative positions is important, it is just as important to find out what *key attributes* people use in comparing institutions, which attributes are most important, and the *relative positions* of the institution and its competitors on the most important attributes. Note that the institution should examine its position in relation to its relevant competitors, not to every school, college, or educational institution in the country or the world. Here is an example.

Yale University admissions officers were interested in how admitted applicants perceived Yale in relation to competing colleges.[5] Researchers asked 800 admitted students and 800 Yale undergraduates to rate the similarity of 136 possible pairs of 17 colleges. Figure 7-7 presents the results. The lines enclose clusters of colleges rated similar in varying degrees. The researchers did not ask respondents what dimensions they used to evaluate similarity, but academic prestige and size seemed to explain their ratings.

In a second study, Yale undergraduates rated Yale and 16 competitors using the semantic differential (see Chapter 2). Factor analysis revealed three main dimensions: academic prestige, active campus life, and agreeableness. Table 7-2 shows the ratings of the 17 colleges on these three dimensions. The results could be charted on a three-dimensional graph to show positions of each college.

In obtaining and using ratings by current students, the planners must keep in mind that students enrolled in the institution may rate their school or college somewhat higher than those not enrolled. Thus, ratings by admitted students who enrolled elsewhere and, where possible, by qualified students who chose not to apply can be important in positioning studies.

Select Desired Position

Having stressed its current position, an institution may (1) decide that its present position is strong and desirable and work to emphasize it with potential

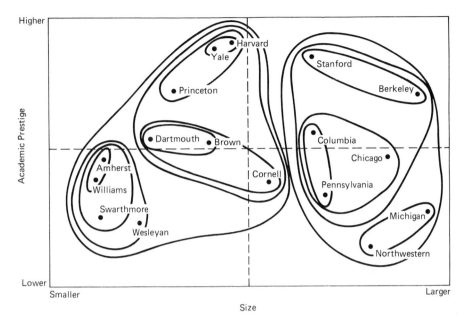

FIGURE 7-7   Perceptual map of college similarity

SOURCE: Robert J. Sternberg and Jeanne C. Davis, "Student Perceptions of Yale and its Competitors," *College and University*, Spring 1978, p. 266.

students and others; (2) develop a new or clarified position for the school and communicate it; or (3) where appropriate, position the school on a new dimension, one that people may value but that they don't routinely use in evaluating the school.

For example, suppose Yale administrators were concerned about Yale's position. Note that Yale was rated at the top on academic prestige but low on agreeableness, whereas Stanford was rated high on both. Yale might accept its position as an academically elite university that isn't particularly pleasant for students. (Some educational institutions may even emphasize their spartan atmosphere and the rigors of being a student there, and attract those who feel a school should be tough and unpleasant.)

Before taking action, Yale administrators would want to look at how students rated Yale on the adjective pairs that made up the agreeableness dimension. Yale was judged about average on scales of pleasantness, happiness, fairness, and roundedness, and slightly below average on beauty. On relaxedness, Yale was judged considerably below average.

After considering the attributes of greatest importance to its current and potential students, Yale will want to prepare a positioning statement that sets forth how the university wants to be perceived in relation to its competition. This statement by itself is not enough; the university must plan and carry out a strategy to achieve this desired position.

TABLE 7-2 Ratings of Yale and competitors by Yale freshmen

	ACADEMIC PRESTIGE	ACTIVE CAMPUS LIFE	AGREEABLENESS
Amherst	.39	−1.04	.47
Berkeley	−.21	1.37	.59
Brown	−.53	.05	.21
Chicago	.11	.35	−2.00
Columbia	.01	.46	−1.99
Cornell	−.19	−.12	−.29
Dartmouth	.15	.28	.99
Harvard	1.31	.40	−.74
Michigan	−2.01	1.63	.38
Northwestern	−1.21	.00	.13
Pennsylvania	−1.18	−.08	−.66
Princeton	.72	−.64	.18
Stanford	.74	.93	1.99
Swarthmore	.05	−1.72	−.54
Wesleyan	−.56	−1.37	.54
Williams	.10	−1.59	.79
Yale	2.33	1.08	−.06

Note: Scores on scales have been reflected so that higher values correspond to greater amounts of the attribute used to name the scale.

SOURCE: Adapted from Robert J. Sternberg and Jeanne C. Davis, "Student Perceptions of Yale and its Competitors," *College and University*, Spring 1978, p. 276.

Plan and Implement Strategy

Suppose Yale decided it wanted to be perceived as the most pleasant school in the Ivy League. It might attempt to change its position by changing its communications to feature the most beautiful areas of the campus and to show clusters of cheerful students, eating lunch on the lawn, commenting on how little stress there is at Yale.

But communications are not enough. Although such communications may change the opinions of some readers, those who have contact with Yale may find that the communications do not match the reality. Instead, Yale would want to consider ways to make campus life more gracious and relaxed and make the campus more beautiful. Or the university may decide that such changes are infeasible or unnecessary and continue to strive to attract students who are not only academically able but who are willing to "trade" greater agreeableness elsewhere for what Yale has to offer.

Changing an institution's position in the academic marketplace is difficult. Old perceptions die hard. The institution must select an appropriate position and then support that position by all means available. For example, suppose a moderately strong, financially healthy university wants to increase its academic prestige. It will want to examine its academic portfolio and select areas for investment. The university may seek donations to bring in distinguished faculty in its strongest departments. It may institute an honors program for undergraduates with especially strong high school records. The news director will try to link the university's name with other, academically stronger institutions. These and other activities must be carefully thought out and orchestrated to obtain the desired effect. And even then, it may be several years before this revised position becomes widely known.

AN EXAMPLE OF STRATEGY FORMULATION

So far in this chapter, we have described the process of reviewing current programs, identifying new program and marketing opportunities, analyzing competitors, and positioning the institution relative to competition. The strategy-formulation process also includes selecting appropriate target markets and designing a marketing mix to serve them. Here we will illustrate target market strategy, competitive positioning strategy, and marketing-mix strategy in terms of the following example.

Desert University [name disguised], located in the Southwest, includes a liberal arts college and several professional schools. One of these, the journalism school, enjoys a good local reputation. Although it has attracted a large number of students in the past, the number of applicants has fallen in recent years because of the growing difficulty of finding journalism jobs for graduates and the low pay. The dean of the journalism school allowed enrollment to decline rather than lower the school's admission standards. The university president, however, is upset with the enrollment decline. The president wants the journalism school to remain at its present size and quality and wants the dean and faculty to develop a marketing strategy for the 1980s that will adapt the school to its best opportunities.

Target Market Strategy

The first step in preparing a marketing strategy is to thoroughly understand the market. We define a *market* as follows:

A market is the set of all people who have an actual or potential interest in a product or service and the ability to pay for it.

Thus, the journalism-student market can be defined as the set of all people who have an actual or potential interest in studying journalism and the ability and qualifications to buy this education.

At the outset, it becomes clear that the national market must be quite large and that Desert University would need only a small share of it to fill its

MARKETS

FIGURE 7-8   Segmentation of the journalism
program/market

classes. But the administration realizes that not every person in this market
would know about Desert University, find it attractive, or be able to attend.
Nor would Desert find every person attractive. When looked at closely, every
market is heterogeneous; that is, it is made up of quite different types of
consumers, or *market segments*. Therefore, the journalism school would benefit
from constructing some market segmentation scheme that would reveal the
major groups making up the market. Then it could decide whether to try to
serve all these segments (*mass marketing*) or concentrate on a few of the more
promising segments (*target marketing*).

There are many ways to segment a market. A market could be segmented
by age, sex, income, geography, lifestyle, and many other variables. The market
analyst tries different approaches until a useful one is found. Suppose the
administration settles on the *program/market segmentation* scheme shown in
Figure 7-8. Three student markets for journalism are shown: college-age learners, adult learners, and practicing journalists. And three product types are
shown: broadcast journalism (radio and TV), print journalism (newspapers and
magazines), and public relations (a program found in most schools of journalism).
Suppose the journalism school at Desert University at present caters to all nine
market segments but is not doing a distinguished job in any. At the same time,
competitors are beginning to concentrate on certain market segments and doing
a first-class job: the University of Texas in training college-age students for
broadcast journalism, Northwestern University in training college-age students
for print journalism, and so on. The dean is wondering whether to pursue target
marketing and, if so, what pattern of target marketing to choose.

The school will recognize that there are five basic patterns of market
coverage possible with a program/market segmentation scheme. They are shown
in Figure 7-9 and are described thus:

1. *Program/market concentration* consists of concentrating on only one market
   segment—here, teaching print journalism to adult learners.
2. *Program specialization* consists of deciding to offer only one program (here,
   print journalism) for all three markets.

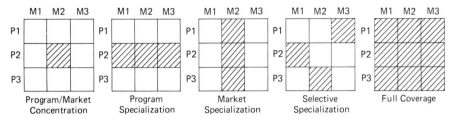

FIGURE 7-9   Five patterns of market coverage

SOURCE: Adapted from Derek F. Abell, *Defining the Business: The Starting Point of Strategic Planning* (Englewood Cliffs, N.J.: Prentice-Hall, 1980), Chap. 8.

3. *Market specialization* consists of deciding to serve only one market segment (adult learners) with all the journalism programs.

4. *Selective specialization* consists of working in several program markets that have no relation to each other except that each constitutes an individually attractive opportunity.

5. *Full coverage* consists of undertaking the full range of programs to serve all the market segments.

After researching these alternatives, the school decides that the most attractive one for the school is program specialization—here, print journalism. The journalism school does not have the funds to buy expensive television and radio equipment and sound rooms for student training, and it would be doing only a second-rate job compared to the University of Texas, with its $12 million facility for teaching broadcast journalism. And the school's program in public relations is quite weak and cannot be the basis for building a distinguished journalism school. The region lacks a good print-journalism school, which happens to be Desert University's strong suit. And it would be best to develop print-journalism programs for all three markets, because the number of college-age students is shrinking.

Having decided on program specialization, the school should now proceed in developing a finer segmentation of the market for print-journalism education. Figure 7-10 shows one possible subsegmentation of the print-journalism market. The columns show different geographical areas from which the journalism school can try to actively recruit students. The school can concentrate on attracting journalism majors from the local area, using easy admission standards, since the market is quite small. Or it can try to compete for students in the Southwest region, which will require a larger recruiting budget and contacts with a larger number of newspapers and magazines for placing students. Or it can try to develop national eminence and attract students from all over the nation. The rows show that journalism majors have different career objectives— some seeking training in news writing, others in feature writing, still others in advertising, and finally, some in managing media organizations. Looking at the subsegmentation, the dean may decide to cultivate the regional market and emphasize careers in news writing and feature writing. Although the school

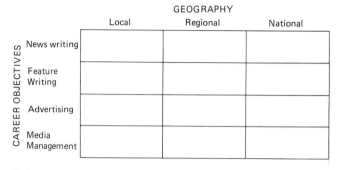

FIGURE 7-10   Subsegmentation of the print
journalism market

will also teach advertising and media management, it will seek to build its reputation as a writer's training school.

Competitive Positioning Strategy

Having selected its target market, the journalism school will now have to develop its competitive positioning strategy vis-à-vis other journalism schools serving the same target market. Suppose there are three other journalism schools in the Southwest that do a good job of training students in print journalism. If the four schools are similar, then high school students going into journalism would not have much basis for choice among the four. Their respective market shares would be left to chance. The antidote for this is *competitive positioning,* defined as follows:

> Competitive positioning is the art of developing and communicating meaningful differences between one's offer and those of competitors serving the same target market.

The key to competitive positioning is to identify the major attributes used by the target market to evaluate and choose among competiitive institutions. Suppose the target market judges journalism schools by their perceived quality (high versus low) and perceived orientation (liberal arts versus vocational). Figure 7-11 shows the perceived competitive positions of the other three journalism schools (A, B, C) and Desert University's journalism school (D). Schools A and B are liberal-arts-oriented journalism schools of low quality, B being somewhat larger and slightly better in quality than A. They are locked in competition for the same students, since their differentiation is negligible. School C is seen as a high-quality vocationally-oriented journalism school and draws those students seeking this type of school. Desert University's journalism school, shown as D, comes closest to being perceived as a high-quality liberal-arts-oriented school. Fortunately, it has no competition in this preference seg-

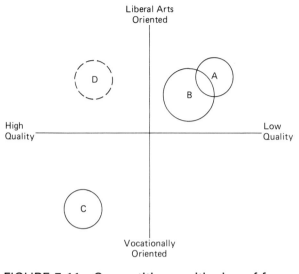

FIGURE 7-11   Competitive positioning of four
journalism schools

ment. The only question is whether there are enough students seeking a high-quality liberal-arts-oriented journalism school. If not, then D is not a viable competitive position, and the administration has to think about repositioning the school toward a part of the market in which the demand is larger.

Marketing Mix Strategy

The next step in marketing strategy is to develop a *marketing mix* and a *marketing expenditure level* that supports the school's ability to compete in its target market. By *marketing mix*, we mean this:

> The marketing mix is the particular blend of controllable marketing variables that the institution uses to achieve its objectives in the target market.

Although many variables make up the marketing mix, they can be classified into four major groups. McCarthy formulated a popular classification called the "four P's": *product, price, place,* and *promotion*.[6] The particular marketing variables under each P are shown in Figure 7-12. The figure emphasizes that the marketing mix must be adapted to the target market.

The institution chooses a marketing mix that will support and reinforce its chosen competitive position. Since the journalism school wants to maintain and project a reputation as a high-quality liberal-arts-oriented journalism school, it will hire high-quality faculty, require students to take many liberal arts courses, develop high-quality school catalogs and brochures, send them to potential students seeking this type of school, and so on. In other words, the

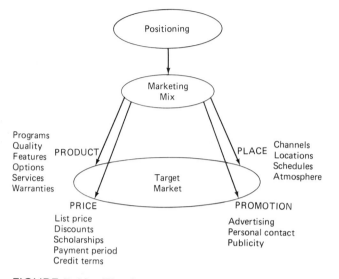

Programs
Quality
Features   PRODUCT
Options
Services
Warranties

PRICE
List price
Discounts
Scholarships
Payment period
Credit terms

Channels
PLACE   Locations
Schedules
Atmosphere

PROMOTION
Advertising
Personal contact
Publicity

FIGURE 7-12   The four P's of the marketing mix

chosen competitive position dictates the elements of the marketing mix that will be emphasized. The marketing mix is presented in detail in Chapters 11 through 15.

As for the marketing expenditure level, this depends on estimating how much money is needed to accomplish the school's enrollment objectives. After projecting the recruiting activities needed, the admissions director can estimate the costs associated with each activity. Another estimate can be derived from past experience. If the school has typically spent about $400 per student recruited and it wants to recruit 100 students, it may need a marketing budget of $40,000. Of course, the school may find the per-student cost to be greater if the market is shrinking or if competitive schools increase their marketing budgets. Or if the school institutes programs that are in high demand, the cost per student may decrease. We shall say more about establishing the marketing budget in Chapter 12.

SUMMARY

Strategy formulation is the institution's effort to figure out its broad strategy for achieving its objectives. First, the institution analyzes its current program portfolio to determine which programs to build, maintain, or terminate. Second, it seeks ideas for new or modified programs and markets by using a program/ market expansion matrix.

Following the choice of particular program/market targets, the institution proceeds to develop marketing strategies for each program market. Marketing strategy is the selection of one or more target-market segments, the choice of a competitive position, and the development of an effective marketing mix to reach and serve the chosen consumers. The marketing mix consists of the particular blend of product, price, place, and promotion that the institution uses to achieve its objectives in the target market.

NOTES

[1] "Policy Document on Discontinuance of Academic Programs at the University of Michigan," in Kenneth P. Mortimer and Michael L. Tierney, *The Three "R's" of the Eighties: Reduction, Reallocation and Retrenchment* (Washington, D.C.: American Association for Higher Education, AAHE-ERIC/Higher Education Research Report #4, 1979), p. 70.

[2] See Gerald D. Newbould, "Product Portfolio Diagnosis for U.S. Universities," *Akron Business and Economic Review*, Spring 1980, pp. 39–45.

[3] These definitions differ somewhat from the definitions used by the Boston Consulting Group.

[4] Robert Lay and John Maguire, "Identifying the Competition in Higher Education—Two Approaches," *College and University*, Fall 1980, pp. 53–65.

[5] The discussion of Yale University draws on Robert J. Sternberg and Jeanne C. Davis, "Student Perceptions of Yale and Its Competitors," *College and University*, Spring 1978, pp. 262–79.

[6] The "four P's" classification was first suggested by E. Jerome McCarthy, *Basic Marketing: A Managerial Approach* (Homewood, Ill.: Richard D. Irwin, 1960).

part III
Understanding Markets

chapter 8
MARKET MEASUREMENT AND FORECASTING

Northwestern University enrolls 4,000 undergraduate students on its main campus on Lake Michigan in Evanston, Illinois. Most undergraduates live on or near campus. Full-time attendance is the norm, reinforced by the set tuition fee per quarter regardless of the number of courses taken. To attract top students and enable them to attend, the university has developed financial aid policies and resources that assist almost 60 percent of undergraduates.

The university's vice president for institutional relations, who oversees the admissions office, became interested in easing access for older students, particularly women, to come to Northwestern as undergraduates. Historically, older students, even those who had once been students at Northwestern, had been discouraged from enrolling in undergraduate programs on the Evanston campus. Instead, they were referred to classes offered in downtown Chicago under the Division of Continuing Education.

The impetus for change came from a 1971 Faculty Planning Committee report urging that the undergraduate student body be more diversified in age and other characteristics. Some faculty decried the "sameness" of the young students they were teaching and felt that older students would contribute different perspectives. The report called for establishing a Program for Returning Students, to appeal primarily to women living near the Evanston campus who had not completed a baccalaureate degree but who had earlier demonstrated "abilities and achievements roughly equivalent to those of Northwestern students."

In 1972, the university reversed the long-standing earlier tradition by agreeing to admit students older than 25 who had one year of acceptable college work. These students would be permitted to attend part-time. A small effort to inform former Northwestern students was made by advertising in an alumni magazine. Yet by 1979, no Program for Returning Students existed, and few women over 25 were enrolled. The director of the recently founded Program on Women noted that although other area institutions were actively encouraging older women to attend, Northwestern had passively waited for them to apply.

In 1979, the combination of early faculty support, pressure from the director of the Program on Women, demographic shifts, and a commitment to equality all encouraged the vice president for institutional relations to move more decisively to determine how many women might be eligible for and interested in completing undergraduate degrees at Northwestern, and to determine their characteristics and preferences. His goal was to use this information to decide whether the number of potential applicants warranted a special program and staff, and what would be the most effective ways to attract and serve this group.

We are now ready to turn our attention to the marketplace and to consider ways to understand and measure it. Analyzing the marketplace includes three major tasks:

1. Market measurement and forecasting: determining the current and future size of the available market for the institution's programs and services
2. Market segmentation: determining the main groups making up a market in order to choose the best target groups to serve
3. Consumer analysis: determining the characteristics of consumers—specifically, their needs, perceptions, preferences, and behavior—in order to adapt the offer to these consumer characteristics

These three tasks make up market analysis. This chapter will deal with market measurement and forecasting. Chapter 9 will deal with segmentation and targeting, and Chapter 10 with consumer analysis.

Market measurement consists of developing quantitative estimates of demand. An institution that has such estimates can analyze market opportunities, plan the marketing effort, and evaluate marketing performance with greater accuracy. Many educational institutions depend entirely on records of past demand or on the experience of other institutions in judging demand for their programs and services. A school that received 1,000 applications each year for the past five years would anticipate receiving about the same number this year. The development office may expect donations to consistently equal or surpass those of previous years as long as the staff carries out the same activities. These are examples of trend extrapolation (discussed in Chapter 5). Although collecting historical data is important, the estimate can prove faulty if underlying forces affecting demand should change. Or a school may look at the success of other schools in attracting students to new programs and conclude that by offering the same programs, it could attract an equal number of students. If the institution could determine the maximum number of potentially interested students, it could evaluate its probability of success in entering this new area.

Educational institutions vary in the level of demand they can serve or wish to serve. The institution's resources (faculty, residence halls, library, and so on) limit the number of students that can be served. The institution wants to enroll a specific number of students, neither more than can be well served nor less than required to ensure that resources are fully utilized. A highly selective school usually wants to generate a large number of applicants, to permit selection of those who best match the school's desired characteristics. Such a school will want estimates of how many students have these character- istics and are potentially interested in attending. Or an educational institution plans to launch a new program or service and wants to be sure that an adequate number of participants exists and can be induced to enroll.

In contrast, public elementary and secondary schools are obligated to serve all those who enroll. Such institutions don't need to generate more demand, but they must be able to predict demand in order to determine the number of teachers, classrooms, and other resources that will be required.

Other institutions want to maximize participation and will expand facilities and offerings to meet whatever level of demand materializes. Such institutions often would like to know the maximum market potential for their programs, so they can assess how much of the market they are attracting and can anticipate likely expansion needs.

Market measurement and forecasting can be used by educational insti- tutions to answer three key questions:

1. *Who is the market?* Defining who is "in the market" assists in determining market size and in designing and promoting programs for them.
2. *How large is the current market?* Measuring the current market demand for a program or service helps the institution set realistic expectations for enroll- ment or participation.
3. *What is the likely future size of the market?* Market forecasting permits the institution to plan ahead. For example, if market demand is likely to drop, a school may prepare to cut back staff or may strive to develop programs that will attract more students. If demand is growing, the institution can plan a response.

These three questions are examined in the following sections.

DEFINING THE MARKET

Every institution faces the task of defining who is in its market. A college realizes that not everyone is in the market for a college education. Of those who do want a college education, some will not attend at all or will attend another institution. Therefore, each institution must distinguish between its potential consumers and nonconsumers.

An institution's market depends on what the institution has to offer. Consider the case of a small private college. We can talk about the market for the college's bachelor's degree, or for its sociology program, or for its specific course on the sociology of religion. The definition of the market will vary in each of the three situations. The more precisely we can define the offer, the more carefully we can determine the market's boundaries and size.

We define a *market* as follows:

A market is the set of actual and potential consumers of a market offer.

The term *consumers* stands for applicants, students, participants, donors, or any other appropriate category. The term *market offer* represents a service, program, idea, product—in fact, anything that might be offered to a market.

A person in the market for something exhibits three characteristics: *interest, income,* and *access.* To illustrate this, we return to the situation described in the introduction.

Northwestern University is thinking of establishing a Program for Returning Students to attract women over 25 to attend the university to complete undergraduate degrees. The vice president wants to determine whether enough women in the community would be in the market to justify establishing a special admissions program.

Two market research studies were carried out to answer this question: (1) derivation of an estimate of the potential market based on available secondary data;[1] and (2) a survey of members of area women's organizations to determine the characteristics, preferences, and requirements of members of such groups who might consider attending Northwestern to complete undergraduate degrees.[2] Some of the examples in this chapter draw on these studies.

A first estimate of market size would be the number of women over 25 in the community with a potential interest in completing an undergraduate degree. We define the *potential market* as follows:

The potential market is the set of consumers who profess some level of interest in a defined market offer.

Now, consumer interest is not enough to define the market. If a price is attached to the offer, potential consumers must have adequate income (or loans or other financial aid) to afford the purchase. They must be able as well as willing to buy. Furthermore, the higher the price, the fewer people will remain in the market.

Market size is further reduced by personal access barriers that might prevent response to the offer. For example, a survey of women interested in attending college found that attending daytime classes was a problem for 77 percent; for 42 percent, commuting to the campus was a problem. These access problems will make the market smaller. The market that now remains is called the *available market*:

The available market is the set of consumers who have interest, income, and access to a particular market offer.

In the case of some market offers, the institution may establish restrictions on whom it will serve. For example, a college may sell football tickets to everyone who wishes to attend a game but may be unwilling to accept everyone who applies for admission as a student. Northwestern was particularly interested in attracting women (1) over 25 years old, and (2) with strong academic potential. These women constitute the *qualified available market*:

> The qualified available market is the set of consumers who have interest, income, access, and qualifications for the particular market offer.

Now the university has the choice of going after the whole qualified available market or of concentrating its efforts on certain segments. We define the *served market* as follows:

> The served market is the part of the qualified available market that the institution puts effort into attracting and serving.

Suppose the university particularly wants to attract women within easy commuting distance of the campus who can afford to attend with little or no financial aid. As a result, it might choose to promote the program primarily through local women's organizations whose members are primarily upper-middle and upper class. In this example, the served market is smaller than the qualified available market.

Once established, a special program for returning women students will attract an actual number of women, who will represent some fraction of the served market. Those who actually enroll are called the *penetrated market*:

> The penetrated market is the set of consumers that are actually consuming the product.

Figure 8-1 brings all the preceding concepts together. The bar on the left illustrates the ratio of the potential market—all interested persons—to the total population, here 10 percent. The bar on the right shows several breakdowns of the potential market. In the figure, the available market—those who have interest, income, and access—constitutes 40 percent of the potential consumers. The qualified available market—those who would meet the institution's admissions requirements—is 20 percent of the potential market, or 50 percent of the available market. Suppose the institution is actively trying to attract half of these; that would be 10 percent of the potential market. Finally, the figure shows that the institution is actually enrolling 5 percent of the potential market.

These definitions of a market are useful in marketing planning. If the institution is dissatisfied with the size of its penetrated market, it can consider several actions, some described in Chapter 7. First, it could try to attract a larger percentage of people from its served market (market penetration). If it

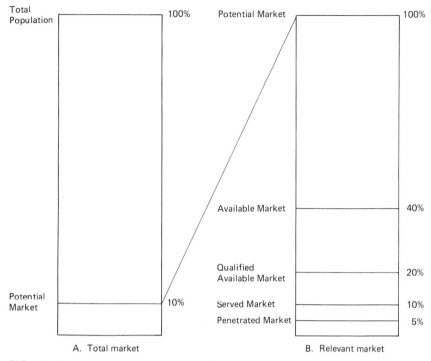

FIGURE 8-1   Levels of market definition

finds, however, that the nonenrolling part of the served market has decided to attend college elsewhere, the institution may seek to widen its served market by promoting the program in other, nearby communities (geographical expansion). Beyond this, some institutions may choose to relax the qualifications for admission in order to expand the qualified available market. The next step would be to consider expanding the available market by lowering tuition or giving more financial aid, improving the convenience of the location and time of course offerings, and doing other things to reduce cost and make the program more accessible. Ultimately, the institution could try to expand the potential market by launching a campaign to persuade women uninterested in attending college that they should be interested in college.

MEASURING CURRENT MARKET DEMAND

We are now ready to examine practical methods of estimating current market demand. A typical educational institution will want to make three types of estimates: *total market demand, area market demand,* and *institution market share.*

Estimating Total Market Demand

Total market demand is defined as follows:

Total market demand for a given product, program, or service is the total volume that would be bought by a defined consumer group in a defined geographical area in a defined time period in a defined marketing environment under a defined marketing program.

Note that total market demand is not one fixed number but depends upon the specified conditions. For example, some educational institutions and programs attract more applicants and students during periods of recession than during prosperity. Students may decide to go to a local community college to study technical and other vocational subjects. Adults may take more leisure courses because the cost of other entertainment is harder to justify. Prestigious institutions often find that applications increase as students decide that a top-quality degree may help them stay ahead during future hard times.

Another condition influencing demand is the institution's marketing program, including the programs and services offered, their prices, the level of expenditures on promotion, and other factors. In most instances, increasing promotional expenditures will yield higher levels of demand—at an increasing rate at first, then slowing down. Beyond a certain level, raising promotional expenditures will not stimulate much further demand, which suggests that market demand has an upper limit, the *market potential*.

We can think of two extreme types of markets. The size of an *expansible market*, such as the market for leisure courses, will be strongly affected by the level of promotional expenditures. On the other hand, a *nonexpansible market*, such as the market for doctoral studies in astronomy, will not be much affected by the level of promotional expenditures. If an institution finds that a market is nonexpansible, it may choose to enter another market with different programs, or it may decide to concentrate its efforts on getting a desired share of the existing market. For example, a university offering a doctoral program in astronomy may accept the fact that the number of people who want to study for doctorates in astronomy is stable, that the level of *primary demand* is fixed. The astronomy department may then concentrate on getting a desired percentage of those students who do want to do graduate work in astronomy to enroll in the department rather than to go to another institution. The department strives to create *selective demand* for its own program rather than for studying astronomy in general.

Once an institution has defined its product, consumer group, geographical area, time period, environment, and basic marketing program, the expected market demand associated with them is called the *market forecast*.

One straightforward approach to estimating demand is the *chain-ratio method*. The chain-ratio method is conceptually similar to the earlier example (in Figure 8-1) showing how the market can be progressively narrowed until

TABLE 8-1 Estimating the market potential for an undergraduate education at Northwestern University among North Shore women between ages 25 and 45

	TOTAL FORECASTED POPULATION 1980
1. *Base market (demographic)* North Shore communities (Evanston, Glencoe, Kenilworth, Wilmette, and Winnetka)	138,000
2. *Population of census tracts with median 1970 income over $15,000 (demographic)*	87,400
3. *Females 25 to 44 (demographic)*	10,300
4. *% upper quartile on IQ* Given the strong relationship between IQ and SES, probably close to 50% 50% × 10,300	5,150
5. *% females 25 to 44 in top quartile on SES, in top quartile of age cohort on academic aptitude, and who did not complete college within five years after high school graduation* Probability of a female (top quartile on SES and academic aptitudes) graduating from a four-year college within five years after high school is .71. Thus, probability of non-completion is .29 .29 × 5,150	1,493
6. *% interested in attending college (stage of readiness)* (Some will decide to continue working, doing volunteer work, etc.)	?
7. *% interested in attending Northwestern (loyalty status)*	?
8. *Further corrections must be made for:* % able to arrange for household help, transportation, family agreement % willing to cope with application process	

SOURCE: Karen F. A. Fox, *Attracting a New Market to Northwestern's Undergraduate Programs: Older Women Living on the North Shore* (Evanston, Ill.: Northwestern University Program on Women, 1979).

the market definition includes the subset of the total market that the institution wants to attract. The chain-ratio method involves multiplying a base number by a succession of percentages that lead to the defined consumer set.

To illustrate the method, we will return to the question facing the vice president for institutional relations: How many women over 25 living near the Evanston campus are likely to have the time, money, and ability to complete undergraduate degrees at Northwestern yet have not already completed college? This question is rather complex, but existing data were located that permitted a useful estimate of market size.[3] Table 8-1 shows the calculations.

Census and other population data indicated that approximately 10,300 upper-income women lived in the vicinity of Northwestern. This number was multiplied by .5, an estimate of the percentage who would have the intellectual ability to succeed at Northwestern,[4] to give 5,150.

But census data do not provide the most crucial information: the prevalence of college noncompletion by upper-socioeconomic-status women with high intellectual ability. Project TALENT found that 29 percent of the high-ability, high SES women in their study had not completed college five years after high-school graduation.[5] Multiplying .29 by 5,150 yielded an estimate of 1,493 women.

This number probably underestimates the total potential market, since it includes only five of the several nearby communities and only upper-SES census tracts. At the same time, it is important to remember that these women may or may not be interested in completing college. Those who are interested may prefer to go to another institution and, even then, may be unable to attend because of family responsibilities, health, or other reasons. Even a highly motivated applicant may be discouraged by the application process, the range of courses available, or some other act or omission by the university. The conclusion is that at least 1,500 women are potential students for Northwestern, that developing a special program for them would be worthwhile, and that the program's success will depend on meeting the special needs of this market.

Estimating Area Market Demand

The market demand for a particular program or service will vary from one geographical area to another. Most institutions want to determine which geographical areas deserve the most attention—usually those having the highest market demand.

There are several ways to estimate the relative attractiveness of different geographical areas. We will illustrate these in connection with the following situation.

St. Clare's School is a Catholic elementary school in Jonesville. The principal believes that the school is not reaching all the Catholic children in the area, and that additional students might come from nearby communities, including Spencer and Dobbs. The principal wants to identify the areas that have the highest potential for providing additional students.

Four methods of estimating area market demand will be described in the following paragraphs.

Area Analysis of Current Enrollment. A common approach is to study the areas that current students come from. The principal can prepare a dot map showing the homes of current students. It may be found that of the 15 percent who live outside Jonesville, 6 percent come from Spencer and 3 percent come from Dobbs. The conclusion may be that Spencer is a better market than Dobbs and that the school should focus recruiting efforts on Spencer.

This conclusion would be premature. Current area enrollment figures reflect not only differences in market potential but also differences in market cultivation. The school may be better known in Spencer, or the pastor of the Catholic parish in Spencer may encourage parents to send their children to the school. Spencer may simply have a larger population or a higher percentage of children than Dobbs. Perhaps the principal should be impressed that any Dobbs parents send their children to St. Clare's, since they have not received as much school publicity and encouragement as have parents in Spencer.

Furthermore, even if Spencer has twice as much market potential as Dobbs, it does not follow that Spencer should get twice as much marketing effort. It may deserve three times the effort, equal effort, or less effort. The decision should be based on estimates of how much response would occur in each community as a result of additional promotional effort.

Single-Factor Index. Here, the principal would try to discover a single measurable factor that would reflect the market potential of different communities. Suppose the principal believes that the best single indicator of market potential for Catholic school attendance is the number of Catholic families in the community. Using this criterion, if Spencer has 400 Catholic families and Dobbs has 200, we could argue that Spencer deserves more marketing effort—indeed, twice the effort given to Dobbs.

Multiple-Factor Index. The principal may decide that the school's whole confidence cannot be placed on a single factor. Instead, two or more factors may better indicate each community's market potential. The problem is to form an index that combines these factors. Suppose the principal believes that two factors are highly associated with interest in attending St. Clare's: (1) the number of Catholic families, and (2) the number of families with incomes over $20,000. Suppose the principal cannot obtain the statistics on two variables combined. Table 8-2 shows how a multiple-factor index can be formed.

The rows list the communities within commuting distance of St. Clare's School. The first two columns list the two factors. The third and fourth columns convert these two factors into percentages expressing each community's share of the total of each column. Thus, Spencer has 20 percent of the Catholic families in the area and 10 percent of the families earning over $20,000. We can take a simple average of the two percentage figures for each community and call this the multiple-factor index number. Spencer can be said to have about 15 percent of the market potential, whereas Dobbs has 25 percent. These numbers can be used to guide the percentage of the promotion budget and effort to expend in each community.

The multiple-factor index can be refined in several ways. First, the prin-

TABLE 8-2 Multiple-factor index

	(1) NUMBER OF CATHOLIC FAMILIES	(2) NUMBER OF FAMILIES EARNING MORE THAN $20,000	(3) PERCENT OF CATHOLIC FAMILIES	(4) PERCENT EARNING MORE THAN $20,000	(5) MULTIPLE- FACTOR INDEX
Spencer	400	200	20	10	15
Dobbs	200	800	10	40	25
.	.	.	.	.	.
.	.	.	.	.	.
.	.	.	.	.	.
	2,000	2,000			

cipal may want to use more than two factors, and this would require additional columns. Second, perhaps unequal weights should be assigned to the factors instead of taking a simple average. For example, the percentage of Catholic families might be weighted double because the principal feels it is a much more important factor than level of family income. Third, some of the factors may be impossible to express in percentage terms, and it may be necessary to convert all the row numbers using standard scales (say, 1 to 10 on a 10-point scale), which are then weighted. The general approach described here is the same one used to determine the "index of consumer buying power" businesses use to determine the market potential of various geographical areas.[6]

Distance-Adjusted Index. A potential consumer's interest in a program or service is likely to vary depending on how far he or she must travel to obtain it. Most people view travel as a cost—in time and money—and will choose outlets nearer their homes when possible. Studies confirm that market potential drops with distance from the site of the offer.[7] For example, over 90 percent of first-time college students attend an institution within 500 miles of their homes.[8]

One simple way to make an adjustment for distance would be to arbitrarily reduce the multiple-factor index value by a fixed number of percentage points for every unit of distance. For example, most of the residents of Spencer are about seven miles from St. Clare's, whereas Dobbs is about four miles from the school. The principal might deduct one percentage point for every mile of distance between the community and the school. Spencer's multiple-factor index would drop from 20 to 13, and Dobbs's index would be reduced from 25 to 21. Thus, Dobbs has almost 50 percent greater potential for enrolling children in St. Clare's than does Spencer.

Estimating Institution Market Share

Knowing the level of one institution's enrollment does not tell the whole story of how well it is doing. Institutions will therefore want to compare their performance with that of competitors to determine how well they are doing.

An institution can estimate at least three different measures of its market share. Ideally, the institution should determine its (1) share of the total market, (2) share of the served market, and (3) share relative to the leading competitor or leading three competitors. Each of these market-share figures yields useful information about the institution's market performance and potential.

FORECASTING FUTURE MARKET DEMAND

Having looked at ways to estimate current demand, we are now ready to examine the problem of forecasting future demand. The ease of accurate forecasting varies widely from one educational service or program to another. For example, the number of first graders in a school district can often be estimated quite accurately two or three years ahead of time, since the eligible children have already been born. The forecasts must take into account migration in and out of the area and possible competition from other schools with first-grade classes. Some public school districts participate in Project Simu-School, which provides computer-based models to forecast projected enrollment, types of instructional programs needed, and cost. The process can take into account population shifts in various parts of the district, teacher salary distributions, and other factors, and can determine whether a certain school should be closed, new facilities built, or how many teachers will be needed and when.[9]

Other educational institutions find that the total market demand and specific institution demand for educational services change significantly from one year to the next, making good forecasting much more challenging and more important. Poor forecasting may mean that too many teachers and staff have been hired and excess capacity is wasted, or, on the other hand, that there is not enough of either. The more unstable the demand, the more critical is forecast accuracy.

The process of forecasting begins with listing all the factors that might affect future demand, then predicting each factor's likely future level and effect on demand. Three broad categories are (1) *noncontrollable macroenvironmental factors*, such as the state of the economy, new technologies, and changes in regulations; (2) *competitive factors*, such as tuition levels at other institutions, new programs, and promotional expenditures; and (3) *institutional factors*, such as the institution's own tuition levels, programs, and promotional expenditures.

A forecast of future demand is always an approximation. A forecast can be based on what people say, what people do, or what people have done. Determining what people say involves conducting *consumer intentions surveys* or getting estimates from people (*middleman estimates*). Building a forecast on what people do involves *market testing*. Determining what people have done involves using statistical tools to analyze records of past buying behavior, using either *time-series analysis* or *statistical demand analysis*. These five methods are described below.

Consumer Intentions Surveys

Demand can be estimated by asking a sample of target consumers to state their intentions for the forthcoming period. Consumer intentions can be obtained in several ways. A "yes-or-no" form of the question would be, "Do you intend to take courses here next year?" This question requires a definite response. Some researchers prefer to give a range of responses: "Will you (a) definitely enroll, (b) probably enroll, (c) probably not enroll, (d) definitely not enroll in courses here next year?" These researchers feel that the "definitely enrolls" would be a fairly dependable minimum estimate, and some fraction of the "probably enrolls" could be added to arrive at a forecast.

More recently, some researchers have recommended using a full purchase probability scale:

Do you intend to enroll in classes here next year?

```
.00      .10    .20    .30    .40    .50    .60    .70    .80    .90    1.00
 +--------+------+------+------+------+------+------+------+------+------+
 No             Slight         Fair           Good           Very         Certain
 choice         possibility    possibility    possibility    probably

                Very           Some           Fairly         Probably       Almost
                slight         possibility    good                          certain
                possibility                   possibility
```

The researcher uses various fractions of the positive responders to form an estimate of the total demand. The forecasted enrollment should be compared to actual enrollment to determine what weights would have improved the forecast.

Middleman Estimates

A forecast can be developed by asking people who are close to the consumers what those consumers are likely to do. For example, the public school district trying to estimate first-grade enrollments may ask each principal for an estimate for the school. The principal is likely to know of plans for new construction, population shifts, parental attitudes, and other factors affecting the estimate.

Asking people close to consumers for their estimates is called grassroots forecasting. In using this method, the grassroots forecasters should be given a set of basic assumptions about the coming year, such as the state of the economy and the institution's expected marketing plans, rather than allowing each expert to make his or her own assumptions.

Market Tests

A direct market test can help forecast the attractiveness of a new program or service or the probable attractiveness of an established one offered in a new format or location. A market test consists of setting up a new program on a small scale or in one or a few locations as a test of the program's feasibility and attractiveness before enlarging the program's scale or extending it to additional locations. Market tests are especially valuable when consumer intentions surveys or middleman estimates are unreliable, such as when an institution is launching a new health promotion program and wants to predict participation, or when a community college plans to offer credit courses in senior citizen centers. Market test techniques are discussed in Chapter 11.

Time-Series Analysis

Instead of costly surveys or market tests, many institutions forecast on the basis of a statistical analysis of past data. The underlying assumption is that statistical analysis of data from past time periods can reveal trends that can be used to predict future demand. *Time-series analysis* is an extension of trend extrapolation, presented in Chapter 5.

A time series of past enrollment in a program can be analyzed into four major components: The first component, *trend* (T), reflects the basic level and rate of change in the size of the market. Trend is found by fitting a straight or curved line through the time-series data. The past trend line can be extrapolated to estimate the next year's trend level.

A second component, *cycle* (C), might also be observed in a time series. Enrollment and donations may be affected by periodic swings in general economic activity. If economic conditions can be predicted for the next period, the stage of the business cycle can be used to adjust the trend value up or down.

A third component, *season* (S), reflects any consistent pattern of applications, enrollments, or donations within the year. The term *season* refers to any recurrent hourly, daily, weekly, monthly, or quarterly pattern. The seasonal component may be related to weather factors, holidays, and so on. The researcher would adjust the estimate for, say, a particular month by the known seasonal level for that month.

The fourth component, *erratic events* (E), includes strikes, blizzards, fads, riots, fire, war scares or wars, entry of new competitors, and other nonrecurring events. This erratic component represents everything that remains unanalyzed in the time series and that cannot be predicted in the future. Therefore, it shows the average size of the error that is likely to persist in time-series forecasting.

Statistical Demand Analysis

Numerous quantifiable factors affect the number of consumers of a program or service. *Statistical demand analysis* is a set of statistical procedures designed to discover the most important real factors affecting enrollment (or donations) and their relative influence. The factors most commonly analyzed in the case of enrollment are academic ability, family income, age, and promotional expenditures.

Statistical demand analysis consists of expressing enrollment (Q) as a dependent variable and trying to explain variation in enrollment as a result of variation in a number of independent demand variables. Multiple regression analysis can be used to statistically fit various equation forms to the data to determine the factors and equations that give the best prediction.[10]

Louisiana State University uses the number of score reports it receives from the American College Testing Program (ACT) as an indicator of the level of student commitment to enroll.[11] Since the typical applicant requests that scores be sent to one or more colleges, the student is indicating something about his or her college intentions. Louisiana State has used the following equation to predict how many new freshman students will enroll in a given year:

$$E = (.4775)SR1 + (.1022)SR2 + (.0720)SR3 + (.0756)(SR4 + SR5 + SR6) + (.4196)SR7$$

where E represents the projected enrollment, SR1 through SR6 are the number of score reports received that indicate LSU as first through sixth choice, and SR7 is the number of supplemental reports. The coefficients equal the percentage of each choice category that has enrolled at LSU in past years. This particular equation is unique to LSU; other institutions would have to calculate their own coefficients based on several years of tracking reports.

SUMMARY

Marketing managers need measures of current and future market size in order to plan. A market is the set of actual and potential consumers of a market offer. To be "in the market," a person must have interest, income, and access to the market offer. The marketer's task is to analyze the various levels of the market, including the potential market, available market, qualified available market, served market, and penetrated market.

The next step is to estimate the size of current demand. Total current demand can be estimated using the chain-ratio method, multiplying a base number by a succession of appropriate percentages to arrive at the defined market. Area market demand can be estimated in four ways: area analysis of current enrollment (or applications or donations), single-factor indexes, multiple-factor indexes, or distance-adjusted indexes. Finally, the institution should compare its performance to similar educational institutions as a group to determine whether its market share is improving or declining.

To estimate future demand, the institution can use one or any combination of five forecasting methods: consumer intention surveys, middleman estimates, market tests, time-series analysis, or statistical demand analysis.

Determining present demand and estimating future demand permit the institution to assess current performance, test the viability of proposed new programs, and plan for needed resources to support future activities.

NOTES

[1] Karen F.A. Fox, *Attracting a New Market to Northwestern's Undergraduate Programs: Older Women Living on the North Shore* (Evanston, Ill.: Northwestern University Program on Women, 1979.)

[2] Yvonne Johns, *A Survey of Older Women as Candidates for Re-Entry at Northwestern University* (Evanston, Ill.: Northwestern University Program on Women, 1979).

[3] Fox, *Attracting a New Market.*

[4] Personal communication from Dr. Lauress Wise of Project TALENT.

[5] John G. Claudy, "Educational Outcomes Five Years after High School," paper presented at the Annual Meeting of the American Educational Research Association, 1971.

[6] See "Putting the Four to Work," *Sales Management*, October 28, 1974, pp. 13ff.

[7] See George Schwartz, *Development of Marketing Theory* (Cincinnati: Southwestern, 1963), pp. 9–36.

[8] Alexander W. Astin, M.R. King, and G.T. Richardson, *The American Freshman: National Norms for Fall 1977* (Los Angeles: Laboratory for Research in Higher Education, Graduate School of Education, University of California, and the Cooperative Institutional Research Program, American Council on Education, 1977).

[9] Janet Weiner, "Enrollment Projections: Plan the Future," *The Executive Educator*, December 1980, pp. 34 and 39.

[10] See William F. Massy, "Statistical Analysis of Relations between Variables," in David A. Aaker, ed., *Multivariate Analysis in Marketing: Theory and Applications* (Belmont, Cal.: Wadsworth, 1971), pp. 5–35.

[11] James H. Wharton, Jerry L. Baudin, and Ordel Griffith, "The Importance of Accurate Enrollment Projections for Planning," *Phi Delta Kappan*, May 1981, pp. 652–55.

chapter 9

SEGMENTING AND SELECTING MARKETS

What are you doing tomorrow morning before breakfast—or after midnight?

If the answer is "sleeping," you're out of step with a growing number of busy, very eager learners who are snatching a little more education during odd hours of the day and night.

Officials of Triton College and Technical Institute, a public community college in a western suburb of Chicago, noticed that their daytime computer-operator courses were overflowing. They decided to launch an experimental series of technical courses running from 11:30 P.M. to 3:30 A.M. to meet the schedule needs of second-shift factory workers. The result was so successful that Triton has more recently begun a 7 A.M. "breakfast college" of 50-minute courses in every field from yoga and algebra to philosophy and investing. Its pitch, with apologies to American Express, is: "Education—don't leave for work without it."

Sandwiching education into odd hours has advantages, but it usually calls for adjustments. Jim Jenkins, who signed up for Triton's nighttime machine-tool course earlier this year, reports that the choice of parking places near the class at that hour was superb—"no more of that driving around, waiting for someone to leave a space." But he says he had his regrets about leaving his wife with the chore of getting up every few hours to tend their infant son.

The hardest part, says Mr. Jenkins, was getting up after only three hours of post-class sleep to get to his 7 A.M. first-shift job. But between having an "excellent teacher who kept us awake" and catnaps at other hours of the day, he says he now is eager to sign up for an advanced machine-tool course on the same "night owl" schedule.

SOURCE: Lucia Mouat, "When Night School Means College Courses at 2 A.M.," *The Christian Science Monitor*, July 21, 1981, p. 2. Reprinted by permission from *The Christian Science Monitor* © 1981. The Christian Science Publishing Society. All rights reserved.

Instead of trying to serve everyone, schools should identify the most attractive parts of the market that they could effectively serve. Triton College serves the "middle-of-the-night" and "breakfast" segments of the community college student market, as well as day students. Not all institutions segment the market and focus their efforts on a specific segment or segments. Three styles are possible.

Mass Marketing. A college could offer one curriculum and try to convince all potential students that this curriculum is best. This is an example of mass marketing, where the college produces and distributes one market offer and attempts to attract every eligible person to use it. The mass marketer pays little or no attention to consumer preferences, but assumes they are all alike.

Product-Differentiated Marketing. An institution using product-differentiated marketing offers two or more programs and, like a cafeteria, invites people to select what they want. The programs might differ in quality, content, or other features. Rather than gearing specific programs to the needs and wants of specific groups, the product-differentiated institution hopes that each potential consumer will find something suitable among its varied offerings.

Target Marketing. Target marketing is the most tailored appoach to satisfying a market. The institution distinguishes among the different segments that make up the market, chooses one or more of these segments to focus on, and develops market offers specifically to meet the needs of each selected target market. For example, the school could develop a program specifically for talented young musicians, emphasizing performance skills and including attendance at musical events in the United States and Europe.

Educational needs and preferences are so varied that many educational institutions adopt either a mass marketing or a product-differentiated marketing approach. Educators should, however, seriously consider the potential contribution of target marketing. Target marketing can provide at least three benefits:

1. *The institution can spot market opportunities better when it is aware of different segments and their needs.* By monitoring these segments, the institution can note those whose needs are not fully met by existing offers.
2. *The institution can make finer adjustments of its programs to match the desires of the market.* It can interview members of the target market to determine their specific needs and desires and how the existing programs should be changed.
3. *The institution can make finer adjustments of its prices, distribution channels, and promotional mix.* Instead of trying to reach all potential consumers with a "shotgun" approach, the institution can create separate marketing programs aimed at each target market (called a "rifle" approach).

To use target marketing, the institution must complete two major steps, shown in Figure 9-1. The first is *market segmentation*, dividing a market into distinct and meaningful groups of consumers which might merit separate products and/or marketing mixes. The second step is *target marketing*, selecting one or more of the market segments and developing a positioning and marketing-mix strategy for each. This chapter describes the major concepts and tools for market segmentation and targeting.

FIGURE 9-1　Steps in market segmentation and target marketing

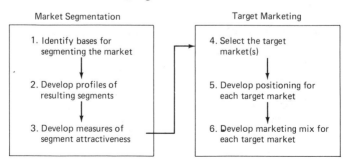

MARKET SEGMENTATION

The markets of an educational institution consist of students, alumni, donors, and people the institution hopes to add to those categories. People differ in age, income, preferences, academic ability, geographical location, and other characteristics. These and other variables can be used to segment a market to the extent that the resulting market segments suggest specific curricula, services, development approaches, and so on, that the school can implement.

Market segmentation is based on the fact that consumer preferences are often clustered. Some people will only be satisfied with a custom-tailored educational program (perhaps private tutors) and can pay the high cost, whereas most people would be very satisfied with a less expensive program aimed at a broader market.

For example, suppose a college is particularly interested in prospective students' preferences for two product attributes—academic rigor and active social life—in order to identify *preference segments*. Three possible patterns could emerge:

1. *Homogeneous preferences.* Figure 9-2,A depicts the case where all the students have roughly the same preference. The market shows no natural segments, at least as far as the two attributes are concerned. We would predict that if students in general had the same preference, colleges would closely resemble each other, because they would all have to please the same kind of student.

2. *Diffused preferences.* At the other extreme, individual student preferences may be so different that they would be scattered fairly evenly throughout the space with no areas of concentration (Figure 9-2,B). We would predict that many different types of colleges would be needed to satisfy the diverse market.

3. *Clustered preferences.* An intermediate possibility is the appearance of distinct preference clusters, called natural market segments (Figure 9-2,C). In this case, we would predict that three basic clusters of colleges would cater to the three types of students.

FIGURE 9-2 Basic market preference patterns

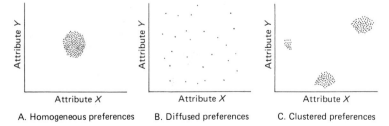

A. Homogeneous preferences   B. Diffused preferences   C. Clustered preferences

Thus, segmentation procedures could reveal the existence of natural market segments, or could be used to construct market segments, or could reveal the lack of any market segments. We now turn to examples of specific variables that can be used in segmenting consumer markets.

Bases for Segmenting Markets

There is no one correct way to segment a market. A market can be segmented using several different variables, singly and in combination, to see which suggest the most useful marketing opportunities.

For example, a Catholic high school might consider the following bases for segmenting the student market:

- *Religious affiliation:* Catholic, non-Catholic
- *Place of residence:* Inside the diocese, outside the diocese; or within 3 miles of the school, 3–10 miles, farther
- *Previous education:* Attended Catholic grade school, did not attend
- *Academic ability:* Top 20%, second 20%, middle 20%, bottom 40%
- *Ability to pay:* Full, some, none
- *Sex:* Female, male

If the high school is supported by the diocese, the school may give preference to Catholic residents of the diocese who are in the top 60 percent in academic ability. The tuition may be kept low, with scholarships to those unable to pay. Preference may be given to those students who attended Catholic elementary schools. In contrast, a highly selective Catholic boarding school may admit only girls in the top 20 percent of academic ability whose families can pay the full expense. Although both schools have segmented the market, each has selected different values of these variables to define the market segments they will serve.

Here we review the major geographical, demographic, psychographic, and behavioristic variables typically used in segmenting consumer markets, shown in Table 9-1. The choice of segmentation variables will, of course, depend upon the problem the institution seeks to clarify. The director of admissions will be interested in understanding the characteristics of applicants and enrollees, whereas the director of development will be interested in the characteristics of donors.

Geographical Segmentation. In geographical segmentation, the market is divided by location—which may be as large as a nation or as small as a neighborhood—based on the notion that consumers' needs and preferences may vary by where they live. Geographical segmentation may be appropriate when a college wants to develop differentiated brochures and student recruitment plans for various regions of the country. Knowing where prospects live may tell the college some useful things about what the students are seeking in

TABLE 9-1   Major segmentation variables for consumer markets

VARIABLE	TYPICAL BREAKDOWNS
Geographic	
Region	Pacific, Mountain, West North Central, West South Central, East North Central, East South Central, South Atlantic, Middle Atlantic, New England
County size	A, B, C, D
City or SMSA size	Under 5,000; 5,000–20,000; 20,000–50,000; 50,000–100,000; 100,000–250,000; 250,000–500,000; 500,000–1,000,000; 1,000,000–4,000,000; 4,000,000 or over
Density	Urban, suburban, rural
Demographic	
Age	Under 6, 6–11, 12–19, 20–34, 35–49, 50–64, 65+
Sex	Male, female
Family size	1–2, 3–4, 5+
Family life cycle	Young, single; young, married, no children; young, married, youngest child under 6; young, married, youngest child 6 or over; older, married, with children; older, married,no children under 18; older, single; other
Income	Under $2,500; $2,500–$5,000; $5,000–$7,500; $7,500–$10,000; $10,000–$15,000; $15,000–$20,000; $20,000–$30,000; $30,000–$50,000; $50,000 and over
Occupation	Professional and technical; managers, officials, and proprietors; clerical, sales; craftsmen, foremen; operatives; farmers; retired; students; housewives; unemployed
Education	Grade school or less; some high school; high school graduate; some college; college graduate
Religion	Catholic, Protestant, Jewish, other
Race	White, black, Oriental
Nationality	American, British, French, German, Scandinavian, Italian, Latin American, Middle Eastern, Japanese
Psychographic	
Social class	Lower lowers, upper lowers, lower middles, upper middles, lower uppers, upper uppers
Lifestyle	Straights, swingers, longhairs
Personality	Compulsive, gregarious, authoritarian, ambitious
Behavioral	
Benefits sought	Academic quality, job skills, social life
User status	Nonuser, ex-user, potential user, first-time user, regular user
Usage rate	Light user, medium user, heavy user
Loyalty status	None, medium, strong, absolute
Readiness stage	Unaware, aware, informed, interested, desirous, intending to buy
Attitude toward program or institution	Enthusiastic, positive, indifferent, negative, hostile

a college and what aspects of the college would be most appealing to them. Community colleges, on the other hand, are chartered to meet the educational needs of those who live within their districts. They thus serve one major geographical segment.

Demographic Segmentation. Demographic segmentation involves dividing the market into groups based on demographic variables such as age, sex, family size, family life cycle, income, occupation, education, religion, race, and nationality. Demographic variables are the most frequently used segmentation variables for three reasons. First, consumer wants, preferences, and usage rates are often highly associated with demographic variables. Second, demographic variables are easier to define and measure than are most other segmentation variables. Third, even when the target market is described in terms of other, nondemographic variables, reaching the desired target market depends upon determining key demographic characteristics of the target market that influence what media they use.

Here we will illustrate how certain demographic variables have been applied creatively in market segmentation.

Age and life-cycle stage. Consumer wants and capacities change with age and life circumstances. A college may offer special summer programs to acquaint high school students with college, a regular curriculum for college students, a continuing education program for adults who wish to get their degrees in the evening, and a summer Elderhostel program to provide educational enrichment programs for adults 60 and over.

Sex. For centuries, sex segmentation was the norm in education. Separate schools and colleges for males and females often had distinct curricula—such as engineering and agriculture at men's colleges and home economics at women's colleges.

The past two decades reveal two trends. First, some single-sex institutions have broadened or merged with others to serve both sexes. The University of Santa Clara, a men's college for 110 years, began admitting women students in 1961. Harvard University and Radcliffe College, which for decades shared courses, merged their academic programs in the 1970s.

Second, many educational institutions are further segmenting the female adult learner market as a basis for offering special programs. Figure 9-3 shows how the marketing specialist for the continuing education division of a state university segmented the female adult learner market. She divided it into "at home" and "working outside the home." The "at homes" are subdivided into homemakers and displaced homemakers. The "working outside the home" segment is also divided into two subsegments. Each of the four subsegments has a different set of motivations for attending college, and different programs are appropriate for each. For example, the homemakers may tend to select courses for self-enrichment and improved homemaking skills; displaced home-

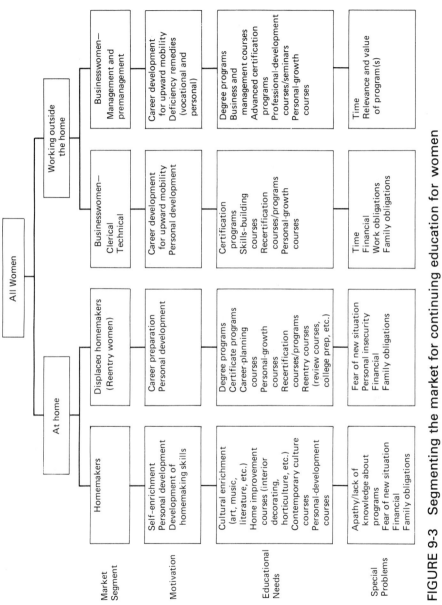

Market Segment	Homemakers	Displaced homemakers (Reentry women)	Businesswomen— Clerical Technical	Businesswomen— Management and premanagement
	At home		Working outside the home	
Motivation	Self-enrichment Personal development Development of homemaking skills	Career preparation Personal development	Career development for upward mobility Personal development	Career development for upward mobility Deficiency remedies (vocational and personal)
Educational Needs	Cultural enrichment (art, music, literature, etc.) Home improvement courses (interior decorating, horticulture, etc.) Contemporary culture courses Personal-development courses	Degree programs Certificate programs Career-planning courses Personal-growth courses Recertification courses/programs Reentry courses (review courses, college prep, etc.)	Certification programs Skills-building courses Recertification courses/programs Personal-growth courses	Degree programs Business and management courses Advanced certification programs Professional-development courses/seminars Personal-growth courses
Special Problems	Apathy/lack of knowledge about programs Fear of new situation Financial Family obligations	Fear of new situation Personal insecurity Financial Family obligations	Time Financial Work obligations Family obligations	Time Relevance and value of program(s)

FIGURE 9-3 Segmenting the market for continuing education for women

SOURCE: Nancy Greene, Division of Continuing Studies, Indiana University—Purdue University at Indianapolis.

makers may seek career preparation. Furthermore, each subsegment faces certain problems in attending college. By addressing the specific problems of each, the university can attract more women to its campus and serve them better.

Psychographic Segmentation. People with similar demographic characteristics may exhibit very different psychographic profiles. In psychographic segmentation, prospects are divided into groups on the basis of their social class, lifestyle, or personality characteristics.

Social class. Social classes are relatively homogeneous and enduring hierarchical divisions in a society. People within each class division tend to share similar values, interests, and behavior. Social scientists distinguish six social classes: (1) upper uppers (less than 1 percent of the population); (2) lower uppers (about 2 percent); (3) upper middles (12 percent); (4) lower middles (30 percent); (5) upper lowers (35 percent); and (6) lower lowers (20 percent), based on measures of income, occupation, educational attainment, and type of residence.[1] Social classes may show distinct preferences for certain educational institutions. Upper-middle-class students may, for example, prefer elite colleges where they will have the opportunity to socialize with higher status peers. Social class may influence a person's willingness to attend any college. A mature woman of the upper class might be reluctant to return to college to earn a degree either because she would be embarrassed to admit that she had not completed college or because attending college would interfere with the social and cultural demands of her lifestyle.

Lifestyle. Different consumer lifestyles exist between and even within social classes. Researchers have found that people's interest in various educational institutions and programs is influenced by their lifestyles, and, in fact, the educational choices they make express their lifestyles. Sun City, Arizona, is a relatively new community where most residents are retired, often with comfortable incomes. Arizona State University has opened a branch campus there to serve the educational interests of this group; and most of the faculty are retired professors who live in Sun City.

Personality. Marketers also use personality variables to segment markets. They strive to endow their products with brand personalities (brand images) that will match and appeal to corresponding consumer personalities (self-images, self-concepts). An educational program with a successful brand personality will prompt potential students or participants to say, "That's my kind of program." A conservative school with a dress code and other rules of student conduct will appeal to students who value social conformity and a familiar and safe environment. Schools that offer students many choices about curriculum and living arrangements will appeal to students who value their independence and who do not feel uncomfortable making decisions.

Behavioristic Segmentation. Sometimes marketers are particularly interested in how consumers respond to an actual program or service, rather than their general lifestyle or personality. Many marketers believe that behavioristic variables are the best starting point for constructing useful market segments, because behavior has direct implications for what institutions and programs consumer segments will choose. Some specific examples follow.

Benefits sought. Consumers can be segmented according to the particular benefit(s) they are seeking through participating in the program. Some consumers look for one dominant benefit; others seek a particular combination of benefits, a *benefit bundle.*[2]

For example, Goodnow surveyed students attending the College of DuPage, a large community college in Illinois, and found five benefit segments: (1) *social/improvement learners,* (2) *learning/career learners,* (3) *leisure/status learners,* (4) *submissive learners,* and (5) *ambivalent learners.* She matched these desired benefits with demographic characteristics and recommended a separate marketing strategy for each benefit segment. The leisure/status learners were typically middle-aged women seeking leisure activities and prestige. They attended noncredit physical-education and creative-arts programs, which met informally in small groups weekday evenings. These programs could appeal to this group's desire for "a night out" and be promoted through a mailed Extension Bulletin, the suburban newspaper, and women's clubs. The other four segments would each call for separate marketing strategies based on the benefit(s) sought and other characteristics of each segment.[3]

User status. Many markets can be segmented into nonusers, ex-users, potential users, first-time users, and regular users of a product.

Usage rate. Many markets can be segmented into light-, medium-, and heavy-user groups of the product, an approach called volume segmentation. Volume segmentation is important, because although heavy users may constitute only a small percentage of the market in numbers, they may account for a major percentage of the total volume of product consumed. Educational institutions often find that some consumers are involved in many aspects of the educational program, and some participate hardly at all. In particular, educational institutions whose tuition revenue is proportional to units taken often prefer to focus on their current light- and moderate-user segments.

On the other hand, some educational institutions, including most community colleges, are mandated to identify and address the educational needs of their communities. A recent report on continuing education for the elderly noted that "the vast majority of those most in need are still unreached," and those who do avail themselves of educational offerings "tend to be those who are already advantaged educationally and economically."[4] An educational institution interested in meeting the needs of the underserved can use volume segmentation to identify this group.

Loyalty status. Loyalty status describes the strength of a consumer's preference for a particular entity. The degree of loyalty can range from zero to absolute. We find consumers who are absolutely loyal to a brand (Budweiser beer, Crest toothpaste, Cadillac automobiles); an organization (the University of Texas, the Republican Party); a place (New England, Southern California); a person (Ralph Nader); and so on. Being loyal means maintaining a preference despite increased incentives to switch to something else.

A school or college may want to analyze alumni loyalty. Four groups can be distinguished: (1) *hard-core loyals,* who are exclusively devoted to the institution; (2) *soft-core loyals,* who are devoted to two or three institutions; (3) *shifting loyals,* who are gradually moving from favoring this institution to favoring another; and (4) *switchers,* who show no loyalty to any institution. Alumni tend to lavish most of their attention and contributions on their undergraduate college, with institutions where they acquired professional certification—law, business, and medical schools—running a close second. Schools also compete for attention with the many other organizations in which alumni may become active. If most of the school's customers are hard-core loyals or even soft-core loyals, the institution probably has a basically healthy alumni base. The school may want to study its "loyals" to find out the basic satisfactions that contributed to their feelings about the school and then work to create these satisfactions for current students and for other alumni.

Stage of readiness. At any one time, some members of the potential market for a product are *unaware* of the product; some are *aware*; some are *informed*; some are *interested*; some are *desirous*; and some *intend to buy*. The distribution of people over stages of readiness makes a big difference in designing the marketing program. When an educational institution launches a new program, most of the potential student market will be unaware of it (see Figure 9-4,A). At this stage, the marketing effort should go into advertising and publicity directed to those most likely to find the program attractive. If

FIGURE 9-4 Stages of market readiness

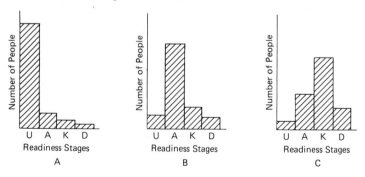

Note: U = unaware, A = aware only, K = knowledgeable, D = desirous

this campaign is successful, more of the market will be aware of the program but will still need more information (see Figure 9-4,B). After knowledge is built up, the advertising should feature the benefits of the program, perhaps including testimonials from program participants, in order to move people into a stage of desire (see Figure 9-4,C). As more people become interested in participating in the program, the institution will need to expand the capacity of the program or refine application procedures to handle the demand.

Attitude. Markets can be segmented according to consumer attitudes toward adopting the program or institution. For example, members of a chapter of Sigma Chi fraternity at an eastern college interviewed incoming freshmen about their attitudes toward fraternities. They found that 10 percent were *enthusiasts,* 20 percent *positives,* 30 percent *indifferents,* 25 percent *negatives,* and 15 percent *hostiles.* Each segment had a distinct consumer profile. Enthusiasts generally come from higher-income, better-educated families living in cities. The fraternity developed a better picture of its natural market and saw some opportunities for converting indifferent people to be more favorable toward fraternity membership.

Multivariable Segmentation. Marketers are often interested in segmenting a market on a combination of several segmentation variables, not just one. SRI International recently developed a multivariable classification of American adults into nine segments based on their values and lifestyles (Figure 9-5). The nine groups are described below, with the current estimated percentage of the U.S. population in each:

- Survivors (4%) are disadvantaged people who tend to be "despairing, depressed, withdrawn."
- Sustainers (7%) are disadvantaged people who are valiantly struggling to get out of poverty.
- Belongers (33%) are people who are conventional, conservative, nostalgic, and unexperimental, who would rather fit in than stand out.
- Emulators (10%) are ambitious, upwardly mobile, and status conscious; they want to "make it big."
- Achievers (23%) are the established, successful people who make things happen, work within the system, and enjoy the good life.
- "I-am-me" (5%) people are typically young, self-engrossed, and faddish.
- Experientials (7%) are people who pursue a rich inner life and want to directly experience what life has to offer.
- Societally conscious (9%) people are usually well-educated, have a high sense of social responsibility, and want to improve conditions in society.
- Integrateds (2%) are people who have fully matured psychologically and who combine the best elements of inner-directedness and outer-directedness.

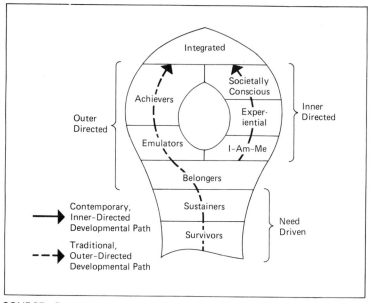

SOURCE: Reprinted with permission of the author and Macmillan Publishing Company from *The Nine American Lifestyles* by Arnold Mitchell. Copyright © 1983 by Arnold Mitchell.

FIGURE 9-5   The VALS typology

Each segment might suggest a different set of educational needs and therefore different programs. An urban community college may attract primarily Sustainers and Belongers. To attract Survivors, the college may choose to provide special services, such as child care, an emergency loan program, and counseling to reduce their distrust of education and of large bureaucracies and to reinforce their motivation to overcome obstacles.

Admissions officers may segment their student markets in terms of academic ability, financial resources, and their match with the institution. Exhibit 9-1 combines these variables to define core markets, wish markets, safety markets, and test markets.

Bases for Segmenting Organizational Markets

Educational institutions may market to other organizations as well as to individuals. A college may want to identify appropriate foundations and corporations to approach for financial support. A business school may want to identify companies interested in sending managers to its training programs. In both cases, the educational institution wants to get other organizations to buy something. The process by which organizations buy things is discussed in the next chapter; here we will consider how a market of organizations can be segmented.

EXHIBIT 9-1   An approach to segmenting prospective students

CORE MARKETS—Student types we are currently attracting

1. Primary Core Market: Students we are most pleased about attracting

2. Secondary Core Market: Students we find acceptable

3. Tertiary Core Market: Students we find barely acceptable

WISH MARKETS—Student types we would like to attract

1. Primary Wish Market: Students we would most like to attract but who prefer other programs to ours (students with high academic and financial ability)

2. Secondary Wish Market: Students we would like to attract but who prefer other programs to ours (students with high academic but low financial ability)

SAFETY MARKETS—Student types we tend to reject but would be willing to accept if our core and wish markets dry up

1. Primary Safety Market: Students with low academic ability and high financial ability

2. Secondary Safety Market: Students with low academic ability and low financial ability

SPECIAL TEST MARKETS—Student types we might reach and serve through special programs

1. Continuing Education Market

2. Summer School Market

Consider the example of a business school interested in providing training programs to company employees. Here are some of the major ways the school might segment companies:

   1. *Organization size.* The companies can be divided into large, medium, and small companies. The business school might find that large companies have "in-house" programs and would be less likely prospects than medium- and small-sized companies that recognize the value of training but have no training staffs.

2. *Geographical location.* Companies can be grouped by their distance from the school—whether they are in the same city as the school, within commuting distance, or beyond commuting distance. The business school may focus on local companies for programs that meet at 5:30, or on commuting-area companies for Saturday programs, and may develop residential short courses for those who cannot conveniently commute to the campus.

3. *Interest profile.* Companies can differ tremendously in their interest in contracting with educational institutions for company training. Companies in certain industries place great value on collaborative relationships with academic institutions and emphasize additional education and training for employees. Other industry groups, including those characterized by high employee turnover, may not be interested in employee training involving universities, preferring to provide essential training on the job.

4. *Resource level.* Companies differ in the resources they have and are willing to budget for training. Even a committed company will be less interested when it is being buffeted by bad economic conditions. The business school will be more successful if it can identify those companies that are likely to have the necessary resources.

5. *Buying criteria.* Companies differ in the qualities they look for in schools that supply training. Some companies emphasize the prestige level of the business school, others the qualifications of the professors who will conduct the specific program, and still others will consider the ties that have developed between the company and the business school over time. If the business school does not have a prestigious reputation, it should focus on companies that are likely to value the strengths the business school and its program do possess.

6. *Buying process.* Companies tend to differ in how much detail they require in training proposals and how long the decision process usually takes. Some companies expect detailed proposals and then take a long time to review, discuss, and evaluate them. The business school may prefer to identify companies that have a good relationship with the school and can make quick decisions based on relatively short proposals.

Requirements for Effective Segmentation

Although markets can often be segmented in several ways, the most useful segmentation approach will have the following characteristics:

• The segments will be *measurable.* The size and characteristics of the resulting segments can be readily determined. A school offering an extremely specialized program may find it very challenging to identify what kind of people find the program attractive and how many there are.

• The segments will be *accessible.* The resulting segments can be reached and served effectively. Certain segments are more difficult to reach than others. Consider trying to reach elderly shut-ins interested in taking tape-recorded "courses" at home. An educational institution may still attempt to locate members of this segment even though they are not easily accessible, but its job is harder.

• The segments will be *substantial*. They will be large enough to warrant a special marketing effort. Educational institutions typically offer programs that they believe will appeal to one or more large segments of the population. On the other hand, some educational institutions are responsible for serving unmet educational needs and will make a point of seeking out those smaller segments that are not served by existing educational programs. The institution needs to determine how large a segment must be to warrant the additional effort to serve it. (The example of Northwestern's program for returning women students in Chapter 8 illustrates this.)

• The segments will be *durable*. The resulting segments are likely to persist over time. Designing educational programs often requires extensive planning time, money, and commitments to teachers and other staff. Educational institutions need to consider whether identified segments will persist long enough to justify these efforts. For example, suppose a college wanted to offer a program to retrain out-of-work engineers for other jobs. This group was a large segment for a few years in the early 1970s. Then the economy picked up, and within a few years, engineers were in such short supply that engineering graduates could expect numerous job offers. Needless to say, a retraining program would soon have become obsolete.

TARGET MARKETING

Segmentation reveals the market segment opportunities facing the institution. Next, the institution has to decide among three broad market coverage strategies, shown in Figure 9-6.

1. *Undifferentiated marketing*. The institution can decide to go after the whole market with one offer and marketing mix, trying to attract as many consumers as possible. (This is another name for mass marketing.)
2. *Differentiated marketing*. The institution can decide to go after several market segments, developing an offer and marketing mix for each segment.
3. *Concentrated marketing*. The institution can decide to go after one market segment and develop the ideal offer and marketing mix.

Here we will describe the logic and merits of each of these strategies.

Undifferentiated Marketing

In undifferentiated marketing,[5] the institution chooses to ignore the different market segments and instead focuses on the common needs of consumers. It designs one program that will appeal to the largest number of consumers.

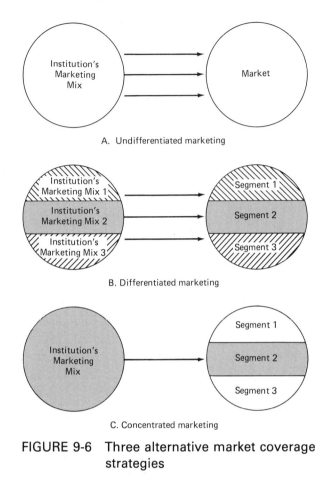

A. Undifferentiated marketing

B. Differentiated marketing

C. Concentrated marketing

FIGURE 9-6   Three alternative market coverage strategies

Undifferentiated marketing is exemplified by a school that offers one program for all students.

Undifferentiated marketing is "the marketing counterpart to standardization and mass production in manufacturing"[6] and, like these, is defended on the grounds of cost economies. The costs of developing, offering, and marketing educational programs are all kept low through limiting efforts to one program. Lower costs, however, are accompanied by reduced consumer satisfaction, since the institution fails to meet varying individual needs. Other institutions may already meet the needs of these "neglected" segments, or competing institutions may step in to serve these segments.

Differentiated Marketing

An institution using differentiated marketing operates in two or more segments of the market but designs separate programs for each segment. Through the use of differentiated marketing, the institution hopes to realize the following benefits:

- To attract more prospective students and donors and to have a bigger effect on each selected market segment
- To strengthen consumers' perceptions of the institution as a specialist in those products/programs it offers
- To create greater consumer loyalty and repeat purchasing, since the institution's offerings have been bent to the consumer's desires rather than the other way around

The institution using differentiated marketing can anticipate more results than one using undifferentiated marketing. Differentiated marketing is usually more costly, however, since the institution has to spend more on marketing research, product/program development, communications, and other tasks. Before deciding whether to adopt differentiated marketing, the institution needs to balance the likelihood of greater effect against higher costs. Some educational institutions push differentiated marketing too far by running more segmented programs than are economically feasible; others fail to recognize real opportunities to serve selected market segments better.

Concentrated Marketing

Concentrated marketing is a special case of differentiated marketing, in which the institution segments the market and then selects one segment as the focus of its marketing efforts. The institution concentrates on serving that one segment well, hoping to achieve the following benefits:

- A strong following and standing in a particular market segment
- Greater knowledge of the market segment's needs and behavior
- Operating economies in production, distribution, and promotion

For example, Gallaudet College provides a liberal arts education for deaf students, and the National Technical Institute for the Deaf at Rochester Institute of Technology offers preparation in technical and other areas.

Concentrated marketing may involve higher than normal risks, in that the selected market segment may decline or disappear. In the early 1900s, National College of Education was the National Kindergarten College, reflecting its specialized program focus. In 1917, it added preparation for elementary school teaching and became the National Kindergarten and Elementary College. By the late 1970s, the now National College of Education faced severe economic difficulties when elementary school enrollments dropped, along with the number of prospective students interested in teaching careers. Fortunately, National College successfully launched additional programs to reduce its dependence on its earlier market segments. The college had moved from concentrated marketing to differentiated marketing.

Choosing a Market Coverage Strategy

The choice of a market coverage strategy depends on several factors. If the institution has *limited resources,* it will probably choose concentrated marketing, because it lacks the resources to serve the whole market or to tailor special programs for more than one segment. If the market is fairly *homogeneous* in its needs and desires, the institution will probably choose undifferentiated marketing, since little would be gained by differentiated offerings. When the institution aspires to be a *leader* in several segments of the market, it will choose differentiated marketing. When *competitors* have established dominance in all but a few segments of the market, the institution might try to concentrate its marketing in one of the remaining segments.

Identifying Attractive Market Segments

Educational institutions usually start out with a strategy of undifferentiated marketing or concentrated marketing, and, if they are successful, they may evolve into a strategy of differentiated marketing. For example, a school may start as a strong academic school but then develop a reputation for activities in the performing arts as well and seek more students interested in music and drama. Whether an institution elects to use a concentrated or differentiated marketing strategy, it must identify the best segment(s) to serve. A market segment is worth further consideration when it satisfies two criteria: (1) The segment is attractive in its own right, and (2) the institution possesses the factors required to succeed in that segment. We will consider each in turn.

Several factors generally contribute to making a market or market segment attractive, independent of the institution that seeks to serve it. The following are the major features:[7]

- *Market size.* Large markets are more attractive than small markets.
- *Market growth rate.* Markets with high growth rates are more attractive than markets with low growth rates.
- *Ability to pay.* Markets that can make larger donations or can pay a higher percentage of educational costs are more attractive than those that cannot.
- *Competitive intensity.* Markets that are served by few competitors or substitute services are more attractive than markets that are served by many and/or strong competitors.
- *Variability.* Markets that fluctuate in size are less attractive than those that are stable or growing.
- *Scale economies.* Markets that can be served at lower unit cost as size increases are more attractive than constant-cost markets.
- *Learning curve.* Markets are more attractive when the institution serving them experiences lower unit costs as it gains more experience serving their needs than where no learning curve exists.

The second issue is whether the institution possesses the necessary success factors to make a strong showing in this market segment:

- *Relative market share.* The higher the institution's relative share of the market it serves, the greater the institution's strength.
- *Price competitiveness.* The lower the institution's costs relative to competitors, the greater its strength.
- *Program quality.* The higher the quality of the institution's offerings relative to competitors, the greater its strength.
- *Knowledge of consumer/market.* The deeper the institution's knowledge of consumers and their needs and wants, the greater its strength.
- *Marketing effectiveness.* The greater the institution's relevant marketing effectiveness, the greater its strength.
- *Geography.* The greater the institution's geographical presence and advantages in the market, the greater its strength.

When an institution evaluates possible segments, both market segment characteristics and institutional success requirements must be carefully weighed. An attractive segment for one school or educational program might be unattractive or inappropriate for another. For example, the adult-learner market might exhibit most of the key factors listed above and be an appropriate match for an urban college or university but be an inaccessible market for a rural institution.

SUMMARY

Educational institutions can take three different approaches to a market. Mass marketing consists of mass-producing and mass-distributing one program, product, or service and attempting to attract everyone to purchase it. Product differentiation consists of producing two or more programs differentiated in style, features, quality, and so on, to offer variety to the market and to distinguish the institution's offerings from those of competitors. Target marketing consists of distinguishing the different groups that make up a market and developing an appropriate program and marketing mix for each target market.

The key step in target marketing is market segmentation, dividing a market into distinct and meaningful groups of consumers which might merit separate programs and/or marketing mixes. Market segmentation is a creative act. The investigator tries different variables to see which reveal the best segmentation opportunities. The major consumer segmentation variables are broadly classified as geographical, demographic, psychographic, and behavioristic. Organizational markets can be segmented by variables such as organization size, geographical location, interest profile, resource level, buying criteria, and buying process. The effectiveness of a segmentation approach depends upon the extent to which the resulting segments are measurable, accessible, substantial, and durable.

The institution then has to choose a market coverage strategy, either ignoring segment differences (undifferentiated marketing), developing differentiated programs for several segments (differentiated marketing), or striving to serve only one or a few segments (concentrated marketing). No one strategy is superior in all circumstances. The institution needs to consider the inherent attractiveness of potential market segments in relation to the institution's strengths.

NOTES

[1] See James F. Engel, Roger D. Blackwell, and David T. Kollat, *Consumer Behavior*, 3rd ed. (New York: Holt, Rinehart & Winston, 1978), pp. 127–28.

[2] See Paul E. Green, Yoram Wind, and Arun K. Jain, "Benefit Bundle Analysis," *Journal of Advertising Research*, April 1972, pp. 31–36.

[3] See Wilma E. Goodnow, "Benefit Segmentation: A Technique for Developing Program and Promotion Strategies for Adults in a Community College," unpublished Ed.D. dissertation, Northern Illinois University, DeKalb, Illinois, 1980.

[4] "Education Found Unused by Adults Who Need It Most," *The Chronicle of Higher Education*, December 15, 1980, p. 6.

[5] See Wendell R. Smith, "Product Differentiation and Market Segmentation as Alternative Marketing Strategies," *Journal of Marketing*, July 1956, pp. 3–8; and Alan A. Roberts, "Applying the Strategy of Market Segmentation," *Business Horizons*, Fall 1961, pp. 65–72. Both articles are included in James F. Engel, Henry F. Fiorillo, and Murray A. Cayley, eds., *Market Segmentation: Concepts and Applications* (New York: Holt, Rinehart & Winston, 1972).

[6] Smith, "Product Differentiation," p. 4.

[7] The criteria for market attractiveness and the institutional success factors are based on the General Electric strategic business planning grid.

chapter 10

UNDERSTANDING CONSUMERS

September 4. Went to the guidance office for information. Got none, but did come away with the feeling that I should consider whether I want an urban or rural campus. Talked with some college students, and they suggested I consider Johns Hopkins.

September 12. Decided to visit some campuses.

September 14. Visited campuses. Current evaluation of schools to be considered: *Johns Hopkins; Rhode Island School of Design.*

September 23. Tried to get information from alumni and student representatives, but didn't find out anything.

October 6. Wrote away for some college literature. Current schools to be considered: *Johns Hopkins; Rhode Island School of Design.*

October 12. Received some unsolicited mail from Columbia. It made me realize that a college's publications are of some importance. Current schools to be considered: *Columbia; Johns Hopkins; Rhode Island School of Design.* I also decided that my level of aspiration with regard to special academic programs is too high, so I revised it.

October 19. Went to the guidance office again, made an appointment for the 21st.

October 21. The counselor gave me some information. Current evaluation of schools to be considered: *Columbia; Johns Hopkins; Rhode Island School of Design.* She also suggested Princeton. Ran into some professionals (in my area of career interest), and they suggested that Brown would be a school to consider and that a college's general reputation is important; not paramount . . . but important.

October 24. Attended College Night; it was a bust.

October 30. Intend to look through some college handbooks.

November 2. Got hold of a handbook today. Current evaluation of schools to be considered: *Brown; Columbia; Johns Hopkins; Princeton; Rhode Island School of Design.*

November 6. I should probably consider applying to Duquesne as a backup.

November 7. Current evaluation of schools to be considered: *Brown; Columbia; Duquesne; Johns Hopkins; Princeton; Rhode Island School of Design.*

[Then followed four and a half months of research, reading catalogs, talking with the counselor, visiting several campuses, and weighing the advantages and disadvantages of many colleges. After submitting several applications, the student gets closer to the final decision.]

March 29. Acceptance received from Boston. Deadline for reply May 1.

March 31. Got some more information from the guidance office.

April 5. One of the teachers suggested I should consider Drexel. He also convinced me that student–teacher ratio is extremely important, although Drexel is only acceptable on this factor.

April 8. Drexel is out; deadline passed.

April 15. Accepted at Union. Must reply by May 1.

April 16. I have decided where I'm going to go. Sent a letter of acceptance to Union and notified Boston that I was not coming. Exhausted!

> **SOURCE:** G. Lewis et al., *Nonroutine Decision Making*, Technical Report, Personnel and Training Programs (Arlington, Va.: Office of Naval Research, 1974), p. 43. Cited in William H. Turner, "Courting the Prospective Student," in David W. Barton, Jr., ed., *Marketing Higher Education* (San Francisco: Jossey-Bass, 1978), pp. 24–27.

The high school student in the passage above has struggled through the process of selecting a college. His search included most of the traditional sources of information and advice—college brochures, campus visits, the guidance counselor, teachers, college night, college students. He considered a variety of institutions, did some analysis of his interests and strengths, submitted several applications, and ultimately selected one of the two institutions that accepted him. Between September 4 and April 16, this student gathered and weighed information and came to a decision. His experience illustrates three steps in the consumer decision process, the focus of this chapter.[1]

Consumer decisions directly affect the institution. Students decide whether to apply and enroll. Alumni consider whether to make donations to their alma mater. A corporation reviews a college's request for funds for a library addition. These and similar decisions have crucial implications for the school or college under consideration, because they influence who the institution's clients will be and what resources it will have to support its work. Knowledge of the consumer is the basis for effective program development, pricing, distribution, and promotion. No wonder then that so many admissions officers and fund raisers wish they had a clearer understanding of what influences the decision to apply, attend, or donate.

When we say "consumer," we mean the person or organization that is the target of the marketing effort. We will deal with *individual consumers* in the first part of the chapter and *organizational consumers* in the second part. In both cases, we will seek to understand the buying process from the consumer's perspective.

The buying process starts before the actual purchase and may have consequences long after the purchase. The school one attends may well affect

FIGURE 10-1   Five-stage model of the consumer buying process

future career, friendships, choice of marriage partner, location of future residence, and life satisfaction. Even making a donation, not typically called a "purchase," involves a "buying process." The buying process has five stages (shown in Figure 10-1), which answer the following questions:

1. What needs and wants give rise to the interest in buying or consuming the program or product? (need arousal)
2. What does the consumer do to gather information relevant to the felt need? (information gathering)
3. How does the consumer evaluate the decision alternatives? (decision evaluation)
4. How does the consumer carry out the purchase? (decision execution)
5. How does the consumer's postpurchase experience with the program or product affect his or her subsequent attitude and behavior toward it? (postdecision assessment)

INDIVIDUAL CONSUMER BEHAVIOR

We will now examine the consumer behavior of individuals seeking to satisfy their own wants. Specifically, we want to understand how consumers make choices among educational programs.

We will examine one "buying" situation—that of students selecting a college. We shall refer from time to time to a hypothetical high school senior named Valerie who is beginning to think about the college-choice process.

Need Arousal

The first task is to understand how consumers develop their initial interest in the product class—in this case, a college education:

- What factors trigger an interest in a product class? (triggering factors)
- What deeper needs and values come into play when the consumer considers the product class? (basic needs)
- What specific wants usually become activated by these needs? (specific wants)

Triggering Factors. A person's interest can be stimulated by *internal or external cues*. An internal cue consists of the person's beginning to feel a need for, or readiness to do, something. The cue might take the form of a physiological stimulus, such as hunger or thirst, or a psychological stimulus, such as boredom or anxiety. An external cue consists of something from the outside coming to the person's attention and stimulating interest in the product class. The external cue can be *personal* (a friend, teacher, or parent) or *nonpersonal* (such as a magazine article or ad). Furthermore, the external cues can be either *marketer-controlled* (such as ads and admissions counselors) or *nonmarketer-controlled* (such as friends and natural settings).

To learn the major types of triggering cues, high school students can be asked to recall what aroused their interest in attending college. Students often mention the following cues:

- Students begin to face the end of high school and wonder what they want to do with their lives.
- High school counselors send forms to students on which they are to indicate their future plans.
- Other students start talking about *their* college plans.
- College brochures arrive in the mail, and the student starts reading them.

Basic Needs. The triggering cues can arouse a set of needs in the person. The cues do not create the needs but only activate existing needs. The marketer's task is to understand which basic needs the institution might serve.

One useful typology of basic needs is Maslow's *hierarchy of needs*, shown in Figure 10-2.[2] Maslow held that people act to satisfy the lower needs first before satisfying their higher needs. For example, a starving man first devotes his energy to finding food. If this basic need is satisfied, he can spend more time on his safety needs, such as eating the right foods and breathing good air. When he feels safe, he can take the time to deepen his social affiliations and friendships. Still later, he can develop pursuits that will meet his need for self-esteem and the esteem of others. Once this is satisfied, he is free to actualize

FIGURE 10-2   Maslow's hierarchy of needs

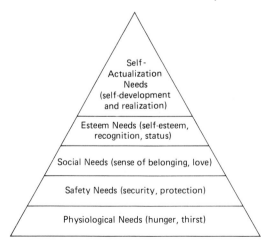

SOURCE: Based on Hierarchy of Needs in "A Theory of Human Motivation" in *Motivation and Personality*, Second Edition, by Abraham H. Maslow. Copyright © 1970 by Abraham H. Maslow. By permission of Harper & Row, Publishers, Inc.

his potential in other ways. As each lower need is satisfied, it ceases to be a motivator, and a higher need starts defining the person's motivational orientation.

We can ask what basic needs are stimulated by the aroused interest in college. Some high school seniors will become concerned about whether they can afford college and meet their basic needs for food and adequate housing. Others will wonder how safe they will be away from home. Still others will be concerned with whether they can find people they like and who like them. And others will be concerned with self-esteem and self-actualization. A college will not be able to give attention to all these needs. Thus, we find colleges that cater primarily to the need for belonging (small schools with small classes, a caring faculty, and a good social life), others to the students' need for esteem (many "name" colleges), and still others to the students' need for self-actualization (schools that emphasize exploring one's values).

Students often want to satisfy several conflicting needs with one decision. Thus, a student may have a high need for both achieving and belonging. This can create internal conflict, resolved either by treating one need as more important or by fluctuating between the two needs at different times. Here, the person's *values* come into play—namely, in choosing among competing ends. Studying people's value systems through interviews and questionnaires can help us understand their behavior.

Specific Wants. People interested in a product class usually have specific wants they would like the product class to satisfy. A college can discover these specific wants by asking students what *attributes* they look for in a college. Those most frequently mentioned by students are (1) academic reputation, (2) cost, (3) setting of campus (urban, rural), (4) distance from home, (5) size of campus, (6) social life, (7) physical look of campus, (8) housing and living, and (9) job placement.[3] Students vary in what they want with respect to each product attribute and its relative importance. We can imagine Valerie, for example, saying that she wants a strong academic college with at least moderate social life, located in the South, medium tuition, good housing, and good job placement. She might add that the first three wants are the most important.

No college can satisfy every student's *hierarchy of wants*, and therefore, the institution must shape itself to meet the want hierarchy of some segment(s) of the college-bound population. The college should review from time to time whether student want patterns are shifting in a way that would favor or disfavor the college's "brand" of education. For example, a college with a weak social program would be increasingly threatened by a shifting preference of college-bound students toward colleges with an active social life.

Information Gathering

Consumers facing a buying decision undertake varying degrees of information gathering, depending on the product class and their own level of need for information. The marketer is interested in the following two questions at this stage:

1. How much information are consumers likely to gather before making a decision in this product class? (information neediness)
2. What information sources will consumers use, and what will be their relative influence? (information sources)

Information Neediness. Consumers vary greatly in their information gathering, from those who jump right into a decision (as with impulse purchases) to those who spend months gathering information before deciding (as with major-expenditure decisions). We can distinguish between two broad levels of information gathering. The milder level is called *heightened attention*. Thus, Valerie may simply become more attentive to information about colleges, noticing news about colleges and listening to friends discuss them. On the other hand, she may undertake an active *information search*, seeking books on the subject, phoning friends, and writing for catalogs. How much she undertakes depends upon the strength of her drive, the amount of information she initially has, the ease of obtaining additional information, the value she places on additional information, and the satisfaction she gets from the search.

Normally, the amount of consumer information gathering increases as the consumer moves to more complex and important buying decisions. Howard has distinguished three buying situations, each calling for a different level of information gathering:[4]

- *Routinized response behavior* The simplest type of buying behavior occurs in the purchase of low-cost, frequently purchased items. For example, people buying aspirin have very few decisions to make because they are well acquainted with the product class, know the major brands, and have a fairly clear brand preference. They do not always buy the same brand, because the choice can be influenced by special deals or a wish for variety. But, in general, consumers do not give much thought, search, or time to the purchase. The goods in this class are often called *low-involvement goods*.

- *Limited problem solving* When consumers confront an unfamiliar brand in a familiar product, they need additional information before making a choice. For example, when a student selects a major, he may ask questions about various fields before choosing. In limited problem solving, buyers are fully aware of the product class (college majors) and the qualities they want (career prospects, interesting courses, and so on) but are not familiar with all the possible fields.

The alert marketer recognizes that consumers in this situation are trying to reduce risk through information gathering. The marketer must design a communication program that will attract attention and describe the product in an appealing way to the target market.

• *Extensive problem solving* Buying reaches its greatest complexity when consumers face an unfamiliar product class and do not know the criteria to use. For example, a college-bound high school senior needs to define the qualities to look for in a college as well as to study specific colleges and how well they deliver these qualities.

The marketer of products in this class must understand the information-gathering and evaluation activities of prospective consumers. The marketer's task is to facilitate the consumer's learning of the attributes of the product class, their relative importance, and the high standing of the particular brand on the more important attributes.

Information Sources. Of key interest to the marketer are the major information sources that the consumer will turn to and the relative influence each will have. Earlier we classified consumer information sources into four groups: (1) *personal nonmarketer-controlled* (family, friends, acquaintances); (2) *personal marketer-controlled* (sales representatives); (3) *nonpersonal nonmarketer-controlled* (mass media, natural settings); and (4) *nonpersonal marketer-controlled* (ads, catalogs). A consumer will normally be exposed to many sources. The marketer's task is to interview consumers and ask what sources of information they sought or received in the course of the buying process. From this, a picture can be drawn of the most frequent sources. Ihlanfeldt identified the major sources for the college choice decision, shown in Figure 10-3.

The relative influence of these information sources can be found by asking consumers to describe the type and amount of influence that different persons

FIGURE 10-3   Information sources influencing the college-bound student

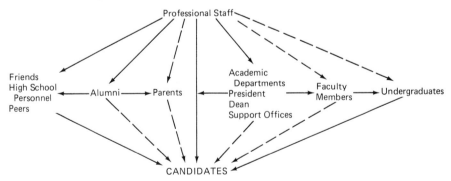

Note: Solid lines imply direct influence in the college-choice process; dashed lines indirect influence.

SOURCE: William Ihlanfeldt, *Achieving Optimal Enrollments and Tuition Revenues* (San Francisco: Jossey-Bass, 1980), p. 129.

had in their decision making. We can identify up to five buyer *roles*:

- *Initiator.* The initiator is the person who first suggests or thinks of the idea of buying the particular product or service.
- *Influencer.* An influencer is a person whose views or advice carries some influence on the final decision.
- *Decider.* The decider is a person who ultimately determines any part of the whole of the buying decision: whether to buy, what to buy, how to buy, when to buy, or where to buy.
- *Buyer.* The buyer is the person who makes the actual purchase.
- *User.* The user is the person(s) who consumes or uses the product or service.

For example, Valerie might report that her uncle initiated her interest in college by asking a year ago where Valerie planned to go to college. Her friends provided considerable information and influence about the types of colleges to consider. Her parents acted both as influencers and as buyers, since they were paying for her education. Valerie, however, made the final decision and was the user of the product.

Not only may Valerie receive different information from each source, but she will also place different value on the information from each source. She consciously or unconsciously gives weight to the *source's credibility* in deciding how to use the information. An information source is more credible when the source is perceived as *trustworthy, expert,* and *likeable.*[5] Thus, Valerie might give more credence to the information provided by an older brother in college than to a college recruiter who she thinks is biased. In addition, Valerie would have a higher *motivation to comply* with her brother's advice than with a college recruiter's advice.

All said, marketers find it worthwhile to study the consumers' information sources whenever (1) a substantial percentage of consumers engage in active search, and (2) consumers show more stable patterns of using the respective information sources. For example, identifying the information sources and their respective influence on the college-decision process could involve asking freshmen how they happened to hear about the college, what sources of information they turned to, what type of information came from each source, what credence they put in each source, and what influence each source of information had on the final decision. The college can use the findings to plan effective marketing communications and stimulate favorable word of mouth. Exhibit 10-1 describes the influences on the college-decision process.

Decision Evaluation

Through the process of gathering information, the consumer forms a clearer picture of the major available choices. He or she eliminates certain alternatives and moves toward making a choice among the few remaining alternatives.

EXHIBIT 10-1 Influences on the college decision process

Colleges are eager to understand the reasons why students select their institutions over others. Many institutions survey students who enroll and those accepted applicants who do not, to find out what influenced their decisions. Here are results of two studies of college applicants:

- Boston College asked more than 2,500 applicants to rate 28 attributes of the college on a five-point scale from 1 = unsatisfactory to 5 = excellent. For those applicants who chose Boston College, statistical analysis revealed that seven attributes were most important: First was financial aid, followed by parents' preference, specific academic programs, size of school, location of campus, athletic facilities, and social activities.
- Students who accepted offers of admission to the University of Santa Clara listed academics as the most important reason for their decision, followed by size, location, campus atmosphere, family living in the area, and curriculum. Only 3 percent mentioned finances. On the other hand, of admitted applicants who chose to go elsewhere, the largest number—30 percent—cited finances as the major reason for not attending Santa Clara.

Both Boston College and the University of Santa Clara are Catholic Jesuit universities with undergraduate and professional schools. Yet the differences in how accepted students rate the value of specific attributes are substantial.

Educational institutions also wonder about the effect of institutional recruiting activities. Admissions offices frequently make visits to high schools, attend college fairs, and send out many pieces of direct mail, and admissions directors would like to know which admissions activities have an effect. Activities that are very effective for many may not work for all institutions. Here is Northwestern's experience:

- Research at Northwestern University found that students uniformly agreed that their contact with Northwestern through visits by the college's representatives to high schools was unimportant in their decision to attend. The director of admissions did not find this surprising, since the decision to attend an expensive private university involves considerable reflection. The studies showed that prospects considered a visit to the campus important, so Northwestern stopped visiting high schools, except private and inner-city schools, where it made effective contacts. Instead, the admissions office created formal and informal programs to bring prospects to the campus, where they stayed in dorms, attended classes, and met and talked with students. These programs addressed the areas that applicants said were most important to them: the availability and quality of the curriculum in the student's preferred area, the reputation of the university, the academic atmosphere of the campus, and the nature of the student body.

Each institution will want to gather information about the effect of its activities, as well as the influences of parents, peers, high school counselors, alumni, and others, on the decision to attend that institution over others. This information provides the basis for informational programs for those sources that are most influential.

SOURCES: John Maguire and Robert Lay, "Modeling the College Choice Process: Image and Decision," *College and University*, Winter 1981, pp. 123–39; Roger Campbell, "Marketing: Matching the Student to the College," *College and University*, Summer 1977, pp. 591–604.

This process of *choice narrowing* can be illustrated for Valerie as she faced the problem of what to do after high school. Figure 10-4 shows her hypothetical movement from a broad set of generic alternatives to a narrow set of brand alternatives. At the beginning, Valerie considered alternatives to college, including working, joining the army, traveling, and doing nothing. Then she considered her needs and values, and this helped her clarify what she really wanted to do. She decided that going to college made the most sense. This raised the next question: What type of college? She could distinguish among three major forms: community college, state university, and private college. Again, she considered her needs and values and concluded that she prefers a private college. Next, she narrowed the possibilities to five private colleges: Cornell, Dartmouth, Duke, Northwestern, and Tulane.

We can now look more closely at how Valerie narrowed her choice to arrive at a decision. Figure 10-5 shows a succession of sets involved in her decision process. The *total set* represents all private colleges that exist, whether or not Valerie knows them; this list runs into the hundreds. The total set can

FIGURE 10-4 Narrowing-of-choice process

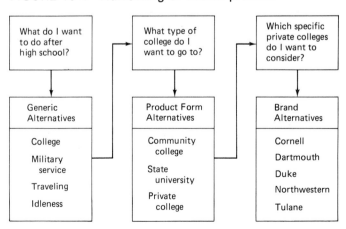

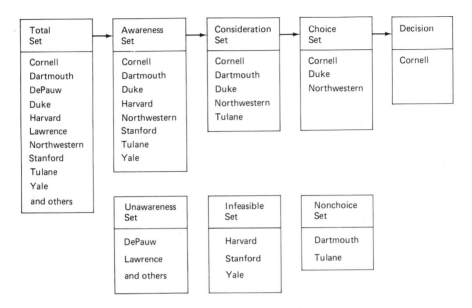

FIGURE 10-5   Successive sets in consumer decision making

be divided into Valerie's *awareness set* (those colleges she has heard of) and her *unawareness set*. Of those she is aware of, she will want to consider only a limited number; they constitute her *consideration set*, and the others are relegated to an *infeasible set*. As she gathers additional information, a few colleges remain strong, and they constitute her *choice set*, the others being relegated to a *nonchoice set*. Let us assume that the student applies to the three colleges in her choice set and receives acceptances by all three. In the final step, she carefully evaluates the colleges in the choice set (we shall examine this process shortly) and then makes a final choice—in this case, Cornell University.

Now we turn to the question, How does the consumer make a choice among the colleges in the choice set? The simple answer is that she forms a set of preferences by some process and chooses her first preference, assuming she is admitted. Here we shall want to explore the process by which the consumer forms her preferences.

We shall return to Valerie trying to make a choice among a set of colleges. We shall assume that her choice set consists of three colleges, to be identified as A, B, and C, rather than using the specific three mentioned earlier. We will assume that Valerie has provided the information shown in Figure 10-6. Six basic concepts are necessary to analyze the consumer evaluation process.

The first concept is the notion of a *choice set*, which we already described as consisting of colleges A, B, and C.

The second concept is that of *product attributes*. We assume that each

College	Academic Quality	Social Life	Location	Cost
A	10	8	6	4
B	8	9	8	3
C	6	8	7	5

(Attribute)

FIGURE 10-6
A high school student's beliefs about three colleges

Note: Ten represents the highest desirable score on that attribute. In the case of tuition, a high number means a low tuition, which makes the college more desirable.

consumer sees a given product as consisting of one or more attributes. These attributes are determined for each product class by asking consumers to name the factors they consider when thinking about the product. In Valerie's case, she named four attributes as most important: academic quality, social life, location, and cost.

Third, the consumer is assumed to have a set of *brand perceptions* about where each brand stands on each attribute. The set of perceptions about a particular brand is known as the *brand image*. Each row of Figure 10-6 represents Valerie's brand image of the corresponding college. A number from 1 to 10 is assigned to represent how much of each attribute Valerie sees the college as possessing.

Fourth, the consumer is assumed to have a *utility function* for each attribute. The utility function describes the consumer's varying level of satisfaction with varying levels of an attribute. For example, Valerie believes that her satisfaction will rise with higher levels of academic quality and social life; she would most prefer a college in the South and least in the West; and her satisfaction falls as the cost rises. If we combine the attribute levels where Valerie's utilities are highest, they make up her ideal college. This college would be the preferred college if it were affordable.

Fifth, the consumer is likely to attach different *importance weights* to the various attributes.[6] The consumer's importance weights can be elicited in at least three ways: (1) the consumer can be asked to rank the attributes in order of their importance (ranking method); (2) the consumer can be asked to distribute 100 points to the set of attributes to indicate their relative importance (constant-sum method); (3) the consumer can be asked to rate the importance of each attribute on a scale going from 0 to 1 (rating method).

Sixth, the consumer arrives at attitudes (judgments, preferences) toward the brand alternatives through some *evaluation procedure*. Unfortunately, there is no one decision evaluation process used by all consumers, or even by one consumer in all buying situations. Consumers apply different evaluation procedures to make a choice among multiattribute objects.[7] The major ones are described in Exhibit 10-2.

EXHIBIT 10-2 Models of consumer decision making

1. *Conjunctive Model.* Here the consumer sets minimum attribute levels that she will consider, then drops from consideration those schools that fall short on any attribute. Valerie might decide that she will consider only colleges with an academic quality greater than 7 *and* a social life greater than 8. Only college B will satisfy her, in this case.

2. *Disjunctive Model.* Here the consumer will consider schools that meet at least one minimum attribute level. Valerie might decide that she will consider only colleges with an academic quality greater than 7 *or* a social life greater than 8. Here, colleges A or B will remain in the choice set.

3. *Lexicographic Model.* Here the consumer will rank the attributes in order of importance. She will compare all the schools on the most important attribute and choose the superior one. If two schools are tied, she repeats the process with the second attribute. Valerie might decide that academic quality is the most important attribute. In this case, she will choose college A.

4. *Expectancy-Value Model.* Here the consumer assigns importance weights to the attributes and chooses the school that maximizes the expectancy value. Suppose Valerie assigned the following importance weights to the four respective attributes: .4, .3, .2, and .1. That is, she assigns 40 percent of the importance to the college's academic quality, 30 percent to its social life, 20 percent to its location, and 10 percent to its tuition cost. To find the expectancy value for each college, these weights are multiplied by the perceptions about the college, and the products are added to give the expectancy value for each college:

$$\text{College A} = .4(10) + .3(8) + .2(6) + .1(4) = 8.0$$
$$\text{College B} = .4(8) + .3(9) + .2(8) + .1(3) = 7.8$$
$$\text{College C} = .4(6) + .3(8) + .2(7) + .1(5) = 6.7$$

We would predict that Valerie will favor college A, since it has the largest expectancy value.

5. *Ideal-Product Model.* Here the consumer decides on the ideal level of each attribute. Suppose Valerie would prefer a college with the levels of 9, 9, 10, and 4 on the respective attributes. The further a college is from these levels, the more likely Valerie would reject it, assuming that she assigns the same importance weights as shown earlier. We multiply the weighted differences of each college from the ideal levels and take the sum. The lower the resulting sum, the closer the college is to Valerie's ideal. The results are shown below (the vertical bars mean that we are interested only in the absolute distance and not in the relative distance):

College A = .4/10-9/ + .3/8-9/ + .2/6-10/ + .1/4-4/ = 1.5
College B = .4/8-9/ + .3/9-9/ + .2/8-10/ + .1/3-4/ = .9
College C = .4/6-9/ + .3/8-9/ + .2/7-10/ + .1/5-4/ = 2.2

We would predict that Valerie will favor college B, because it is the smallest weighted difference from her ideal college.

6. *Determinance Model.* A consumer might ignore attributes that may be important but are pretty much at the same level for all colleges. Suppose the three colleges all have excellent music programs. In spite of the fact that Valerie may attach high importance to a music program, it will have no determinance on her college choice, since all colleges in her set are equal on this attribute. Determinant attributes are those that are both important and highly variable in the product class.

In the college-decision process, the prospective students and their families are not the only decision makers. Except in the case of public institutions which are required to accept all applicants meeting minimum standards, colleges also engage in a decision-making process. The admissions committee has a choice set of applicants to evaluate according to a set of academic and personal attributes to which the committee will attach importance weights. At Dartmouth College, for example, each application is read by three admissions officers, who rate the students on a scale of 1 to 9 on their academic and personal attributes, 18 being a perfect rating.[8]

Marketers can gain useful insights by interviewing a sample of consumers to find out how most of them form their evaluations in that product class. Suppose the admissions director discovers that most prospective students form their preferences by comparing actual colleges to their ideal college. Suppose college A, which would be the second choice to people like Valerie (according to the ideal-product model), wants to strengthen its chances of attracting students like Valerie. It can consider at least six alternative strategies.[9]

1. *Modifying the product.* The college could alter its attributes to bring it closer to this segment's ideal college. For example, college A could improve its social life so it gets a higher rating. This is called *real repositioning.*

2. *Altering perceptions of the product.* The college could try to alter students' perceptions of where it actually stands on key attributes. Thus, Valerie may believe that the tuition is higher than it actually is, and marketing communications can be used to correct this perception. This is called *psychological repositioning.*

3. *Altering perceptions of the competitors' brands.* The college could try to alter students' perceptions of where a leading competitor stands on different attributes. This is called *competitive repositioning.*

4. *Altering the attribute-importance weights.* The college could try to persuade

students to attach more importance to those attributes that the college happens to excel in. For example, college A can attempt to persuade students that academic quality is the most important aspect of any college.

5. *Calling attention to neglected attributes.* The college could try to persuade students to pay attention to an attribute that they are normally unaware of or indifferent to. If college A is located near a skiing area, it might tout skiing as a fringe benefit of attending college there.

6. *Shifting the ideal product.* The college could try to persuade students to change their ideal levels for one or more attributes. College A might try to convince students that a location in a cold climate is ideal, since they can get more studying done.

The college will need to carefully evaluate these alternative strategies according to their feasibility and cost. The difficulty of implementing each strategy, such as repositioning the college or shifting the importance weight, should not be minimized.

Decision Execution

The evaluation stage leads the consumer to form a ranked set of preferences among the alternative products in the choice set. Normally, the consumer will move toward the purchase of the most preferred product. He or she will then form a purchase intention, depending on acceptance. However, at least three factors can intervene between a purchase intention and its being converted into a purchase decision. These factors are shown in Figure 10-7.[10]

The first is the *attitude of others.* Suppose Valerie prefers college B but her father prefers college A. As a result, Valerie's *purchase probability* for college A will be somewhat reduced. The extent to which a preference will shift depends upon two things: (1) the intensity of the other person's negative attitude toward the consumer's preferred alternative, and (2) the consumer's motivation to comply with the other person's wishes. The more intense the

FIGURE 10-7   Steps between decision evaluation and decision execution

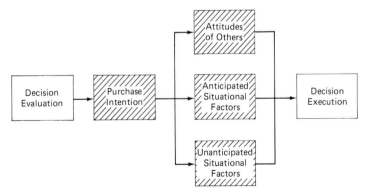

other person's negativism and the closer the other person is to the consumer, the more the consumer will revise downward his or her purchase intention.[11]

Purchase intention is also influenced by *anticipated situational factors.* The consumer forms a purchase intention on the basis of such factors as expected family income, expected total cost of the product, and expected benefits of the product.

When the consumer is about to act, *unanticipated situational factors* may arise that prevent carrying out the purchase intention. Valerie may learn that she cannot get a college loan to attend college. She may not like the looks of the campus when she visits it. She may be turned off by some of the students or professors she meets. Unanticipated factors in the *critical contact situation* can have a great influence on the final decision.

Thus, preferences and even purchase intentions are not completely reliable predictors of actual buying behavior. They give direction to purchase behavior but fail to include a number of additional factors that may intervene.

A person's decision to modify, postpone, or avoid a purchase decision is heavily influenced by *perceived risk.* Marketers have devoted considerable effort to understanding buying behavior as risk taking.[12] Consumers cannot be certain about the performance and psychosocial consequences of their purchase decisions. This produces anxiety. The amount of perceived risk varies with the amount of money at stake, the amount of attribute uncertainty, and the amount of consumer self-confidence. A consumer develops certain routines for reducing risks, such as decision avoidance, information gathering from friends, and preference for well-known products and institutions. The marketer must understand the factors that provoke a feeling of risk in the consumer and must attempt to provide information and support that will help reduce this risk.

Postdecision Assessment

After making the decision and enrolling, the student will experience some level of satisfaction or dissatisfaction that will influence her behavior. Valerie's satisfaction with her decision has important implications for the college and for her college career. A satisfied student will keep enrolling each term and will also tend to say good things about the school to others. According to a marketer, "Our best advertisement is a satisfied customer." On the other hand, a dissatisfied student will probably drop out or, at any rate, bad-mouth the college.

Educational institutions can take positive steps to help students feel good about their choice. A college can send a warm congratulatory letter to recently admitted candidates. It can invite their suggestions and complaints after they have spent a few months on the campus. The college can develop effective communications describing its philosophy and aspirations to reinforce the students' reasons for coming. Such postpurchase communications can reduce the amount of consumer postpurchase dissatisfaction.[13] Of course, the college must do more than communicate a positive image; it must deliver the quality and attributes that attracted students in the first place. We will have more to say about satisfaction in Chapter 16.

We have now completed the exposition of the consumer buying process and its five stages of need arousal, information gathering, decision evaluation, decision execution, and postdecision assessment. We deliberately chose an example involving extensive problem solving in which the consumer normally passes carefully through each stage.

But we should note that even in this buying situation, some consumers will pass through the process much faster than others, and may even skip certain stages. We can imagine the high school senior who immediately thinks of one college he would like to attend, sends in his application, receives acceptance, and matriculates. He engages in hardly any information gathering or decision evaluation. And when we examine other buying situations of a less demanding character—such as buying a magazine or enrolling in a one-day seminar—the buying process may be greatly contracted. Also, the stages in the buying model are sometimes reversed.[14] For example, a consumer may decide to enroll in an adult education course, then develop feelings of satisfaction, and then seek more information about other courses.

The model of the buying process that we have presented features important aspects of buying but does not imply that all consumers in all buying situations move smoothly and deliberately through each stage in the order shown. The purpose of the model is to help marketers raise and answer key questions about the behavior of consumers, by providing clues on how to better attract, serve, and satisfy a given group of consumers. For example, Figure 10-8 shows the types of information that correspond to each stage in the college decision process.

We have focused on the similarities among consumers as they go through the buying process, rather than on their differences. Each consumer will be

FIGURE 10-8   Interaction between information and the college-
decision process

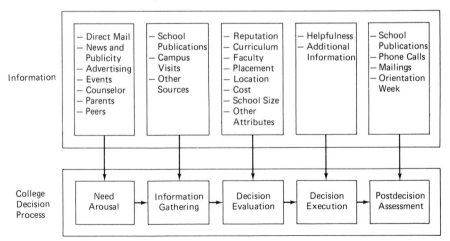

uniquely influenced by *cultural factors* (subculture and social class), *social factors* (reference groups, family roles, and statuses), *personal factors* (age and life cycle, occupation, economic circumstances, lifestyle, personality, and self-concept), and *psychological factors* (motivation, perception, learning, beliefs, and attitudes).[15] Many of these factors have been discussed in the preceding chapter on market segmentation.

ORGANIZATION BUYER BEHAVIOR

Educational institutions market to organizations as well as to individuals. Here are some examples:

- A college seeks a foundation grant to upgrade its engineering facilities. It must identify likely foundations and determine their "buying criteria" for choosing among the proposals they receive.
- A hospital health promotion program wants to provide stress-management and other courses for area employees under company sponsorship.
- Companies from all over the United States send their employees to North Carolina State University for short courses on all facets of textile production. The university would like to attract more participants.

Since educational institutions offer programs and services to other organizations, they need to understand the buying organizations' needs, resources, policies, and buying procedures. They need to take into account several considerations not normally found in consumer marketing:

- Organizations buy goods and services in order to make profits, reduce costs, serve their internal clientele's needs, and meet social and legal obligations.
- More people tend to participate in organizational buying decisions than in consumer buying decisions. The participants in an organizational buying decision usually vary in their organizational responsibilities and in the criteria they apply to the purchase decision.
- Organizational buyers operate under formal policies, constraints, and requirements established by their organizations.
- Selling to organizations tends to involve more personal contact and negotiation than does consumer marketing.

We are now ready to examine how organization buyers move through the buying process. As an illustration, we will assume that a university hopes to attract large corporate donations to endow scholarships.

Need Arousal

The first step calls for identifying corporate prospects. The university's prospect list would include corporations that have made generous gifts in the past as well as other corporations that are likely to have some interest in education and/or the university itself.

The marketer's next step is to try to understand the basic needs and wants of target organizations. This is fairly straightforward in the case of corporations, whose main objectives are to make money, save money, and be good corporate citizens. The university cannot directly help corporations make or save money, but it can appeal to the corporation's wish to be a good corporate citizen. Most corporations welcome favorable publicity about their "good deeds." The university can meet this need by offering to name some of the scholarships after the corporation.

The university needs to analyze the mission, goals, plans, and criteria of each corporate prospect so that it can develop appropriate appeals. The university might appeal to a major motion picture company or to a corporation headed by a person known for an interest in the performing arts to endow scholarships in theater and dramatic arts. In presenting its case to the corporation, the university must address the issues uppermost in the minds of the corporate contacts and decision makers.

Information Gathering

The corporation will normally need time to consider the university's proposal and to gather information. The type and amount of information will depend on the buying situation and on the corporation's familiarity with the university. Robinson et al. distinguished among three types of buying situations that they called "buyclasses":[16]

1. *Straight rebuy.* Here the organization is buying something similar to what it bought before. For example, a corporation might already be donating to the university each year, and in the absence of major new factors, it might approve a donation comparable to the last year's. A straight rebuy is analogous to routinized response behavior in the individual consumer buying situation. The corporation will not need much information, because the purpose and the university are known from previous dealings.

2. *Modified rebuy.* In the modified-rebuy situation, the organization is considering some change from its past purchases. The task calls for limited problem solving and hence more information than in the case of a straight rebuy. Thus, corporations that have made annual donations may want specific information to evaluate whether the university really needs more endowed scholarship funds before making a decision to contribute a large sum for one project.

3. *New task.* The new task faces an organizational buyer when presented with a new offer of an unfamiliar kind from an unfamiliar seller. An example would be a Japanese corporation's being asked to donate to an American university to improve Japanese-American relations. If the Japanese corporation is

intrigued with the idea, it will face extensive problem solving and will need to gather considerable information prior to making any decision.

To what source of information is the buyer likely to turn? One source is the educational institution, which can increase the probability of a donation by supplying relevant and credible information to the buying (or donating) organization. In developing its marketing plans the university should also anticipate other information sources that the organization buyer is likely to tap.

Decision Evaluation

Each buying organization will have certain well-established ways of evaluating different types of expenditures, including donations. Straight-rebuy decisions may be in the hands of a single officer who makes the decision in a fairly routine way. Modified rebuys may be in the hands of a small, middle-management committee. New tasks may be in the hands of a high-level management committee with members representing different areas of expertise. Many large corporations have offices that manage corporate philanthropy and coordinate the decision process.

The university must attempt to identify the people in the corporation who are likely to affect the decision. This *buying center* is "all those individuals and groups who participate in the purchasing decision-making process, who share some common goals and the risks arising from the decisions."[17]

The university's task is to identify the members of the buying center and then figure out (1) in what decisions they exercise influence, (2) what their relative degree of influence is, and (3) what evaluation criteria each decision participant uses. This knowledge can help the university in approaching the *key buying influencers.*

Organization buyers are subject to many influences when they meet to make their buying decisions. Part of the process is highly rational. A corporation will rate a request for a donation on such attributes as (1) the university's credibility; (2) its efficiency; (3) effect of the proposal on profits, costs, and other dimensions; (4) amount of goodwill created; and so on. To the extent that the process is a rational one, the university will want to make the strongest case in rational terms.

Other factors also play a part in the organization buying process. A study of buyers in ten large organizations concluded:

> Corporate decision makers remain human after they enter the office. They respond to "image"; they buy from companies to which they feel "close"; they favor suppliers who show them respect and personal consideration, and who do extra things "for them"; they "overreact" to real or imagined slights, tending to reject companies which fail to respond or delay in submitting bids.[18]

The university should take these human and social factors into account when dealing with organization buyers.

Decision Execution

After the corporation has decided to make a donation, the corporation and the university have to negotiate the exact terms and timing of various steps. Thus, the corporation would need to decide on the exact amount, how to pay it, and what compliance conditions to establish. Any of these steps can involve further negotiation. The university should anticipate these issues of detail and be prepared to work them through smoothly.

Organization buyers have also been known to cancel or withdraw at the last minute. The buyer may have heard something negative about the institution or might have encountered a cash-flow problem. The practical implication is that the university's work is not done after it receives news of a favorable decision. The alert institution will keep in touch with the corporation to make sure the agreement is enacted smoothly and that no snags develop.

Postdecision Assessment

The corporation will usually expect regular reports to make sure that the university is performing according to expectations. For example, the university should keep the corporate donor informed of the recipients and their academic achievements. By demonstrating responsible performance, the university will be able to go back to the same corporate donor some years later and ask for another large donation based on the satisfactory results it has produced.

SUMMARY

At the heart of marketing analysis is understanding the consumer's needs, wants, and buying behavior. We can distinguish between individual and organizational buying behavior.

Individual buyers tend to pass through five stages in connection with a purchase. The first stage is need arousal. Understanding need arousal involves determining what factors triggered interest in the product category, what basic needs became involved, and what specific wants became activated by these underlying needs. The second stage, information gathering, consists of the prospective buyer's seeking out information from personal and impersonal sources. At the third stage, decision evaluation, the consumer evaluates alternatives and develops a preference for one of them. The fourth stage, decision execution, describes additional factors (the attitudes of others, anticipated and unanticipated situational factors) that influence the final choice. The fifth stage, postdecision assessment, involves the buyer in reviewing the purchase, experiencing satisfaction or dissatisfaction, and taking postpurchase action.

The educational institution that seeks to provide services to or receive donations from other organizations needs to understand the organizations' needs and wants and to identify people who will influence the decision. Organizations go through the same five stages in buying a good or service or in making a donation as do consumers. The buying center consists of individuals who participate in the purchasing decision-making process. The number and behavior of members of the buying center vary with the complexity, expensiveness, and riskiness of the purchase.

NOTES

[1] Several models of the consumer buying process have been developed by marketing scholars. The most prominent models are in John A. Howard and Jagdish N. Sheth, *The Theory of Buyer Behavior* (New York: Wiley, 1969); Francesco M. Nicosia, *Consumer Decision Processes* (Englewood Cliffs, N.J.: Prentice-Hall, 1966); and James F. Engel, Robert D. Blackwell, and David T. Kollat, *Consumer Behavior*, 3rd ed. (New York, Holt, Rinehart & Winston, 1978).

[2] Abraham H. Maslow, *Motivation and Personality* (New York: Harper & Row, 1954), pp. 80–106.

[3] Patrick E. Murphy, "Consumer Buying Roles in College Choice: Parents' and Students' Perceptions," *College and University*, Winter 1981, p. 146.

[4] Howard and Sheth, *The Theory of Buyer Behavior*, pp. 27–28.

[5] Herbert C. Kelman and Carl I. Hovland, "Reinstatement of the Communicator in Delayed Measurement of Opinion Change," *Journal of Abnormal and Social Psychology*, Vol. 48 (1953), 327–35.

[6] The importance of an attribute should be distinguished from its salience. The attributes that come to a consumer's mind when asked to name a product's attributes are called the salient attributes. They may be salient because the consumer was just exposed to a commercial message mentioning them or had a problem involving them, hence making these attributes "top-of-the-mind." The consumer, when prompted, may recall other attributes that are equally important. We are more interested here in attribute importance than attribute salience. See James M. Myers and Mark I. Alpert, "Semantic Confusion in Attitude Research: Salience vs. Importance vs. Determinance," *Advances in Consumer Research*, 1976, pp. 106–10.

[7] See Paul E. Green and Yoram Wind, *Multiattribute Decisions in Marketing: A Measurement Approach* (Hinsdale, Ill.: Dryden Press, 1973), Chap. 2.

[8] "Days and Nights at the Round Table: How Dartmouth Admits Its Freshmen," *The Chronicle of Higher Education*, April 20, 1981, p. 9.

[9] See Harper W. Boyd, Jr., Michael L. Ray, and Edward C. Strong, "An Attitudinal Framework for Advertising Strategy," *Journal of Marketing*, April 1972, pp. 27–33.

[10] See Jagdish N. Sheth, "An Investigation of Relationships among Evaluative Beliefs, Affect, Behavioral Intention, and Behavior," in *Consumer Behavior: Theory and Application*, John U. Farley, John A. Howard, and L. Winston Ring, eds. (Boston: Allyn & Bacon, 1974), pp. 89–114.

[11] See Martin Fishbein, "Attitude and Prediction of Behavior," in *Readings in Attitude Theory and Measurement*, Martin Fishbein, ed. (New York: John Wiley, 1967), pp. 477–92.

[12] See Raymond A. Bauer, "Consumer Behavior as Risk Taking," in Donald F. Cox, ed., *Risk Taking and Information Handling in Consumer Behavior* (Boston: Division of Research, Harvard Business School, 1967); and James W. Taylor, "The Role of Risk in Consumer Behavior," *Journal of Marketing*, April 1974, pp. 54–60.

[13] See James H. Donnelly, Jr., and John M. Ivancevich, "Post-Purchase Reinforcement and Back-Out Behavior," *Journal of Marketing Research*, August 1970, pp. 399–400.

[14] Michael L. Ray, *Marketing Communication and the Hierarchy of Effects* (Cambridge, Mass.: Marketing Science Institute, November 1973).

[15] For a discussion of these factors, see Philip Kotler, *Marketing Management: Analysis, Planning and Control*, 5th ed. (Englewood Cliffs, N.J.: Prentice-Hall, 1984), pp. 124–142.

[16] Patrick J. Robinson, Charles W. Faris, and Yoram Wind, *Industrial Buying and Creative Marketing* (Boston: Allyn & Bacon, 1967).

[17] Frederick E. Webster, Jr., and Yoram Wind, *Organizational Buying Behavior* (Englewood Cliffs, N.J.: Prentice-Hall, 1972), p. 6.

[18] Murray Harding, "Who Really Makes the Purchasing Decision?" *Industrial Marketing*, September 1966, p. 76. This point of view is further developed in Ernest Dichter, "Industrial Buying is Based on Same 'Only Human' Emotional Factors That Motivate Consumer Market's Housewife," *Industrial Marketing*, February 1973, pp. 14–16.

part IV
Establishing
the Marketing Mix

chapter 11

DESIGNING
EDUCATIONAL
PROGRAMS

New York University (NYU) enrolls 35,000 students in several undergraduate colleges and professional schools, including law, business, science, arts, and education. In the early 1970s, NYU faced a number of formidable problems, including (1) a mounting annual deficit of several million dollars; (2) declining enrollment; (3) lack of a strong image in New York City; and (4) a number of weak educational programs. The deficit grew so worrisome that NYU began to consider closing down some programs, such as its School of Social Work, which involved a high cost per student to operate. It ultimately dropped its School of Engineering and also sold its University Heights campus to the city of New York for $62 million.

Then new leadership came to NYU and worked hard to turn this battle-scarred university into a high-quality, innovative institution of national stature. Raising entrance requirements in many of its schools resulted in fewer but better students. New buildings were added, including a $25 million library. NYU carried out marketing research, which indicated that it did not have a strong image and was often confused with the City University of New York. It hired the marketing firm of Barton-Gillette to revise its brochures and to improve its advertising and public relations. Soon people were hearing more and better things about NYU. It was becoming the university to watch in New York City.

NYU began to innovate programs instead of sitting back and offering the same ones year after year. Deans and chairpeople were appointed who had a more entrepreneurial view of their markets. They were going to "find new needs and fill them."

The university's new entrepreneurial spirit is well illustrated by the program it pioneered in 1978 to meet the educational needs of jobless Ph.D.s. NYU's business school noted the large number of Ph.D.s in such fields as history and literature who could not find teaching jobs in their field or receive job offers from companies because they lacked business training. Many were reduced to driving taxis or waiting on tables. NYU designed a six-week summer program to teach enrolling Ph.D.s the rudiments of business—finance, accounting, economics, marketing, and management—to ease them into the world of business. It also worked on changing the antibusiness attitudes and dress of some of these students, to remove these impediments to their being hired. The course ended with career counseling and visits from corporate recruiters. As a result of this training, most of the Ph.D.s received good job offers. This program, pioneered by NYU, has since been initiated by the University of Texas, the University of Virginia, the Wharton School at the University of Pennsylvania, Harvard, and the University of California at Los Angeles.

NYU has also added an early-morning breakfast-and-lecture series for about 100 invited executives. The lectures, mostly on nonbusiness topics—including opera, physics, and philosophy—are free, but university officials hope that the series will pay off in goodwill and contributions.

The most basic decision an educational institution makes is what programs and services it will offer to its students, alumni, donors, and other markets and publics. An institution's mix of offerings establishes its position vis-à-vis other educational institutions in the minds of consumers and determines how consumers will respond. We have only to consider a cosmetology school and a liberal arts college. Each school will attract a distinct clientele and be in competition with a distinct set of other institutions. Institutions with similar programs will find their markets and publics differentiating between them on the basis of the combination of programs and their quality.

Although few educators think of their programs and services as products, marketers use the word *product* as an all-inclusive term for what the institution offers to a customer. We define *product* as follows:

> A product is anything that can be offered to a market for attention, acquisition, use, or consumption that might satisfy a want or need. It includes physical objects, programs, services, persons, places, organizations, and ideas. Other names for a product would be the offer, value package, or benefit bundle.

Examining the institution's programs and making program decisions raise the following questions:

1. How can the institution identify the main components of its program mix? (*product-mix decisions*)
2. How can the institution better understand what it offers to its consumers? (*product-item decisions*)
3. How can the institution more effectively launch new programs? (*new-product decisions*)
4. What changes in marketing strategy are called for at different stages in the product life cycle? (*product life-cycle decisions*)

These questions are considered in the following sections.

PRODUCT-MIX DECISIONS

Most educational institutions offer multiple products. New York University offers degree programs in law, business, liberal arts, and many other fields; a summer program for Ph.D.s interested in business careers; a lecture series for executives; and numerous other programs.

An institution's *product mix* consists of all the product lines and items that the institution makes available to consumers. A *product line* is a group of products that are closely related in some way—because they either function in a similar manner, are made available to the same customers, or are marketed through the same outlets. For example, many colleges offer educational products (classes, library, campus lectures, and so on), recreational products (athletic facilities and clubs, film series, parties, and the like), personal-growth products (counseling center, religious organizations, advisors), curative products (health center), and future-planning products (career counseling, placement service, and so on). Each of these product categories can be considered a product line.

Suppose the college is thinking of expanding its product mix. The college could add more product lines, such as residential services—dormitories. Or it could add more products to an existing product line; for example, it might add a new degree program or lecture series. Or suppose the college needs to reduce the number of programs to bring down its costs or to attain a more specialized position in the marketplace. It might drop an entire product line—say, by closing its health center and sending students to local doctors—or drop a few items from one or more product lines, such as dropping an academic major that is no longer in demand.

An educational institution should evaluate its product mix periodically, and particularly when considering modifications. Some products are more central than others. For this reason, educational institutions should use the academic portfolio model (presented in Chapter 7) to assess the quality, centrality, and market viability of various products before adjusting the product mix. It will find that some—specifically, educational offerings—are *essential products* that it cannot do without, and others, such as recreational activities, are *ancillary products*. Furthermore, certain programs will play a major role in attracting consumers; these are called *product leaders* or *flagship products*. For example, students and donors will be attracted to a college with a strong reputation in at least one field. Often an institution will seek to add a *star product* or *crown jewel* to its mix, and then showcase that in its literature and promotion. The crown jewel may be an outstanding scholar on the faculty, a nationally ranked medical school, or some other person or program that establishes the institution's quality or uniqueness.

PRODUCT-ITEM DECISIONS

Educational institutions spend much time and effort making decisions about individual products—specific programs, academic majors, courses, and workshops. These educational products are services the institution provides to students and participants. What distinguishes services from other products is that services are intangible. We define a service as follows:

A service is any activity or benefit that one party can offer to another that is essentially intangible and does not result in the ownership of anything. Its production may or may not be tied to a physical product.

A service, like any other product, can be analyzed on three levels—the *core*, *tangible*, and *augmented* levels. By understanding these levels the marketer can fine-tune the service to be most attractive to consumers.

Core Product

At the most fundamental level stands the *core product*, which answers the questions, What is the consumer really seeking? What need is the product really satisfying? The marketer's task is to understand the product from the consumer's perspective. By uncovering the essential needs that underlie every product, the marketer can describe product benefits, not just product features. The core product stands at the center of the total product, as illustrated in Figure 11-1.

The core product may differ from one consumer to another. Consider the case of Avon cosmetics. The company's representatives sell cosmetics, but many of its customers are buying hope—for beauty, admiration, and romance. Other customers buy the Avon products to collect the distinctive bottles and jars they

FIGURE 11-1   Three levels of product

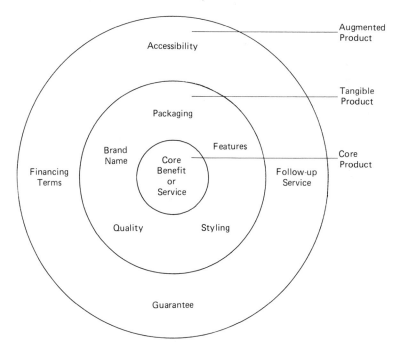

come in. Still others buy the products because the Avon representative's visit alleviates their loneliness.[1] The same is true of educational services. A college provides instruction, but some students are seeking marketability, and others are seeking a good time before going to work. A Sunday school may offer religious instruction, but some participants are seeking peace of mind or salvation.

Tangible Product

The core product is almost always embodied in some tangible form, even in the case of a largely intangible service.[2] Consider a student in a classroom. The core product that the student may want is information. The *tangible product* may take the form of a classroom where the student sits at a desk facing the blackboard, and the instructor stands in back of a lectern and reads from notes, occasionally making diagrams on the board. Clearly, this is not the only form that the tangible product can take, as witness the growing popularity of computer-aided instruction. We could imagine the same student sitting in front of a computer terminal, seated in a carrel designed for comfort by a human-engineering specialist. The student can type in a request for a lesson and wait for the information to appear on the monitor screen. After reading each set of instructions, the student responds to short questions that test his or her understanding.

The tangible product can be described as having up to five characteristics: *styling, features, quality level, packaging,* and a *brand name.* We will examine each of these five characteristics of the tangible product in more detail, because each can be modified by the marketer to make it more attractive to consumers.

Styling. Styling means giving the service a distinctive look or "feel." Much of the competition in durable goods—such as automobiles or watches— is style competition. Style is also expressed in the design of schools and other buildings where educational services are offered. Services themselves can be styled: Consider the style of the individualized instruction just described compared to the classroom setting.

An educational institution should consider style when planning a new service or evaluating an existing one. Ideally, the institution will design the style for the intended market rather than impose a style on it. For example, if a college wants to attract high school students to a summer workshop, the styling should be selected with high school students in mind. An educational institution may also find that its style is no longer appropriate or effective with its current target audience, in which case it may want to consider modifying its style to meet changing market preferences.

Features. Features are individual components of the tangible product that could be easily added or subtracted without changing the service's style or quality. Consider an elementary school that is seeking to expand enrollment. There are many feature improvements it could offer; for instance:

1. Expanding its hours so that children of working parents could be supervised before and after regular school hours

2. Adding more playground equipment

3. Offering a free course in effective parenting

The use of features has many advantages. The institution can go after specific market segments by selecting those features that would appeal to them. Features are also a tool for differentiating the institution's products from those of competitors. Features have the advantage of being easy to add or drop quickly, and they can be made optional at little expense. Novel features are often newsworthy and can be used to get media publicity.

Quality. Quality represents the perceived level of performance in a service. The quality of a service is particularly important precisely because quality can vary so much, depending on the provider of the service—including the provider's skills, motivation, and mood—and on how much control the institution can exercise over service providers. Consider the case of colleges A and B. College A is a publish-or-perish institution where professors are judged primarily by their research output, not by their classroom performance. College B, on the other hand, insists on high-quality teaching and drops instructors who do not meet this standard. Whether college A will continue to attract enough students depends upon the extent to which prospective students get information about this quality difference and care enough about quality teaching to have it determine their college choice.

Packaging. Packaging is the container or wrapper surrounding the specific product or service. We know that good packaging can add value beyond that perceived in the product itself; consider the fancy perfume bottle and its contribution to the aura of the perfume. In the case of a service, packaging is the contribution of the larger context in which the service is obtained. Thus, a college campus's environment serves as the packaging of the academic product:

> The architecture, topography, and landscaping of a campus should support the educational function of the university. . . . The campus should evoke the feeling of a tone poem, a festival, a composition that washes over the inhabitants. It should combine all the senses—sight, sound, touch, taste, and scent—becoming a street scene, a block party, a family gathering, a tactile encounter, a tribute to the intermeshing of the sights and sounds of human beings.[3]

Of course, not every school campus can be a "tone poem," but reflecting on how the campus is experienced may at least suggest priorities for improvement.

Branding. The products and services of an educational institution can be branded—that is, given a name, term, sign, symbol, or design, or some combination, that identifies them with the institution and differentiates them from competitors' offerings. Branding can add value to the institution's offer and more satisfaction for the consumer. College football teams, for example, generate loyalty and enthusiasm in part because they carry the brand name of the school and the team. Likewise, a well-titled program or idea will attract more favorable attention than one with a name that is dull or a turnoff. For example, people are apt to think better of a program called "individualized learning" than one called "programmed instruction," because the first name suggests personal attention, whereas the latter suggests a rigid process.

Augmented Product

The marketer can offer the target market additional services and benefits that go beyond the core product and the tangible product, thus making up the augmented product. A college can offer lifetime use of the career placement center, membership in the alumni organization, perhaps access to college classes to update skills in the future. Of the hundreds of educational institutions, many are seeking or will seek ways to augment their services to attract more customers. To paraphrase Levitt, the new competition is not between what educational institutions offer in the classroom but between what they add to their standard offerings in the form of packaging, services, advertising, financing, delivery arrangements, and other things that people value.[4]

Thus we see that a service (or other product form) is not a simple thing but a complex offer consisting of a core need-satisfying service, a set of tangible characteristics, and a set of augmenting benefits. The institution should examine each of its services and design them in a way that will distinguish them from competitors' offers and convey the intended qualities to the target market.

NEW-PROGRAM DEVELOPMENT

Educational institutions differ in their need for and interest in ideas for new programs and services. Some are fully occupied in providing their current services; others are looking for new courses or programs to meet the changing interests of the public. Some hope that a new program or service can keep them from sliding into oblivion.

Educational institutions often assume that designing and launching a new program is a simple task. The following situation is typical of many efforts to develop new educational programs.

A university's school of education had seen its undergraduate enrollment dive during the 1970s and was concerned about keeping viable graduate programs as educational administration and college teaching positions dwindled. The faculty held a meeting to decide how to restructure the school's graduate programs. After existing courses were listed on the blackboard, faculty in each subarea met to consider what new courses to add. The faculty group then completed the diagram of courses and discussed how to recruit prospective students. Faculty members called out names of nearby colleges that might have students interested in graduate programs in education. The colleges were listed on the blackboard, and each faculty member selected two campuses to visit. The meeting closed with the decision to place ads in college newspapers announcing when faculty members would be available to discuss the programs. The whole process took about three hours.

Although common, this approach is unlikely to be successful. The faculty planners ignored important considerations in planning for new programs and services. They never considered what would be the best program ideas based on career possibilities or student interests. They did not analyze past trends in graduate enrollment at the university and its competitors for clues about what students wanted, nor did they conduct market research to determine which programs would be most interesting to students. Finally, the recruiting "plan" used a shotgun approach of highly doubtful effectiveness.

Most educational institutions think that new-program planning must be informal, because they lack the time and money to do the job right. On the contrary, precisely because they have scarce resources, they cannot afford to waste them on thrown-together programs. Consumer-products companies can afford to launch many new products that fail, because they can recoup their losses and make a profit on those that succeed. Even then, effective consumer-products companies invest heavily in developing each new product.

Figure 11-2 shows the development process for new programs and services. *Opportunity identification* involves selecting the best program areas and generating ideas that could be turned into new programs. *Design* entails converting the ideas into a form that can be implemented, including the description of the program, preparation of materials, and development of a marketing strategy. If the resulting design looks promising, *testing* begins—testing of the program, its market potential, and its appeal to consumers. Only then is the program introduced. After *introduction*, the new program must be managed (*management*) to ensure that it will continue to be successful. This section describes each step in the context of De Paul University's interest in launching a new program. The same process is applicable to any new product or service.[5]

Opportunity Identification

De Paul University wanted to expand its educational services in the greater Chicago area. De Paul needed to determine what types of educational programs seemed most promising and what specific ideas merited further consideration.

Market Definition. De Paul is already in the education business and is looking for new educational services it could provide. The university will want to find unmet educational needs or wants and then consider whether De Paul has the resources and interest to provide programs to meet them.

FIGURE 11-2 New-program and service development process

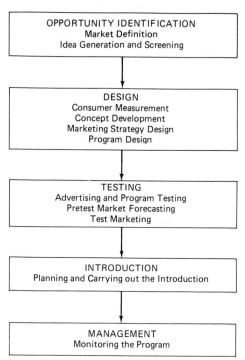

SOURCE: Adapted from Glen L. Urban and John R. Hauser, *Design and Marketing of New Products*, © 1980, pp. 33. Reprinted with permission of Prentice-Hall, Inc., Englewood Cliffs, N.J.

The De Paul planning group identified the following potential markets that might be entered: womens' studies, black studies, dentistry, evening degree programs for adults, and weekend graduate business programs. De Paul did not have the resources to enter all these markets and had to identify the most attractive one. An attractive opportunity should be attractive both (1) in itself, and (2) in relation to the institution. Table 11-1 lists factors to consider in each step. De Paul can evaluate each of the five markets in terms of its size, growth rate, and other characteristics. The planning group will then want to consider how well each market matches the university's capabilities. A particular program area may be a good opportunity for one institution but not for another.

At this stage, the institution also needs to consider what consumers it

TABLE 11-1   Factors to consider in
             determining attractive markets

Market Characteristics
    Size of market
    Growth rate of market
    Cost to enter this market
    Time needed to become established
    Likelihood of competition
    Investment required
    Availability of required resources

Match to Institution's Capabilities
    Have financial resources required
    Match to present location/distribution system
    Match to marketing capabilities
    Utilize existing personnel and facilities
    Compatible with existing programs and services
    Management skills and experience with this market

SOURCE: Adapted from Glen L. Urban and John R. Hauser, *Design and Marketing of New Products* (Englewood Cliffs, N.J.: Prentice-Hall, 1980), p. 88.

wants to appeal to, because this will affect which program area will ultimately be chosen and how the particular program will be designed and promoted. The planning group needs to segment the consumer markets for each program and identify the segments that have the most potential. The result will be an evaluation of the characteristics of each new program area and a clearer picture of which segments each might address. De Paul University decided that a degree program for adults presented the best opportunity.

Idea Generation and Screening. Once the institution has defined promising program areas and consumer markets, the planning group develops ideas to take advantage of the identified opportunities.

Ideas come from many sources. Current or potential consumers may have ideas about new programs or modifications of existing ones. Their ideas can be gathered through direct surveys, projective tests, focus groups, and letters and complaints. The institution should also watch its competitors to see what new services they launch and with what success. The institution's administrators, faculty, and staff are another good source of ideas, along with outside consultants, educational associations, and others who are familiar with the field.

New-program ideas are usually prompted by *inspiration, serendipity, consumer requests,* or *formal creativity techniques.* Institutions have little influence in the first two processes, other than maintaining an open atmosphere and encouraging creativity. They should carefully study customer requests in search of good ideas. They can also employ creativity techniques to encourage group members to come up with promising ideas.[6] Of the many such techniques, two widely used ones are these:

1. *Brainstorming.* In this approach, a group tries to generate a large number of diverse ideas. The brainstorming may start with a task, such as, "Think of new ways to provide degree programs to working adults." No criticism is allowed while ideas are being generated, and group members are encouraged to build on other people's ideas. After the group runs out of ideas, the members discuss and evaluate the ideas that have been given.

2. *Synectics.* This group approach begins with stating the problem, describing its background, and reviewing past solutions. Goals and statement of the characteristics of the ideal solution are formulated. The group then generates a large number of ideas. One promising idea is selected, developed, and—if acceptable—added to a list of possible solutions. The group then considers the other ideas it has generated.

The resulting ideas can be reviewed and used in designing the new program and its marketing mix.

Design

Designing the new program involves more than preparing a list of courses or features. The design step includes gaining a clear understanding of what consumers want and using that knowledge to guide the design of the program and the marketing mix.

Concept Development. The institution needs to be able to describe its proposed program ideas to consumers to get their reactions. An educational institution cannot "show" the proposed program to potential customers, so it must prepare a verbal description. De Paul began with a product idea, a possible program described in objective and functional terms, that the university could offer to the market. A product concept has a particular subjective consumer meaning that the institution tries to build into the product idea. Starting with the product idea, an adult degree program, the following product concepts could be created:

Concept 1. An evening program with a liberal-arts orientation, mostly required courses, and no credit for past experience

Concept 2. An evening program with a career-development orientation, much latitude in course selection, and credit for past experience

Concept 3. An evening program with a general-education orientation for people over 50 years of age who want a bachelor's degree

Each concept should then be prepared in written form in enough detail to allow consumers to understand it and express their reactions. Here is an example of concept 2 in more elaborate form:

An evening program, called the School for New Learning, with a career-development orientation and much latitude in the courses that can be taken. The program would be open to people over 24 years of age; lead to a bachelor's degree; give course credit for past experiences and skills that the person has acquired; give only pass-fail grades; and involve a "learning contract" between the student and the school.

Target consumers are identified and asked for their reaction to this and other concepts. Table 11-2 shows the types of questions that might be asked. For example, the last question in the table goes after the consumer's intention to buy: "Would you (definitely, probably, probably not, definitely not) enroll in this program?" Suppose 10 percent of the target consumers said "definitely" and another 5 percent said "probably." De Paul could apply these percentages to the size of the entire target market to estimate the total number of enrollees. Even then, the estimate is at best tentative, because people often do not carry out their stated intentions. Nevertheless, by testing the alternative concepts with target consumers in this way, De Paul would learn which program concept has the best market potential and get ideas for improvements.

Marketing Strategy Design. Many educators assume that the marketing strategy is developed after the program is ready to offer to the market. In fact, the marketing strategy is as much a part of the success of the new program as the program itself and requires attention during the design stage. The preliminary marketing strategy may, of course, be modified throughout the development process.

The marketing strategy should be spelled out in three parts. The first part describes the size, structure, and behavior of the target market, the intended positioning of the new program in this market, and the enrollment and income goals in the first few years. Thus:

The target market is adults over 24 living in the greater Chicago area who have never obtained a bachelor's degree but have the skills and motivation to seek

TABLE 11-2 Major questions in a concept test for a new educational program

1. Is the concept of this adult degree evening program with its various features clear to you?
2. What do you see as reasons why you might enroll in this program?
3. What expectation would you have about the program's quality?
4. Does this program meet a real need of yours?
5. What improvements can you suggest in various features of this program?
6. Who would be involved in your decision about whether to enroll in this program?
7. How do you feel about the tuition cost of this program?
8. What competitive programs come to mind, and which appeals to you the most?
9. Would you enroll in this program? (Definitely, probably, probably not, definitely not.)

one. This program will be differentiated from other programs by offering course credit for relevant past experience, as well as in its career-development emphasis. The school will seek a first-year enrollment of 60 students with a net loss not to exceed $100,000. The second-year aim will be an enrollment of 100 students and a net income of at least $20,000.

The second part of the marketing strategy statement outlines the new program's intended price, distribution strategy, and marketing budget for the first year:

The new program will be offered at the downtown location of De Paul University. All courses will take place once a week in the evening from 6:00 to 9:00. Tuition will be $500 per course. The first year's promotion budget will be $80,000, $50,000 of which will be spent on advertising materials and media and the remainder on personal contact activities. Another $10,000 will be spent on marketing research to analyze and monitor the market.

The third part of the marketing strategy statement describes the intended long-run enrollment and profit goals and the marketing-mix strategy over time:

The university ultimately hopes to achieve a steady enrollment of 400 students in this degree program. When it is built up to this level, a permanent administration will be appointed. Tuition will be raised each year in line with the rate of inflation. The promotion budget will stay at a steady level of $50,000 per year. Marketing research will be budgeted at $10,000 annually. The target income level for this program is $100,000 a year, and the net income will be used to support other university programs that are not self-supporting.

These budget figures were derived by estimating the revenues and costs of the program for different possible enrollment levels. Breakeven analysis (see Chapter 13) is the most frequently used approach. Suppose De Paul learns that it needs an enrollment of 260 students to break even. If it manages to attract more than 260 students, this program will produce a net income; otherwise, if there is a shortfall, De Paul will lose money.

Program Design. A program concept is not a program. The program elements must be carefully designed to embody the program concept and to reflect the best preliminary marketing strategy. De Paul University's program design will include planning the overall structure of the academic program and setting admissions requirements and procedures. Then each course will need to be designed to fit the purpose of the program and the students who will attend. The program planners, together with faculty, will need to examine individual courses and plan course sequences that will carry out the program concept. Thought will have to be given to how student achievement will be assessed. Faculty training in teaching mature students may be important to the program's success and be included in the program design.

Testing

Testing is part of every phase of the new-program development process. Just as the product concepts were reviewed by potential consumers, the materials, schedules, advertising, and other components of the new program should be consumer-tested before they are printed or distributed. For example, a sample of prospects might be asked to comment on a mockup of the brochure describing the new program. This review usually results in valuable suggestions for improvement.

Market Testing. When the organization is satisfied with the initial design, materials, and schedules, it might set up a market test whereby the program and marketing strategy are introduced into an authentic consumer setting to learn how many consumers are really interested in the program. Thus, De Paul might decide to mail 10,000 brochures to strong prospects in the Chicago area during the month of April to see whether at least 30 students can be attracted. If more than, say, 30 students sign up, the market test will be regarded as successful, and full-scale promotion can be launched.

Test Markets. Test markets are the ultimate form of testing a new program. The institution can measure the viability of the new program without installing it wholesale throughout the system. Suppose the State University of New York (SUNY) was considering a new program. Since SUNY consists of 64 campuses, SUNY could develop the program and test it at one of the campuses to see how well it worked. Or it could test the new program at two campuses, each campus promoting it a different way to test the cost-effectiveness of different promotion approaches. If the new program proved successful in one or both test markets, it could then be launched at other campuses where appropriate.

Introduction and Management

When the design and testing steps are complete, the institution will be ready to introduce the new program. The timing and skillful management of the program introduction are important. The institution should begin informing potential consumers well in advance of the program, but not so early that waiting for it to start dampens their enthusiasm. By the same token, the institution should not wait until the last minute to begin promoting the program; otherwise, interested people will have other commitments and be unable to attend.

The tasks involved in the introduction should be clearly spelled out on a chart that indicates when each task must be completed and who is responsible. If program materials are delayed or faculty members are unclear about their roles, program participants will question their initial attraction to the program and perhaps drop out, creating "lost business" and bad word of mouth as well.

Those responsible for managing the new program should follow through with planned monitoring activities to ensure that the program is executed as designed and that participants are satisfied. Controls should be established to determine if enrollment, revenue, and costs are within the target ranges.

THE PRODUCT LIFE CYCLE

New programs, if they succeed, become old programs. A program's characteristics and marketing approach cannot remain optimal indefinitely. Broad changes in the macroenvironment and changes in consumers and competitors usually call for significant adjustments in the program and its marketing strategy. The nature of the appropriate adjustments can be conveyed through the concept of the *product life cycle.*

Many programs and services can be viewed as having something analogous to a "life cycle," being well received at their introduction and then moving into a period of decline. One only has to think of buggy whips and home ice delivery. The life cycle of a typical program or service exhibits an S-shaped curve marked by the following four stages:

- *Introduction* is a period of slow growth as the program is introduced in the market.
- *Growth* is a period of rapid market acceptance.
- *Maturity* is a period of slowdown in growth because the program has received acceptance by most of the potential consumers.
- *Decline* is the period when consumer interest shows a strong downward drift.

The product-life-cycle concept can be applied to a *product class* (educational services), a *product form* (college), or a *brand* (Boston State College). Product classes have the longest life cycles; educational services can be expected to be around indefinitely. Product forms tend to exhibit more standard product-life-cycle histories. As for brands, specific institutions or programs, they are the most likely to show finite histories.

Not all programs and services exhibit an S-shaped life cycle. Two other common patterns are these:

- *Cyclical pattern.* Some programs show a cyclical pattern (Figure 11-3, A). For example, engineering schools go through alternating periods of high enrollment and low enrollment, reflecting changes in the demand for and supply of engineers. Programs with a cyclical pattern should not be eliminated during the decline stage but should be maintained as much as possible, awaiting the next boom.
- *Fad pattern.* Here a new program appears, quickly attracts attention, is adopted with great zeal, peaks early, and declines rapidly (Figure 11-3, B). The acceptance cycle is short, and the program tends to attract only a limited following of people who are looking for excitement or diversion. Some community colleges offer a constantly changing list of leisure offerings to meet public interest in short-lived topics that are not part of the regular curriculum.

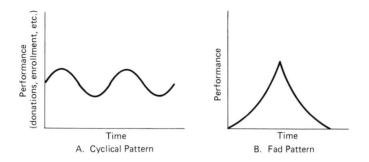

FIGURE 11-3   Two anomalous product-life-cycle
patterns

We will now return to the S-shaped product life cycle and examine the characteristics and appropriate marketing strategies at each stage.

Introduction Stage

The introduction stage of the product life cycle takes place when the new program is first made available in the marketplace. The introduction into one or more markets takes time; growth is apt to be slow. The institution needs time to expand its capacity—to locate more classroom space or hire more instructors, for example—and to work out "bugs" in the design. Potential consumers may be reluctant to try something new, and if the new program or service is expensive, only a few consumers may be interested enough to spend the money when it is first introduced.

Costs are high during the introduction stage, because the institution must invest in the new endeavor and in advertising while there are few consumers. Heavy promotional expenditures are necessary (1) to inform potential consumers of the new and unknown program, and (2) to induce them to try the program. At this stage, there are few if any competitors. All the providing institutions strive to attract the early adopters—those people who tend to be the first to try new programs and services. These early adopters have several distinguishing characteristics:

> The relatively earlier adopters in a social system tend to be younger in age, have higher social status, a more favorable financial position, . . . and a different type of mental ability from later adopters. Earlier adopters utilize information sources that are more impersonal and cosmopolite than later adopters and that are in closer contact with the origin of new ideas. Earlier adopters utilize a greater number of different information sources than do later adopters. The social relationships of earlier adopters are more cosmopolite than for later adopters, and earlier adopters have more opinion leadership.[7]

Management should keep these characteristics in mind in designing their introduction plans.

Growth Stage

If the new program satisfies the market, many consumers will be attracted to it. Other consumers will follow the lead of the early adopters, especially if there is favorable word of mouth. New competitors may enter the market, attracted by the institution's success. They may introduce feature, style, and packaging variations, in order to expand the market. During this stage, the institution tries to sustain rapid market growth as long as possible in several ways:

1. It undertakes to improve program quality and add features.
2. It vigorously searches out new market segments to enter.
3. It keeps its eyes open for new ways to gain additional attention for its program or service.
4. It shifts its promotion from building awareness of the program or service to trying to bring about conviction and purchase.

Maturity Stage

At some point, a program's rate of growth will slow down, and the program will enter a stage of relative maturity. Most programs are in the maturity stage of the life cycle. This stage normally lasts much longer than the previous stages, and it poses some of the most formidable challenges to marketing management.

The beginning of a slowdown in the rate of growth usually produces overcapacity; too many institutions providing a certain program while demand is falling. This overcapacity leads to intensified competition among the institutions. Competitors engage more frequently in price-cutting (through scholarships, credit for life experience, and so on) and increase their promotional budgets. Some institutions strive to improve their programs. Still others resort to modifying their consumer mix or program/service mix—for example, by admitting less-qualified students or adding new programs. These steps often result in higher costs. Some of the weaker competitors start dropping out. What remains eventually is a set of well-entrenched competitors striving to maintain or gain a competitive advantage that will help them survive.

Decline Stage

Programs may eventually enter a stage of declining demand. The decline may be slow or rapid. Enrollments and donations may plunge. More typically in education, enrollment or other indicators of consumer interest may petrify at a low level for many years.

Commonly, interest declines for several reasons. The market may lose interest because a particular program or major is no longer "in fashion" or does not meet consumer needs. Changes in technology or the economy may affect what educational services people seek. No matter what the reason, some changes must be made or the institution will suffer.

As interest declines, some programs will be eliminated. Responding to funding cuts, the University of Washington made plans to eliminate many degree programs, including urban planning, Near Eastern languages, kinesthesiology, nutrition, children's drama, textiles, art education, and dance. To other programs, the university planned to admit fewer students—dentistry, medicine, education, social work, architecture, and public administration.[8]

Remaining programs may reduce their offerings, withdraw from smaller market segments, or close satellite facilities. They may cut their promotion budgets and perhaps their prices. On the other hand, some educational institutions faced with declining programs will increase their promotion budgets, add new courses, and keep raising prices to meet higher costs. In general, this strategy works only when the institution has successfully identified an opportunity in which it has distinctive competence and a differential advantage, along with a growing market.

Unless strong retention reasons exist, carrying a weak program is very costly. The cost of maintaining a weak program is more than the financial loss. The weak program tends to consume a disproportionate amount of administrative time and requires both advertising and other attention that might be better spent making the "healthy" programs more successful. The program's weakness can create consumer misgivings and cast a shadow on the institution's image. The biggest cost may lie in the future. When not eliminated at the proper time, these programs delay the aggressive search for replacements; they create a lopsided program mix, long on "yesterday's breadwinners" and short on "tomorrow's breadwinners;" and they depress current cash and weaken the institution's foothold on the future.

In the face of declining interest, some institutions will abandon the market earlier than others. Those that remain often enjoy a temporary increase in consumers as they pick up those of the withdrawing institutions. For example, as several universities dropped Master of Arts in Teaching (M.A.T.) programs in the 1970s, the remaining programs received more applicants for a few years. But each institution faces the issue of whether it should be the one to stay in the market until the end.

If it stays in the market, the institution faces further strategic choices. It could adopt a *continuation strategy*, in which case it continues its past marketing strategy: same market segments, channels, pricing, and promotion. In this case, the number of consumers will probably shrink. Or it could follow a *concentration strategy*, concentrating its resources in the strongest markets while phasing out its efforts elsewhere. Thus, an M.A.T. program could prepare only science and mathematics teachers, since teaching positions in those fields are plentiful. Finally, it could follow a *harvesting strategy*, in which case it sharply reduces its expenses to increase its positive (or decrease its negative) cash flow, knowing that these cuts will accelerate the rate of decline and the ultimate demise of the program.

When a program has been singled out for elimination, the institution faces some decisions. First, it might decide to move the program to another institution or simply drop it. For example, when Northwestern was considering dropping its elementary-teacher-training program, one proposal was to send Northwestern students to nearby National College of Education to take the necessary elementary-education courses while enrolled at Northwestern. Second, the institution has to decide whether to drop the program quickly or slowly. Third, it must decide what level of service to maintain to cover existing students or customers. Educational programs often require several years of study; therefore, an educational institution usually cannot in good faith drop a program without transition plans to allow currently enrolled students to complete it.

SUMMARY

Most educational institutions offer multiple products. A product can be defined as anything that can be offered to a market to satisfy a need. The term *product* can refer to physical objects, programs, services, persons, places, organizations, and ideas.

Most educational institutions specialize in offering programs and services. An institution's program mix consists of all the programs it offers. Some of its programs constitute its essential products, and others are ancillary products. Institutions often seek to offer a flagship or crown-jewel product to gain publicity and enhance the institution's reputation.

A service is an activity or benefit that one party can offer to another that is essentially intangible and does not result in ownership of anything. A service, like any other product, can be analyzed on three levels. The core product answers the question, What need is the product really meeting? The tangible product is the perceptible elements of the service—its features, styling, quality level, packaging, and brand name. The augmented product consists of the tangible product and the additional services and benefits, such as follow-up service and guarantees. As competition increases, institutions augment their product offers to compete.

Planning new programs is a demanding process. The development process has five main steps. Opportunity identification involves selecting the best areas for further analysis and generating ideas that could be turned into new programs. The design step involves converting the ideas into implementable form, including describing the program, preparing the materials, and developing a preliminary marketing strategy. The testing step includes testing the design, its market potential, and its appeal to consumers. Introduction is the actual launch of the program. The final step is managing the new program over time to ensure its success and profitability.

Programs typically pass through a product life cycle consisting of four stages: introduction, growth, maturity, and decline. Each stage of the life cycle presents new marketing challenges and requires adjustments in the marketing mix.

NOTES

[1] See Ben M. Ennis and Kenneth J. Roering, "Services Marketing: Different Products, Similar Strategy," in James H. Donnelly and William R. George, eds., *Marketing of Services* (Chicago: American Marketing Association, 1981), pp. 1–4.

[2] See G. Lynn Shostack, "Breaking Free from Product Marketing," *Journal of Marketing*, April 1977, pp. 73–80.

[3] William F. Sturner, "Environmental Code: Creating a Sense of Place on the College Campus," *Journal of Higher Education*, February 1972, pp. 97–109.

[4] Theodore Levitt, *The Marketing Mode* (New York: McGraw-Hill, 1969), p. 2.

[5] This section draws on Glen L. Urban and John R. Hauser, *Design and Marketing of New Products* (Englewood Cliffs, N.J.: Prentice-Hall, 1980).

[6] James L. Adams, *Conceptual Blockbusting*, 2nd ed. (New York: W.W. Norton, 1979).

[7] Everett M. Rogers, *Diffusion of Innovations* (New York: The Free Press, 1962), p. 192.

[8] Barry Mitzman, "U. of Washington Plans to Drop 24 Degree Programs," *The Chronicle of Higher Education*, November 10, 1982, p. 3.

chapter 12

PRICING EDUCATIONAL PROGRAMS

Attend Harvard for two bushels of wheat? Almost. In 1910, the Lowell family gave a large endowment to start an evening extension program at Harvard University. The endowment came with the stipulation that the tuition charge for each course should not exceed the cost of two bushels of wheat, then about $5.

The earliest extension students paid $5 per course, and the price held for four decades, as automation of agriculture and economic conditions kept the price of wheat stable at $5 for two bushels. Educational costs increased, of course, and by the early 1960s, Harvard Extension had to raise tuition prices. The spirit of the Lowell family's bequest was preserved by keeping the tuition low and by raising it in multiples of the price of two bushels of wheat. The tuition rose to $20, $30, $35, and up.

Harvard Extension currently enrolls more than 10,000 students in evening classes. The program has an open-admissions policy, and students who successfully complete the entire program receive a bachelor's degree. And in 1984, each four-unit semester course cost $150; the price of two bushels of wheat was about $7.

> **SOURCE:** Mr. John Adams, Assistant Director, Harvard University Extension, February 22, 1982.

Educational institutions have a strong interest in the price question, because most depend on tuition and fees to keep operating. Tuition covers an average of two-thirds of the operating expenses of private colleges and universities, with variations from zero to over 100 percent. Cooper Union in New York City is probably the last tuition-free private four-year college in the United States. Noted for strong programs in architecture, art, and engineering, Cooper Union was founded in 1859 by self-made millionaire Peter Cooper. The college has a $35 million endowment and owns the land under the Chrysler Building, for which it receives about $3 million in annual rent. At the other end of the spectrum are the profit-making schools at which tuition exceeds operating expenses. Many small, nonprofit colleges rely on tuition for 80 to 90 percent, whereas at most state colleges and universities, tuition covers less than 20 percent of operating expenses.

We frequently think of price as the monetary cost of obtaining a good or service. Prices are called by various names:

> Price is all around us. You pay RENT for your apartment, TUITION for your education, and a FEE to your physician or dentist. The airline, railway, taxi, and bus companies charge you a FARE; the local utilities call their price a RATE; and the local bank charges you INTEREST for the money you borrow. The price for driving your car on Florida's Sunshine Parkway is a TOLL, and the company that insures your car charges you a PREMIUM. The guest lecturer charges an HONORARIUM to tell you about a government official who took a BRIBE to help a shady character steal DUES collected by a trade association. Clubs or societies to which you belong may make a special ASSESSMENT to pay unusual expenses. Your regular lawyer may ask for a RETAINER to cover her services. The "price" of an executive is a SALARY; the price of a salesman may be a COMMISSION; and the price of a worker is a WAGE. Finally, although economists would disagree, many of us feel that INCOME TAXES are the price we pay for the privilege of making money! [1]

Price includes other elements as well. For example, *list price* refers to the stated price of the product or service. The *actual price* may be greater or smaller, depending on the presence of a *premium* or *discount*. A school or college may set its tuition price but then give *scholarships*, which in effect "discount" the list price for needy students. If students or their families choose to borrow money to pay educational expenses, they will be interested in the *credit* terms—that is, the monthly cost and time period of payments. Many schools provide for *deferred* or *credit-card payment*.

Educational institutions routinely make price decisions. Annually the chief financial officer will review tuition rates and room and board fees to determine needed increases. From time to time, application, registration, health-service, and other fees need to be revised. The school's nondegree programs need to be priced as part of the marketing mix. In most colleges and universities, trustees review and approve these prices; state legislatures are involved in tuition decisions for most state universities. In either case, tuition is often adjusted incrementally, by adding some "reasonable" percentage increase across the board.

In this chapter, we will take a broader view of pricing for educational programs and services, looking at price in terms of consumer demand and competition as well as the more frequently used cost-based pricing. We will consider five pricing issues:

1. How do consumers perceive price?
2. What pricing objectives are appropriate?
3. How does the institution select a pricing strategy?
4. How are prices established?
5. What are the effects of price changes?

HOW CONSUMERS PERCEIVE PRICE

Educational administrators who set prices often overlook the meaning of price and price changes to consumers. For example, the actual charges made by a school or college are not the only cost to the consumer. As Adam Smith noted long ago, "The real price of everything, what everything really costs to the man who wants to acquire it, is the toil and trouble of acquiring it." In addition to the price, consumers might have to face other costs: *effort costs, psychic costs,* and *time costs.* Some high school students avoid applying to colleges that require an essay as part of the application. Some select a college close to home because they feel living at home will reduce the psychic pressure of being a college student.

Consider the case of encouraging people to enroll in smoking-cessation classes. A prospect's resistance to attending can be based on (1) an actual price of $50 for the class, (2) the time costs and trouble of traveling a long distance to the class site, and (3) the fear of hearing about the risks of smoking and thinking about the health damage already done. The health education center offering the program must recognize that the $50 price is not the only deterrent and that finding ways to reduce other consumer costs may increase participation.[2]

The Price/Quality Relationship

Research confirms that consumers often use the price of a product or service as an *indicator of its quality*.[3] When price differences among various brands are slight, consumers will not use price as a basis for deciding which to purchase. But when confronted with several imaginary brands of the same product, research subjects tended to choose the higher-priced brand when the price difference between brands was large. Consumers tend to rely on price more frequently in making an important decision, especially when they lack self-confidence in making the decision.[4]

In practice, consumers seem wary of schools that charge significantly less than comparable schools. They may wonder what is wrong with the school and presume that other, more expensive schools offer a better education. Acknowledging this price/quality relationship, some schools have substantially raised their tuition charges in the hope of raising institutional prestige and attractiveness while covering a greater share of educational costs.

Effective Price

The consumer is interested in the *effective price*, not just the "list price." In higher education, the effective price to a student and his or her family is the net amount they must pay after financial assistance is subtracted.

Even though tuition charges have increased over time, financial aid from institutional and government sources helps to reduce the cost. A comparison of state university tuition with that of a private institution may overlook the greater financial assistance at the private institution that narrows the price gap. For example, tuition, room, and board at the University of Santa Clara, a private institution, rose 13 percent for 1982–83, but financial aid for students was increased 18.5 percent.

Reducing Price by Reducing Time

The effective price of the total program can also be reduced in other ways besides direct financial aid. For example, Boston University offers a six-year B.S./M.D. program for outstanding entering freshmen, who thus save two years of tuition and foregone income. The combined program in effect contains a very attractive financial aid package and attracts top students to the university. Of course, any program that reduces the length of time a student is enrolled will also reduce the institution's per-student revenue.

Some institutions are generous in granting credit based on examinations or life experience. Reducing the number of courses the student needs for a degree decreases the institution's per-student tuition revenue. Offering such programs can provide some benefits to the institution in attracting mature students discouraged at the alternative of many years of formal college courses to get a degree, but the institution should do some deep soul-searching about what the student may be missing in academic experience and rigor by substituting life-experience credits for academic study.

Price Barriers

Students and families or companies that pay the tuition may have a psychological *price barrier* beyond which they will decide the price is too high and select a lower-priced school. This is analogous to the "sticker shock" automobile shoppers experience when they see the total price, including all accessories, additions, and services, not just the quoted base price. For example, a university developed a specialized training program for high-level executives. To cover the university's costs (including research and development costs, overhead, and contribution to university overhead) and offer the program in an ideal setting and manner, the university would need to price the program at $7,000. Since area companies seemed to consider $5,000 a psychological price barrier for such programs and experienced "sticker shock" at amounts over that, the university decided to reduce some of the features in order to offer the program at $5,000. If the program is highly successful, its features and price can be increased when it is repeated.

Although some people experience a price barrier, others make less price distinction at high price levels than at low ones. For example, the price difference between, say, a state college at $1,000 per year and a private college at $5,000 is sufficiently large that some parents who have adjusted their thinking to accept the higher cost of a private college find the increment from $5,000 to $10,000 for an elite college to be less of a psychological barrier.

Price in the Marketing Mix

Finally, price is just one component of the marketing mix that influences consumers' choices. Prospective students will be interested in the school's program, quality, and features; the location; and communications by and about the institution. Many students will pay more for a high-quality education. If the institution is attractive and conveniently located, this can outweigh some price differences. A college that is well-known and well-respected will command more attention and attract more applications than one that is a well-kept secret.

By understanding how consumers perceive price, the educational institution can anticipate how consumers are likely to respond. The institution should strive to create value for consumers by integrating all four elements of the marketing mix, and not focus solely on price.

SETTING THE PRICING OBJECTIVES

Determining a price or setting a pricing policy begins with deciding the objectives the institution wants to achieve. Often the possible objectives are in conflict, and a choice must be made. For example, a church-sponsored school may want to keep tuition low to enable as many children as possible to receive a religious education, yet the school recognizes it must charge enough (or compensate with donations) so that it will not lose money and be forced to close. On the other hand, some schools, including many vocational schools, are for-profit businesses.

Three pricing objectives can be distinguished: *surplus maximization, usage maximization,* and *cost recovery.* Rather than selecting one pricing objective for all programs, an educational institution may use different objectives for different programs. For example, a private school may aim for surplus maximization for fund-raising events and partial cost recovery for academic programs.

Surplus Maximization

Most educational institutions are legally constituted as nonprofit institutions. One might expect, then, that nonprofit educational institutions would never use the principle of profit or surplus maximization. This is not so. In many situations, a school will want to set its price to yield the largest possible surplus. (The definition of a surplus is the difference between total revenue and total cost.) For example, a college development office will set the ticket price for a major benefit dinner with the objective of maximizing its receipts over its costs.

Surplus-maximizing pricing is not the same as charging "what the traffic will bear," because this might drastically reduce attendance and result in less net revenue. Instead, the development office would want to know how the quantity of tickets sold is affected by price, and how later donations are affected. Nor would the development office spend the smallest possible amount on promotion to keep costs low, since it is aware that more money spent on promotion may increase the number of tickets sold and thus increase revenue.

Usage Maximization

Some educational institutions want to maximize the total number of users of their service in order to benefit users and society. Public schools, most community colleges, and public libraries generally pursue this goal. Since they are supported by tax funds, they need to show a large number of students or users to justify the amount of revenue they receive each year. To attract the greatest number of users, public schools and libraries set a zero price for most users, and community colleges charge very low fees.

Although a zero or very low price usually stimulates higher usage, the institution may find that some people undervalue its offerings. Cooper Union, despite its free tuition, experienced no significant increase in applications over the years. It finally began actively recruiting students and increasing public awareness of the college. Some parents gladly pay tuition for their children to attend private schools because they believe that the free public schools are of lower quality, even when the reverse may be the case. On the other hand, an educational institution may find that charging relatively low prices for its programs will attract more participants whose future support for the institution will more than make up for the lower prices.[5]

Cost Recovery

Many educational institutions are interested in breaking even each year—that is, ending the year with a zero surplus. (In practice, colleges and universities aim to end the fiscal year with a cushion of around 5 percent, since an exact match of revenues and expenses is impossible.) Such institutions aim to provide as much service as they can as long as their revenues just cover their costs. To break even, the institution may set a price to cover all the fixed and variable costs (as well as overhead) of the program or service; this is *full cost recovery*. But even though educational institutions may use full cost recovery to set prices for training programs for industry, they often use *partial cost recovery* as the goal for most academic programs. Tuition is often set to cover some share of operating expenses, with capital expenditures and remaining operating expenses coming from endowments, current contributions, and bond issues.

Examining the Revenue Function

The basic definition of revenue is price times quantity. But stating the revenue function more completely can reveal ways in which an institution can increase its revenue. Let's consider the case of a private university that gets its revenue from four main sources: student payments for tuition and room and board; payments for other services; sponsored research; and donations and return on endowment.

Revenue	=	Average annual tuition per student per year	×	Number of students enrolled
	+	Average room and board payment per person per year	×	Number of students in residence halls
	+	Net revenue from other services— conferences, programs, facilities, rentals, etc.	+	Net contribution to overhead from sponsored research
	+	Donations	+	Return on endowment

Specifying the revenue function helps pinpoint positive marketing actions that can increase revenue. The university can generally improve its revenue by increasing any one or more of the factors, as long as an increase in price, for example, is not offset by a decrease in quantity. First, the university can consider raising tuition, which most universities do annually. It can seek to attract and retain more students. It can increase room and board charges (increases usually pegged to cost increases) or, if rooms are vacant, consider ways to increase the attractiveness of campus living or set policies requiring students to live on campus for at least part of the time they are enrolled. The university can rent its facilities for conferences or offer workshops and other programs for the general public that will return a surplus. It will also want to encourage sponsored research, improve the effectiveness of its fund-raising efforts, and arrange for the best possible management of its endowment to maximize the return to the university.

Educational institutions strive to increase revenue to meet rapidly rising costs. If the university can find ways to reduce some costs, the pressure on revenues is somewhat reduced. Implementing energy-conservation measures, eliminating nonessential expenditures, and reducing waste can reduce the cost side of the budget equation.

CHOOSING A PRICING STRATEGY

After the institution has defined its pricing objective, it can consider the appropriate pricing strategy. Pricing strategies tend to be cost-oriented, demand-oriented, or competition-oriented, or to reflect some combination of these approaches.

Cost-Oriented Pricing

Cost-oriented pricing refers to setting prices largely on the basis of costs, either marginal costs or total costs including overhead. Two examples are markup pricing and cost-plus pricing. They are similar in that the price is determined by adding some fixed percentage to the unit cost.

Markup pricing is commonly found in retail trades, where the retailer adds predetermined but different markups to various goods. College bookstores use markup pricing in pricing various items. *Cost-plus pricing* is used to describe the pricing of jobs that are nonroutine and difficult to "cost" in advance, such as putting on a special training program for a company.

Many educational institutions have historically charged less than their costs (called *cost-minus pricing*). Tuitions at private colleges often cover far less than the total cost of services; the remaining costs are covered by donations and interest on endowment funds. Tax appropriations cover the remaining operating costs at public institutions.

Breakeven analysis is the most widely used form of cost-oriented pricing. Breakeven analysis is used to determine, for any proposed price, how many units of an item would have to be sold to fully cover the costs; this is known as the *breakeven volume*. To illustrate, the director of a summer computer camp wants to set a tuition for an eight-week summer session that would cover the total cost of operation and wants to determine how many campers must enroll to do this. The director would calculate the fixed costs of the camp— real estate taxes, interest charges, physical property, insurance, building maintenance, vehicle expense, and so on—and the variable cost per camper—food, computer rental, counselor salaries, camper insurance, and so on. Finally, the camp director initially considers charging $1,000 tuition per camper. The number of campers needed to break even is determined by the intersection of the total revenue curve and the total cost curve. (See Figure 12-1.) The breakeven volume can be directly calculated for any proposed price by using the following formula:

$$\text{Breakeven volume} \quad = \quad \frac{\text{Fixed cost}}{\text{Price} \ - \ \text{Variable cost}}$$

Given fixed costs of $200,000 and variable costs of $500, the breakeven volume would be 400 campers at a tuition of $1,000.

If the camp fails to attract at least 400 campers at $1,000 each, it will suffer a loss varying with the number of campers attracted. If the camp attracts more than 400 campers at $1,000 each, it will generate a surplus. If the camp director thought of charging $700 tuition, he would have to attract 1,000 campers to break even.

Cost-oriented pricing is popular for situations where costs are relatively easy to determine. If similar programs have similar costs, prices are likely to be similar. Cost-oriented pricing is often considered fairer to both consumers

FIGURE 12-1　Illustration of breakeven analysis

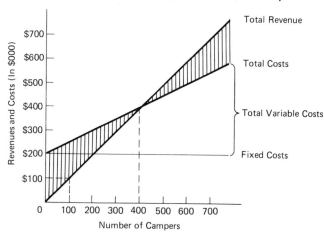

and institutions. Institutions do not take advantage of consumers when the demand rises, yet they receive a price that covers cost (or a designated share of cost). Thus, the popularity of cost-oriented pricing rests on its administrative simplicity, competitive harmony, and perceived fairness.

In contrast to the simplicity of the example above, cost-based pricing is exceedingly difficult to apply to components of an educational program. First, cost is determined after the fact, based on actual expenditures, and cost for educational inputs is difficult to estimate into the future. Second, the institution must decide whether and how to include the cost of instruction or the cost of education, the latter including allocation of costs for library and computing facilities, overhead, and so forth.

Third, costs can be heavily influenced by how the institution or department allocates resources and by demand levels, since cost is usually stated as cost per course or per credit hour. Consider the simplified illustration below, which assumes that instructional cost equals instructor salary and hypothesizes two different enrollment levels for a given course:

INSTRUCTOR	SALARY PER COURSE	ENROLLMENT	COST PER STUDENT
Full professor	$10,000	60/20	$167/$500
Assistant professor	5,000	60/20	$83/$250
Lecturer	2,500	60/20	$42/$125

Depending on availability and course assignments of faculty, the cost per course could range from $2,500 to $10,000. Depending on enrollment, the per-student cost can range from $42 to $500.

Suppose that in the preceding year, the course was taught by a full professor and that enrollment was 20, yielding a cost per student of $500. (Again, this simplified example assumes that total cost equals salary cost and that tuition equals cost per student.) Basing the next year's tuition on this cost may misrepresent the true cost. Furthermore, determining tuition price on cost alone ignores the effect on cost of who is assigned to teach it, and ignores the effect of instructor inputs on demand. If a distinguished full professor is scheduled to teach the course, 60 or more people may enroll; if an unknown, part-time lecturer teaches, the enrollment may be 20 or fewer. At these extremes, the costs per student converge, but in the second case, fewer students have been served and perhaps at a lower standard. For the coming year, the planners will look back at the current year's experience and face the same dilemma in using costs to determine price.

Rather than calculating instructional costs on a per-course basis, the institution may calculate average costs for all courses or for departments, majors, lower/upper division courses, or some other categories. In any event, nonprofit schools rarely pass on the full cost of instruction to students, so they are engaged in partial cost recovery, not full cost recovery. We will have more to say about differential pricing in the next section.

Demand-Oriented Pricing

Demand-oriented pricing sets price based on the level of demand rather than on costs. The institution estimates how much value consumers see in the market offer and prices accordingly. An executive conference with nationally recognized speakers will command a higher price than a program taught by skilled but unknown presenters.

The premise of demand-based pricing is that price should reflect the *perceived value* of the offering in the consumer's mind. A corollary is that the institution should invest in building up the perceived value of the offer if it wants to charge a higher price. Thus, a private college that builds a reputation for excellence in teaching and placement can charge a higher tuition than can an average private college.

One form of demand-oriented pricing involves charging different prices for a particular program or service. This practice is termed price discrimination or *differential pricing*. Many schools are looking carefully at differential pricing and several already charge differential tuition fees on the following bases [6]:

- *By program*—by student major, e.g., business, engineering, arts and sciences, law, medicine, etc.; or by cluster of majors, e.g., humanities, social sciences, physical and life sciences
- *By student level*—undergraduate and graduate, lower division and upper division; grad 1 and grad 2; by individual class
- *By student courseload*—by student credit hours or for student credit hour intervals (e.g., 10–18 hours at a fixed rate
- *By type of student*—degree versus nondegree (since nondegree students generally require fewer support services)
- *By residency status*—for publicly supported institutions which distinguish between resident and nonresident students
- *By course*—each course, or for each course in a cluster of disciplines
- *By time/place of offering*—differentials for summer session, evening classes, or for classes offered at different sites (e.g., at a company).

Differential pricing works only when certain conditions are met.[7] First, the student market must be segmentable by category, and each segment must show different intensities of demand. For example, differential pricing would fail if day students all decided to attend evening classes owing to lower tuition. If courses in the mathematics department cost less than in the quantitative methods department of the business school, students might prefer to enroll in mathematics department courses. Second, there should be no chance that members of the segment paying the lower price could turn around and resell the product to the segment that would otherwise pay a higher price. For this reason, students are limited in the number of reduced-price tickets they can purchase for school athletic and other events. Third, there should be little chance that competing institutions can attract the higher-paying segment with a lower-priced program or service. Finally, the cost of segmenting and policing the market to verify eligibility for special prices should not exceed the extra revenue derived from differential pricing.

Differential pricing may imply that some people or groups are being treated unfairly, but this is usually not the case. In fact, given the different costs of providing courses in English composition and more expensive courses in mechanical engineering, having students pay the same tuition regardless of major field means that some students are paying more than their share of instructional costs and subsidizing others. The most common form of differential pricing is the granting of scholarship assistance based on financial need. The purpose of scholarship assistance is to enable students to purchase educational services that they would otherwise not be able to afford.

Differential pricing has an important policy consequence. When all courses and fields of study cost the same, price is not a factor in student choice. If high-cost and/or high-demand programs are priced significantly higher than others, price-sensitive students may make curricular and thereby career decisions based on tuition-cost differences. The same effect occurs when scholarships and loans are given for study in specific fields, as with the National Defense Education Act to encourage students to go into teaching in the 1960s.

Competition-Oriented Pricing

When an institution sets its prices chiefly on the basis of what competitors are charging, its pricing policy can be described as *competition-oriented*. It may choose to charge (1) *the same as competition*, (2) *a higher price*, or (3) *a lower price*. The distinguishing characteristic is that the institution does not maintain a rigid relationship between its price and its own costs or demand. That is, its costs or demand may change, but it maintains its price position in relation to its competitors. Conversely, the same institution will change its prices when competitors change theirs, even if its own costs or demand have not changed. Since consumers often use price as an indicator of quality, a school may consciously set its tuition level to establish its position in relation to other institutions. For example, a college that wants to be perceived as comparable to a set of other colleges may set its tuition at or close to their tuition level.

Going-rate or *imitative pricing* means the institution tries to keep its price at the average level charged by other, similar institutions. Where costs are difficult to measure, the going price often represents the collective wisdom of educational institutions concerning the appropriate price. Charging a going price helps maintain harmony between institutions by reducing price competition. The difficulty of predicting how consumers and competitors will react to price differentials is another reason for going-rate pricing.

Going-rate pricing is often used when institutions offer standard programs or services. When a school offers a program identical to that available elsewhere, it has little choice in setting its price. For example, a parochial school that charged a much higher tuition than other, nearby schools would attract few students unless it were truly distinctive in some important way. At the same time, an institution with a standard program or service need not charge less than the going-rate price as long as it can attract enough students at that price.

Where programs differ, institutions have more latitude in their price decisions, since program differences make price differences less salient. A private educational institution often tries to establish its price level with respect to its competitors, assuming the role of a high-tuition, medium-tuition, or low-tuition school. Educational offerings and marketing programs are made compatible with this chosen pricing zone, or vice versa. The other institutions then respond to competitive changes in price to maintain their pricing zone.

SETTING THE PRICE

Setting prices for most educational programs should take into account cost-oriented, demand-oriented, and competition-oriented factors. Most institutions have focused on costs and have not viewed pricing from a marketing perspective.

For example, tuition increases are often determined in the following cost-oriented manner: The chief financial officer determines expected operating expenses for the coming year and projects revenues from endowment, donations, and other sources. Subtracting expenses from revenues determines the amount that must be covered by tuition. This amount is divided by the projected number of students or courses to determine the tuition level per student or course.

Public institutions, dependent on state appropriations, typically set fees based on the gap between what legislators (and the taxpayers they represent) will approve and their operating costs. When appropriations are cut, operating costs must be reduced (despite reductions in educational quality) or student tuition and fees must go up—or both.

Such cost-oriented pricing only very indirectly reflects the market forces of demand and competition. According to Ihlanfeldt, the institution should consider (1) the effects of a given pricing policy on the nature and mission of the institution, (2) the effects of a given pricing policy on enrollment, and (3) the degree to which a particular pricing policy may encourage acceleration and therefore decrease per-student revenue.[8] In addition, the institution must weigh (4) prices charged by comparable competing institutions, and (5) the effects of its own price level and price changes on the actions of such competitors. These considerations provide a basis for setting prices.

The traditional one-price-for-all-students approach is increasingly being replaced by a price schedule with one level of tuition for undergraduates, another for graduate students in arts and sciences, and still another for each professional school. Such variations may be based on differences in costs of instruction, anticipated earnings of graduates, and demand by various market segments, as we have noted above.

Consider the case of Northeastern University in Boston. Tuition increases were for decades based on adding a flat percentage each year based solely on covering costs. In fact, its overall price structure was significantly below those of such competitors as Boston University and Boston College. Northeastern then instituted differential tuition based on program and year, such that business students pay more than humanities students and upperclassmen pay more than freshmen and sophomores.

A number of basic pricing approaches have been adopted or proposed. Here we will consider *unit pricing, two-part pricing, term pricing,* and *scaled pricing.*[9] These approaches can each be applied to variable or one-price-for-all situations. Each pricing approach will have a different effect on students' educational plans and on the institution's revenues, as we will illustrate.

Unit Pricing

Institutions with many part-time students often set tuition on a per-unit or per-course basis. This approach is easy to administer, provides great flexibility for students, and encourages attendance by more part-time students. On the other hand, the institution cannot forecast enrollment and tuition revenue as accurately. The students who took one course last term may take three this term, or vice versa. There are no built-in price incentives for students to take additional courses, so the institution's revenue depends on external forces that might encourage or discourage taking courses, such as the job market. Nor does unit pricing account for the costs associated with recruiting, record keeping, and providing counseling services, which do not vary whether the student takes one course or more.

Two-Part Pricing

Two-part pricing addresses the latter two limitations of unit pricing. This approach adds a flat charge for each student to the total tuition based on a per-course or a per-unit formula. The fixed cost might vary from program to program, or be the same for all. Part-time students would have a greater incentive to take more courses per term than under unit pricing.

Term Pricing

Under this approach, a student may take as many (or as few) courses as desired for the same fixed tuition each term. This approach encourages students to take a full course load and penalizes part-time students. Term pricing encourages some students to accelerate their programs to complete at least one whole term early, since to take even one course the last term would represent no cost saving. Some colleges discourage acceleration by requiring every student to pay four academic years of tuition.

Scaled Pricing

Under scaled pricing, a student would pay a larger tuition charge for the first and second courses, then a smaller charge for additional courses. This approach covers the administrative costs as in two-part and term pricing, while offering the flexibility of unit pricing for part-time students and a price incentive for full-time students. An institution wanting to discourage acceleration could set a higher tuition price for each additional course over the normal course load.

Other Approaches

Educational institutions are giving serious thought to pricing their programs and services in new ways that may better serve potential students and the schools. Here are some examples:

Negotiated Tuition. Some Catholic high schools offer parents the option of "negotiating" the amount of tuition they feel they can pay, ranging from zero to full cost.[10]

Quantity Discounts. A college might offer a discount for five, ten, or more registrations for the same course or program, submitted together. This would encourage people to discuss their educational plans with their friends and colleagues and might increase demand for selected programs.

Time-Based Discounts. An educational program might offer a discount to students who register and pay early, since this gives the school a more accurate basis for planning. Several colleges have offered "guaranteed tuition" plans that involve paying the entire four years' tuition in advance at the first year's tuition rate. The college invests the unused portion, yielding interest income equal to the tuition increases for future years.

Work Contribution. Berea College admits only students with financial need, and all students work on campus as part of their tuition and expenses (see Exhibit 12-1). Many colleges and universities have College Work-Study Programs as part of students' aid packages. Such work programs, like scholarships, provide ways to reduce the financial cost of attending college.

EFFECTS OF PRICE CHANGES

Most educational institutions are constrained to increase prices to meet costs and maintain quality. A very few have experimented by reducing prices to stimulate demand. Price reductions involve risk. If they diminish the quality of the educational program, such institutions will have even more trouble asking for and receiving an adequate price in the future. Any price change will affect consumers and competitors, so the success of the change depends on how they

EXHIBIT 12-1   Financing an education at Berea College

Berea College provides financial assistance and work experience for its students while carrying out its commitment to serve the Southern Appalachian region and to demonstrate that "work, manual and mental, has dignity." Admissions preference is given to students whose families would have a difficult time financing a college education without assistance. In effect, financial need is a requirement for admission.

Student labor has been a part of the Berea program since 1859 and is central to the financial aid program for students, the economics of the college, and the social and economic experiences of the student.

Each student receives a labor grant of $1,700, which is applied to the annual tuition of $5,600. The remaining tuition cost of $3,900 is met by federal, state, and other scholarships. Any remaining cost is guaranteed by Berea College.

The student and the family are expected to contribute toward living expenses of $1,812 per year and books and personal expenses of about $840. Each student receives an hourly wage of from $1.15 to $2.35 for 10 to 15 hours of work weekly, in addition to the $1,700 labor grant.

The effect of these policies is that no Berea student directly pays the full cost of education. The cost is met by direct labor, outside aid programs, and Berea scholarship funds.

SOURCE: Based on the *Berea College Catalog, 1983–85.*

respond. Predicting consumer responses to price changes is both difficult and important. Here we will consider ways to assess probable consumer reactions to price changes.

Price Elasticity of Demand

The traditional analysis of consumers' reactions to price change assumes that all consumers learn of the price change and take it at face value. *Price elasticity of demand* is a ratio that reflects how much demand changes as the price rises. It is defined as the ratio of the percentage change in demand caused by a percentage change in price.

In practice, price elasticity of demand is extremely difficult to measure. Price elasticity depends on the magnitude of the contemplated price change: It may be negligible with a small price change and substantial with a large one. Price elasticity also varies with the original price level. A 10 percent increase over a current price of $200 may exhibit quite a different elasticity of demand than a 10 percent increase over a current price of $4,000. Finally, long-range price elasticity is apt to be different from short-range elasticity. Students may remain at a school for a while after a price increase because transfering to a less expensive school takes time, but they may eventually transfer. In this case, demand is more elastic in the long run than in the short run. Or the reverse might happen: Students may leave in anger after a tuition increase but return later. Therefore, educational institutions may not be able to evaluate the wisdom of a price change for some time after it is made.

How Consumers Interpret Price Changes

In discussing elasticity, we assumed that price changes would be interpreted simply as price changes. An example is the experience of Biscayne College. After it lowered its tuition by over 10 percent, applications almost doubled the first two months. But the college's potential students and its publics might instead interpret a tuition reduction to mean that:

- The quality of the school will go down.
- The school is in financial trouble, and this is a last-ditch effort to stay open.

A tuition increase might also be interpreted in unexpected ways:

- The school is going to improve.
- The school has been undercharging in the past.

These perceptions might lead consumers to react to a price change quite differently from what the school expects. For example, a higher tuition might actually increase the number of applicants, because a higher price might imply higher quality and prestige.

Educational institutions should be aware that low prices and small price changes are not necessarily better accepted than realistic ones.

One Catholic school promoted the fact that its tuition was "affordable"—well below tuition levels at nearby, comparable schools. Price increases were so modest that the school's tuition increasingly lagged behind that of its principal competitor, and deficits made it impossible for the school to improve its program in areas where it was at a competitive disadvantage. Its altruistic efforts to hold down prices and price increases hurt its image and depressed enrollment, rather than enhancing them.

A parish elementary school in a wealthy suburb maintained its in-parish tuition at $350 year after year by subsidizing the school from parish contributions. The tuition was one-half to one-third of tuition at nearby parish schools. The school had a long waiting list, but the building and grounds were in disrepair, and the school had depleted the parish resources needlessly.

Both these schools would have been better served by setting realistic prices and making appropriate annual changes.

Price increases for an educational program should be supported by a communications campaign that indicates the amount and timing of the increases, reasons that necessitate them, and institutional efforts to reduce their effect (such as increases in financial aid and additional fund-raising efforts). Information on the increase should be made well in advance, to help applicants and current students make plans to accommodate the increased cost as well as to minimize resentment that the news of the price increase came "too late to do anything." The institution also needs to keep reminding students (and their parents) of the institution's strengths, so that the increased price is more acceptable.

SUMMARY

Pricing decisions are important to educational institutions, because they depend on revenues to operate. When they set or change prices, they need to understand how consumers perceive price. In addition to monetary prices, consumers face effort costs, psychic costs, and time costs. They often use the price as a measure of quality of a service or program. They are particularly interested in the effective price, the net amount they must pay, rather than the list price. With these factors in mind, the institution should consider ways to reduce the nonmonetary costs of its services while enhancing the perceived quality.

An institution can be guided by any of three objectives in setting its price: surplus maximization, usage maximization, or cost recovery. Examining its revenue function may indicate ways in which the institution can increase revenues.

In practice, price-setting strategies are cost-oriented, demand-oriented, competition-oriented, or a combination of these. In setting tuition prices, the institution should consider its mission as well as market demand and competition. It may decide on unit pricing, two-part pricing, term pricing, scaled pricing, or a variation of these.

Institutions planning to change an existing price should take into account how consumers and competitors will respond to the price change. Price increases should be announced well in advance and be accompanied by a communications campaign explaining reasons for the increase and institutional responses.

NOTES

[1] From *Marketing Today*, third edition, by David J. Schwartz. Copyright © 1981 by Harcourt Brace Jovanovich, Inc. Reprinted by permission of the publisher.

[2] For a discussion of how marketers can reduce time and effort cost, see Karen F.A. Fox, "Time as a Component of Price in Social Marketing," in Richard P. Bagozzi et al., *Marketing in the 80s: Changes and Challenges* (Chicago: American Marketing Association, 1980), pp. 464–67.

[3] See Kent B. Monroe, "Buyers' Subjective Perceptions of Price," *Journal of Marketing Research*, February 1973, pp. 70–80.

[4] Benson Shapiro, "Price as a Communicator of Quality: An Experiment," unpublished doctoral dissertation, Harvard University, 1970.

[5] See Charles B. Weinberg, "Marketing Mix Decision Rules for Nonprofit Organizations," in Jagdish Sheth, ed., *Research in Marketing*, Vol. 3 (Chicago: JAI Press, 1980), pp. 191–234.

[6] See Marilyn McCoy, "Differential Tuition at the University of Colorado," University of Colorado Office of Planning and Policy Development, August 1983, for results of a survey of state universities' use of differential tuition and for an excellent discussion of policy implications.

[7] See George Stigler, *The Theory of Price*, rev. ed. (New York: Macmillan, 1952), pp. 215ff.

[8] William Ihlanfeldt, *Achieving Optimal Enrollments and Tuition Revenues* (San Francisco: Jossey-Bass, 1980), p. 115.

[9] See Ihlanfeldt, *op. cit.*, pp. 117–20, for a fuller discussion of these approaches.

[10] "The Pay-What-You-Can Plan," *Time*, March 29, 1982, p. 61.

chapter 13

MAKING EDUCATION AVAILABLE

Karen Donnellon never dreamed of being able to resume her education—until a community college made her an offer she couldn't turn down. She was 19 years out of high school at the time, married, active in church and politics, and employed in a demanding full-time job.

"I felt like an antique," she recalls. "I was out of date and stagnant. I had always wanted higher education but didn't think I had a chance."

Donnellon lives in the small community of Vinton, in east central Iowa. The nearest colleges are about 25 miles away in Cedar Rapids. But a new telenetwork instructional program at Kirkwood Community College in Cedar Rapids enabled her to attend college classes without traveling. Students in Vinton and six other rural Iowa communities receive their instruction via telephone.

The Kirkwood telenetwork is simple. Some classrooms on the Cedar Rapids campus are equipped with telephone transmitting and receiving equipment that relies on microphones and speakers instead of ordinary telephones. Six similarly equipped classrooms are scattered in smaller towns throughout the seven counties served by the college. Students are encouraged to attend classes near their homes, but the instructor can teach from any of the seven sites. The telenetwork system allows for discussions among students "attending" a given class from a variety of locations. . . .

The telenetwork makes the delivery of college instruction to small groups in rural areas economically feasible. Such students, hampered by long distances from campus and rising gasoline prices, might otherwise be forced to forgo higher education. . . .

The telenetwork has also simplified delivery of an educational program for inmates at the state reformatory for men in Anamosa. Telenetwork classes in the reformatory are supplemented by professional counseling, library services, and basic education services provided inside the walls.

The telenetwork is a first step toward more sophisticated methods. Last fall, the college began to broadcast two-way microwave color television instruction to outlying class sites. Through a series of grants from the Public Telecommunications Facilities Program of the Department of Commerce, the college eventually plans to use interactive television as widely as it presently uses the telephone/telenetwork.

> **SOURCE:** Bill F. Stewart, "Telephone/Telenetwork Instruction in a Community College," *Phi Delta Kappan*, vol. 62, No. 7 (March 1981), 521–22.

The basic distribution question for an educational institution is, How can we make our programs and services *available and accessible* to our target consumers? Availability and accessibility are not the same thing. Suppose a college ran a program to enhance the skills of elementary school teachers, but the college was located an hour away from where most of the teachers lived and worked. Suppose, further, that the program was offered from 9 to 12 on weekday mornings from September to May—precisely the hours when even nearby teachers would be working. We would say that the program, although available, was not accessible to those for whom it was planned. For such a program to succeed, the college must increase its accessibility, perhaps by offering the program closer to the potential participants and by scheduling it for late afternoons, weekends, or concentrated summer sessions.

The location and scheduling of programs are critical. Offering a high-quality, appropriately priced program is not enough. Students may avoid classes in rundown, dangerous urban areas because the surroundings are unpleasant and unsafe. Likewise, they may avoid rural campuses that seem isolated and boring. Gone are the days when would-be students put up with long journeys to attend schools with limited curricula, spartan dormitories, and restrictive rules. In the 1980s, few educational institutions can claim a captive market; students have many educational options. At the same time, there are under-served markets for education. For instance, adults who want to earn a bachelor's degree through evening or weekend courses often find few options. Less than 25 percent of bachelor's-degree-granting institutions provide all the necessary courses, and then in only a few fields.[1]

Some educational institutions, recognizing these market changes, have adopted new schedules, delivery systems, and locations to retain and serve their markets. Realistically, few institutions can make fundamental changes in the short term. They can, however, consider how to improve their use of existing resources in making educational offerings available. Then they can begin planning ways to modify or expand current systems to create more consumer satisfaction. This chapter considers a series of questions to guide the planning process:

1. How do educational institutions tend to select their locations?
2. How are educational programs and services made available to consumers?
3. How should educational institutions develop their distribution strategy?

Our discussion of distribution strategy includes consideration of the following issues:

- How should new locations be selected?
- Should additional facilities be established?
- What alternative channels could be used?
- How can middlemen be used?
- Can facilitating intermediaries be used?

HOW HAVE EDUCATIONAL FACILITIES BEEN LOCATED?

Most educational institutions already have facilities at one or more fixed locations. When they begin to consider how to serve their markets more effectively, their thinking about distribution patterns and systems is colored by their existing investment in facilities.

The question of where to locate facilities was answered years ago, often for pragmatic reasons:

1. The land (and even buildings) may have been donated. Leland and Jane Stanford founded Stanford University on their 8,000-acre farm; the College of Notre Dame moved from San Jose to the donated Ralston estate in Belmont, California.

2. Centralized facilities were established for administrative convenience and economies, as in the case of many state universities.

3. A location may have been selected because a site was available or because the land was relatively inexpensive. Public school sites were included in plats of the Northwest Territory, along with additional lots to be farmed to provide the teacher's salary. Sites set aside for public schools were often those deemed unsuitable for farming.

The location of facilities can have a tremendous symbolic and political significance. For example, the concept of the "neighborhood school" is so well established that public outcry is virtually assured whenever a school is closed, even when the closure is fiscally imperative and the merger of schools will ensure a continued—or improved—level of instruction and services.

Past decisions about the location of educational facilities may create later imbalances. A number of states founded their land-grant institutions a century ago in small towns, away from what are now major population centers. Liberal arts colleges have often been located in rural areas and small towns, based on the notion that a bucolic setting is particularly conducive to morality, reflection, and learning. In his speech at the 1965 groundbreaking for Eisenhower College, Dwight D. Eisenhower expounded this view:

> I believe that the liberal arts college should seek its natural habitation in rural areas. Let the universities go to the cities where they have the benefits of great lawyers, great engineers, great people all around them. In this period of maturing in a liberal college, let's have the finest faculty, let's bring in the knowledge lecturers, and let's do it in an atmosphere and an environment where the student's standards of respect for law, his moral standards, his willingness for accommodation with his fellow students will be expanded and strengthened.[2]

Of the institutions located for the preceding reasons, some are flourishing while others are struggling. These educational facilities may once have been well located, but shifts in population, and particularly in their target markets, have reduced the locations' appropriateness. Yet the cost of leaving existing facilities behind and moving to new ones may be prohibitive. Caught in this dilemma, some institutions close, and others make strategic alterations to serve new markets.

HOW ARE EDUCATIONAL PROGRAMS AND SERVICES MADE AVAILABLE?

In responding to this question, educators usually think first of providing classroom instruction to students. A more complete picture shows a variety of educational programs and services, each provided to consumers in a different way. For example, a university may offer a lecture course in introductory psychology for undergraduates, a correspondence course for armed forces personnel, and a short course on the psychology of personnel administration via television for professionals.

Educational institutions often have several different programs, and they need to plan an appropriate strategy for providing each one. How these programs and other outputs are made available constitutes the institution's *delivery* or *distribution system*. Consider the case of Iowa State University, a 25,000-student land-grant university in Ames. Its product line includes educational programs, extension services, publications, cultural and athletic events, research findings in agriculture and other fields, veterinary care, and, at one time, packaged cheese! The university also "produces" intangible products, such as lasting friendships among students and feelings of pride on the part of the state's residents.

Analyzing the distribution system involves tracing the steps by which the product or service gets from the producer to the final consumer. Most services are created and delivered directly by the producer to the consumer—the lawyer advising the client, the doctor treating a patient, the teacher instructing a group of students. The teacher is usually the creator of the instructional plan as well as the performer. (Of course, in many instances, the content of the lesson draws on the research and ideas of other scholars.) We can diagram the process by which the course is distributed, as shown in Figure 13-1, A.

Another important instructional program at Iowa State is carried out by home-economics and agricultural extension agents who inform Iowa homemakers, farmers, and commercial enterprises of research findings that affect their activities. The research is conducted at Iowa State and other centers around the world. The "ag extension" agent's task is to inform farmers of new practices, to provide printed information, and to look for problem areas that might warrant future research. The agent may also appear on television or radio or prepare news stories featuring useful information for farmers. The distribution process for Iowa State's extension services is shown in Figure 13-1, B.

The university also produces books and cheese. The Iowa State University Press obtains manuscripts from authors, and edits and prints them. The books are sold in the Press's own shop, as well as through the traditional distribution channels, shown in Figure 13-1, C. At one time, students in the dairy industry program made several varieties of cheese during the autumn for sale in gift packages just before Christmas at the Dairy Industry Building and through a few local grocery stores (see Figure 13-1, D.)

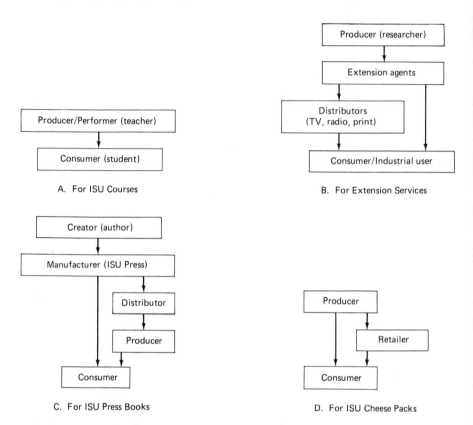

FIGURE 13-1   Distribution processes for four Iowa State University
products

In deciding how to distribute its programs and products, Iowa State must consider the nature of each as well as the important characteristics of the consumer who will ultimately benefit from it. A workable distribution system successfully gets the right product or service to the consumer who wants it, at a cost that both producer and consumer can afford. A superior distribution system accomplishes the same task in a way that makes the product easier to obtain and/or reduces the cost for one or both parties. Planning a distribution system entails answering the questions that follow.

DECISION PROBLEMS IN DISTRIBUTION

Planning an effective distribution system involves understanding the consumer, the institution's mission and resources, and the nature of the program, service, or product to be distributed. Let us consider the major decisions educational institutions often face in designing and operating their distribution systems.

What Should Be the Distribution Objectives?

The institution first needs to consider appropriate distribution objectives. The most basic is what level of convenience should be offered to the target market. Obviously, cost will be an issue, but the institution might begin by trying to describe the maximum level of service it could offer. For an educational institution, the maximum level of service might be to provide individual instruction in each student's home upon request. Once the norm for children of the very wealthy, private tutors are no longer practicable. Few consumers would pay for the extra convenience, and the supplying institution could not afford the cost of providing this level of service to everyone. In England, Oxford and Cambridge Universities have combined lectures, individual study, and sessions with tutors for centuries. International College in Los Angeles arranges for students to work directly with one of more than 100 tutors (Exhibit 13-1).

Few institutions can provide the maximum level of service, but preparing the description may suggest alternative ways to provide services that come

EXHIBIT 13-1 International College revives personal tutors

Centuries ago, young men thought nothing of traveling modest distances to study with a master tutor. Present-day students at Los Angeles's International College are following in their footsteps, except that in some cases, they have to travel halfway around the world before they begin their studies. Ravi Shankar, for example, insists that his students fly to India for their lessons in classical sitar; Yehudi Menuhin conducts class in London; author Lawrence Durrell teaches in the south of France; and writer-philosopher Russell Kirk invites students to live with him and his family in their rambling home in rural Michigan.

The Los Angeles campus is a cluster of modest offices. The mechanics of the program are simple. Undergraduate and graduate students (the latter usually professionals in their 30s and 40s) pay $4,600 tuition for the opportunity to work and study closely with the tutor of their choice, wherever in the world he or she may be. Those classes that aren't taught far afield are generally held in homes, offices, and workshops scattered throughout southern California.

International's tutors are an informal group, tending to meet with their students just once or twice a week for a few hours, relying on them to work independently. Instruction is low-key, often taking the form of bright, penetrating conversation between two close friends. At the end of the eight-month semester, the tutor writes a detailed narrative of the student's accomplishments and notifies the college when a degree is earned.

SOURCE: Based on Mark Jones, "International College—In the Footsteps of Socrates," *Change*, Vol. 10, No. 2 (February 1978), 16–19. A publication of the Helen Dwight Reid Educational Foundation. (Tuition given is for 1984.)

closer to the maximum than was formerly thought possible. Thus, although schools may not be able to provide personal tutors, they may develop structured home-study courses or organize groups of students who tutor each other. Or the institution may reduce students' time cost by offering courses to workers on employers' premises. Employees at Digital Equipment Corporation in Maynard, Massachusetts, may earn degrees, from a B.S. in business administration to an M.B.A. or an M.S. in electrical engineering, by taking on-site courses taught by traveling faculty from Boston University, Worcester Polytechnic University, and Clark University.[3]

Educational institutions must usually offer less than the maximum consumer convenience in order to keep down the cost of distribution. Thus, a public school district will have one or more elementary and secondary schools, and students will have to travel to the schools. Schools may have to increase class sizes or eliminate certain courses when qualified instructors or other necessary resources are lacking. Students may have to wait longer for teacher assistance. Since virtually all educational institutions have limited resources, they must base their distribution planning on a clear picture of the level and quality of service they will offer.

Making programs available and accessible involves more than convenient locations or innovative delivery systems. Unlike physical products, which can be purchased and used at the buyer's convenience, educational services often require that the service provider—the teacher—and the consumer—the student—coordinate their activities so they can be available in the same place at the same time. Many would-be students cannot attend during traditional class hours, and some colleges are beginning to adapt to their time constraints. Evening courses are widely available, and some colleges offer late evening and even nighttime courses to accommodate those who work late shifts. Others offer "early-bird" classes so people can attend class on their way to work. The University of Chicago offers a master of business administration degree to qualified middle-management executives who are able to attend all-day classes on alternate Fridays and Saturdays for two years. Other institutions offer courses on weekends or during lunch hour. These examples demonstrate how educational institutions can modify locations and schedules to meet their distribution objectives.

Should New Facilities or Channels Be Established?

Educational institutions with new or growing markets need to consider whether to offer some of their programs in other locations or through different channels. Institutions that provide direct services are like retail stores, where people can come to make their selection and purchase. Like retail businesses, they must decide how many outlets to operate. The most economical decision is to operate a single outlet and have all customers come to it. For example, many small high schools were established in widely separated rural towns. As recently as the 1960s, the senior-class play at one Iowa high school had only two roles, and both members of the senior class performed! Beginning in the 1950s, most of the small high school districts were consolidated into larger districts that could provide a wider range of subjects, vocational training, and other services.

The cost of running a state university used to be minimized by operating a single campus. Years ago, the University of California was located in Berkeley, and the University of Wisconsin was in Madison. Gradually these universities established branches, often by incorporating existing colleges and universities. The aim was partly to make educational opportunities more accessible to residents (and taxpayers) in other parts of their states and partly to keep a single campus from becoming too large and impersonal. Now most states have systems of state colleges and universities, as well as locally supported community colleges, where they each once had one or two institutions. Once these universities decided to distribute their offerings throughout the state, they encountered all the classic distribution problems faced by business firms: how many branch locations should be established, how large they should be, where they should be located, and what specializations should be featured at each branch.

Some private institutions have opened satellite branches in areas of strong population growth, sometimes competing directly with public institutions. Satellite branches can make the institution's programs attractive to new markets while relieving space limitations or inadequacies on the main campus, as well as locating the educational programs closer to key supporting facilities. For example, Roosevelt University, a 7,000-student private institution in downtown Chicago, opened three satellite campuses in rented facilities in the more affluent suburbs of Arlington Heights, Waukegan, and Glenview, and offers complete degree programs.

A few educational institutions have expanded their facilities by holding classes in unusual classroom settings. The principal value is in increasing accessibility.

Indiana University–Purdue University at Indianapolis offers credit courses in the training rooms of department stores in local shopping malls in its Learn & Shop Program. The program offers plenty of free parking space, excellent teaching facilities provided free by the stores, regular faculty, university credit, and the same tuition as on-campus courses. The University of Wisconsin Extension provides volunteer "traveling teachers" to nursing homes, retirement communities, senior centers, and other organizations for the elderly, to offer classes in more than 20 subjects.

Whether the institution uses rented or loaned facilities, converts existing ones, or builds new ones, it faces the task of deciding where the new facilities should be located. Figure 13-2 shows the steps involved in the decision process.[4] First, the institution evaluates its current distribution pattern to determine

FIGURE 13-2   The decision process for locating facilities

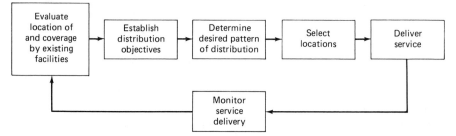

SOURCE: Adapted from Charles W. Lamb, Jr., and John L. Compton, "Distributing Public Services: A Strategic Approach," in Philip Kotler, O. C. Ferrell, and Charles Lamb, *Cases and Readings in Marketing for Nonprofit Organizations* (Englewood Cliffs, N.J.: Prentice-Hall, 1983), p. 211.

whether it adequately meets current and projected needs and matches the institution's resources. Second, if the current pattern has some inadequacies, the institution determines its revised distribution objectives. It may state its objectives in terms of percentage of the community that enrolls in courses, size of enrollment, or some other consumer behaviors that can be measured.

Third, the institution considers its desired pattern of distribution. For educational programs, this step involves deciding whether to have one facility to serve everyone, or to establish multiple locations. This decision depends on consumers' ability and willingness to travel to facilities. We know that most college students attend a college close to home. Although some students will travel hundreds of miles to enroll in a high-quality, prestige college, community colleges draw from a relatively small geographical area. If the institution wishes to maximize attendance, facilities should be convenient. At the same time, the institution must balance the cost of multiple locations with the state or local funding and consumer revenue that will be generated if the multiple locations succeed in bringing in more students.

Fourth, the institution selects the location(s). At the outset, the institution should identify the location (or locations) that would provide the best access for the target markets and then compromise from that optimum location as little as possible in settling on the final site. Determining appropriate locations will depend on residential and work patterns, commuting routes, demographic characteristics of various areas, and location of competing and complementary institutions.

Consider how a major public urban university with 20,000 students planned where to locate a satellite campus to consolidate dispersed off-campus courses.[5] The planning task force mapped where current students lived, drawing on data from computerized student-record files, to identify strong and weak attraction areas. Next, the planners analyzed population trends and delineated four major growth centers located just outside the perimeter highway around the city, each within 25 minutes of downtown.

The planners then identified five market segments for the satellite campus—traditional students, workers seeking job-skills courses, married reentry women, remedial-needs students, and people seeking leisure and personal development courses—and located concentrations of these groups on an area map. The planners assessed the location and reputation of the university's 18 competitors and determined that the university had higher status and stronger regional and national reputation than all but one of them, a private university with much higher tuition.

The next step was to select the specific sites. Four criteria were used:

1. The sites should be located near population growth areas and defined market segments.
2. The sites must be highly accessible—i.e., near major thoroughfares and public transportation.
3. The sites should be located near services for students—restaurants, shops, service stations, etc.
4. The cost of the potential sites should not be exorbitant.

The planners identified four potential sites within or near regional shopping centers and office parks where leasable space and adequate parking were available. One "best" site was selected after economic feasibility studies of each site. Figure 13-3 shows the perimeter highway and the four growth areas, and the stars mark the four potential sites.

The planners next surveyed four of the five market segments to answer three questions: (1) What is the level of interest among potential students for a satellite campus? (2) What classes would respondents like to take? and (3) What schedules would be most attractive? With this information, the university planners could implement the satellite campus program.

Although some educational institutions are expanding, most have fixed facilities, and some face declining demand. Buildings cannot be moved as population shifts or surroundings change, but buildings or parts of buildings can be leased, sold, or closed. Some public schools are leasing school facilities to day-care centers, fine arts programs, and other education-compatible users, and other schools have been sold and converted into shopping centers, apartment buildings, and corporate headquarters buildings.[6] Some educators recommend that high schools with declining enrollments could attract and serve new markets, including adult education programs, and might even take on new functions.[7]

How Should Facilities Look?

The most important factor in facilities planning is how well the facilities will serve the planned educational activities there.[8] Educational institutions should also consider the "look" of their facilities, because the atmosphere in

FIGURE 13-3   Location of proposed satellite campus sites

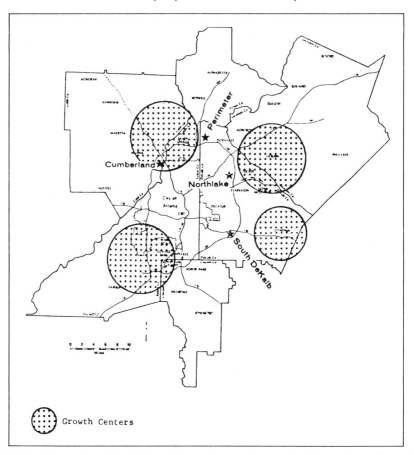

SOURCE: Wayne G. Strickland, "The University and the Community: Planning for an Alternative Form of Educational Service Delivery," *Planning for Higher Education*, Summer 1980, p. 14.

which educational services are delivered can affect consumers' attitudes and behavior. Private colleges and universities are often particularly aware of the value of having an attractive campus. Many have taken pains to maintain their original architectural style and master plan, or at least to integrate newer buildings by using materials that blend with the earlier style. Newer institutions have the opportunity to develop and follow a unified plan from the start.

Marketing planners in the future will use atmospherics as consciously and skillfully as they now use price, advertising, personal selling, public relations, and other tools of marketing. *Atmospherics* describes the conscious designing of space to create or reinforce specific effects on consumers, such as feelings of well-being, safety, intimacy, or awe.[9]

An educational institution designing a facility for the first time faces four major design decisions. Suppose a university business school is planning a facility to use for its executive M.B.A. program and other executive training programs. The four decisions are as follows:

1. *What should the building look like on the outside?* The building can look like a villa, a bank, an office building, or another genre. The decision will be influenced by the site where the building will be located, and by the message that the business school wants to convey to potential students and program participants.

2. *What should be the functional and flow characteristics of the building?* The planners have to consider how the building will be used and what types of spaces are needed. In addition to classroom spaces, study areas and areas for meals and social hours will be needed. The rooms and corridors must be designed in a way to handle all those likely to be attending programs in the building at one time.

3. *What should the building feel like on the inside?* Every building conveys a feeling, whether intended or not. In designing the interior, the planners need to consider whether it should be bright and modern, somber and business-like, or warm and relaxing. Each feeling will have a different effect on the participants and their overall satisfaction with the programs offered there.

4. *What materials would best support the desired feeling of the building?* The feeling of a building is conveyed by visual cues (color, brightness, size, shapes), aural cues (volume, pitch), olfactory cues (scent, freshness), and tactile cues (softness, smoothness, temperature). The planners need to choose colors, fabrics, and furnishings that create or reinforce the desired feeling.

The same questions arise for other educational facilities. Each facility will have a look that may add or detract from consumer satisfaction and employee performance. The latter point deserves special emphasis. Since the employees work in the facility all day long, the facility should be designed to support them in performing their work with ease and cheerfulness. Granted, many educational institutions are financially pressed and cannot afford the facilities that would be desired in principle. But they should pay attention to small details of present facilities and take even minor steps to improve their comfort and effectiveness.

What Alternative Channels Could Be Used?

Some educational institutions are turning to the telephone, television, radio, newspapers, computers, and tape recorders to serve their current markets or to attract new ones. In some countries of the world, many students attend classes by radio or television. In the early 1980s, a third of a million Chinese were enrolled in courses given by 29 "television universities," and many other students took courses by radio. In the United States, these approaches often supplement more traditional learning settings, but their popularity is growing. Educational institutions considering the use of new instructional technologies need to ask three questions: Is the new technology likely to be more effective than the one it replaces? Is the alternative channel appropriate for the intended market? and, What will be the additional resource costs and added benefits of adopting the new channel?

Let's consider some of the present and future innovations in delivering instruction:

- PBS TV stations offer credit and noncredit courses on oceanography, personal computers, home decorating, and other subjects via the Electric Classroom. Texts and supplemental materials can be ordered and delivered by mail.

- The Stanford Instructional Television Network (SITN) provides more than 170 Stanford graduate courses in all fields of engineering and in computer science, mathematics, applied physics, and statistics. The network broadcasts 12 hours a day on four channels to employees in 100 companies and research organizations. These students can communicate directly with the professor via two-way radio. Academically qualified employees of SITN members may enroll as fully matriculated graduate students in the honors cooperative program at Stanford. Others may take the courses as nondegree students or auditors.

- The future "electronic classroom" might include the transmission of holographic images. Imagine a "celebrity" teacher entering a holography studio at 8:45 A.M. At 9:00, he starts teaching, and his three-dimensional image is transmitted simultaneously into 50 college classrooms, some of which may be thousands of miles away. Students in these classrooms see him in three-dimensional full color, waving his hands, pacing the floor, furrowing his brow. In this manner, one gifted teacher presents the course instead of 50 average teachers, thereby providing better instruction with enormous cost savings. There would be phone hookups in each of the 50 classrooms to permit students to raise questions directly with the "holographic" professor.[10]

Whereas electronic classrooms require students and instructors to "meet" at prearranged times and places, other instructional technologies are more flexible:

- Oakton Community College in suburban Chicago offers telecourses in accounting, child psychology, and other subjects. The student registers at the college, buys a workbook, watches thirty 30-minute videotapes, and, when ready, takes an examination. The videotapes can be viewed either on a local television station at scheduled times or on videocassettes in selected public libraries that have agreed to carry them.

- Foothill Community College in Los Altos Hills, California, offers courses by newspaper and by audio cassette. Audio-cassette courses include oral communication, contemporary music, and San Francisco history (which includes independent sightseeing trips), topics particularly well suited to the approach.

How Can Middlemen Be Used?

Educational institutions usually produce and then deliver their services directly to the consumer. Yet in the business sector, *middlemen* (including *wholesalers, retailers,* and *brokers*) are commonly used to assist in getting the product from the producer to the final consumer. What are the advantages of using middlemen that might also apply to educational institutions?

Many educational institutions cannot afford to distribute their programs without assistance from volunteers. For example, the Chicago Lung Association offers classes for people who would like to stop smoking, as well as for sufferers from asthma and emphysema who need help in coping with their disabilities. If the association's resources were unlimited, it might hire a large team of public-health professionals to teach these courses. Instead, volunteers are recruited and trained to conduct structured sessions independently.

Even if an institution has the funds to distribute its programs and services directly to the consumer, middlemen may be less expensive and generally more efficient because of their experience, specialization, and contacts. For instance, many smokers say they would like to stop and also say that their physician's advice to stop would make a difference. Yet many doctors say they don't know what to do. Therefore, the Cancer Information Office of the National Institutes of Health decided to prepare and distribute "Helping Smokers Quit" kits to physicians. Each kit includes copies of a questionnaire on smoking habits for patients to complete in the waiting room and give to the doctor; a booklet advising the doctor how to influence the smoker to quit; copies of a follow-up letter and booklet on typical side effects of quitting smoking, to be mailed by the office assistant a week after the appointment; and wall charts for the office. The kit helps the doctor act as a middleman between the National Institutes of Health and the patient.

Can Facilitating Intermediaries Be Used?

Facilitating intermediaries are individuals or organizations that provide marketing services such as marketing research and advertising. (In the commercial sector, a company may employ facilitating intermediaries to provide shipping, warehousing, and financing as well.) When an institution needs these services, it must decide whether to hire from the outside or to provide its own services internally. It may hire a marketing research firm or decide to design and conduct its own marketing research study. It may hire an advertising agency or design its own advertisements.

The institution must weigh the quality, cost, and other factors involved in performing the service internally versus buying the assistance of others. In some instances, outside specialists can contribute valuable information and services beyond the reach of any one institution. For example, The College Board and American College Testing will provide mailing lists of high school students with specified demographic and academic characteristics. A college using this service can focus its direct-mail campaign on prospects whose profiles match those of its currently enrolled students. Many institutions contract with outside services to develop and produce brochures and catalogs.

SUMMARY

Distribution, the third major component of the marketing mix, is the process by which an institution makes its programs and services available and accessible to its target markets. Since educational services usually cannot be "stored up," educational institutions need to consider how to make their services as convenient as practicable in terms of both location and schedule.

To design an efficient distribution, delivery, or dissemination system, an institution must first decide on what level of convenience it can and should offer to its target market. Often the institution cannot offer the maximum level of consumer convenience—completely personalized service—and current facilities may be poorly matched to the institution's needs. The institution should then consider opening additional facilities and/or using alternative channels to serve its markets. Finally, the institution should consider using middlemen or intermediaries to provide services to assist in the distribution task.

NOTES

[1] "Notes on Continuing Education," *The Chronicle of Higher Education*, April 6, 1981, p. 2.

[2] Cited in *Choices*, Eisenhower College Bulletin, 1980–81, p. 1.

[3] "Earning an Undergraduate Degree at the Plant," *Business Week*, August 4, 1980, pp. 76–77.

[4] This section draws on Charles W. Lamb, Jr., and John L. Compton, "Distributing Public Services: A Strategic Approach," in Philip Kotler, O.C. Ferrell,

and Charles Lamb, eds., *Cases and Readings in Marketing for Nonprofit Organizations* (Englewood Cliffs, N.J.: Prentice-Hall, 1983), pp. 210–21.

[5] Wayne G. Strickland, "The University and the Community: Planning for an Alternative Form of Educational Service Delivery," *Planning for Higher Education*, Summer 1980, pp. 7–15.

[6] C. William Brubaker, "What to Do With Surplus School Space," *American School & University*, February 1980, pp. 36–41.

[7] Terrence E. Deal, "High Schools without Students: Some Thoughts on the Future," *Phi Delta Kappan*, Vol. 64 (March 1983), 485–91.

[8] S. Aaron Hyatt, "Facilities Planning for Academic Results," *Planning for Higher Education*, Vol. 9 (December 1980), 10–13.

[9] For more details, see Philip Kotler, "Atmospherics as a Marketing Tool," *Journal of Retailing*, Winter 1973–74, pp. 48–64.

[10] Philip Kotler, "Educational Packagers: A Modest Proposal," *Futurist*, August 1978, pp. 239–42.

chapter 14

COMMUNICATING WITH PUBLICS

Few if any educational institutions set out to mislead their publics, but some, driven by the desire to "put their best foot forward," may issue communications that present a sanitized version of reality, which may ultimately hurt the institution.

In contrast, the director of Stanford University's News Service starts from the position that "in times of crises, candor pays." Robert W. Beyers underscored the importance of candor by pointing out that "if the institution makes no effort to tell both sides of a controversy, it relinquishes that function to the media . . . and/or its critics." He added a remark sometimes attributed to Henry Ford II: "The facts about this place can never be as bad as the fiction."

What makes Bob Beyers' approach remarkable is that it stands in stark contrast to what is routinely considered good college public relations. On most campuses, the emphasis is still on telling only what's good about the college, while doggedly trying to prevent bad news from getting out. Beyers believes that such an approach is ineffective: "Any institution that tries to hide its warts will lose its esteem first with its own constituents, later with the general public."

The daily routine has the News Service staff spending about half its time outside the office, pursuing news leads, asking people what they have seen, heard, or done that might be newsworthy. Interesting stories in the student publications are checked for accuracy and then released to the news media. The News Service also monitors half a dozen daily newspapers, 50 magazines, and as many broadcasts as possible to provide information to the campus community.

Over the years, Beyers has had a good deal of experience with skeptical colleagues at other colleges who are convinced—probably with good reason—that similar devotion to candor would threaten their job security. He has an object lesson for them: "Bad news may have good results. Several years ago, quite a few Stanford faculty members were upset when one of their colleagues was quoted in *Time* magazine as saying that the library was the worst he'd ever seen at a major university. Yet that frankness helped the campus attract an outstanding librarian—and he, in turn, promptly enlisted the critic's support in building a better collection."

SOURCE: Fred M. Hechinger, "To Tell the Truth," *Change*, April 1978, pp. 56–57. A publication of the Helen Dwight Reid Educational Foundation.

Educational institutions need effective communications with their markets and publics. The three preceding chapters have explained the marketing aspects of program development, pricing, and distribution decisions. But developing good programs and services, pricing them attractively, and making them readily available to target consumers is not enough. The institution must also inform consumers and others about its goals, activities, and offerings and motivate them to take an interest in the institution.

This communication takes many forms. Educators usually think in terms of catalogs and bulletins describing their institution and its programs. Colleges, schools, and other educational institutions communicate about themselves by their very existence, whether or not they have a formal communications program. Many are rethinking their communications efforts, both formal and informal.

The educational communicator must start with a clear picture of the communications tasks facing the institution. The following tasks are typical:

- To maintain or enhance the image of the institution
- To build alumni loyalty and support
- To attract prospective donors
- To provide information about the institution's offerings
- To attract prospective students and encourage application and enrollment
- To correct inaccurate or incomplete information about the institution

In addition, the institution must determine and meet the information needs of faculty, staff, current students, and others in the internal environment.

Communications involves an exchange between the institution and the audience. The communicator must consider the institution's purpose for preparing the communication and the purpose(s) for which the audience will be paying attention to it. Only then can the form, content, and delivery of the message be planned to match the audience and achieve the intended purpose.

Most educational institutions use both public relations and advertising. *Public relations* consists of efforts to obtain favorable interest in the institution and/or its programs by planting significant news about them in publications or obtaining favorable unpaid presentation on radio, television, or in other media. *Advertising* consists of paid presentation and promotion of ideas, products, programs, or services—whether in magazines or newspapers, on television, radio, billboards, or bus cards, or through catalogs, direct mail, or some other medium. We believe that public relations and advertising are overlapping approaches and that educational institutions will usually need both approaches to carry out their communications tasks.

In this chapter, we address the following questions:

1. What are the steps in planning an effective communication?
2. What is public relations?
3. What are the steps in the public relations process?
4. What are the main public relations tools?
5. What are the hallmarks of an effective communications program?

PLANNING EFFECTIVE COMMUNICATIONS

Communications planning should start with an understanding of eight elements of every communication. The exchange aspect of every effective communication is diagrammed in Figure 14-1. There are two parties—a *sender* and a *receiver*. One or both send a *message* through *media*. To communicate effectively, senders need an understanding of the needs and wants of receivers. The senders

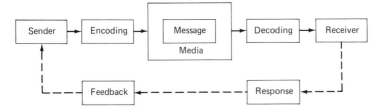

FIGURE 14-1   Elements in the communication process

must be skillful in *encoding* messages that reflect how the target audience tends to *decode* messages. They must transmit the message over efficient media that reach the target audience. They must develop *feedback* channels so they can know the audience's *response* to the message. Marketing research will be required at each stage: to identify potential audiences, segment them, determine their information needs, develop appropriate messages, and measure audience response.

The communications planning flow should begin with considering the target audience and work backward to the communicator. The marketing communicator must make the following decisions: (1) identify the target audience, (2) clarify the response sought, (3) develop a message, (4) choose the medium or media, (5) select source attributes, and (6) collect feedback. These planning steps are essential for effective communications, whether advertising or public relations is used. We will consider these basic elements, then show how they are implemented in public relations and, in Chapter 15, in advertising.

Identifying the Target Audience

An effective communication speaks directly to the concerns of a specific person or group. A college will want to identify the key audiences and their specific concerns in order to provide information tailored to their needs. For example, parents may be particularly interested in educational costs and faculty quality, whereas high school seniors may be more interested in social activities and students' evaluations of the educational experience.

Potential target audiences include all the institution's publics and markets. The institution will need to develop a communications program for each target audience, not just the two or three key audiences. For example, a college may identify its main audience as prospective students, but at various times, it will need to communicate with its other publics and markets—including alumni, current students, their parents, donors, and the general public.

Clarifying the Response Sought

A purposeful communication is designed to obtain a response from the receiver. The response may be a change in awareness of the institution and its programs, or a change in attitude—being favorably impressed by the quality of a program, for example. Or the institution may be seeking a behavioral response—a request for additional information, an application, or a donation. Only by determining the desired response can the institution shape the best message and later assess its effectiveness.

Developing the Message

Having defined the response desired from the target audience, the communicator then develops a communication. An ideal communication would manage to *get attention, hold interest, arouse desire*, and *obtain action* (known as the *AIDA model*). In practice, few messages will take the consumer all the way from awareness through action. The institution may need to use different messages and different types of communication at various stages of the communications process.

For example, a prospective donor may have first had contact with the college when attending a conference there. Impressed by the campus and the college's faculty and staff, the would-be donor takes the time to read news stories that tell about events at the college and reinforce his interest. He may meet alumni of the college socially and listen attentively to their reminiscences. If his interest becomes known (and based on his "giving potential"), he may be contacted by a representative of the college's development office or even by the college president to discuss the college's plans and needs. In this case, the college is engaging in event creation to get attention, relying on informal personal contact by alumni along with publicity to hold his interest, and depending on professional personal contact to arouse desire and obtain action— a donation.

A message has both *content* and *format*. Preparing the content requires understanding the target audience and what will motivate them to respond. The communicator then needs to select a format that attracts attention, arouses interest, and presents the message clearly.

Choosing Media

The communicator must select efficient media or channels of communication. Channels of communication are of two broad types, *personal* and *nonpersonal*.

Personal Communication. *Personal communication* includes direct communications from representatives of the institution (such as alumni admissions representatives, development staff, admissions officers); and word-of-mouth influence through conversations with neighbors, friends, family members, and associates—a highly persuasive form of communication. Personal influence is often a potent factor in decisions to apply to, attend, or donate money to an institution.

Institutions can stimulate personal-influence channels to work on their behalf. They can (1) identify individuals and groups that are influential and devote extra effort to them; (2) create opinion leaders by supplying them with information and asking them to help the institution (say, in fund raising or admissions); (3) work through community influentials, such as club presidents, elected officials, and others; (4) feature influential people in press releases and advertising; and (5) develop advertising that is high in "conversation value."[1]

Nonpersonal Communication. *Nonpersonal channels* include all channels of communication that do not involve direct person-to-person contact: newspapers, magazines, radio, television, billboards, events, and direct mail.

Communication through nonpersonal channels can encourage and reinforce personal communications. After seeing a news story on a new career-planning course at the local community college, a woman may tell her neighbor about the course. A high school student may talk with a college counselor about a number of colleges and then read brochures from those colleges with increased interest. Therefore, educational institutions should strive to combine personal and nonpersonal channels of communication according to their communications objectives.

Selecting Source Attributes

A communication's effect on an audience will be influenced by how the audience perceives the communicator. Messages delivered by highly credible sources will be more persuasive. Three factors underlie *source credibility*: expertise, trustworthiness, and likability.[2] *Expertise* is the degree to which the communicator is perceived to possess the necessary authority for what is being claimed. Students or recent graduates are usually perceived as experts on the college experience. Professors rank high on expertise when speaking about their areas of specialization. *Trustworthiness* is related to how objective and honest the source is perceived to be. Audiences tend to put more trust in friends and others like themselves than in strangers or recruiters. *Likability* is related to how attractive the source is to the audience. Qualities such as candor, humor, and naturalness tend to make a source more likable. The most highly credible source, then, would be a person who scored high on all three dimensions.

Collecting Feedback

The communicator must research the message's effects on the target audience. This may involve keeping records of coupons returned requesting further information, applications or donations received, or other measures of attention and interest. The communicator may survey target-audience members and ask them whether they recognize or recall the message, how they felt about the message, their previous and current attitudes toward the institution that sponsored the message, and their intentions to apply, enroll, or donate.

This section has considered the basic elements in planning effective communications. The following sections focus on public relations.

PUBLIC RELATIONS

People often equate public relations with publicity—obtaining publication of favorable stories about the institution—but that is only part of the public relations task. The most frequently quoted definition of *public relations* is the following:

> *Public relations* is the management function that evaluates public attitudes, identifies the policies and procedures of an individual or an institution with the public interest, and executes a program of action to earn public understanding and acceptance.[3]

This definition emphasizes understanding the institution's publics and reflecting the real character of the institution.

Every school, college, or other educational institution is involved with public relations in some way, since each must deal with a variety of publics. The local community, politicians, the news media, and others—all may take an active or reactive interest in the institution's activities. In many instances, the institution's top administrator plays a major role in public relations. Arnold points out that the first two letters in *president* and *principal* are PR.[4] A national sample of community college presidents reported that they have as much influence on institutional image as do more formal public relations activities, through their relationships with other community leaders and internal publics, and through activities directly connected with their colleges.[5]

Presidential public relations is not a recent phenomenon. The history of American higher education includes numerous dynamic, high-profile presidents who saved foundering institutions or carried reasonably successful ones to positions of greater luster. Here are two examples:

In his 1869 inaugural address as president of Harvard College, Charles W. Eliot described the president's duties as follows: "He must . . . influence public opinion toward advancement of learning; and . . . anticipate the due effect on the university of the fluctuations of public opinion on educational problems . . . [and] of the gradual alteration of social and religious habits in the community. The university must accommodate itself promptly to significant changes in the character of the people for whom it exists."[6]

William Rainey Harper, president of the University of Chicago from 1891 to 1906, was a masterful early practitioner of public relations and a model for other university presidents. His determination was to make Chicago "from the beginning an institution of the highest rank and character." To achieve this end, he courted influential Chicagoans, held convocations to build goodwill, and established both external and internal publications that candidly described the university's activities and even its financial circumstances. He established an information office to answer questions and guide visitors. Distressed that the press overlooked the university or lapsed into inaccurate reporting, Harper hired a publicity director who enjoyed the confidence of both the faculty and the press community. Harper also used staged events to focus attention on the university—lavish celebrations of its fifth, tenth, and fifteenth anniversaries. Harper viewed public relations as a positive approach to gaining funds, faculty, and students to build the University of Chicago.[7]

Of course, every other member of the institution is also, to a degree, a representative whose words and actions can influence public opinion about it. But institutions usually recognize the advantages of a more formal public relations operation. In fact, many public relations activities date back to the first two decades of this century: Harvard, Yale, Columbia, the University of Chicago, the University of Pennsylvania, and the University of Wisconsin set up influential publicity offices to spread the institutions' fame and to attract students and donors.

Nowadays, responsibility for recruiting students resides in the admissions office and fund raising with the development office, and a public relations officer or office may consult with them as well as handle other public relations tasks. The public relations office may monitor the institution's public image and advise administrators on areas of image strength and weakness. It may work with admissions and development officers to plan publications and manage their production. And the public relations office may prepare and distribute press releases about admissions and fund-raising activities as well as other campus stories.[8]

On some campuses, public relations, admissions, and fund raising are all directed by a vice president for external relations. The person at this level sits in on all meetings involving public-sensitive information and actions and advises on policy and implementation. In other institutions, public relations means getting out publications and handling special events. In such cases, the public relations people are not involved in policy or strategy formulation, only tactics. The institution can realize several advantages by formalizing its public relations operation: (1) better anticipation of potential issues; (2) better handling of these issues; (3) consistent public-oriented policies and strategies; and (4) more professional written and oral communications.

THE PUBLIC RELATIONS PROCESS

Public relations practitioners view themselves as the caretakers and enhancers of the institution's image. At various times, they are assigned the task of forming, maintaining, or changing attitudes. In this connection, they carry out the five-step process shown in Figure 14-2. We will examine each step below.

Identifying the Institution's Relevant Publics

An institution would like to have the goodwill of every public that it affects or is affected by. But given limited public relations resources, it has to concentrate its attention on certain publics.

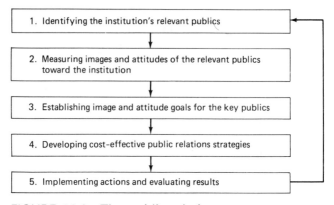

FIGURE 14-2   The public relations process

An educational institution's primary publics are those that it relates to on an active and continuous basis—its students, donors, faculty and staff, trustees, and the community. If the goodwill of any of these groups disappears—students stop coming, donors stop giving, faculty and staff start quitting, trustees lose their interest, or the community becomes hostile—the institution is in deep trouble.

The publics are related not only to the institution but also to each other in many important ways. A particular public may strongly influence the attitudes and behavior of other publics toward the institution. Consider a school whose students are highly satisfied. Their enthusiasm will be transmitted to their parents and to friends who might be potential students. Their enthusiasm will reinforce the faculty's attention to teaching. As alumni, they will be more generous donors and supporters of the school. Thus, students influence the attitudes and behavior of other school publics.

Measuring Images and Attitudes of the Relevant Publics

After identifying its various publics, the institution needs to assess how each public thinks and feels about it. Some idea of each public's attitude can be obtained simply through regular contacts with members of that public. But impressions based on casual contact cannot necessarily be trusted.

A college wanted to rent its stadium facilities to a professional football team for five Sundays as a way to acquire more revenue. The college's administrators thought that most local residents and city council members would be agreeable. However, when the plan became public, local citizens organized themselves and attacked the college, calling it insensitive and arrogant. They complained that the football crowd would use up parking spaces, leave litter, walk on lawns, and be rowdy. Many citizens, including city council members, revealed negative attitudes toward the college. The college's administration dismissed the community spokesman as a minority, unrepresentative of community opinion, and were shocked when the vote went against the college.

Formal marketing research is essential to effective public relations. A focus group discussion with six to ten members of a key public can reveal their knowledge and feelings about the institution. Although the resulting observations may not be fully representative, they normally contribute valuable perspectives and raise questions that the institution will want to explore more systematically. Eventually, the institution may find it worthwhile to conduct formal field research on its image and issues of concern in the form of a public opinion survey. The public opinion survey measures such variables as awareness, knowledge, interest, and attitude toward the institution.

Establishing Image and Attitude Goals for the Key Publics

Through periodically researching its key publics, the institution will have some hard data on how these publics view it. The findings can be assembled in the form of a scorecard, such as the one illustrated for a college in Table 14-1. The scorecard becomes the basis for developing a public relations plan for the coming period. The college's scorecard shows that high school counselors have a medium amount of knowledge about the college and a negative attitude. Since high school counselors have a role in the college-choice decision, the institution needs to develop a communications program that will improve high school counselors' knowledge and attitudes toward the college. The objective should be made even more specific and measurable, such as "80 percent of the high school counselors should know at least four key things about the college, and at least 60 percent should report having a positive opinion about the college, within two years." Making the objectives concrete helps determine the necessary activities and budget and provides a basis for evaluating the success of the plan.

The next item on the scorecard indicates that communication also has to be directed at high school seniors to increase their knowledge and improve their attitudes toward the college. As for alumni, their knowledge and attitude are ideal, and the college's job is simply to maintain their enthusiasm. As for the general public, the college may decide to do nothing. In this case, the general public's knowledge and attitude are not that important in attracting

TABLE 14-1 Scorecard on a college's publics

PUBLIC	KNOWLEDGE	ATTITUDE	PUBLIC'S IMPORTANCE
High school counselors	Medium	Negative	High
High school seniors	Low	Neutral	High
Alumni	High	Positive	High
General public	Low	Neutral	Low

students, and the cost of improving the situation would be too high in relation to the value.

Developing Cost-Effective Public Relations Strategies

An institution usually has many options in trying to improve the attitudes of a particular public. Its first task is to understand why the attitudes have come about, so that the causal factors can be addressed by an appropriate strategy. Let us return to the college that found it had weak community support when it wanted to rent its stadium to a professional football team. In digging deeper into the negative citizen attitudes, administrators discovered that many local citizens harbored resentments against the college, including complaints that (1) the college never consulted citizens or citizen groups before taking actions, (2) the college discriminated against local high school students, preferring to draw students from other parts of the country, (3) the college did not actively inform the local community about campus events and programs, and (4) the college owned local property that was tax-free and thus raised the taxes of the citizens. Essentially, the community felt neglected and exploited by the college.

The diagnosis suggests that the college needs to change its ways and establish stronger contacts with the community. It needs to develop a *community-relations program*. Here are some of the steps it might take:

1. Identify the local opinion leaders—prominent businesspeople, news editors, city council members, heads of civic organizations, school officials—and build better relationships through inviting them to campus events, consulting with them on college–community issues, and sponsoring luncheons and dinners.
2. Encourage the college's faculty and staff to join local organizations and participate more actively in community campaigns such as the United Way and American Red Cross Blood Bank program.
3. Develop a speakers' bureau to speak to local groups such as the Kiwanis, Rotary, and so on.
4. Make the college's facilities and programs more available to the community.
5. Arrange open houses and tours of the campus for the local community.
6. Participate in community special events such as parades, holiday observances, and so on.
7. Establish a community advisory board of community leaders to act as a sounding board for issues facing the college.

Each project involves money and time. The institution will need to estimate the amount of expected attitude improvement with each project in order to arrive at the best mix of cost-effective actions.

Implementing Actions and Evaluating Results

The actions must be assigned to responsible people, along with concrete objectives, time frames, and budgets. The public relations office should oversee the effort and monitor the results. Evaluating the results of public relations activities, however, is not easy, since it is hard to separate them from the effects of other marketing activities.

Consider the problem of measuring the value of the institution's publicity efforts. Publicity is designed with certain audience-response objectives in mind, and these objectives determine what is measured. The major response measures are exposures, awareness/comprehension/attitude change, and changes in behavior.

The easiest and most common measure of publicity effectiveness is the number of *exposures* created in the media. Most publicists supply the client with a "clippings book" showing all the media that carried news about the institution. This exposure measure is not very satisfying. There is no indication of how many people actually read, saw, or heard the message, and what they thought afterward. Furthermore, there is no information on the net audience reached, since publications have operlapping readership.

A better measure calls for finding out what change in public *awareness/ comprehension/attitude* occurred as a result of the publicity campaign (after allowing for the effect of other promotional tools). This requires the use of survey methodology to measure the before–after levels of these variables. The best measure is the effect of the campaign on people's actions—donating to the college, applying, and so forth.

Certain public relations activities will be found to be too costly in relation to their results and might be dropped. Or the public relations objectives might be recognized as too ambitious and require modification. Furthermore, new issues will arise with certain publics and require redirection of the public relations resources. As the public relations office implements these actions and measures the results, it can return to the earlier steps, reassess where the institution stands in the minds of specific publics, and determine what improvements to pursue. Thus, the public relations process is continually recycling, as the arrow in Figure 14-2 indicates.

PUBLIC RELATIONS TOOLS

Here we want to examine the major public relations media and tools in more detail. They are (1) written material, (2) audiovisual material, (3) institutional-identity media, (4) news, (5) events, (6) speeches, (7) telephone information services, and (8) personal contact.

Written Material

Institutions rely extensively on written material to communicate with their target publics. Colleges use annual reports, catalogs, employee newsletters, alumni magazines, posters, flyers, and so on.

In preparing each publication, the public relations office must consider *function, aesthetics,* and *cost.* For example, the function of an annual report is to inform interested publics about the institution's accomplishments during the year, with the ultimate purpose of generating confidence in the institution and its leaders. The annual report should be readable, interesting, and professional. A mimeographed annual report suggests a poor and amateurish organization. On the other hand, if the annual report is too slick, readers may question why the institution is spending so much on printing instead of on other things. Cost acts as a constraint in that the institution will allocate a limited amount of money to each publication. The public relations department has to reconcile considerations of function, aesthetics, and cost in developing each publication.

Audiovisual Material

Audiovisual material—such as films, slides-and-sound, and audio cassettes—are coming into increasing use as communication tools. In the old days, college recruiters would make a presentation, answer questions, and pass out brochures to the high school seniors gathered to hear about the college. Today's recruiter, in contrast, comes prepared to deliver an effective audiovisual presentation. Some colleges now provide high school counselors with videotapes showing the campus and describing what the college has to offer. Interested high school students can select and view tapes on several colleges in one visit to the counselor's office.

Institutional-Identity Media

Normally, each of the institution's separate materials takes on its own look, a situation that not only creates confusion but also neglects an opportunity to create and reinforce an *institutional identity*. In an overcommunicated society, educational institutions have to compete for attention. They should at least try to create a visual identity that the public immediately recognizes. The visual identity is carried through the institution's permanent media, such as logos, stationery, brochures, signs, business forms, business cards, buildings, and uniforms.

The institutional-identity media become a marketing tool when they are attractive, memorable, and distinctive. The task of creating a coordinated visual identity is not easy. The institution should select a good graphic-design consultant. A good consultant will try to get management to identify the essence of the institution, and then will try to turn it into a big idea backed by strong visual symbols. The symbols are adapted to the various media so that they create immediate institutional recognition in the minds of various publics. Barton-Gilette, a New York communications firm, designed an apple logo for all New York University's publications to identify the university with New York City, "the Big Apple."

News

The public relations office should also find or create favorable news about the institution and market it to the appropriate media. The appeal of publicity is that it is "free advertising." As someone said, "Publicity is sent to a medium and prayed for, while advertising is sent to a medium and paid for." However, publicity is far from free, because special skills are required to write good publicity and to "reach" the press. Good publicists cost money.

Publicity has three qualities that make it a worthwhile investment. First, it may have *higher veracity* than advertising, because it appears as normal news and not sponsored information. Second, it tends to catch people *off guard* who might otherwise actively avoid sponsored messages. Third, it has high potential for *dramatization*, because news of a noteworthy event arouses attention.

Consider a college suffering from low visibility that adopts the objective of achieving more public recognition through news management. The public relations director will review the college's various components to see whether any natural stories exist. Do any faculty members have unusual backgrounds, or are any working on unusual projects? Are any new and unusual courses being taught? Are any exceptional students with unusual backgrounds enrolled? Are any interesting events taking place on campus? Is there a story about the architecture, history, or aspirations of the college? Usually a search along these lines will uncover hundreds of stories that can be fed to the press with the effect of creating much more public recognition of the college. Ideally, the stories chosen should symbolize the kind of college this college wants to be. The stories should support its desired market position.

A good public relations director understands that the media seek interesting and timely stories, and that educational institutions must compete for attention with all the other events of the day. The director will make a point of knowing as many news editors and reporters as possible and providing them with press releases.

In addition to press releases, the public relations office should also respond to media requests to interview faculty and other campus figures. When a news story breaks, various media may seek out academic experts for comment. The public relations director should be knowledgeable about faculty areas of expertise and be able to recommend appropriate interviewees. Some campus public relations directors help faculty prepare for such interviews.

Events

An institution can increase its newsworthiness by creating events that attract favorable attention from target publics. Thus, a college seeking more public attention can host academic conferences, present well-known speakers and public figures, mark important occasions in the life of the college, and provide press releases on notable people and events at the college. Each well-run event impresses the immediate participants and provides the basis for several stories directed to relevant media vehicles and audiences. Exhibit 14-1 describes how one community college uses events to attract students to take math courses.

Speeches

The public relations director will look for effective spokespersons for the institution and will try to arrange speaking engagements. If a college's president

EXHIBIT 14-1 Using events to attract students

The mathematics department at Lane Community College in Eugene, Oregon, sponsors special events to interest students in taking math courses. Casey Fast, the chairman of the mathematics department, describes one such event:

"We decided to honor National Metrics Week. In our building and hallways we decided to present a complete display of all the present uses of the metric system; i.e., tire sizes, metric tool kits, dress patterns, recipes, and so on. We held a bake sale from a metric cookbook. We had a microcomputer with a conversational program on metrics. We had free metric measuring sticks. All of this was good, but I knew it was not quite enough to really pique the public interest. After all, many people do not like the metric system and they certainly won't drive across town to honor something they don't like."

"I suggested that we hold a funeral to bury the present archaic, inefficient English System of Measurement. While many of my colleagues felt that a funeral was morbid, depressing, embarrassing and downright sick, I met their criticisms with positive questions like

1. Did you know that a local funeral home has donated a coffin?
2. Did you know that the Science Department has donated a skeleton and old measuring utensils to put in the coffin?
3. Did you know that Performing Arts has provided costumes for the pall-bearers?
4. Did you know that the school's Dixieland Band will play?
5. Did you know that every TV station in town wants to record the event?"

The funeral procession started across campus with only about 25 people, but within five minutes grew to several hundred. The event drew coverage from National Public Radio as well as the local television stations, and attracted interest from potential students and community residents.

SOURCE: Adapted from Casey Fast, "Educational Marketing Methods at Lane Community College," March 1979.

is articulate and attractive, the public relations director will try to line up appearances on national and local TV and radio talk shows and at major conventions. The director can also set up a speakers' bureau for delivering appropriate talks to community organizations.

Telephone Information Services

A relatively new public relations tool is a telephone number through which members of the public can get information about the institution. Triton Community College, for example, set up a telephone number that gives recorded information about the college, registration times, and costs. Some school districts have set up "homework hotlines" where teachers are available in the evenings to help students—and their parents—with homework problems. These telephone services are ways for the institution to show that it cares about the public and is ready to serve it.

Personal Contact

We have already referred to the importance of top administrators as spokespersons for the institution. Others associated with the school also have a public relations role: admissions officers, development officers, volunteer fund raisers, faculty, staff, current students, and alumni, among others. The impressions they make can have a significant impact on how the institution is perceived.

THE EFFECTIVE COMMUNICATIONS PROGRAM

An educational communications program involves both public relations and advertising (in Chapter 15). A typical school or college issues many communications and wants to get the most benefit from the time and money spent on them.

An effective marketing communications program has several hallmarks. First, effective marketing communications are *coordinated*. Rather than issuing a jumble of bulletins, brochures, and press releases, the institution analyzes its various markets and publics to determine each group's communications needs. It considers what response it wants from each group—for example, donations from alumni and applications from well-prepared high school seniors—and develops a communications program for each. Rather than depending on one communications form or medium, the institution will want to use a carefully planned combination of direct mail, advertising, publicity, and special events to achieve its communications objectives.

The institution will want to use a *single logo* and theme on publications and other communications to increase institutional recognition as well as identification of each communication with the institution. The quality of content and style will be consistent, and layout and production qualities will be appropriate to the communications objective. (For example, a brochure for potential large donors will be more lavish than a listing of the coming semester's course schedule.) To achieve quality and consistency, the institution will need one or more highly skilled professionals who review all official publications and, at the very least, have an opportunity to recommend improvements before publication and dissemination. This function may be headed by a director of communications.

Where possible, the institution will want to *personalize* its communications. With word processing, the admissions office can send personalized responses to inquiries. Other communications, to current students, parents, and donors, can likewise include a personal salutation. Despite broad awareness that many letters are "computer-generated," such touches still reflect well on the institution that uses them. Beware of defeating their efffect by "signing" such personalized communications with a rubber stamp!

Effective marketing communications are *authentic*. There is no place for deception or puffery. Those who visit the college or decide to enroll will soon find the gaps and be resentful. Furthermore, an educational institution cannot and should not present inconsistent pictures of itself and its offerings to different groups. For example, admissions brochures and other recruiting communications should meet a "reality test"—review by currently enrolled students and others who are knowledgeable about the institution.

Finally, educational institutions must remember that an effective marketing communications program, although important, is but one element in the institution's marketing effort. The institution must ensure its performance and viability through sound program, pricing, and distribution decisions as well.

SUMMARY

Every educational institution constantly communicates about itself through its programs, students, alumni, campus, and formal communications program. Communications form one of the four elements of the marketing mix. The main types of marketing communications are public relations and advertising. This chapter discusses the steps in preparing an effective communication and the role of public relations in an institution's communications program.

Planning an effective communication involves (1) identifying the target audience, (2) clarifying the response sought, (3) developing a message, (4) choosing the medium or media, (5) selecting source attributes, and (6) collecting feedback.

The task of public relations is to form, maintain, or change public attitudes towards the institution. The process of public relations consists of five steps: (1) identifying the institution's relevant publics, (2) measuring the images and attitudes held by these publics, (3) establishing image and attitude goals for the key publics, (4) developing cost-effective public relations strategies, and (5) implementing actions and evaluating results.

Public relations practitioners must be skilled communicators, adept at developing written material, audiovisual material, institutional-identity media, news releases, events, speeches, and telephone information services, and at facilitating favorable personal contact by administrators and others associated with the institution.

An effective communications program requires strong professional skills and cannot be left to chance. The institution's publications should be reviewed for quality and consistency of content and style. Wherever possible, communications should be personalized. The institution should ensure that communications are accurate and do not use puffery.

NOTES

[1] See Thomas S. Robertson, *Innovative Behavior and Communications* (New York: Holt, Rinehart & Winston, 1971), Chap. 9.

[2] Herbert C. Kelman and Carl I. Hovland, " 'Reinstatement' of the Communicator in Delayed Measurement of Opinion Change," *Journal of Abnormal and Social Psychology*, 48 (1953), 327–35.

[3] *Public Relations News*, October 27, 1947.

[4] Ken Arnold, "Principal: The First Two Letters Are P.R.," *Thrust*, October 1977, p. 28.

[5] Gerald S. Nagel, "How Can I Improve the Image of the College?" *Community College Review*, Summer 1981, pp. 24–27.

[6] Scott M. Cutlip, " 'Advertising' Higher Education: The Early Years of College Public Relations," *College and University Journal*, Fall 1970, p. 21.

[7] Scott M. Cutlip, " 'Advertising' Higher Education: The Early Years of College Public Relations—Part II," *College and University Journal*, January–February 1971, pp. 25–28.

[8] Thomas Huddleston, Jr., "Getting It Together," *Techniques* (American College Public Relations Association), April 1974, pp. 7–8.

chapter 15

ADVERTISING EDUCATIONAL PROGRAMS

In 1982 Marymount College Tarrytown received an unsolicited offer of assistance from honorary alumna Mary Wells Lawrence, president of Wells, Rich, Green advertising agency in New York City. The agency offered to design an ad for use during the celebration of the college's 75th Jubilee during the 1982–83 academic year. The next week saw a creative team from the agency on campus to interview Sr. Brigid Driscoll, Marymount's president, and administrators from admissions, career services, communications, and development, as well as several key faculty.

The manager of the college's news bureau and the director of development worked closely with the agency as the campaign was prepared.

WE PUT WOMEN IN THEIR PLACE.

DR. EUGENIE DOYLE '43
DIRECTOR OF PEDIATRIC
CARDIOLOGY
N.Y.U. MEDICAL CENTER

LORET MILLER RUPPE '57
DIRECTOR
PEACE CORPS

MARY ANNE DOLAN '68
MANAGING EDITOR
*LOS ANGELES
HERALD EXAMINER*

MARIKO ARMITAGE '71
LONDON TRADER
SALOMON BROTHERS

Imagine what the women who graduate from Marymount four years from now will do.

To find out about becoming one of them, call Micheileen Doran, our Director of Admissions, at (914) 631-3200. Or send in the coupon.

When it comes to helping you find your place in the world, there's no place like Marymount.

Name _____

Address _____

City _____ State _____ Zip _____

Telephone No. _____

High School _____

Year of Graduation _____

Field of Interest _____

Send to: Director of Admissions,
Marymount College, Tarrytown, NY 10591

MARYMOUNT COLLEGE TARRYTOWN

The president also attended the agency's presentation and kept in touch with the planning process.

In October the agency presented two ideas for campaigns. The favored campaign idea featured alumnae who had achieved leadership positions in their careers. After receiving photographs from selected alumnae, the ad agency went to work to design an ad that would attract attention, arouse interest, and convey the campaign theme: Marymount College Tarrytown is a women's college that prepares women for distinguished careers in many fields.

The ad appeared in the *New York Times* and in several local newspapers in the spring of 1983, and it was reproduced and included in a regular mailing to parents, trustees, and major donors. It was very well received by the general public, alumni, parents of students, and students. The ad succeeded in presenting Marymount as a college that offers excellence in education to women who will achieve excellence in their careers.

> **SOURCE:** Vivian S. Frommer, Director of Communications, Marymount College Tarrytown. Ad used with permission.

The idea of advertising strikes some educators as new, yet educators were using advertising as long as 2,000 years ago. The Greek sophists, like doctors and other wandering professionals of their day, publicly "made high display of their acquirements, and gave exhibitions of eloquence and of argument to show the value of their wares."[1] In more recent times—1869—an ad for Harvard College appeared on the outside cover of Harper's Magazine, and created an uproar. According to one commentator, "Such a thing had never been heard of before. It was as if Noah had put up posters on the cliffs of Armenia to announce that the ark was to open on such a day."[2]

Because of—or despite—these early practitioners, some educators resist the idea of paid advertising, feeling that it demeans educational programs and should be unnecessary. They overlook other forms of paid advertising already widely used: The typical college prints bulletins, sends direct mail, and places program announcements in the press. On the other hand, some educators may expect too much from advertising or try to accomplish large objectives with inadequate skills and resources, and thus be disappointed. Sometimes an institution mistakenly believes that advertising can save a weak program. Still other institutions, ambivalent about the propriety of advertising, produce am-

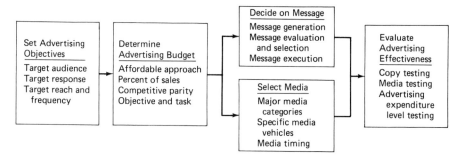

FIGURE 15-1   Major decisions in advertising management

ateurish and ineffective ads and then complain that advertising does not work. In fact, advertising can play a role in an institution's communications program and can enhance rather than demean the institution that uses it appropriately.

More and more schools and colleges are turning to advertising. Advertising consists of *nonpersonal forms of communication conducted through paid media under clear sponsorship.* Advertising can take many forms and serve many purposes. It involves such varied media as *magazines* and *newspapers, radio* and *television, outdoor displays* (such as posters, signs, billboards, skywriting), *direct mail, novelties* (blotters, calendars, pens, pencils), *cards* (bus, subway), *catalogs, directories,* and *circulars.* Advertising can serve to build the long-term image and reputation of the institution (*institutional advertising*) or of a particular division or product line, to provide information about a specific program or event, and for other purposes.

To develop an effective advertising program, the institution must make five major decisions. It must:

1. Set advertising objectives
2. Determine the advertising budget
3. Decide on the message
4. Select media
5. Evaluate advertising effectiveness

These decisions are diagrammed in Figure 15-1 and are discussed in the following sections.

SET ADVERTISING OBJECTIVES

An effective communications program must start with clear communications objectives. These objectives must flow from prior decisions on the institution's strategy—the target market, market positioning, and marketing mix. Some of the objectives will be addressed with public relations and other communications approaches, and others can best be addressed by advertising. The overall marketing strategy defines the role advertising will play in the total marketing mix.

Developing advertising objectives calls for defining the target audience, target response, and target reach and frequency.

Identifying the Target Audience

A marketing communicator must start with a clear target audience in mind. ("Target audience" is analogous to "target market" and refers to the audience we particularly want to reach with our communications.) The audience may be potential users of the institution's services, current users, deciders, or influencers. It may consist of individuals, groups, particular publics, or the general public. The target audience will critically influence the communicator's decisions on *what* is to be said, *how* it is to be said, *where* it is to be said, and *who* is to say it.

Consider the case of a small private college in Iowa called Pottsville.

Pottsville is seeking applicants from Nebraska, and it estimates there are 4,000 graduating high school seniors who might be interested in Pottsville College. The college must decide whether to aim its communications primarily at high school counselors in Nebraska or at the high school students themselves. Beyond this, it may want to develop communications to reach the parents and other influentials in the college decision process. Each target audience would warrant a different communications campaign, of which advertising might be a part.

Defining the Target Response

Once the target audience is identified, the marketing communicator must define the target response that is sought. The ultimate response is usually some action, but action is the end result of what may be a long process of consumer decision making. The marketing communicator needs to know in which stage the target audience stands at present and to which stage it should be moved.

Any member of the target audience may be in one of the six action-readiness states with respect to the institution or its offerings. These states—*awareness, knowledge, liking, preference, conviction,* and *action*—are described below.[3]

1. *Awareness.* The first step is to determine the target audience's awareness of the institution. The audience may be completely unaware of the school, know only its name, or know one or two things about it. If most of the target audience is unaware, the communicator's task is to build awareness, perhaps even just name recognition. This calls for simple messages repeating the name.

Even then, building awareness takes time. Pottsville College has no name recognition among high school seniors in Nebraska. The college might set the objective of making 70 percent of these students aware of Pottsville's name within one year.

2. *Knowledge.* The target audience may be aware of the college but not know much about it. Thus, the communicator's objective will be to transmit some key information. Thus, Pottsville College may want its target audience to know that it is a private four-year college in eastern Iowa that has distinguished programs in ornithology and thanatology. After the communications campaign, it can sample the target-audience members to measure whether they have little, some, or much knowledge of Pottsville College, and the content of their knowledge. The particular set of beliefs that the audience has of an institution is called the *image.* Institutions must periodically assess their public images as a basis for developing communications objectives.

3. *Liking.* If the target-audience members know the institution, the next question is, How do they feel about it? We can imagine a scale covering *dislike very much, dislike somewhat, indifferent, like somewhat, like very much.* If the audience holds an unfavorable view of Pottsville College, the communicator has to find out why and then develop a communications program to build up favorable feeling. If the unfavorable view is rooted in real inadequacies of the college, then a communications campaign would not do the job. The task would require first improving the college and then communicating its quality.

4. *Preference.* The target audience may like the institution but may not prefer it over others. It is one of several acceptable institutions. In this case, the communicator's job is to build the consumers' preference. The communicator needs to present information on the institution's quality, value, performance, and other attributes. The communicator can gauge the success of the campaign by surveying members of the audience to see if their preference for the college is stronger after the campaign.

5. *Conviction.* A target audience may prefer a particular institution but may not have developed a conviction to select it. Thus, some high school seniors may prefer Pottsville to other colleges but may not be sure they want to go to college. The communicator's job is to build conviction that going to college is the right thing to do. Building conviction that one should select a particular institution is a challenging communications task.

6. *Action.* A member of the target audience may have conviction but may not quite get around to taking action. He or she may be waiting for additional information, may plan to act later, and so on. A communicator in this situation must encourage the consumer to take the final step.

The six states simplify to three stages known as the *cognitive* (awareness, knowledge), *affective* (liking, preference, conviction), and *behavioral* (action). The communicator normally assumes that consumers pass through these stages in succession. The communicator must then identify the stage that characterizes most of the target audience and develop a communications message or campaign that will move them to the next stage. Rarely can one message move the audience through all three stages. Most communicators try to find a cost-effective communications approach to moving the target audience one stage at a time.

Some marketing scholars have challenged the idea that a consumer passes through *cognition* to *affect* to *behavior* in this order. Ray has suggested that some consumers pass from *cognition* to *behavior* to *affect*.[4] An example would be a student who has heard of Pottsville, enrolls there without much feeling, and afterward develops a strong liking (or disliking) for the place. Ray has also suggested that sometimes consumers pass from *behavior* to *affect* to *cognition*. Thus, a student may sign up for a course that he or she knows nothing about except that friends are taking it, develop a favorable feeling, and finally begin to understand the subject. Each version of the sequence has different implications for the role and influence of communications on behavior.

Determining Target Reach and Frequency

The third decision is the determination of the optimal *target reach and frequency* of the advertising. Since funds for advertising are usually limited, not everyone in the target audience can be reached and reached with sufficient frequency. Therefore, marketing management must decide what percentage of the audience to reach with what exposure frequency per period. For example, Pottsville College could decide to use direct mail and to buy 4,000 advertising exposures. This still leaves several choices on target reach and frequency. For example, the college could send one letter to 4,000 different students. Or it could send two different letters a week apart to 2,000 students. The key issue is how many exposures are needed to create the desired response, given the market's state of readiness. One exposure could be enough to convert students from being unaware to being aware, but it would not be enough to convert students from awareness to preference.

DETERMINE ADVERTISING BUDGET

Setting the advertising budget will depend on the advertising objectives and the advertising program to carry them out. Some media will be far more expensive than others, and the communications planner must develop an affordable budget to carry out the identified tasks.

Suppose Pottsville College wants to send two letters to each of 2,000 students, yielding a total of 4,000 exposures. Suppose the average mailing piece will cost $2 to design and mail. Then Pottsville will need a rough advertising budget of $8,000 to accomplish its objective.

In addition to setting the total size of the advertising budget, marketers must plan how to allocate the budget over different market segments, geographical areas, and time periods. In practice, advertising budgets are allocated to different segments depending on some indicator of market potential. For example, Pottsville might spend twice as much on advertising to students who live closer to Pottsville than to those farther away, if the college had reason to believe that Nebraska students prefer to go to a college reasonably near their homes. In fact, however, the budget should be allocated to different segments according to their expected marginal response to advertising. A budget is well allocated when it is not possible to increase total market response by shifting dollars from one segment to another.

Some educational institutions receive *donated* or *reduced-cost advertising*. A notable example is the American Negro College Fund campaign. The copy is produced by a volunteering advertising agency, which provides this service as a member of the Advertising Council of America, and the media donate broadcast time and space as a public service. The colleges that benefit from this advertising have no control over the place or timing of its appearance, but they have many of the advantages of a professional advertising program.

DECIDE ON MESSAGE

Given the advertising objectives and budget, the next step is to develop a creative message. Advertisers and their agencies go through three steps: message generation, message evaluation and selection, and message execution.

Message Generation

Message generation involves developing several alternative messages (appeals, themes, motifs, ideas) that are planned to elicit the desired response in the target market.

Messages can be generated in several ways. One approach is to talk with members of the target market and other influentials to determine how they view the institution or program, and have them talk about it and express their desires about it. This can be done through personal interviews or through focus group discussions (presented in Chapter 3). A second approach is to hold a brainstorming session at which key personnel in the institution generate advertising ideas.

A third approach is to use some formal deductive framework for coming up with advertising messages. One framework calls for generating three types of messages: rational, emotional, and moral.

1. *Rational messages* aim at passing on information and/or serving the audience's self-interest. They attempt to show that the institution or program

will yield the expected functional benefits. Examples would be messages discussing a program's quality, economy, value, or performance.

2. *Emotional messages* are designed to stir up some negative or positive emotion that will motivate action. Communicators have worked with fear, guilt, and shame appeals, especially in connection with getting people to start doing things they should (brushing their teeth, practicing breast self-examination) or stop doing things they shouldn't (smoking, overimbibing, overeating). Advertisers have found that fear appeals work up to a point, but if too much fear is aroused, the audience will block out the message. Communicators have also used such positive emotional appeals as love, humor, pride, and joy.

3. *Moral messages* are directed at the audience's sense of what is right and proper. They are often used in messages exhorting people to support such social causes as a cleaner environment, equal rights for women, and support for higher education. An example is the United Negro College Fund's appeal: "A mind is a terrible thing to waste."

Figure 15-2 shows an ad that combines both moral and rational appeals. The "waste not, want not" proverb sets the tone of the ad, which points out to businessmen and women that a donation to the United Negro College Fund helps ensure that they will be able to hire well-qualified college graduates as employees in the future.

Maloney proposed another deductive framework.[5] He suggested that buyers may be expecting any of four types of reward from a product: *rational, sensory, social,* or *ego-satisfaction.* And they may visualize these rewards from *results-of-use experience, product-in-use experience,* or *incidental-to-use experience.* Crossing the four types of rewards with the three types of experience generates twelve types of advertising messages, illustrated in Table 15-1.

A third framework examines the product's actual and desired positions and looks for the themes that would shift the market's view of the product in the desired direction. The advertisement may try to change the belief about the product's level on some attribute or the perceived relative importance of different attributes, or to introduce new attributes not generally considered by the market. For example, Drake University wanted to attract more students from the Chicago area by emphasizing that Drake was "away from home" but near enough to Chicago to get home quickly. Billboards were used near O'Hare Airport and a Loop-bound expressway announcing, "Drake University: Only 65 minutes from O'Hare to Des Moines."

Message Evaluation and Selection

The task of selecting the best message out of a large number of possibilities calls for evaluation criteria. Twedt has suggested that contending messages be rated on three scales: *desirability, exclusiveness,* and *believability.*[6] He believes that the communications potency of a message is the product of the three

WASTE NOT.
WANT NOT.

When you need to fill a position,
you'll have a qualified graduate
that you helped educate.

**GIVE TO THE
UNITED NEGRO COLLEGE FUND.
A MIND IS A TERRIBLE THING
TO WASTE.**

Photographer: Dwight Carter
A Public Service of This Magazine &
The Advertising Council
© 1981 United Negro College Fund, Inc.

FIGURE 15-2 United Negro College Fund ad

factors, because if any of the three has a low rating, the message's communications potency will be greatly reduced.

The message must first say something desirable or interesting about the
program or institution. This is not enough, however, since others may be
making the same or very similar claims. Therefore, the message must also say
something exclusive or distinctive. Finally, the message must be believable or
provable. If consumers are asked to rate different messages on desirability,
exclusiveness, and believability, these messages can be evaluated for their
communications potency.

TABLE 15-1   Examples of twelve types of appeals

TYPES OF POTENTIALLY REWARDING EXPERIENCE WITH A PRODUCT	POTENTIAL TYPE OF REWARD			
	RATIONAL	SENSORY	SOCIAL	EGO SATISFACTION
Results-of-use experience	1. Get the training to get ahead	2. Yoga classes to relax body and mind	3. Join a select group—our alumni	4. For women who are going places
Product-in-use experience	5. The program based on your schedule	6. Excitement in learning	7. The friendly college	8. Add some class to your life
Incidental-to-use experience	9. Free child care while you attend class	10. The thrill of the Homecoming game—autumn at the U.	11. Make the friends you'll keep all your life	12. The school for the discriminating student

SOURCE: Framework from John C. Maloney, "Marketing Decisions and Attitude Research," in *Effective Marketing Coordination,* George L. Baker, Jr. ed. (Chicago: American Marketing Association, 1961).

Message Execution

The *words* must be memorable and attention-getting, especially in the headlines and slogans that lead the reader into the ad. There are six basic types of headlines: news ("New Music Program for Senior Citizens"); question ("Having Trouble Helping Johnny Do Homework?"); narrative ("I'll Be Marching Down the Aisle with My Son in June"); command ("Put Some Class in Your Life"); 1-2-3 ways ("6 Ways to Get Ahead"); and how-what-why ("What You Should Know About College").

Any message can be put across in different *execution styles*. Suppose a multicampus community college district wants to encourage enrollments in evening programs for career training and job upgrading. The budget will stretch to allow locally broadcast 30-second television spots to motivate people to sign up for this program. Here are some major advertising execution styles that can be considered:

1. *Slice-of-Life.* An interviewer regretfully tells a woman in her mid-30s that she just doesn't have the educational requirements for the job she wants. The same woman, in a number of quick shots, is similarly turned down by other interviewers. She thinks to herself, "I'm going to take advantage of Western Community College's new programs." In the next scene, an interviewer (perhaps the original one!) stands up, shakes her hand, and congratulates her on earning the qualifications and getting the new job.

2. *Lifestyle.* A small group of men and women on a coffee break wearily share their ideas on what they have planned for that evening. When the round robin of mundane, boring suggestions finally comes around to Jane, she says brightly, "I'm starting my new class at Western Community College. It sounds really interesting, and I can upgrade my data-processing skills to get that promotion in the computer department." Everyone congratulates her and then sinks back—thinking of his or her own dull evenings ahead.

3. *Fantasy.* Jane steps forward to get a transfer from the bus driver. She imagines him as the college president in a cap and gown, proudly handing her a diploma. The busful of weary commuters becomes a smiling crowd of well-wishers as she joyfully realizes her dream of finishing college.

4. *Mood.* The camera catches campus scenes of students laughing and joking, helping each other with homework, asking questions in lectures, and cheering a school team. The entire mood is upbeat, aware, alert, fast-paced, and convivial.

5. *Musical.* The strains of "Pomp and Circumstance" are interspersed with collegiate songs and currently popular music while the film shows appropriate scenes from college life matching the music.

6. *Personality symbol.* The president of Western Community College is shown giving a "fireside chat" to a small group of admiring students.

7. *Technical expertise.* A number of job-placement counselors and employment recruiters introduce themselves and talk briefly of the success they've had in placing graduates of Western Community College's evening programs.

8. *Scientific evidence.* An economist presents the statistical evidence of increased earnings potentials for graduates of programs similar to those of Western Community College, and the results of studies on the increased job satisfaction for the graduates.

9. *Testimonial evidence.* The ad shows a number of recent program graduates saying such things as, "This is my new office!" and "This is my new paycheck!"

The communicator must also choose the *tone* for the ad. The ad could be serious, chatty, humorous, and so on. The tone must be appropriate to the target audience and target response desired.

Format elements such as ad size, color, and illustration will make a difference in an ad's impact as well as its cost. A minor rearrangement of elements within the ad can improve its attention-getting power. For example, large ads and four-color ads gain more attention, but these advantages must be weighed against the additional cost.

The importance of specific format elements varies from one medium to another. If the message is to be carried in a print ad, the communicator has to develop the elements of headline, copy, illustration, and color. If the message is to be carried over the radio, the communicator has to carefully choose words and voice qualities (speech rate, rhythm, pitch, articulation). The "sound" of an announcer promoting an educational program has to be different from that of one promoting a used-car dealer. If the message is to be carried on television or given in person, then all of these elements plus body language (nonverbal cues) have to be planned. Presenters have to pay attention to their facial expressions, gestures, dress, posture, and hair style.

A study of television and print advertising found that the ads that scored above average in recall and recognition had the following characteristics: innovation (new product or new uses), "story appeal" (as an attention-getting device), before-and-after illustration, demonstrations, problem solution, and the inclusion of relevant characters that become emblematic of the brand (cartoon figures or actual people, who are not necessarily celebrities).[7]

SELECT MEDIA

Media selection is another major step in advertising planning. Some media thinking should take place before the message-development stage and even before the advertising-budget stage, to determine which media are used by the target audience and which are most efficient costwise in reaching it. This information affects the size of the advertising budget and even the type of appeal to use.

There are three basic steps in the media selection process: choosing among major media categories, selection of specific media vehicles, and timing.

Choosing Among Major Media Categories

The first step is to determine how the advertising budget will be allocated to the major *media categories*. The media planner has to examine the major media categories for their capacity to deliver reach, frequency, and results. Table 15-2 presents profiles of the major advertising media. In order of their advertising volume, they are *newspapers, television, direct mail, radio, magazines,* and *outdoor*. Each major media category has its own advantages and limitations. They are listed after each media category in the table. Media planners make their choice among these major media types by considering the following variables:

1. *Target-audience media habits.* For example, radio and television are the most effective media for reaching a broad teenage audience.
2. *Product.* Media types have different potentialities for demonstration, visualization, explanation, believability, and color. For example, television is the most effective medium for demonstrating a complex product or service.
3. *Message.* A message announcing a public lecture tomorrow will require radio or newspapers. A message containing a great deal of technical data might require specialized magazines or mailings.
4. *Cost.* Television is very expensive, and newspaper advertising is quite expensive. What counts, of course, is the cost per thousand exposures rather than the total cost.

On the basis of these characteristics, the media planner has to decide on how to allocate the given budget to the major media categories.

Selecting Specific Media Vehicles

The next step is to choose the specific media vehicles within each media type that would produce the desired response in the most cost-effective way. Consider a business school that wants to advertise executive education programs in the San Francisco area. Possible vehicles include *The Wall Street Journal, Time, Business Week* (each in specially targeted West Coast editions), the *San Francisco Chronicle,* the *San Francisco Examiner,* the *San Jose Mercury-News,* and so on. The media planner contacts each vehicle or turns to several volumes put out by Standard Rate and Data that provide circulation and cost data for different ad sizes, color options, ad positions, and quantities of insertions. Beyond this, the media planner evaluates the different publications on qualitative characteristics such as credibility, prestige, geographical editioning, occupational editioning, reproduction quality, editorial climate, lead time, and

TABLE 15-2 Profiles of major media categories

MEDIUM	EXAMPLE OF COST (1984)	ADVANTAGES	LIMITATIONS
Newspapers	$21,000 for one-page weekday in the *Chicago Tribune*	Flexibility; timeliness; good local market coverage; broad acceptance; high believability	Short life; poor reproduction quality; small "pass-along" audience
Television	$6,000 for 30 seconds of prime time in Chicago	Combines sight, sound, and motion; appealing to the senses; high attention; high reach	High absolute cost; high clutter; fleeting exposure; less audience selectivity
Direct mail	$800 for names and addresses of 20,000 individuals in a category (on labels but not including printing and postage)	Audience selectivity; flexibility; no ad competition within the same medium; personalization	Relatively high cost; "junk mail" image
Radio	$400 for one minute of prime time in Chicago	Mass use; high geographical and demographic selectivity; low cost	Audio presentation only; lower attention than television; nonstandardized rate structures; fleeting exposure
Magazines	$60,000 for one-page, four-color ad in *Newsweek*	High geographical and demographic selectivity; credibility and prestige; high-quality reproduction; long life; good pass-along readership	Long ad purchase lead time; some waste circulation; no guarantee of position
Outdoor	$7,500 prime billboard cost per month in Chicago	Flexibility; high repeat exposure; low cost; low competition	No audience selectivity; creative limitations

psychological impact. The planner makes a final judgment as to which specific vehicles will deliver the best reach, frequency, and results for the money.

Media planners normally calculate the *cost per thousand persons reached* by a particular vehicle. Table 15-3 presents some examples of vehicles the executive program might use. For comparison, each analysis is for a one-eighth-page ad.

TABLE 15-3   Comparison of three newspapers

VEHICLE	COST	CIRCULATION	COST PER THOUSAND
The Wall Street Journal (Western Edition)	$1,730	427,000	$4.05
The San Francisco Chronicle and San Francisco Examiner—business sections (must be purchased together)	$2,170	695,000	$3.12
The San Jose Mercury and News (morning and evening papers)	$730	228,000	$3.20

In general, the media planner would rank the various publications according to cost per thousand exposures and favor those with the lowest cost per thousand, all things being equal. In this case, the planner would initially favor the *San Francisco Chronicle* and *Examiner*.

The cost-per-thousand criterion provides a crude initial measure of a media vehicle's exposure value. Several adjustments need to be applied to this initial measure. First, the measure should be adjusted for *audience quality*. For an executive-program advertisement, a newspaper read by 1 million executives will have an exposure value of 1 million, but, if read by 1 million retirees, would have close to a zero exposure value. In this instance, the media planner will want to weigh the preponderance of top business executives who read *The Wall Street Journal* against the fact that a smaller percentage of *San Jose Mercury-News* and *San Francisco Chronicle/Examiner* readers happen to be executives. And then the planner must weigh this against the fact that *Wall Street Journal* Western Edition readers are spread over the western states, whereas the readers of the other papers are concentrated in the San Francisco Bay area, where the executive program will be held.

Second, exposure value should be adjusted for the *audience attention probability*. Readers of the San Jose and San Francisco papers may pay more attention to ads than do the readers of *The Wall Street Journal*. Third, the exposure value should be adjusted for the *editorial quality* (prestige and believability) that one vehicle might have over another. Business executives may be more attracted to a program that is advertised in *The Wall Street Journal*.

The business school would also use direct mail to reach executives in area firms. Assuming that appropriate mailing lists are available, direct mail is the most carefully targeted and usually most cost-effective medium. For this reason, colleges purchase mailing lists from American College Testing or use the College Board's Student Search Service.

Developing an effective direct-mail program calls for each of the steps presented in this chapter. Exhibit 15-1 presents guidelines for using direct mail.

EXHIBIT 15-1 Using direct mail effectively

Direct mail is the major medium for reaching potential students and donors. In direct mail, the institution makes an offer to the recipient and seeks to obtain a direct response from him or her.

The format of a direct mailing ranges from a self-mailer brochure to a package that includes a letter, color booklet, application, and return card. Direct-mail experts strongly recommend including a letter in most cases: "Let a brochure do the telling, but a letter do the selling." Mailings that include a letter usually get a much better response rate than identical mailings without a letter.

Institutions that use direct mail skillfully are enthusiastic about its performance. Here are some guidelines for enhancing the effectiveness of direct mail:

1. Target your most promising audiences. The institution should take pains to purchase lists that carefully match the intended target-market segments. To purchase lists that are not well matched can be extremely costly in wasted time, materials, and postage, which could be better used on more appropriate audiences. Prospective-student lists that generate the highest response rate usually correspond closely to the institution's current student profile.

2. Frame the right message for the right audience. The materials must reflect an understanding of the recipients and of how your program or institution can meet their needs. The average person will spend only a few seconds glancing at a piece of third-class mail. The message must pique the reader's interest or it will be discarded.

High school students interviewed about college mailings said they liked letters personalized with their names; concise fact sheets that helped them sort out the colleges that would interest them; prepaid return postcards to ask for information or to indicate they were not interested in the college; attractive envelopes that encouraged students to open them. They did not like first-contact letters that "came on too strong," in some cases virtually guaranteeing admission; initial packets that contained too much material, including application forms and catalogs; and manila envelopes.

3. State the benefits to the reader of making a positive response. People usually respond best to a clearly stated personal benefit of taking the requested action. Direct-mail pieces often reflect some confusion between features and benefits. Features are attributes of the program or institution: "The college is located in downtown Manhattan" is a feature; but "At XY College you can see the best of America's performing arts in your own backyard" is a benefit. The benefits may be stated as testimonials from satisfied students or donors.

To clarify which benefits to offer, the staff preparing the mailing pieces should answer such questions as these: What benefits will people receive from attending this program/making a donation/enrolling in this institution? Why should people come/donate? What will they get out of it?

4. Send the message at an appropriate time. The best-prepared message will be ignored if it comes at the wrong time, whether too early or too late. January, February, August, October, and November are usually the best months for college mailings. Since high school seniors are usually actively filing applications for college in the fall, direct mail from colleges that comes at the beginning of the senior year tends to be the most effective in leading to actual applications than do mailings earlier or later. Continuing education programs usually send out announcements about eight weeks before a scheduled program: Earlier, the mailing may be put away and forgotten; later, the recipient may have already made conflicting commitments. Fund raisers select times that are likely to be attractive to prospective donors, such as end-of-the-year appeals to those who are considering the tax advantages of contributing.

5. Tell the reader what response you want. Some fund raisers and admissions staff feel shy about coming out and asking the reader to take some action, and thereby fail to get any response at all. They hope that the reader will draw the desired conclusion from the materials without being told. The letter and brochure should state the desired response—to send for further information, to write for an application, to send a check—and the response card should be easy to complete and be postage-paid. Gone are the days when educational institutions could fall back on the excuse that if people really cared, they would respond anyway.

6. Plan follow-up mailings or other contact. Don't assume that once is enough. A college admissions office may plan a succession of materials to send to those who ask for more information—a brochure on the student's area of interest, financial aid information, a campus viewbook, application materials, an invitation to the campus, perhaps phone calls from admissions staff. Those who do not respond may receive one or two additional mailings inviting an expression of interest, before the school concludes the recipient is no longer a prospect.

7. Measure your results. Only by keeping track of response rates can the institution determine which lists and which materials are most effective. Those using direct mail should code each response card to indicate from which list the name came. By selection of the best segments to target and the most effective approaches, the costs of direct mail can be greatly reduced over time.

SOURCES: Based on material from Barry Druesne, Jan Harvey, and Mary Zavada, "College Mailings: What Works," *The College Board Review*, Summer 1980, pp. 12–17; Joseph Merante, "Direct Marketing Goes to College," *The College Board Review*, Winter 1980–81, pp. 10–12; and Jeffrey B. Nelson, "Promoting Education by Mail," *CASE Currents*, April 1980, pp. 28–31.

Deciding on Media Timing

The third step in media selection is *timing*. One aspect is that of *seasonal timing*. For most institutions and programs, there is a natural variation in the intensity of interest at different times of the year. Interest in school issues wanes during the summer; high school students may be apathetic about considering colleges until their junior or senior year. Most marketers prefer to spend the bulk of the advertising budget just as natural interest is beginning to ripen in the product class and during the height of interest.

The other aspect is the *short-run timing* of advertising. How should advertising be spaced during a short period—say, a week? Consider these possible patterns: The first is called *burst advertising* and consists of concentrating all the exposures in a very short space of time—say, all in one day. Presumably, this will attract maximum attention and interest, and if recall is good, the effect will last for a while. The second pattern is *continuous advertising*, in which the exposures appear evenly throughout the period. This may be most effective when the audience needs to be continuously reminded. The third pattern is *intermittent advertising*, in which intermittent small bursts of advertising appear in succession, with periods of no advertising in between. This pattern is presumably able to create a little more attention than continuous advertising and yet has some of the reminder advantages of continuous advertising.

EVALUATE ADVERTISING

The final step in the effective use of advertising is that of *advertising evaluation*. The most important components are copy testing, media testing, and expenditure-level testing.

Copy testing can occur both before an ad is put into actual media (copy pretesting) and after it has been printed or broadcast (copy posttesting). The purpose of *ad pretesting* is to make improvements in the advertising copy to the fullest extent prior to its release. There are two major methods of ad pretesting:

1. *Direct ratings.* Here, a panel of target consumers or of advertising experts examines alternative ads and fills out rating questionnaires. Sometimes a single question is raised, such as, "Which of these ads do you think would influence you most to enroll at Pottsville?" Or a more elaborate form consisting of several rating scales may be used, such as the one shown in Figure 15-3. Here the person evaluates the ad's attention strength, read-through strength, cognitive strength, affective strength, and behavioral strength, assigning a number of points (up to a maximum) in each case. The underlying theory is that an effective ad must score high on all these properties if it is ultimately to stimulate taking action. Too often, ads are evaluated only on their attention- or comprehension-creating abilities. At the same time, it must be appreciated that direct-rating methods are judgmental and less reliable than harder evidence of an ad's actual effect on a target consumer. Direct-rating scales help to screen out poor ads rather than to identify great ads.

2. *Portfolio tests.* Here, respondents are given a dummy portfolio of ads and asked to take as much time as they want to read them. After putting them down, the respondents are asked to recall the ads they saw—unaided or aided

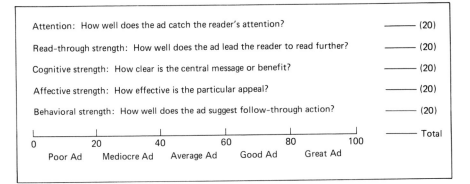

FIGURE 15-3　Rating sheet for ads

by the interviewer—and to play back as much as they can about each ad. The results are taken to indicate an ad's capacity to stand out and to be understood.

There are two popular *ad posttesting methods,* the purpose of which is to assess whether the desired effect is being achieved:

1. *Recall tests* These involve finding people who are regular users of the media vehicle and asking them to recall advertisers and products contained in the issue under study. They are asked to describe everything they can remember. The administrator may or may not aid them in their recall. Recall scores are prepared on the basis of their responses and are used to indicate the power of the ad to be noticed and retained.

2. *Recognition tests* Recognition tests call for sampling the readers of a given issue of the vehicle—say, a magazine—asking them to point out what they recognize as having seen and/or read. For each ad, three different Starch readership scores (named after Daniel Starch, who provides the leading service) are prepared from the recognition data:

- *Noted.* The percentage of readers of magazine who say they had previously seen the advertisement in the particular magazine
- *Seen/associated.* The percentage of readers who say they have seen or read any part of the ad that clearly indicates the names of the school (or program) of the advertiser
- *Read most.* The percentage of readers who not only looked at the advertisement but say that they read more than half the total written material in it.

The Starch organization also furnishes Adnorms—that is, average scores for each product class for the year, and separately for men and women for each magazine, to enable advertisers to evaluate their ads in relation to competitors' ads.

It must be stressed that all these efforts rate the communications effectiveness of the ad and not necessarily its effects on attitude or behavior. The latter are much harder to measure. Most advertisers are satisfied to know their ads have been seen and comprehended and are unwilling to spend additional funds to determine the ads' effectiveness.

Another advertising element that is normally tested is media. *Media testing* seeks to determine whether a given media vehicle is cost-effective in reaching and influencing the target audience. A common way to test a media vehicle is to place a coupon ad and see how many coupons are returned. Similarly, an institution can keep track of media vehicles used, their cost, and the number of inquiries generated by each. Table 15-4 shows part of an inquiry cost analysis for a private school in the Midwest. Another media-testing device is to compare the ad readership scores in different media vehicles as a sign of media effectiveness.

Finally, the advertising-expenditure level itself can be tested. *Expenditure-level testing* involves arranging experiments in which advertising-expenditure levels are varied over similar markets to see the variation in response. A "high-spending" test would consist of spending twice as much money in a territory similar to another to see how much more response (inquiries, applications, and so on) this produces. If the response is only slightly greater in the high-spending territory, it may be concluded, other things being equal, that the lower budget is adequate.

TABLE 15-4 Inquiry cost analysis

REFERRAL SOURCE	TOTAL COST	INQUIRIES	(ENR)	COST/INQ.
Directories:				
Porter Sargent's *Handbook*	$ 195	3	(2)	65.00
Bunting & Lyon's *Blue Book*	425	1		425.00
Publications & Periodicals:				
Vogue magazine	51	16	(1)	3.19
Ebony magazine	none	3	(1)	none
Harper's Bazaar magazine	none	4		none
Illinois Dental Journal	105	1		105.00
Wisconsin Bar Journal	85	1		85.00
Wisconsin Alumni Magazine (2x)	200	1	(1)	200.00
Purdue Alumni Magazine (2x)	230	3		76.67
National Observer	168	22		7.64
Chicago Tribune	361	2		180.50
Radio:				
WGBM-AM	2,625	12	(1)	218.75
WAIT-FM	4,690	10		469.00
WLAK-FM	4,900	2		2450.00
Totals	$14,035	81	6	173

SUMMARY

Advertising consists of nonpersonal forms of communication conducted through paid media under clear sponsorship. While some educators resist the idea of paid advertising, every institution that produces catalogs, bulletins, and direct mail is already engaged in advertising. With careful planning, the institution can make its advertising more effective.

An advertising program calls for five major decisions: setting the advertising objectives, determining the advertising budget, deciding on the message, selecting media, and evaluating advertising effectiveness. The institution should identify the target audience, describe the desired response, and determine the target reach and frequency. The advertising budget can be set based on what is affordable and what is required to accomplish the institution's advertising objectives. The message decision calls for generating messages, evaluating and selecting among them, and executing them effectively. The media decision calls for choosing among major media categories, selecting specific media vehicles, and deciding on media timing. Finally, evaluating advertising results helps to determine the cost-effectiveness of the advertising and to suggest changes in future advertising.

NOTES

[1] See Arthur H. Glogau, "Advertising Higher Education," *College and University Journal*, Spring 1964, pp. 34–39, for examples of higher education advertising through the centuries.

[2] Edward Everett Hale, *Harvard*, Outlook, February 27, 1909, p. 457.

[3] There are several models of buyer readiness states. For a discussion of these models and their implications for advertising, see Richard Vaughn, "The Consumer Mind: How to Tailor Ad Strategies," *Advertising Age*, June 9, 1980, pp. 45–46.

[4] Michael L. Ray, *Marketing Communication and the Hierarchy of Effects* (Cambridge, Mass.: Marketing Science Institute, November 1973).

[5] See John C. Maloney, "Marketing Decisions and Attitude Research," in George L. Baker, Jr., ed., *Effective Marketing Coordination* (Chicago: American Marketing Association, 1961).

[6] Dick Warren Twedt, "How to Plan New Products, Improve Old Ones, and Create Better Advertising," *Journal of Marketing*, January 1969, pp. 53–57.

[7] David Ogilvy and Joel Raphaelson, "Research on Advertising Techniques That Work—and Don't Work," *Harvard Business Review*, July–August 1982, pp. 14–18.

chapter 16

ATTRACTING
AND RETAINING
STUDENTS

Hood College, in western Maryland, blossomed in the 1970s. Enrollments tripled, annual giving shot up more than sevenfold, budgets rollercoasted from surplus to deficit to surplus again, and a graduate school came into being—all signs of vitality that seers would hardly have predicted for a small-town liberal arts college for women, particularly in early 1973.

In that year, Hood's admissions picture was bleak. In seven of the eight preceding years, the number of students enrolled declined. The outlook for the fall term of 1973 was grim, for even the most optimistic estimates indicated that fewer than 160 students would matriculate. Hood's situation was not unique: Many women's colleges were experiencing application declines, and in response, many went coed; but Hood decided to remain a women's college. The key question for Hood was how to stop and reverse the enrollment decline.

Fortunately, in 1973 Hood College enjoyed a reputation as a sound, well-managed institution, providing a quality liberal arts education for young women, and was highly regarded in the region—the Middle Atlantic states and southern New England. Furthermore, Hood revitalized its academic program, incorporating practica, internships, and volunteer work in career-relevant areas. These strengths did not prevent Hood from facing an enrollment decline but did make it better prepared to take action to reverse it.

The new president brought two consultants to campus in April 1973. Their first task was to institute measures to attract every possible prospect for that fall. One stopgap measure involved the design, production, and distribution of a poster-folder, which was sent to selected high schools for posting as well as to every high school student whose name was still on Hood's prospect list. The poster-folder was sent to alumnae to give them an understanding of the college at that time, as well as to urge them to refer the names of prospective students. Under the direction of the consultants, the admissions staff phoned every admitted student who had not yet made a commitment to attend Hood. When the college opened in the fall, 170 of the 176 new students who had made deposits matriculated.

But these were only temporary measures. The real job lay in creating and implementing a program to attract many more students for the next year. The president's goal was to enroll 250 new freshmen in September 1974, an increase of almost 50 percent over 1973. The consultants went to work.

Students provide most educational institutions with their reason for being. Without students, schools would close their doors, not just because tuition revenues would drop but because the schools would no longer have clients to receive the classes, counseling, and other services that the institutions were established to provide. And they would stop graduating new alumni who in future would provide financial support and recognition.

Recruiting students has been going on for millenia. Itinerant teachers in ancient Greece relied on tuition from their student followers. In the nineteenth century, new American land-grant colleges frequently had to promote the advantages of college study among a primarily rural population, using brochures and scholarship offers.

The rapid post–World War II expansion of public colleges, universities, and community colleges, together with increased financial aid and loan programs, encouraged many more high school graduates to consider higher education. During the era of expansion, many institutions were flooded with applicants. The admissions office's task was to select the best applicants for admission.

Times have changed. Many educational institutions now confront threatening demographic realities—including fewer young adults, population migrations from the Northeast and Northwest to the Southwest and West, and shifting demand from the traditional liberal arts to career preparation. Surprisingly, many administrators and admissions officers have been complacent about the implications of the declining student pool and increasing intrainstitutional competition for students. A 1979 College Board survey of 1,463 college admissions officers found that only 14 percent of institutions responding expected enrollments to drop more than 5 percent below 1978 figures.[1] In a separate survey the same year, Dominick et al. found that over 40 percent of the private-college admissions officers did not believe that their institutions would be strongly affected by decreasing high school enrollments. The authors concluded that "the optimism of the private colleges seems inconsistent with current trends and may be more a reflection of wishful thinking."[2]

This complacency is now being replaced with increased attention to re-

SOURCES: Donna Shoemaker, "Institutional Strategies: Hood College," *Educational Record*, Winter 1982, pp. 53–57; and "A Case History of How a College Increased Its Freshman Enrollment 100% in One Year," *Insights*, June–July 1974, pp. 1–14.

cruiting. Over 90 percent of college admissions officers in the Dominick survey agree that "the admissions office will more strongly rely on marketing techniques to attract students" and that "the college will be involved in more aggressive recruiting strategies.[3] Four out of five colleges in a College Board survey reported that admissions staff visit high schools "very frequently" to recruit students.[4] Other frequently used activities include direct mail and attendance at college nights and college fairs. Table 16-1 shows reported increases in the use of many recruitment tools between 1975 and 1980. Over half of all institutions are preparing new promotional literature, and over one-third are increasing the recruiting budget above inflation, increasing travel, buying national mailing lists, and conducting special marketing research studies.[5]

When enrollment starts to decline, colleges usually adopt one of three responses. Some proceed to do more of what they have been doing in the past: The admissions director hires more admissions counselors to make more high school visits; the brochures are printed in four colors with new photographs, and more are mailed. This approach may temporarily attract more interest but is doomed to failure from the start. This we would term a "sales" approach, focusing on ways to "sell" the product of a college education.

A second group of schools will take the "sales" approach a step further. They will turn to the "hard sell," believing that since heavy media advertising seems to sell beer and cake mix, it will have a tremendous effect on applications and enrollment. The school may even come up with gimmicks and "deals" to attract more of the available students to attend. As part of the "hard sell" approach, admissions counselors are urged to try to convince each prospect that the school can deliver exactly what he or she wants. In desperation, some schools turn to recruiting wealthy if not always academically able foreign students, and/or hire aggressive recruiters who receive commissions for each student who enrolls.

The result of a "hard-sell" approach is often an advertising glut, potential applicants turned off on the school, and disappointed enrollees who will soon drop out and discourage their friends from applying. Moreover, the admissions director will be looking for new admissions staff, since the professional admissions counselors will balk at misrepresenting what the school has to offer. In fact, if the school has so little to offer prospective students, the trustees and top administration should take a searching look at the school's mission and programs and consider if it should redirect its efforts or even close down.

A third group of schools will turn to a marketing approach. They conduct marketing research to understand students' wants and needs. They provide programs and services that match the institution's mission and resources as well as student needs. They schedule and locate, price, and promote these offerings to attract and serve students' needs. These institutions reflect a commitment to educate and serve.

The preceding chapters have presented the marketing approach. In this chapter, we consider the steps in applying marketing to student recruitment,

TABLE 16-1 Changes in recruitment program, 1975–1980 (percentage of admissions directors reporting increased activity)

ACTIVITY	PUBLIC RESEARCH UNIVERSITIES (119)	PUBLIC 4-YEAR COLLEGES (354)	PUBLIC 2-YEAR COLLEGES (909)	PRIVATE UNIVERSITIES (65)	PRIVATE 4-YEAR COLLEGES (812)	PRIVATE 2-YEAR COLLEGES (238)	ALL INSTITUTIONS
Prepare new promotional literature	54	58	38	64	66	60	54
Increase budget (above inflation)	29	36	27	57	55	80	43
Recruit adult students	39	44	48	14	30	20	38
Increase travel	31	48	35	57	32	50	37
Conduct special market research	33	26	20	50	51	40	35
Involve academic department in recruitment	44	36	23	14	38	50	33
Buy national mailing lists	45	33	16	36	43	30	31
Contact special groups (church, youth)	18	25	20	17	38	40	29
Recruit part-time students	26	34	29	8	21	30	27
Recruit minorities	62	41	15	36	23	20	25
Use alumni in recruiting	24	22	4	71	36	20	22
Attend workshops	15	21	16	23	27	20	22
Increase staff	19	27	8	36	31	30	21
Award no-need financial aid	24	18	12	15	17	30	17
Set up cooperative recruitment programs	11	18	11	14	20	20	16
Set up special admissions task force	39	26	7	15	20	10	16
Recruit handicapped	15	13	20	15	1	0	11
Use outside consultants	0	5	7	17	11	20	9
Recruit foreign students	3	11	4	29	13	10	9
Recruit veterans	10	15	10	0	4	0	8
Recruit U.S. students from overseas schools	0	3	0	21	8	10	5

SOURCE: 1981 National Enrollment Study. Cited in J. Victor Baldridge, Frank R. Kemerer, and Kenneth C. Green, *The Enrollment Crisis: Factors, Actors, and Impacts*, AAHE-ERIC/Higher Education Research Report No. 3, 1982 (Washington, D.C.: American Association for Higher Education, 1982), pp. 32–33.

from identifying problems through designing programs for student retention. We will use Hood's experience and those of other institutions to illustrate the process. Although most of the examples are drawn from colleges and universities, the underlying issues and the critical tasks are similar for private elementary and secondary institutions.

This chapter presents the steps in the student-recruitment process, and then discusses ways to measure and increase student satisfaction to improve retention.

THE STUDENT-RECRUITMENT PROCESS

The student-recruitment process consists of the following steps:

1. Identify enrollment problems and needs in relation to resources and mission.
2. Define enrollment goals and objectives in line with institutional strategy.
3. Conduct research to segment the potential student market, to identify target markets, to understand the student decision process, and to determine market size and potential.
4. Determine the marketing strategy for recruitment, including the target market(s), marketing mix, and marketing expenditure level.
5. Plan and implement action programs.
6. Evaluate results and procedures, including cost-effectiveness of recruitment efforts and satisfaction of enrolled students.

We will consider each step in turn.

Identify Problems

The first step is to identify the institution's problems as they may affect the institution's ability to attract and retain students. Declining enrollment is rarely the only problem an educational institution faces, but other problems are often overlooked until a significant drop in enrollment galvanizes the administration into full consciousness of the institution's plight. The curriculum may be outdated, or nearby institutions may have built higher-quality, competitive programs, but these may not be perceived as serious threats until they take their toll on enrollment.

To get a picture of the institution's application and enrollment situation, the trends should be graphed. Figure 16-1 shows Hood College's total applicants, total acceptances, and total new students enrolled for 15 years. The highest number of applications and acceptances came in 1965, after which the number of applicants began to decline sharply at Hood and most other women's colleges. The graph shows that as applications declined, a higher percentage were admitted. The admissions staff worked doubly hard to keep in contact with those admitted to encourage them to enroll.

FIGURE 16-1   Applicants, acceptances, and matriculants at Hood
College, 1960–1974

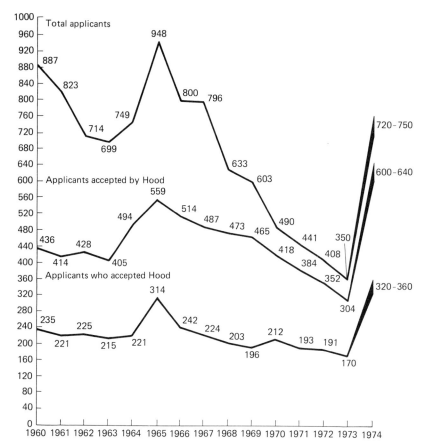

SOURCE: "A Case History of How a College Increased Its Freshman Enrollment 100% in One Year," *Insights*, June–July 1974, p. 2.

What can the college expect if no corrective action is taken? The college should make enrollment estimates based on the most objective, hard-headed data available, perhaps indicating two or three alternative scenarios. Figure 16-2 projects what would happen to Hood's enrollment if the trends of the previous five years were to continue. The modest increases in new transfer students could not compensate for continued declines in new freshmen. Corrective action was necessary if Hood was to regain the enrollment levels of the past.

Application and enrollment trends and projections can help document the extent of the enrollment problem, but alone they shed little light on the problems contributing to the decline. In Chapter 6, we presented approaches

FIGURE 16-2   Projections of enrollment trends

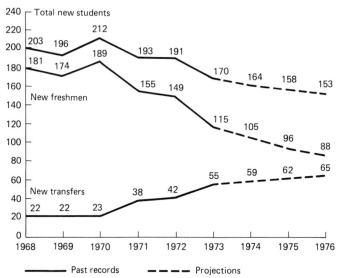

SOURCE: "A Case History of How a College Increased Its Freshman Enrollment 100% in One Year," *Insights*, June–July 1974, p. 3.

to assessing the institution's strengths, weaknesses, threats, and opportunities. In Chapter 18, we shall present guidelines for auditing the institution's marketing effectiveness. The institution's leaders must thoroughly review the findings of these analyses to guide necessary changes in curriculum, services, teaching quality, and other aspects in addition to admissions.

Hood College had already established internships, field experiences, and special programs to give students practical exposure to various academic disciplines and related careers. A biology major might intern at the Frederick Cancer Research Center of the National Cancer Institute; the dietetics major could get practical experience at the Johns Hopkins Hospital in Baltimore; political-science majors could participate in field study with various federal agencies in Washington, D.C. (Later, in the mid-1970s, the college added a professional dimension to each liberal arts area.) These curriculum changes required the joint efforts of faculty and administrators.

The decision to remain a women's college did create some problems for Hood. With a declining applicant pool overall, women's colleges found their student market shrinking. Many became coeducational by admitting men or by merging with all-male colleges. Those choosing to remain women's colleges had to contend with a growing student preference for coeducational schools. Forty-four percent of Hood's "lost prospects" said that Hood's major disadvantage was that it was not coed; only 8 percent saw it as an advantage of attending Hood.

Recognizing these problems and confirming the college's mission as a women's college provided a basis for moving to the next step, defining goals and objectives.

Define Goals and Objectives

The school's administration must decide on appropriate recruitment and admissions goals and objectives in line with its overall institutional strategy. For example, a college's goal may be to maintain the number and quality of students enrolled; to increase enrollment; to improve the quality of admitted students; to attract a certain number of students to a new program; or some other goal. A school's specific situation and goals will shape its admissions objectives and specific actions to achieve them.

In Hood's case, admissions had become increasingly less selective over the years preceding 1973. The president's stated objective was to enroll 250 new freshmen in September 1974. The longer-term objective was to increase the total number of new students (freshmen, transfer, and continuing education) to 350, the capacity of the existing physical facilities. Then, by increasing the number of applicants, the college hoped to become progressively more selective.

Setting enrollment objectives raises three questions. First, what is the institution's optimal level of student enrollment? This number is often based on historical experience or on the highest number ever enrolled. As long as dormitory space and other housing do not impose constraints on size, tuition-dependent schools often yearn to accommodate as many tuition-paying students as possible by increasing class size.

The second question is, What level of enrollment can the institution realistically expect to draw? Setting realistic enrollment objectives requires good data and careful analysis. The initial enrollment objective may be based on strong optimism, but the operational enrollment objective must be based on strong data.

Third, what level of student quality do we want? Most schools want to attract academically talented students, but many do not have the faculty, curricula, and other attributes that permit them to compete with academically elite institutions for these students. Non-elite colleges need to be realistic about whom they can serve well, keeping in mind that an effective college academic program can make a tremendous contribution to students who may enter with weak academic backgrounds and skills. For example, Erskine, a Presbyterian College in South Carolina, enrolls students with average SAT scores in the mid-to-high 400s. It graduates three-fourths of its entering freshmen, 32 percent of whom continue to graduate and professional schools.[6]

When application rates are softening may be a constructive time to consider these questions. Top administration and the admissions office should review the institution's resource commitments (people and buildings), along with financial, demographic, and other marketing-relevant data that bear on these decisions. The result should be a realistic target enrollment and quality level to guide planning for housing, student services, faculty hiring, and course planning and scheduling, as well as admissions.

In addition to setting goals for the number and quality of entering students, the admissions director should consider other recruiting and admissions goals and objectives. Hood's admissions office established five promotion goals:

1. To change the image of the college from a good traditional girls' school to an exciting, high-quality college for women, which emphasizes the new women's concerns and careers in a personable atmosphere
2. To more effectively communicate the "new" image of the college to a target audience in particular market segments
3. To improve the publications program—better appeals and more information, expanded use of printed materials
4. To expand the inquiry base through increased mailings, posters, advertising, special events, career workshops, counselor luncheons, and alumnae
5. To better promote financial aid, early acceptance, transfer programs, and career-oriented curricula[7]

To carry out these goals, the admissions office established specific objectives— school visits, campus events, interviews, and professional training, among others. This listing of goals and objectives, combined with marketing research, provides the basis for setting marketing strategy.

Conduct Marketing Research

Marketing research can help the institution answer such questions as these:

- What have been our rates of applications, acceptances, and enrollments over the past several years?
- What have our yield ratios been?
- What is the market size and potential?
- Who are our primary and secondary markets?
- What are the characteristics of our current students?
- What are the characteristics of applicants who are accepted and do not enroll?
- What sources of information do they use in the college decision process?
- Who are the college's competitors?

Many admissions offices already have vast amounts of data on inquiries, school visits made, number of interviews, applications, and so forth. These data are often ignored when times are good; and when application rates slump, the admissions staff is often so pressured to "do something" that the data continue to gather dust while the staff makes more high school visits. These data are important indicators of what the institution has done and with what effect, and they must receive close scrutiny. Hood's admissions-office staff pulled together

records on the number of inquiries, applications, deposits, rejections, acceptances, matriculants, high school and junior college visits, campus interviews,
annual reports, monthly breakdowns, and any other data relevant to the admissions picture. Where unavailable, the data were reconstructed as closely as
possible. Past admissions efforts were reviewed. [8]

The data must be compiled and presented in a format that can be used
in decision making. This usually means graphing it to show trends over the
past five to ten years. The school will want to graph (as with Figure 16-1 on
Hood College) the number of applicants, acceptances, and matriculants. In
addition, the admissions staff can easily calculate the various *yield ratios* and
graph those—number of acceptances divided by number of applications, number of matriculants divided by number of acceptances, and number of matriculants divided by number of applications. With a personal computer and spread
sheet and graphics software, these data can be recorded and displayed quickly.

Where tuition revenues are based on number of courses rather than
number of students, the admissions staff should also review trends in the total
number of credit hours taken each term over the past several years. For example, the part-time M.B.A. program in a university school of business found
enrollment numbers down, but the total number of credit hours was equal to
that of the previous year—indicating that although there were fewer students,
they were taking more units. Schools with significant part-time enrollments
should graph the average number of units per student over a period of several
years to determine trends in course loads. If a school wants to maintain a certain
level of tuition revenue and the average number of units per student is dropping, the school must either encourage students to take more courses or recruit
additional students to close the gap.

Analyzing the characteristics of current students helps identify where the
college should recruit and what types of students it is likely to attract. As a
rule, a college will have an easier time attracting students like its current
students than attracting prospects who are significantly different. From student
records, the institution can create a profile of current students by age, sex,
place of residence, prior school attended, academic background, test scores,
and academic performance at the college. A residential college can usually
identify its primary and secondary markets by noting the locations and characteristics of the high schools from which applicants come. Much of these data
can come from summary records from the College Board combined to show
differences in yield over several years.

An institution's *primary market* is one from which it receives a large
number of applications over time. The primary market may be defined in terms
of individual secondary schools, a number of secondary schools, or a given
geographical area. Typically, a high percentage of primary-market candidates
who submit applications are accepted and elect to attend the institution. Often
an institution will find that its primary market is located within a 300-mile
radius of the institution. A *secondary market* is one from which the school has

received a steady flow of applications over a period of three to five years but from which few of the admitted students have enrolled. The secondary market is substantially larger than the primary market, but the yield rate is lower.[9]

Colleges that use the Scholastic Aptitude Test of the College Entrance Examination Board can obtain detailed analyses of applicant and enrollment data. The College Board provides each participating school with a 24-page Admissions Yield and Retention Report that describes the school's yield ratios with respect to characteristics of the school's applicants, accepted students, and enrollees and those of college-bound high school seniors in the region. With this information, the school can examine its success in attracting students. The report also includes comparative data on yield ratios with other colleges of the same type. One summary report lists the top 70 high schools from which applicants come, along with sex, SAT mean scores, high-school percentile rank, estimated parental contribution, and chosen area of study. This report identifies the high schools that should receive admissions-office attention. A comparison with past years would reveal changes in the importance of specific feeder high schools. Another report helps define the college's competition by ranking the 35 colleges most frequently applied to by applicants to the college. The American College Testing Program provides similar reports for colleges that use its score results.

In summary, the most important information for recruiting and admissions purposes may already exist in some form. The task is to locate it, organize it, express it in usable form (often graphically), and then draw conclusions from the data that can guide the choice of actions. The most critical step is to implement the plan that grows out of the data. Too often, the available data are ignored, and planning is based on hunches rather than on available information.

Although existing data can answer many questions, institutional research is needed to answer questions that will affect recruiting strategy. The institution will want to know what attracted some students to apply and enroll, whereas others chose to attend another school. Many institutions survey admitted students and those who inquired, whether or not they followed through with an application. Typical surveys ask for respondents' personal and academic characteristics; their evaluation of the school in comparison with specific other colleges to which they applied; their evaluation of various contacts with the school and other sources of information; and a comparison of financial aid offers.[10]

Regardless of the group surveyed, the questionnaire should be carefully developed to be clear and complete and should be reproduced in a professional and easy-to-answer manner. Survey data can be analyzed using the widely available Statistical Package for the Social Sciences (SPSS) or, in the case of personal computers, other survey-analysis software.

Hood College conducted a survey as part of its admissions research program:

A key part of the market research was an opinion-and-attitudes questionnaire that produced an 87% return from 1,000 students and young women who had inquired about Hood in 1972–73. The questions were framed by professionals so the answers would best reveal the respondents' evaluation of the weaknesses and strengths of the college as well as the factors that played a part in the candidate's decision— whether that decision was for or against the college.

This questionnaire was administered, in written form, to freshmen and upper-classmen (keeping the responses of these two groups separate). By phone it was administered to a list of "lost acceptances" and "lost inquiries" to see what motivated these women to turn down Hood for another college.[11]

With the results of such surveys, the school can prepare a profile description of the students who choose to attend and those who go elsewhere. This *student profile* summarizes the student characteristics that will influence the recruiting and admissions process. If the college is satisfied with students who fit the current profile, the admissions staff may decide to continue recruiting in the same or similar high schools. The college may believe it can take steps to attract and serve those who now attend other colleges; or it may conclude that those students would be dissatisfied and/or would not be good prospects for the college. If it finds it is losing good prospects, the college will want to determine what changes in recruiting, financial aid, academic programs, or other areas would be required to successfully attract them, and then institute changes where appropriate. To attract students who are significantly different from the current profile, the college will need to segment and select target markets, then develop an attractive marketing mix to reach and serve each target market.

The institution will also want to carry out studies of the factors that weigh most heavily in students' application and enrollment decisions, of who has an influence on such decisions, of rates of retention and of transfer to other institutions, of the relative attractiveness of competing institutions, and of other factors that bear on student attraction and retention. To attract participants to short courses and special events, the institution should ask current participants what media they use, in order to identify places to promote future programs.

The college will also want to know the size of its potential student market by various categories, discussed in Chapter 8. The potential market for any one institution will be determined by numerous institutional characteristics and by demographic realities. A college that draws only recent high school graduates must contend with a pool that is declining overall. If the college offers only limited financial aid, it must compete for an even smaller student pool. For these reasons, many educational institutions are striving to identify new markets for their programs.

Determine Marketing Strategy

Marketing strategy includes selecting the most promising target markets; setting the marketing mix of product, price, place, and promotion; and setting the marketing expenditure level. Once the strategy is determined, the school can plan for implementation.

Selecting Target Markets. If recruiting resources were unlimited, every institution could attempt to appeal to each potential student. In practice, such a strategy is unworkable and wasteful, since recruiting is expensive and each institution can serve only a small percentage of the total available market. Instead, each institution focuses its attention on one or a few target-market segments. At the undergraduate level, state universities focus their recruiting on graduates of high schools in their states. At the graduate level, specific departments may target the best graduating seniors in those disciplines from colleges in the region or the entire nation. Church-sponsored institutions usually target church members. For example, North Park College in Chicago is the only college in the United States under the auspices of the Evangelical Covenant Church and recruits church members nationwide.

Target-market selection requires a thorough understanding of the topics presented in earlier chapters, including characteristics of current students, consumer decision making, key demographic and other macroenvironmental trends, and the institution's mission, resources, and goals. The institution must then segment its current and potential markets and determine where it can best meet the needs of potential students. Existing data, together with additional marketing research, can reveal the most important student characteristics and the sources of information upon which students base their decisions to apply and enroll. This understanding is essential for planning a sound recruitment program.

Hood College's decision to remain a women's college guided its choice of three target markets. First, the college continued to seek recent high-school-graduate women who would be attracted to a women's college for "the modern woman." Second, the college set up a continuing education program to attract older women students. Third, it began an intensive program for Hispanic women, often underrepresented in higher education. In addition, the college now enrolls some local men as commuter students, but this is not a target market for Hood.

Setting the Marketing Mix. Previous chapters have discussed the four elements of the marketing mix: product, price, distribution, and promotion. Each selected target market may require a different marketing mix, or at least some modification of the basic marketing mix. For example, when Hood decided to serve Hispanic women, it built on a strong Spanish department and a three-year grant from the Fund for Improvement of Post-Secondary Education to develop a bilingual, bicultural curriculum and to sensitize the campus to the special needs of these women.

Developing the appropriate marketing mix must involve the whole institution. To be attractive to prospects, an educational institution must provide a sound and appropriate educational program, at a price students and their families are willing and able to pay (with assistance as necessary), in a reasonably attractive place. All these features need to be communicated to prospective students in a timely, interesting, and accurate manner.

Often this communications task is deemed the only responsibility of the admissions office. In fact, the chief admissions officer should be involved in institutional planning that affects programs, pricing, and distribution. The admissions officer knows the school's enrollment history and trends and has information directly from students about their desires and impressions. He or she should also have a sound grasp of societal trends that may affect enrollment. Ignoring these insights in the planning process leads to situations like this:

When the first information-science major in the country was developed at a private college some time ago, the enthusiastic chairman of the department anticipated that several hundred freshmen would be attracted to it the first year. The admissions director suggested that 25 would be more realistic; and the matriculated statistic in September proved to be 23. While the chairman knew that information science was a good program for eventual employment, he did not realize that high school counselors were not yet briefed that this major dealt with computers; parents were not prepared to pay for a course of study they did not understand; and, for the most part, high school seniors had already made other career and college choices by the time the program was announced. [12]

Had the admissions director been closely involved in planning, he could have pointed out the need to train admissions staff and high school counselors on information science and could have curbed the enthusiasm of the department chairman.

The admissions office typically controls the communications function as it relates to recruiting students. The admissions staff will prepare (or direct the preparation of) brochures, letters, and other mailings to prospects and applicants; attend college fairs and college nights; arrange campus visits and make visits to high schools; and maintain contact with high school and community college personnel who may advise or refer students. (Private precollegiate institutions will use variations of these activities.)

The admissions office must plan an appropriate, cost-effective communications program for each target market. Figure 16-3 shows the questions the planners should consider in preparing the recruitment strategy. A community college mandated to serve the entire community will probably send periodic mailings to all area households, in addition to holding information sessions for high school seniors, reentry students, and other defined groups. Some schools that enjoy high demand will do no advertising or direct mail to prospects and will not attend college fairs; instead, they will emphasize alumni and admissions-office contacts with the best applicants. A school launching a new program needs to identify the best prospects and determine the best ways to reach them.

Setting the Marketing Expenditure Level. The admissions-office budget should be set to cover the necessary marketing tasks to accomplish the institution's admissions goals. A 1983 national survey found that the average cost

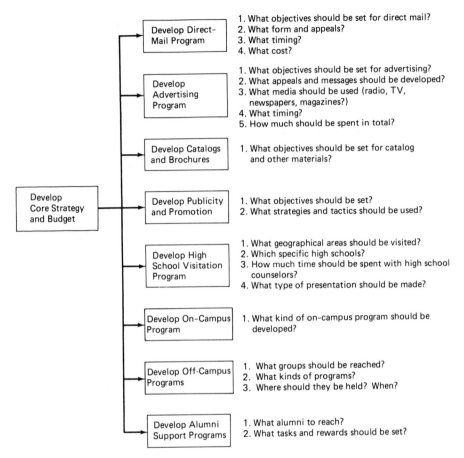

FIGURE 16-3 Elements of core strategy

of recruiting and admitting one college student in 1981–82 was $151, up from $128 in 1980–81. Selective liberal arts colleges spent the most, an average of $709, private colleges averaged $455, and public colleges spent $64.[13] These costs included salaries of admissions directors, counselors, and other staff; and travel, telephone, printing, supplies, postage, and other items.

As the potential applicant pool shrinks, each institution must work harder to attract students. Rising costs of printing and postage are also a factor. The admissions director and staff must determine which recruiting activities are most important and allocate funds accordingly. By the same token, an institution can rarely afford to "squeeze" the admisssions-office budget without serious risks to enrollment numbers and/or quality.

Plan and Implement Action Programs

The admissions office needs to translate its strategy into action programs, including what will be done, who will do it, and when. The action plan answers each of the questions shown in Figure 16-3 in detail, as well as any other specific institutional concerns. The action plan should provide for periodic reviews of how well the plan is succeeding, so changes can be made where indicated.

Planning should lead to improved performance. To be useful, the plan must be carried out in a smooth, professional, and timely manner. The plan should be appropriate for the institution and for the target markets it is designed to attract and serve.

Handling Inquiries. The admissions office will need smooth procedures for responding to inquiries. The simple mailing of a catalog and application forms has, for many schools, been replaced by a series of publications, direct mailings, phone conversations, campus visits, and personal contacts. Office staff should be prepared to respond promptly and thoughtfully to requests for information. This process should be periodically reviewed. One college sent inquiries to the campus computer center, where the data-entry operator was to code and enter records on inquiries, then mail out application packets. However, the operator was not briefed on the need to send packets out on a daily basis, and by November, she was six weeks late in mailing out 1,600 applications. Needless to say, the admissions office took back the task of mailing applications.[14]

The Admissions Decision Process. The timetable for admissions decisions varies by type of institution. The most selective universities require completed applications early in the year and announce admissions decisions in late spring. Other private institutions have implemented "immediate-decision" programs to speed the review and notification process and thereby encourage qualified applicants to enroll:

About a quarter of Bard College's applicants participate in sessions held on the Bard campus and in several other cities. Each applicant brings a completed application, test scores, and an essay and participates in a two-hour faculty-led seminar based on assigned readings. While students are involved in the seminar, Bard admissions officers review the applicants' files. Following lunch, each student has a half-hour interview with an admissions counselor, who concludes with the school's admissions decision. This admissions approach gives prospective students a sense of what education at Bard will be like and permits both applicants and admissions officers to explore the match between the student and the college.

Coordination with Financial Aid. Cost is a major factor in the college decision process. The admissions staff needs to work closely with the campus financial aid office to ensure that prospects receive and complete aid forms and that each eligible student is offered an equitable and attractive aid package. Some institutions are implementing an *enrollment management* approach in which admissions, financial aid, and the registrar's office coordinate all aspects of the process as a team.

Follow-up. Applicants should be notified of acceptance or rejection as promptly as possible in accordance with announced procedures. Some schools use a "rolling admissions" process, making and sending admissions decisions throughout the year; others have one or more notification dates.

The admissions process does not conclude when notifications have been sent. The school needs to encourage accepted applicants to enroll and to keep the school informed of any changes in plans. It also needs to provide information about housing, orientation schedules, advising, and registration. Additional timely information about the institution and its programs may help students confirm their decision to enroll. Rollins College in Florida helps freshmen preregister by telephone in early June with a faculty advisor. At the same time, students can get answers to other questions about the college. These and other follow-up efforts can encourage the transition from admitted student to enrolled and committed student.

What of the applicants the school does not accept? By applying, applicants are expressing a serious interest in the school. How rejected applicants are treated shapes their future image of the school and what they say to others about it. A responsive, marketing-oriented school notifies rejected applicants as promptly as possible so that they can make other plans. Some rejected applicants will want to discuss reasons why they were not accepted or to "plead their case."

Evaluate Results and Procedures

Five types of evaluation should be routinely carried out: First, the admissions office will want to review the *total number and quality of applications* received and the institution's success in meeting its enrollment number and quality objectives. Figure 16-4 shows a recruitment-yield pyramid that illustrates the admissions office's effectiveness at each stage in the recruitment process.

Second, the admissions office should *survey admitted students* who enroll and those who do not enroll to find out how they differ in demographic characteristics, interests, abilities, and perceptions of the institution.

Third, the *cost-effectiveness* of advertising, school visits, and other recruitment efforts should be evaluated. An evaluation of advertising effectiveness is shown in the preceding chapter. In a similar manner, the school can evaluate travel expenditures by how many contacts were made, how many applied and

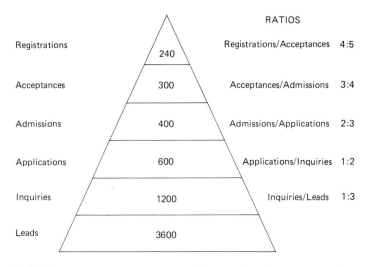

FIGURE 16-4   Recruitment-effort evaluation

enrolled, and the salary and travel costs involved. Of course, recruitment efforts are likely to have a wider effect than such evaluations can reveal. For instance, visits to high schools may increase the visibility of the college with younger students and with guidance counselors, and the results may not be measurable for a few years.

Bradley University surveyed matriculants and nonmatriculants about the importance of various recruiting activities and used these ratings to evaluate the cost-effectiveness of each technique. For example, Bradley considered two recruiting programs that would each cost about $5,000 a year: purchasing a toll-free telephone line, and flying high school counselors to the campus. The survey results showed that 69 percent of students think that college response to their questions is important, whereas only 38 percent believe that the high school counselor's advice is important. On this basis, the admissions office decided to install a toll-free line.[15]

Fourth, the admissions director and staff should review their *recruiting procedures* qualitatively. Improved procedures might reduce paperwork and delays for applicants, identify new information needs or formats, provide an enhanced image for the institution, and/or increase staff time for other tasks. The review may also suggest places where additional training would enhance staff confidence and performance.

Fifth, the admissions office should later review data on *student satisfaction, academic performance*, and *retention* to assess how well the students they admit match what the institution offers. Satisfaction and retention are considered in the following section.

IMPROVING RETENTION

Retaining matriculated students is just as important as attracting and enrolling them. Students are not a captive audience. Each matriculated student renews his or her enrollment decision every term. The busy or dissatisfied student may cut back on the number of courses or drop out completely. Nondegree students may decide to take courses at a different institution each term or to take none at all.

In a recent survey, 85 percent of college presidents agreed that "[their] institution should devote more attention and resources to the issue of student retention and reducing the dropout rate."[16] Presidents of colleges with enrollment problems identified student attrition as the number-one cause.[17]

Attrition rates vary by type of institution. Figure 16-5 shows freshman attrition rates for seven types of institutions. The 1981 National Enrollment Survey and other findings lead to the following conclusions:

- In four-year institutions, roughly half the students who enter never graduate from the same institution. Among the half who leave the institution, however, a substantial number transfer to other colleges and eventually finish. Still, roughly 30 percent of the freshmen entering four-year colleges never finish a bachelor's degree.

FIGURE 16-5 Freshmen attrition by institution type

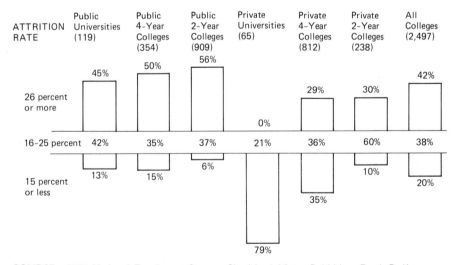

SOURCE: 1981 National Enrollment Survey. Cited in J. Victor Baldridge, Frank R. Kemerer, and Kenneth C. Green, *The Enrollment Crisis: Factors, Actors, and Impacts*, AAHE-ERIC/Higher Education Research Report No. 3, 1982 (Washington, D.C.: American Association for Higher Education, 1982), p. 36.

- Community colleges have a much higher dropout rate than four-year institutions have. Approximately 60 percent of the entering freshmen in community colleges never complete an associate degree, and over 80 percent never complete a bachelor's degree.
- Private four-year institutions have slightly higher graduation rates for students five years after admission than do public four-year institutions (roughly 53 percent).
- The more prestigious and selective the institution, the lower its attrition rate. Very selective institutions have low dropout rates; at the other end, "open-admission," unselective community colleges have extremely high dropout rates.
- Institutions that are heavily populated by commuter students have higher dropout rates, and institutions with strong residential dormitory programs have lower dropout rates. [18]

The retention issue is important for several reasons. A responsive institution wants to create as much satisfaction as it reasonably can. Pragmatically, satisfied students are less likely to drop out. Considering the limited pool of potential college students and the effort and other costs of recruitment, the school should make a concerted effort to retain students who, with some help, could succeed at the institution.

The institutional costs of attrition are substantial. The institution loses the tuition revenue and enrollment-dependent public subsidies. A dropout may mean an unused dormitory space and loss of a year's dormitory fees. Serious dissatisfaction leads not only to a high dropout rate but also to a weakened institutional image among prospective candidates, making recruitment even more difficult. The admissions staff must seek out and enroll more students to replace those who drop out, often accepting weaker candidates to meet enrollment quotas. Four-year public institutions (depending on type) must enroll from 160 to 311 freshmen in order to graduate 100 seniors. The range among private four-year colleges is 120 to 192. [19] The importance of creating more satisfaction and improving retention cannot be overemphasized.

In Chapter 2, we introduced the concept of satisfaction and discussed its relationship to the goals of the institution. In this section, we present specific ways to assess student satisfaction. Then we discuss the steps in a successful retention program.

Assessing Student Satisfaction

Student satisfaction, in spite of its central importance, can be difficult to measure. Students will differ in what characteristics of the school are related to their satisfaction and how much of each characteristic they feel is essential. Some students may be disappointed because the foreign language department is weak; others will be oblivious to the foreign language department but be tremendously disappointed if the school's football team is on probation and can't play in bowl games.

To overcome the difficulty of measuring satisfaction directly, some institutions look primarily at objective measures related to enrollment. They reason that if a student enrolls and stays, the student is probably satisfied. Such schools will look at the following measures:

- Rates of increase in number of applications and in percentage of those admitted who matriculate.
- The school's share of the relevant student market. For example, of all National Merit Scholars living west of the Rockies, what percent chose this school? Or, of all the schoolage children of families belonging to this parish, what percentage are sending their children to the parish school?
- The number of well-qualified children of alumni who enroll and the number of families in which two or more children choose to attend the school. These measures may indicate high satisfaction.
- The school's retention rate. Of those students who matriculate, what percentage stay through graduation?

These indirect, objective measures are important, but by themselves they are insufficient to assess satisfaction. When a school has no competitors or when there are more applicants than it can serve, these measures may be high and yet not reflect actual satisfaction, because students have no alternatives. Even when a school does not have a monopoly, applications and enrollments may remain strong for a while even after satisfaction has started to decline, because of students' inertia. Dissatisfied students may decide to "stick it out" because they are close to graduating or because transferring would be difficult or costly.

The school needs to supplement these indirect measures of satisfaction with other information obtained from students themselves. We will turn to these other measures of satisfaction next.

Student Panels. A small group of students may be selected to make up a panel that will be sampled from time to time about their feelings toward the school or any of its services. Panel members may volunteer, be named by the student government as liaisons to the administration, or be selected at random and invited to participate. Some provision is usually made to rotate membership on the panel to get fresh views from new people. Such panels often provide valuable information. At the same time, the panel may represent only the views of those who are involved enough to serve on a panel. It is even possible that those who will serve are more loyal to the school and thus less likely to see its faults.

Student Satisfaction Surveys. Some schools conduct periodic surveys of student satisfaction. They send questionnaires or telephone a random sample of students to determine what they like and dislike about the school. Three types of questions for measuring student satisfaction will be described here.

Directly reported satisfaction. A school can distribute a questionnaire to a representative sample of students, asking them to state their felt satisfaction with the school as a whole and with specific components. Students can be interviewed in person, on the telephone, or through a mail questionnaire.

To measure felt satisfaction, the questionnaire would contain questions of the following form:

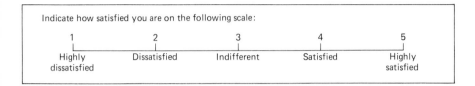

The student responds by circling the number on the scale from 1 to 5 that describes his or her level of satisfaction. Although five intervals are used in this example, some scales use as few as three intervals, others as many as eleven. The numbers assigned to the intervals are arbitrary, except that each succeeding number is higher than the preceding one. There is no implication that these are unit distances—that the respondent who marks 5, "highly satisfied," is twice as satisfied as the student who marks 3, "indifferent."

When the results are in, a histogram can be prepared showing the percentage of students who fall into each group for each questionnaire item. Of course, students within any group, such as the "highly dissatisfied" group, may have very different intensities of dissatisfaction, ranging from feelings of mild disappointment with the school to intense anger.

If the histogram is highly skewed to the left, with the preponderance of students dissatisfied, the school is in deep trouble. If the histogram is bell-shaped, the school has some satisfied and some dissatisfied students, and a large group that is more or less neutral. If the histogram is highly skewed to the right, the school can be assured that it is delivering satisfaction to most students. Repeating this survey at regular intervals points up any significant changes in the distribution. Furthermore, the respondents should be asked to respond to similar scales for the various components of the school, such as its academic program, extracurricular program, housing, and the like. With this information, the institution could investigate the contribution of satisfaction with various components to overall satisfaction with the school.

The data may also be presented as shown in Figure 16-6, which reports percentages of college sophomores and seniors who said they were generally pleased with each area surveyed. The survey found that the vast majority of college students are satisfied with their academic programs and professors, but many complain that support services—such as academic advising, career counseling, and job placement—are inadequate. Seniors tend to be more dissatisfied with the services than sophomores do.

Derived dissatisfaction. The second type of question measures derived dissatisfaction, on the premise that a person's satisfaction is influenced by his

FIGURE 16-6   Student satisfaction with college

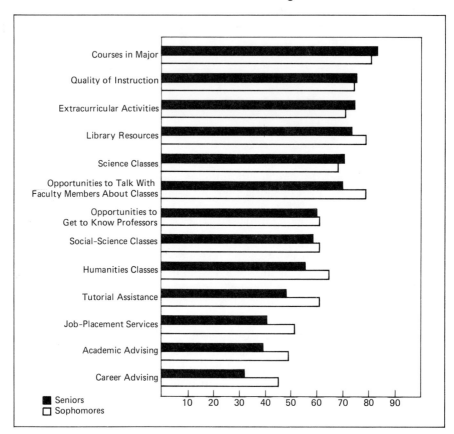

SOURCE: Higher Education Research Institute, University of California, Los Angeles. Chart by Tyler Young appeared in *The Chronicle of Higher Education*, July 27, 1983, p. 3. Copyright 1983 by *The Chronicle of Higher Education*. Reprinted with permission.

or her expectation as well as the perceived state of the object. Each person is asked to respond to a pair of questions about each component of the college; for example:

> The quality of the academic program:
> a. How much is there now?
> (min)   1   2   3   4   5   6   7   (max)
> b. How much should there be?
> (min)   1   2   3   4   5   6   7   (max)

This type of question provides more useful information than the previous method does. By averaging the scores of all the respondents to part *a*, the researcher learns the average perceived level of that attribute of the object. The dispersion around the average—measured by the standard deviation—shows how much agreement there is in the responses. If all students see the college's academic program as approximately 2 on a seven-point scale, this means the program is pretty bad. If, on the other hand, students hold widely differing perceptions of the program's actual quality, administration will want to determine what personal or group factors might account for them.

The next step is to average the responses given to part b. This number represents the average student's view of how much quality he or she expects in the academic program. The measure of dispersion will indicate how much variation there is in student opinion about the desirable level of quality.

Next, we can derive a "need-deficiency" score by substracting the answer for part a from that for part b. In this case, suppose the respondent circles 2 for part a and 5 for part b. The need-deficiency score is 3. The greater the need-deficiency score, the greater the respondent's degree of dissatisfaction (or the smaller the degree of satisfaction).

By finding the need-deficiency score for each component of the college's program, the administration can better understand current student moods and make necessary changes. If this survey is repeated at regular intervals, the college can detect new need deficiencies as they arise and take timely steps to remedy them.

Importance/performance ratings. Another type of question asks students to rate several services on (1) the importance of each service, and (2) how well the school performs each service. Figure 16-7, A shows hypothetical student responses to fourteen services. The importance of a service is rated on a four-point scale of "extremely important," "important," "slightly important," and "not important." The school's performance is rated on a four-point scale of "excellent," "good," "fair," and "poor." For example, the first service, academic program, might receive a mean importance rating of 3.83 and a mean performance rating of 2.63, indicating that students feel it is highly important but is not being performed very well.

The hypothetical ratings of all 14 services are displayed in Figure 16-7, B. The figure is divided into four sections. Quadrant A shows important services that are not being offered at the desired performance levels. The school should concentrate on improving these services. Quadrant B shows important services that are being performed well. The school should concentrate on maintaining these services. Quadrant C shows minor services that are being delivered in a mediocre way but that do not need any attention, since they are not very important. Quadrant D shows a minor service that is being performed in an excellent manner, a case of possible "overkill." This rating of services according to their perceived importance and performance provides the school's administration with guidelines on where to concentrate their efforts.

Table 16-2 shows another example of importance/performance ratings. As part of Stanford University's annual Senior Survey, students about to graduate

Service	Service Description	Mean Importance Rating[a]	Mean Performance Rating[b]
1	Academic program	3.83	2.63
2	Housing quality	3.63	2.73
3	Food quality	3.60	3.15
4	Athletic facilities	3.56	3.00
5	Social activities	3.41	3.05
6	Faculty availability	3.41	3.29
7	" "	3.38	3.03
8	" "	3.37	3.11
9	" "	3.29	2.00
10	" "	3.27	3.02
11	" "	2.52	2.25
12	" "	2.43	2.49
13	" "	2.37	2.35
14	" "	2.05	3.33

Extremely Important

A. Concentrate Here | B. Keep Up the Good Work

1 2 4 3 5 6 7 8

Fair performance 9 | 10 Excellent performance

11 12 13

14

C. Low Priority | D. Possible Overkill

Slightly Important

B.

[a] Ratings obtained from a four-point scale of "extremely important." "important," "slightly important," and "not important."

[b] Ratings obtained from a four-point scale of "excellent," "good," "fair," and "poor." A "no basis for judgment" category was also provided.

A.

FIGURE 16-7 Importance and performance ratings for several college services

were asked to rate various aspects of their college experience on three five-point scales—an absolute scale, relative to their expectations, and importance to them. By examining the results of such studies, the institution can identify areas for improvement. These studies demonstrate the institution's concern for students and provide the basis for a retention program.

Key Steps in a Retention Program

An institution interested in increasing retention will enjoy more success if two conditions are met. First, there must be a visible institutionwide commitment to student retention, reflected in formal and informal reward systems. Second, all units of the school that come in contact with students must be part of the solution, not admissions or advising alone.[20]

Set Up a Retention Steering Committee. A retention program needs designers and champions. The committed institution should establish a retention steering committee to fill these roles. Each department and other functional area of the school should set up its own retention committee to develop plans for its own area. Each area committee should send one member to serve on the universitywide committee to ensure representation. Steering-committee members should be committed to the shared goal of improving programs and services for students.

TABLE 16-2 Stanford seniors' evaluations of the undergraduate program (percentages)

A. With regard to your undergraduate program, please assess:	ON AN ABSOLUTE SCALE						RELATIVE TO YOUR EXPECTATIONS					IMPORTANCE OF THE ITEM TO YOU				
	Not applicable or blank	Very poor	Poor	Average	Good	Excellent	Much Worse	Worse	About as expected	Better	Much Better	Very slight	Slight	Moderate	Great	Very great
1. The overall quality of your undergraduate education at Stanford.	0%	0%	1%	5%	51%	44%	1%	18%	49%	27%	5%	0%	0%	6%	36%	58%
2. The general quality of the courses within your major.	0	0	3	19	49	29	3	22	42	25	7	0	1	12	39	48
3. The coherence of your overall program of study.	1	1	7	32	46	15	1	22	51	21	6	2	6	33	39	20
4. The adequacy of your training for graduate or professional schools.	18	1	5	18	46	30	2	16	51	25	6	2	7	29	36	26
5. The adequacy of your general or liberal education.	1	1	7	25	42	26	2	20	45	25	9	1	4	19	38	37
6. Your experience at a Stanford overseas campus.	59	0	2	6	19	73	2	6	16	34	42	0	0	12	29	59
7. The contribution of your campus living arrangements to your intellectual life and learning.	2	7	14	22	32	25	8	19	30	26	18	4	9	28	30	30

SOURCE: *Campus Report*, Stanford University, November 16, 1983, p. 2.

Assess the Retention Situation. To understand the institution's retention situation, the steering committee needs to (1) determine the institution's past record on retention, and (2) determine factors related to attrition. These steps help determine in what ways the institution is successful and what aspects need to be changed to enhance retention.

Most schools have highly accurate counts of applications received, applications accepted, students enrolled in a given term, and degrees granted, yet they may be unaware of their retention rate. The most direct approach is to determine the number who entered in a given class and the number of those students who graduated within a certain period. The retention rate is the percentage of those entering who graduate within a certain period, typically four or five years for a four-year degree program.

Figure 16-8 illustrates the retention problem of one part-time degree program that takes an average of three years to complete. Simply comparing the number of new students enrolled and the number of degrees granted each year shows that about one-third of matriculating students do not complete the program. To improve the diagram's accuracy, we would compare the number of matriculants in a given year with the number of graduates three years later. Such an analysis reveals that approximately 40 percent do not complete the program. This statistic should raise questions about student selection and curriculum and teaching quality. The high attrition rate might also reflect a job transfer to another state, increased work responsibilities that prevent part-time study, or transfer to a full-time program, all circumstances beyond the institution's control.

A second approach is a longitudinal study assessing each student's enrollment status at several intervals. The most comprehensive type of longitudinal study examines the complete enrollment histories of all students in an

FIGURE 16-8 The attrition gap for a part-time program

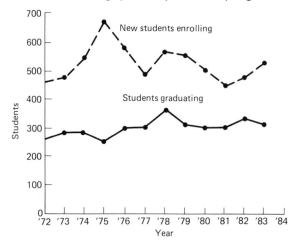

entering class over a period of several years on a term-by-term basis. Once longitudinal data files are compiled, researchers can (1) identify the cumulative percentage of an entering class in each of several retention and attrition categories at several points over a period of time; and (2) place each student into the appropriate retention or attrition category at the end of the set longitudinal period.

Where complete individual enrollment histories are conveniently available, students who entered several years before can be studied. The steering committee may also launch a retention study of the current entering class, with the results used to track the effectiveness of retention efforts in future years. In either event, each student's enrollment status is noted each term—enrolled, voluntarily withdrawn while in good standing (including reason, if known), disciplinary dismissal, academic dismissal, graduated, and so forth. Some students labeled "dropouts" may be "stopouts" who will return within a year or two, or "attainers" who have achieved their personal goals (such as to prepare to transfer or for a job) and then leave without graduating.[21] A longitudinal approach can best differentiate between attrition categories.

Determine Why Students Leave. In some cases, the reasons for withdrawal appear obvious—academic or disciplinary dismissal, for example. But the concerned institution seeks to identify the controllable factors that lead to such events. For example, in the case of academic dismissal, should the student have been admitted? Was the student inadequately prepared for the academic demands of the institution? Could these deficiencies be identified in the applicant file? Did the student get inadequate guidance in identifying areas needing improvement? Did the student have personal problems that could have been alleviated by appropriate counseling, financial assistance, or other help?

Students who leave voluntarily should be interviewed or surveyed to determine their reasons for leaving and their future plans. They may drop out because of family obligations, illness, financial problems, lack of academic skills or motivation, desire to work or travel, or dissatisfaction with the school. They may drop out for a time and then return, or they may transfer to schools that are closer, or less expensive, or that in other ways better meet their needs. Many "dropouts" eventually complete degree requirements at the same or other institutions. By understanding the reasons for transferring or dropping out, the institution can determine how to improve its programs and other factors that affect retention.

Encourage an Attitude of Service to Students. Enhancing retention may call for substantial changes in programs, facilities, support services, and other areas. But often the first and most important step is to foster a campuswide attitude of serving students. The official tone of the campus is set by faculty, administrators, secretaries, and other staff. Important steps include making current personnel aware of their importance, providing training, and hiring with students in mind. Exhibit 16-1 illustrates the importance of serving students.

EXHIBIT 16-1 Influences on student retention

During her senior year in high school, Jane wrote to Eucalyptus University as part of the routine of applying to colleges. After two weeks, she received a mimeographed letter outlining the personal nature of a Eucalyptus U. education. The accompanying application forms were more complex than an income tax form and, of course, asked for $20.

Several days later, Jane telephoned Eucalyptus U. After 17 rings, an operator answered and placed her on "hold" for four minutes. When the operator returned to the phone, she asked, "Are you through?" And when Jane finally reached the admissions office, a secretary told her, "The director is not taking any calls, and the rest of the staff is out. Could you call back tomorrow?"

Jane was persistent and scheduled a visit to Eucalyptus. There were no directional signs when she drove onto the campus, so she found a parking space near what looked like an administration building. It wasn't. She met two professors and a student—and none of them knew where the admissions office was.

Twenty minutes later, success. The admissions office was busy and loud, but finally a receptionist confronted Jane: "Do you have an appointment?" Jane said she did, but the receptionist informed her that the director was not available and that she would have to see a student assistant (who turned out to be transferring from Eucalyptus and was less than enthusiastic about the university).

In spite of her experiences, Jane enrolled that fall. Registration was like a lottery; she was enrolled in two classes, via computer, that were completely out of her field. She was interested in pre-law, and her assigned counselor was from the chemistry department. There was a major error in her tuition bill. Her dorm room had not been cleaned, and her roommate was taking drugs. It took two weeks to get her room changed, and she fell behind on her homework.

One of Jane's professors made her buy two textbooks—both of which he had written. Another was late every day and missed several classes altogether. Another just read his notes—and didn't even do that very well.

But one professor cared, counseled, and gave Jane the attention that made the difference. Jane is still attending Eucalyptus U. because one person understood that colleges exist to serve their students.

Young, sensitive minds need support, not confrontation—and this does not apply only to the classroom. Telephone operators, secretaries, groundskeepers, business-office personnel, and other staff members are part of the lifeblood of a college. They often lack degrees and professional training, but their roles are important. They greet students, bill them, comfort them, delay them, frustrate them, inform them.

Administrative personnel in student-affairs offices have a special function. They provide the "home-away-from-home" counsel that makes a student comfortable. Theirs should not be a job but a labor of love. They ought to ask themselves questions of this sort:

- Are the forms, guidelines, rules, and regulations necessary? Or are they part of a system that just evolved?
- Can students understand the regulations that *are* important? Or are they written in "educationese"?
- Within reason, is the office door open, or just slightly ajar?
- Are students involved in the planning and implementation of policies that affect them?

The role of the faculty member is even more basic: to be the teacher he or she always wanted to be. A caring professor sees a student as both a consumer and a product. While the student is learning and paying a price in time and money, a product is developing. The result can be positive or negative, and those who influence the result have a grave responsibility. The most positive words a college can hear about itself are, "The professors really care." If faculty members approach each class, each term, each year with enthusiasm, the college is alive and well.

SOURCE: Dennis L. Johnson, "One Professor Cared," *The Chronicle of Higher Education,* April 19, 1976. Copyright 1975 by Editorial Projects in Education. Reprinted with permission of *The Chronicle of Higher Education.*

Establish a Good Student–Institution Match in Recruiting and Admissions. Programs to enhance retention begin when the admissions office plans its recruiting strategy. The college should recruit and admit students who are qualified to benefit from its programs and who "match" the current student body in interests and ability. If the college decides to attract a new market— for example, older women as commuting students—it should consider in advance the necessary staff, support services, and facilities to succeed with this new group.

The institution must provide complete, accurate, and timely information to help students make the enrollment decision. A student who makes a poor choice of institution or program of study will probably have low morale, perform poorly, and drop out.

Facilitate the Student's Transition Into the Institution. Once the new student is admitted, the college needs to help the student get started "right" through appropriate placement in courses, orientation to procedures and support services, and activities that create a sense of identification and belonging.

Provide Counseling and Advising. Counseling and advising should be available from the very beginning. On a residential campus, many students are living away from home for the first time and are dealing with complex personal issues of identity, competence, and choice. They also face family illness, death, and other human crises and may well need personal counseling at these times. If such circumstances lead them to drop out, they will be more likely to return if they have received such help.

Academic advising is often mentioned as important to retention. Students who are performing well academically and who have a sense of purpose (such as a career direction) are less likely to drop out. To some extent, academic advising can be effective in helping students identify strengths and weaknesses, improve study skills, and determine academic and career interests. But to be effective, such advising must be of high quality, and students must make use of it. A survey of deans found that although 95 percent of undergraduate students consider dropping out at some time, only a third seek advice from professors.[22] Often students withdraw without any interaction with college faculty, administrators, or staff. The institution that waits for students to come for help will probably have little or no influence on their decisions to withdraw.

Providing high-quality advising requires committed, competent advisors. If professors are uninterested or unavailable—or are perceived as such—students will not go to them for advice. Good academic advising cannot be mandated. At some institutions, faculty advisors are selected and receive additional training and released time. Other institutions have professional academic advisors.

Most institutions would like to concentrate their retention efforts on the most dropout-prone students. Unfortunately, prediction is difficult. The only reliable predictor is college grades, but that predicts only academic dropouts. Counseling and advising programs to reduce attrition need to be directed toward all students and need to begin as soon as students arrive on campus.

Create a Caring, Responsive Environment. The purpose of these efforts is to create the academic and social conditions that foster personal growth, academic success, and a sense of belonging. The institution committed to retaining students needs to examine its efforts and take steps to create the kind of atmosphere that encourages students to stay.

SUMMARY

Attracting students is often an educational institution's key marketing task. Schools and colleges seek to enroll students who will benefit from what the institution has to offer. Although publicly supported colleges accept students who meet specific criteria, selective public and private institutions want to attract many applicants so that they may admit the very best. Once the institution has enrolled qualified students, the next task is to ensure that students' reasonable expectations are met so that the student will complete the program and become a satisfied graduate.

The student recruitment process consists of six steps: identifying enrollment problems, defining enrollment goals and objectives, researching the potential student market, setting marketing strategy, planning and implementing action programs, and evaluating results and procedures.

Retaining students is just as important as attracting and enrolling them, since students are not a captive audience. The institution will want to create a high level of satisfaction. Satisfaction is a state in which a person feels that a performance or outcome has fulfilled his or her expectations. Responsive educational institutions will make use of complaint systems, satisfaction surveys, and surveys of needs and preferences to determine how well students' expectations are being met and to identify areas for improvement.

An effective retention program must include all points of contact between the student and the institution. The retention process should include eight steps: set up a retention steering committee, assess the retention situation, determine why students leave, encourage an attitude of service to students, establish a good student–institution match in recruiting and admissions, facilitate the student's transition into the institution, provide counseling and advising, and create a caring, responsive environment.

NOTES

[1] *Undergraduate Admissions: The Realities of Institutional Policies, Practices, and Procedures*, a Report of a Survey Conducted by the American Association of Collegiate Registrars and Admissions Officers and the College Board (New York: College Entrance Examination Board, 1980), p. 51.

[2] Charles A. Dominick, Russell H. Johnson, David W. Chapman, and John V. Griffith, "College Recruiting in the Next Ten Years," *National ACAC Journal*, February 1980, p. 3.

[3] *Ibid.*, p. 4.

[4] *Undergraduate Admissions*, p. 41.

[5] J. Victor Baldridge, Frank R. Kemerer, and Kenneth C. Green, *The Enrollment Crisis: Factors, Actors, and Impacts*, AAHE-ERIC/Higher Education

Research Report No. 3, 1982 (Washington, D.C.: American Association for Higher Education, 1982), p. 30.

[6] David Riesman, "The Evangelical Colleges: Untouched by the Academic Revolution," *Change*, January/February 1981, pp. 13–20.

[7] *Master Plan 1973–74*, Hood College Admissions Office.

[8] "A Case History of How a College Increased Its Freshman Enrollment 100% in One Year," *Insights*, June–July 1974, pp. 1–14.

[9] William Ihlanfeldt, *Achieving Optimal Enrollments and Tuition Revenues* (San Francisco: Jossey-Bass, 1980), pp. 77–81.

[10] For other examples, see Ihlanfeldt, *Achieving Optimal Enrollments*, pp. 37–46.

[11] "A Case History," p. 5.

[12] Clifford C. Campbell, "The Administration of Admissions," in *Marketing Higher Education: New Directions for Higher Education* (San Francisco: Jossey-Bass, 1978), pp. 52–53.

[13] Beverly T. Watkins, "The Cost of Recruiting a Student Is on the Rise," *The Chronicle of Higher Education*, May 4, 1983, p. 7.

[14] Campbell, "The Administration of Admissions," p. 62.

[15] Thomas Huddleston and Frank A. Wiebe, "Understanding the Nature of the Student Market for a Private University," *Journal of College Student Personnel*, November 1978, p. 522.

[16] Baldridge et al., *The Enrollment Crisis*, p. 35.

[17] Verne A. Stadtman, *Academic Adaptations: Higher Education Prepares for the 1980s and 1990s* (San Francisco: Jossey-Bass, 1980), Table 39.

[18] Baldridge et al., *The Enrollment Crisis*, p. 37.

[19] C. Henderson and J.C. Plummer, *Adapting to Changes in the Characteristics of College-Age Youth*, Policy Analysis Service Reports, Vol. 4, No. 2 (Washington, D.C.: American Council on Education, 1978), p. 31.

[20] Lee Noel, "First Steps in Starting a Campus Retention Program," in Lee Noel, ed., *Reducing the Dropout Rate* (San Francisco: Jossey-Bass, 1978), pp. 87–88.

[21] Edwin A. Rugg, "Design and Analysis Considerations for Longitudinal Retention and Attrition Studies," *College and University*, Winter 1983, pp. 119–34.

[22] Judi R. Kesselman, "The Care and Feeding of Stop-outs," *Change*, May 1976, pp. 13–15.

chapter 17

ATTRACTING
FINANCIAL
SUPPORT

Toward the end of 1978, when theologian James L. Laney had been president of Emory University for little more than a year, he went to see the university's most prominent benefactor, the Coca-Cola magnate and philanthropist Robert W. Woodruff. Laney carried a piece of paper on which he had drawn up a wish list of the campus's priority needs. Laney had listed scholarships and distinguished professorships and a few buildings, all of which would amount to such an expense that it was unlikely Emory could afford them anytime soon from present income. The preacher had come prepared to plead an "effective case" for Emory's needs in the years of his presidency.

The soft-drink tycoon had in the previous fifty years, since 1937, given the university more than $100 million, continuing the philanthropy of the first president of Coca-Cola, Asa G. Candler, whose interests had been in theology and medicine. Nearly all of Woodruff's gifts, however, had been directed to the Medical Center, including the School of Medicine, the creation of a cancer clinic, the construction of a medical administration building and the advancement of the School of Nursing, which was named after his wife, the late Nell Hodgson Woodruff. More recently, in the 1970s, he had underwritten the cost of a chemistry building and of White Hall, a main classroom building that also houses the offices of Emory College.

This widening of Woodruff's philanthropic interest in Emory was encouraging to Laney. Beyond that, Laney evidently got the impression that Woodruff liked him personally and professionally, that Woodruff saw in him a good manager of money and men, as Woodruff himself had been across town at the world headquarters of Coca-Cola. Like Woodruff, Laney seemed to possess a world view and talked about wanting to do something great. At Laney's inauguration in 1977, Woodruff was photographed as he placed a hand on the new president's shoulder. That remains one of Laney's favorite photographs and hangs on his office wall.

The two men had met in 1975, when Laney was still dean of Emory's School of Theology, but their close relationship did not develop until the theologian became president of the university. That day in 1978, Laney did not press too hard with his list.

"Here's what we need, Mr. Woodruff," he said.

"Well, I'll be!" said Woodruff. He just looked at the piece of paper.

It was around this time, Laney recalls, that Woodruff could be seen on fine Saturday mornings as his chauffeur drove him around the campus. "He would drive around and look," says Laney, "at all the buildings."

Almost a year passed before, late in 1979, Laney could announce Woodruff's generous decision. Turning 90 years old, he was transferring 3 million shares of Coca-Cola stock to Emory as a special endowment. When the accountants finished figuring the value, they totaled the gift at about $105 million, with an annual yield of $6.9 million in dividends. Thus, over a ten-year period, Emory could count on spending about $69 million.

SOURCE: Leonard Ray Teel, "Emory University Decides How to Allot $100,000,000," *Change*, May/June 1981, pp. 12–13. A publication of the Helen Dwight Reid Educational Foundation.

In addition to attracting students, educational institutions must attract financial support to carry on their activities. Most private educational institutions are not-for-profit organizations and rely on tuition from students, on income from endowment funds, and on donations and grants. Public schools, colleges, and universities rely principally on allocations from the public treasury, although many are increasing tuition, and some are more actively seeking alumni donations, foundation grants, and corporate grants.

Of the $64.9 billion in charitable money raised by all nonprofit organizations in 1983, 14 percent ($9 billion) was raised by education, outranking all other areas of voluntary support except religious institutions.[1]

Fund raising has evolved through various stages. Its earliest stage was begging, with needy people and groups importuning more fortunate people for money and goods. Some schools and colleges still believe that the more needy they present themselves to be, the more willing people will be to give money. The next stage of fund raising relied on the premise that people would be more willing to give if they got something tangible in return. Of course, to make a surplus, the fund-raising institution had to rely on volunteers to make cakes for bake sales or on donated goods for auctions, and so forth. The success of such fund-raising activities often depended more on people's interest in the products for sale than on their interest in supporting the institution.

More recently, fund raising is viewed as *development*, whereby educational institutions build up different classes of loyal donors who give consistently and receive benefits in the process of giving. A development perspective starts from the position that the school or college is worthy of support and that prospective donors who value what it has to offer will contribute if an opportunity is presented.

Virtually everything the institution does has an effect on its ability to attract and maintain the support and enthusiasm of its markets and publics— not only donors, but also students, faculty, staff, the general public, and others. In this view, development is really a part of an overall *institutional advancement program* that includes public relations, communications, alumni programs, and anything else that generates satisfaction and potential support—including campus landscaping and the reputation of the school's athletic teams:

In 1957, Stanford University received a letter in pencil on a scrap of paper:

"Gentlemen, My name is Max Herman Stein, born Nov. 12, 1883.

"I have an estate which I believe to be worth in excess of $200,000. This I intend to bequeath to Stanford."

Stein's only previous contact with the university came during a period of work as a gardener on a nearby estate. He chose Stanford partly because of its clean record in the Pacific Coast Conference football scandal of the time, and a visit to the campus convinced him he had made the right choice. Since his death in 1958, the Max H. Stein Professorship in Physics has supported two Nobel laureates.[2]

Some institutions are short on both fund-raising expertise and money. Many rely on short-range fund-raising tactics when they should be working to establish the school's credibility and worthiness so that people will want to give money toward its success. In Exhibit 17-1, the director of education for a Catholic archdiocese contrasts a long-term development approach and a short-term "fund-raising" approach.

We use *fund raising* in this chapter to refer to the institution's activities to obtain financial support. The development approach to fund raising reflects the marketing view that the institution must analyze its position in the marketplace, concentrate on those donor sources whose interests are best matched to it, and design solicitation programs to supply needed satisfactions to each donor group. This approach involves carefully segmenting the donor markets; measuring the giving potential of each donor market; assigning executive responsibility for developing each market through research and communication approaches; and developing a plan and budget for each market based on its potential.

This chapter will analyze fund raising from a marketing perspective, considering the following topics:

1. Laying the groundwork for fund raising
2. Setting fund-raising goals
3. Organizing for fund raising
4. Researching and approaching donor markets, including individual givers, foundations, corporations, and government
5. Coordinating fund-raising activities
6. Evaluating fund-raising effectiveness

EXHIBIT 17-1 The contrast between development and fund raising

DEVELOPMENT	FUND RAISING
BASIC APPROACH/CONCEPTS	*BASIC APPROACH/CONCEPTS*
• Commitment of chief administrator and board to the development program	• Panic reactions to negative deficits start process of fund raising
• Complete integrity	• Crisis orientation
• Principal concern is top-quality education	• Project-oriented; year-to-year
• Good business management procedures are absolute necessity	• Temporary solutions
• Long-range planning	• Limited objectives—short range
• Public relations as prerequisite	• Shaky, unreliable, insecure
• Invite substantial investments	• Immediate solution demanded
• Goals and objectives clearly written	• Amateur approach; stopgap measures
• Negotiate from position of strength	• No planned continuing efforts: hit and miss; no long-range plan
• A positive attitude is paramount and permanent	• Band-Aid approach
• Publics must be involved with the institution on a continuing basis	• Negotiate from position of weakness—"help," "need," "poor," "assist"
	• Rely on gimmicks

EXHIBIT 17-1   The contrast between development and fund raising (continued)

DEVELOPMENT	FUND RAISING
PROGRAMS AND PROJECTS (activities) • Establish endowment fund • Estate-planning programs • Annuity programs • Marketing research program—needs of people • Life insurance benefits solicited • Business and industry grants • Research major prospects • Involve influential, affluent people • Encourage writing wills • Scholarship programs • Proposals to foundations • Long-range planning • Written, distinctive philosophy • Policy, practice, and procedure manuals	*PROGRAMS AND PROJECTS* (activities) • Bingo (a major form of financial support) • Car wash • Annual bazaar • Thanksgiving raffle • $10-a-plate dinner • Cadillac ball • Sales program and advertising • Magazine sales • Candy drives • Festivals • Annual book fair • Bash • Slave auction • Las Vegas Night • Mardi Gras
RESULTS (effects) • Large private donations received on a consistent annual basis • Money programmed for five to ten years down road • Working from clearly projected 5-year plan • Positive attitude developed • Problems are looked upon as challenge • Obstacles are seen as opportunities • Annual reports of progress to all publics • Supporters of program have strong interest in programs • Function charts developed • Life insurance policies/dividends received • Foundation grants • Private dollars generated • Insurance dollars attracted	*RESULTS* (effects) • Recurring financial crisis • Confused job specs • Job descriptions out of date • Working one year at a time • Raising money on crisis orientation • No clear-cut goals or objectives • High staff turnover • Vague financial reporting • No records of past progress or reasons for change • Changes made for the sake of change • Unwritten assumptions • Vague organization chart • Do nothing to educate public about values of education nor their role in supporting education • Fails to get people involved in programs

SOURCE: Rev. John Flynn, cited in *Catholic School Management Letter* (24 Cornfield Lane, Madison, Connecticut 06443), September 1980, p. 2.

LAYING THE GROUNDWORK FOR FUND RAISING

The contribution of institutional strategic planning is nowhere more apparent than in fund raising. The institution that has gone through the strategic planning process presented in this book has the following advantages:

- The institution is aware of the major threats and opportunities that the environment poses and has developed contingency plans for dealing with them.
- It has identified its key publics, has determined their images of the institution, and has developed communications programs for them.
- It has a thorough understanding of its major markets—students, donors, and others—and their expectations of the institution.
- It has identified its competition and has determined how to position itself in ways that are valued by its markets and publics.
- The institution has analyzed its strengths and weaknesses as a basis for remedying weaknesses and communicating its strengths.
- It has clarified its mission and has identified the overall goals and objectives it will pursue.
- It has analyzed the programs and services it offers and has made decisions about which to drop, modify, build, or add.
- It has reviewed its organizational design to provide the structure and organizational culture that support its other activities.
- The institution has effective systems for obtaining and disseminating important information to support research, planning, implementation, and control tasks.
- It has rank-ordered its goals and objectives and has determined the financial resources needed to attain them.
- It can answer the prospective donor who wants evidence that the institution knows where it is going and will spend donated money wisely to further significant goals.

With this preparation at the institutional level, the development staff can proceed to determine (through additional research, if necessary) the best features of the institution that would merit donor support; set fund-raising goals; research donor markets; and develop and implement fund-raising action plans.

SETTING FUND-RAISING GOALS

Educational institutions typically set annual and long-range goals for fund raising. As an example, the University of Santa Clara set the following goals for a five-year campaign to raise $50 million:

1. To provide the annual operating support needed for ongoing university programs and operations and to expand and strengthen annual giving programs
2. To increase the university's endowment so that income from endowment investments will underwrite at least 10 percent of the educational and general expenses

3. To provide the funds for the construction of two urgently needed facilities and the renovation of four existing structures

In this case, the goals state the uses for the donated funds, rather than just the desired total amount. In the process of developing fund-raising goals, the school's leadership will consult with key people, including deans and department chairs, to determine their most pressing needs as well as the projects they would undertake if additional resources were available. These needs and "wishes" should reflect strategic planning at the school and department level. These lists need to be combined and the projects prioritized as a basis for determining the amount the institution would like to raise and the amount that is of greatest importance.

The institution may set goals for particular donor groups. For example, one large university set the following goals for a class that was marking its twentieth reunion:

1. Participation by 75 percent of class members
2. $200,000 overall dollar goal, which, if reached, will earn an additional $25,000 from five classmates
3. Establish a $25,000 class endowment fund composed of gifts that are over and above regular annual contributions

For the class that was graduated only five years earlier, the goals are much more modest: to increase class participation and to establish a $15,000 class endowment fund with gifts that are over and above annual contributions.

Most institutions set a total goal each year for contributions, because this allows the institution to (1) establish a budget for fund-raising activities, (2) motivate the staff and volunteers to high exertion, and (3) measure fund-raising effectiveness.

Educational institutions arrive at their fund-raising goals in different ways, such as these:

1. *Incremental approach.* Here, the institution takes last year's contribution total, increases it to cover inflation, and then modifies it up or down depending on the expected economic climate.

2. *Need approach.* Here, the institution forecasts its financial needs and sets a goal based on them. Thus, a university's administration will estimate the future building needs and costs, faculty salaries, energy costs, and so on, and set the portion that has to be covered by fund raising as its target.

3. *Opportunity approach.* Here, the institution makes an estimate of how much money it could raise from each donor group with different fund-raising approaches and expenditures, with the objective of maximizing the net surplus. This approach is often used before a major capital campaign; the development office conducts a feasibility study before announcing the campaign goal.

Educational institutions often use a combination of these three approaches. They look for growth from year to year, they keep in mind the continuing and special needs for which the institution needs money, and they consider the giving potential for each donor group.

After setting its fund-raising goal, the institution has to develop an overall strategy, identifying the most promising donors and determining how to present its case to the donors. The institution needs to prepare a case statement, explaining the institution's worthiness, its needs, and reasons why support is justified. It may base its appeal on loyalty, on identification with earlier distinguished benefactors, or on some other major motive for giving. The institution has to decide how to allocate scarce staff time to different donor groups and geographical areas.

The role of the vice president for development in influencing the institution's objectives and strategies varies greatly. Some institutions treat the development officer as a technician rather than a policy maker. The president and/or board decides how much money is needed, selects the broad fund-raising strategy, and then assigns its implementation to the development officer. This, unfortunately, robs the institution of a valuable contribution that the development officer can make. Some institutions give more scope to the development officer: He or she participates with the institution's top administrators and trustees in setting dollar goals and fund-raising strategy, and in developing the institutional positioning strategy. By establishing a sound institutional position, the development officer can raise money more easily.

ORGANIZING FOR FUND RAISING

Educational institutions must develop an organized approach to fund raising. Small schools may have one person who is chiefly responsible for fund raising. This person may be the school's head or a director of development. He or she will be responsible for identifying fund-raising opportunities and activating others—administrators, trustees, faculty, and alumni and other volunteers—to assist when needed.

Large colleges and universities will have entire development offices consisting of several staff members plus volunteers numbering into the hundreds. In these large institutions, development staff members take responsibility for either specific donor markets, services, marketing tools, or geographical areas. We shall illustrate this by showing how a large private university organizes its fund raising.

A model organization for university fund raising is shown in Figure 17-1. The board of directors has the ultimate responsibility for overseeing the financial health of the university and does this by making personal and company contributions, arranging donor contacts, and advising on development strategy, as well as by oversight of endowment and investment strategy. The college pres-

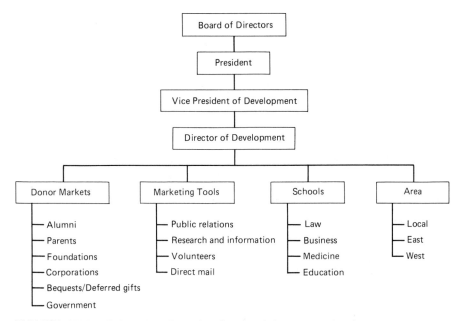

FIGURE 17-1   A large university fund-raising organization

ident is the chief fund raiser when it comes to meeting major prospects and asking for their support. The vice president for development is the chief planner of the fund-raising strategy for the institution and also personally asks for money from potential donors. Day-to-day administration is often handled by a director of development, to free the vice president for development for strategic planning and coordination of the functions that report to him or her, which may include public relations, publications, and alumni affairs. The remaining development staff carries out specialized activities. Some of the staff are specialized to donor markets—thus, there are directors of alumni giving, foundations, corporate giving, and so on. Other staff members manage marketing functions, such as public relations, research, and volunteers. Others handle various schools, where they get to know the faculty and fund-raising needs and opportunities.

The staff's effectiveness is amplified by managing a large number of volunteers—such as alumni, friends of the institution, deans, faculty, students, and so on. For example, Stanford runs a special program called the Inner Quad program to solicit and recognize donors of over $1,000 annually. This program is run by eight professional staff members working through 250 volunteers operating in 16 regions of the country. In this case, the staff really functions to activate the volunteers who are the main fund-raising arm of the university.

The institution's effectiveness in fund raising is also affected by the quality of its information system. The development office needs to maintain up-to-date and easily accessible files on donors and prospects (individuals, foundations, corporations, and so on) so that past and/or potential giving can be identified and previous solicitations can be reviewed. By computerization of the files so that data can be retrieved by year, school, giving level, and other key variables, the fund raiser is in a much better position to allocate his or her time effectively.

RESEARCHING AND APPROACHING DONOR MARKETS

Educational institutions obtain their donated funds from four major donor markets: *individuals, foundations, corporations*, and *governments*. In this section, we will examine the characteristics of each donor market and show how these shape fund-raising activities.

Effective fund raising relies heavily on marketing research. The development staff needs to thoroughly understand the actual and potential donor groups and to determine ways to further segment these groups into more homogeneous groups that are similar in some important way that affects their ability and/or willingness to give. The staff members need to identify specific prospects for larger gifts, to develop a profile of their interests and affiliations, and to rate them on their giving potential and the strength of their motivation to give. The development office needs to draw on results of prior or new image studies on how donor segments perceive the institution. To tailor the case for giving still further, the development staff needs to understand the donor decision process, including identifying the most salient motivations for giving, strengthening and creating ties with the institution, and encouraging a habit of giving. Accurate identification of donors followed by appropriate cultivation is at the heart of successful fund raising.

The most successful approach is to present giving as an *investment* in some aspect of the institution that the donor cares about. For some individual donors, this will be the athletic program; for others, the business school; and for still others, scholarships for students in the performing arts. Corporations typically support projects that offer them some short- and/or long-term potential benefits, such as goodwill or better-trained employees. When the institution presents the prospective donor with an attractive investment opportunity, an exchange is likely to take place. We will have more to say about motives for giving as we take up each major donor group.

Individual Donors

Individuals are the major source of donations to educational institutions. For a group of 71 American colleges and universities, close to 60 percent of the money donated was in the form of gifts and bequests from individuals, with foundation and corporate philanthropy making up the rest.[3] Of course, institutions vary greatly in the percentage of funding received from individuals.

In order to develop effective approaches, the development staff needs to segment this group in a meaningful way. Donor markets can be segmented on geographic, demographic, psychographic, and behavioristic variables (see Chapter 9).

Segmentation can suggest the benefits which each group wants from giving. Of course the development office should be careful to check their hunches about donor motivations by asking them what benefits are most important to them. Some people give, and say they expect nothing back. But actually they have "expectations." They expect the institution to use the money efficiently; they expect the fund raiser to show gratitude; and so on. Even the anonymous giver, while wanting no acknowledgment, may privately enjoy the self-esteem of being "big enough" to give money without requiring recognition. One group of donors to a university might respond to "pride," another to "let's catch up to the competition."

Another important basis for segmentation is the donor's "giving potential." Fund raisers distinguish between small, medium, and large donors. Educational development officers typically find that about 90 percent or more of the money is donated by less than 10 percent of the donors. Thus many fund raisers prefer to concentrate all or most of their energy on large potential donors, feeling that attracting a few large gifts would produce more funds than attracting many small gifts. If a college fund raiser spends thirty hours with a wealthy alumnus who ends up giving $1 million, the fund raiser's productivity is much greater than trying to raise $100 from each of 10,000 alumni. For this reason many college fund raisers in the past neglected building up the number of alumni givers and concentrated instead on increasing the size of the average gift received. This is now changing, as more colleges are seeking to involve all alumni in school support and giving, while maintaining efforts to attract large gifts.

The usual approach for attracting large gifts is *personal solicitation*, either by someone in the development office, an administrator (the president, a dean, or a principal, for example), a trustee, or another highly credible spokesperson for the institution. If the spokesperson is a trustee or graduate, he or she should already be donating at the level expected from the prospect. For example, a trustee calling on a prospect for a $5,000 donation to a capital campaign should ideally have already given that amount.

Personal solicitation consists of five steps: *identification, introduction, cultivation, solicitation,* and *appreciation.* The development office first identifies wealthy individuals who could conceivably have a strong interest in the institution. The staff then identifies others who might supply information and arrange an introduction. The development director, trustee, or other representative cultivates the person's interest without asking for any money. Asking too early may result in a refusal or a smaller donation than is possible. Some fund raisers will spend considerable time cultivating wealthy individuals. Eventually they do ask for money, and upon receiving it, they express their appreciation and provide appropriate recognition to the donor. Since personal solicitation requires time and great tact, it is usually reserved for wealthy donors. If the institution has qualified volunteers (often alumni), this same approach can be very successful in soliciting smaller donations. But for gifts below a certain amount, the development office will probably choose to use other approaches, such as direct mail, which are more cost-effective.

Some universities are skillful in hosting weekend retreats for wealthy prospects to attract their financial support. One well-known private university invited 50 of its wealthiest alumni to an all-expense-paid weekend on the campus, flying them in on private planes from their homes in various parts of the country. These alumni were put up in the best hotel, treated to some fine lectures, led in a religious service by the university president, and treated to a football game won brilliantly by the school's team. The spirits were so high that the average alumnus attending that weekend gave a check to the university for over $100,000.

Large-individual-gift fund raising is often most effective when the institution has developed a "wish list" of exciting projects and lets the prospective donor see the list, as in the case of Emory University. Large institutions classify their wished-for gifts in several financial sizes, ranging from the purchase of laboratory equipment for under $10,000 to the construction of an entire building for over $5 million. One of the most powerful appeals is an offer to have donors' names (or the names of loved ones) attached to campus buildings, distinguished chairs, and the like. In addition, fund raisers can offer these donors several ways to make their gifts, including direct cash payment, gifts of stock and other property, deferred gifts, such as trusts and annuities, and bequests whereby donors assign part or all of their estate to the institution upon their death. Schools and colleges have developed a variety of gift plans that can be tailored to the needs of individual wealthy donors.

Most donors will not be especially wealthy, but their support is important for three reasons. First, from a fund-raising perspective, their donations, although relatively modest, do contribute to achieving the institution's financial objective. Second, today's small givers may become large givers as their financial circumstances and interest in the institution grow. Third, educational institutions do not live by money alone. By the act of contributing money, donors are acknowledging and reinforcing a tie to the institution. Donors at any level will typically feel more interest in the institution and its success. Their financial resources may be modest, but they are in a position to speak well of the school and to encourage others to attend, to donate, or to support the school in other ways.

Obviously, a school or college development office cannot spend a lot of time personally cultivating every small donor. It must rely on other, more cost-effective ways of contacting and motivating them. The two most frequently used approaches are direct mail and phonathons.

Direct Mail. Direct mail is the least expensive way to communicate with individual donor prospects. A further advantage is that mailing lists can be updated by requesting an address correction from the postal service.

A typical direct mail communication will include three items:

- A *letter* from a member of the donor's graduating class (if an alumnus), from the president or principal, or from some other person who is likely to be known and respected by the recipient, asking the recipient to contribute
- A *brochure* that presents the case for supporting the institution
- A *reply card and envelope* or other response piece for the recipient to send in a contribution

A brochure without a letter is rarely as effective as a combination of the two. A truism of fund raising is that people give to people. A brochure alone doesn't establish the personal connection that prompts people to give. Likewise, the skilled development officer recognizes the importance of making it easy for the prospect to give. Without a reply card, the prospect may never get around to writing to the development office; without a postage-paid envelope, the prospect may never get around to finding a stamp and putting the contribution in the mail.

Designing and producing effective solicitation letters, brochures, and response pieces is ideally carried out by people with skill and experience in preparing direct mail. Fund-raising professionals recognize the importance of communications that appropriately reflect the institution's character and quality. Sloppy or discordant communications reflect poorly on the institution and discourage support.

Phonathons. Phonathons have become an important fund-raising tool because they are more personal and thus more effective than direct mail and less time-consuming and intrusive than face-to-face contact. They also marshal volunteers' enthusiasm for the institution.

A phonathon consists of a group of volunteer callers who meet in a room specially equipped with a telephone for each person, for the purpose of calling donor prospects to ask for contributions. Since most phonathons are scheduled in the evening hours when volunteers and prospects are not at work, the facilities may be a large office donated by a company for the evening. Volunteers usually have something in common with the people they will be calling. For example, they may have graduated the same year or majored in the same field. Parent volunteers will call other parents. Each volunteer caller receives printed information explaining the aim of that evening's phonathon and answering such essential questions as, "Why are alumni gifts important?" "Who are our prospects?" and, "How much should I ask for?" The instructions usually include a sample conversation as a guide.

After completing a successful call, the volunteer writes a short thank-you note to accompany the remit card. For example, for a donor who says yes and names an amount, the note might read, "Dear Paul, Your thoughtful gift of $100 means a lot to the university. Sure hope you can make it to the campus for the reunion." For someone who says maybe: "Dear Sue, Thanks for considering a gift to the university. Even $25 can make a difference when you add everyone's gifts up. I hope you'll participate. Regards." Such personal notes cement the person-to-person contact made over the telephone.

The development office needs to remember that volunteers are donors too. The office might provide sandwiches and a pep talk before starting in on the evening's calls, with coffee and snacks during the evening. The organizers should, of course, warmly thank the volunteers for their contribution of time, effort, and caring in helping the institution.

Foundations

Colleges and universities are the primary beneficiaries of foundation grants, receiving 40 percent of all foundation-grant dollars awarded. These grants total about 20 percent of all gifts to higher education in the United States.

There are some 22,000 active grant-making foundations in the United States. They are of four basic types:

1. *Family foundations*, set up by wealthy individuals to support a limited number of activities of interest to the founders. Family foundations typically do not have permanent offices or full-time staff members. Decisions tend to be made by family members and/or counsel. Development offices often find that soliciting donations from a family foundation consists of soliciting the founders of the trust as they would other wealthy individual donors.

2. *General foundations*, set up to support a wide range of activities and usually run by a professional staff. General foundations range from extremely large organizations—such as the Ford Foundation and the Rockefeller Foundation—that support a wide range of causes and give most of their money to large, well-established institutions, to more specialized general foundations that give money to a particular cause, such as education (Carnegie Foundation).

3. *Community trusts*, set up in cities or regions and made up of smaller foundations whose funds are pooled for greater effect.

4. *Corporate foundations*, set up by corporations with funds coming from endowment or from current income. (Corporations may donate up to 5 percent of their adjusted gross income to charitable causes.)

We will first discuss issues relevant to all four types of foundations and then turn to corporate foundations for further attention.

Researching Foundations. With 22,000 foundations, the fund raiser needs to know how to locate the few that would be the most likely to support a given project or cause. Fortunately, there are many resources available for researching foundations.[4] The best single source is the Foundation Center, a nonprofit organization with reference collections in New York, Washington, Cleveland, and San Francisco and cooperating collections in every state. Many libraries around the country also carry valuable materials describing foundations. The most important materials include these:

1. *The Foundation Grants Index,* which lists the grants that have been given in the past year by foundation, subject, state, and other groupings. The fund raiser could, for example, look up "medical education," find all the grants made to support medical education, and identify the most active foundations in this area of giving.

2. *The Foundation Directory,* which lists more than 3,100 foundations that either have assets of over $1 million or award more than $100,000 annually. The directory describes the general characteristics of each foundation, such as type of foundation, type of grants, annual giving level, officers and directors, location, particular fields of interest, contact person, and so on. The directory also contains an index of fields of interest, listing the foundations that have a stated interest in each field and whether or not they gave money to this field last year.

3. The *Taft Foundation Reporter,* which presents comprehensive profiles and analyses of private foundations, and the *Taft Corporate Directory,* which covers corporate foundations and corporate nonfinancial support, such as loaned executives and equipment donations. Entries include extensive information on each foundation, including recent giving pattern by type of grant, areas of interest, and geographical emphasis, as well as the history of the donors and of the foundation, and application procedures.

4. *The National Data Book,* which includes all the currently active grant-making foundations in the United States. The *Data Book* lists foundations by state in descending order of their annual grant totals, and gives information on location, principal officer, market value of assets, grants paid, and gifts received. This book includes community foundations.

5. *The Foundation News,* which is published six times a year by the Council on Foundations and describes new foundations, new funding programs, and changes in existing foundations.

6. Annual reports from foundations that look promising. Such reports include the foundation's history, current assets, geographical limitations to its giving, the range of grants, the current focus of activity, and whom to contact. The annual report will also give specific guidelines for making an application to the foundation, including whether to submit a letter of inquiry or preliminary proposal, or to submit only completed proposals.

7. *COMSEARCH Printouts,* produced by the Foundation Center, which are computer-sorted listings of foundation grants in more than 60 major giving categories.

The key concept in identifying foundations is that of *matching.* The educational institution should search for foundations matched to its *interests* and *scale of operation.* Too often, a small college will send a proposal to the Ford Foundation because it would like to get this well-known foundation's support. But the Ford Foundation accepts only about one out of every 100 proposals and may be less disposed toward helping small colleges than more regional or specialized foundations would be.

Preparing the Proposal. After identifying several foundations that might have high interest in its project, the institution should try to determine their level of interest before investing a lot of time in proposal preparation. Most foundations are willing to respond to a letter of inquiry, phone call, or personal visit regarding how interested they are likely to be in the project. If the foundation officer is encouraging, the fund-seeking institution can then make the investment of preparing an elaborate proposal for this foundation.

Writing successful grant proposals is becoming a fine art, with many guides currently available to help the grant seeker.[5] Each proposal should contain at least the following elements:

1. A *cover letter* describing the history of the proposal, and who, if anyone, in the foundation has been contacted
2. The *proposal*, describing the project, its uniqueness, and its importance
3. The *budget* for the project
4. The *personnel* working on the project, with their résumés

The proposal itself should be compact, individualized, organized, and readable. In writing it, the institution should be guided by knowledge of the "buying criteria" that the particular foundation uses to choose among the many proposals it receives. Many foundations describe their criteria in their annual reports or other memos; or their criteria can be inferred from the characteristics of the recent proposals they have supported, or by talking to knowledgeable people. Among the most common guiding criteria used by foundations are these:

1. The importance and quality of the project
2. The neediness and worthwhileness of the institution
3. The institution's ability to use the funds effectively and efficiently
4. The importance of satisfying the people who are doing the proposing
5. The degree of benefit that the foundation will derive in supporting the proposal
6. The contribution this project might make if it serves as a model for other institutions

If the proposing institution knows the relative importance of the respective criteria, it can do a better job of selecting the features of the proposal to emphasize. For example, if the particular foundation is influenced by who presents the proposal, the institution should sent its highest-ranking officials to the foundation. On the other hand, if the foundation attaches greatest importance to the quality of the written proposal, the institution should edit and present the proposal very carefully.

Educational institutions should not contact foundations only on the occasion of a specific proposal. Many colleges and universities cultivate a handful of appropriate foundations in advance of specific proposals. This is called "building bridges," or *relationship marketing*. One major university sees the Ford Foundation as a "key customer account." The development officer arranges for various people in the university to get to know people at their corresponding level in the foundation. One or more members of the university's board arrange to see corresponding board members of the foundation each year. The university president visits the foundation's president each year for a luncheon or dinner. Members of the university's development staff cultivate relations with foundation staff members at their level.

When the university has a proposal, it knows exactly who should present it to the foundation and whom to see there.[6] Furthermore, the foundation is more favorably disposed toward the university because of the long relationship and special understanding they enjoy. Finally, the university is able to do a better job of tracking the proposal as it is being reviewed by the foundation.

Corporations

Corporations represent another distinct source of funds. In 1982, American business contributed $1.1 billion of the $9 billion that was given to higher education.[7]

Corporate giving differs from foundation giving in a number of important ways. In the first place, corporations regard gift giving as a minor activity, whereas for foundations, it is the major activity. Corporations may vary their giving with the level of current and expected income. They have to be sensitive to the feelings of their stockholders, to whom they have the first obligation, in terms of both how much to give to charity and what charities to support. Corporations are more likely to avoid supporting controversial causes than are foundations. Some large corporations handle the many requests for support they receive by setting up a foundation so that corporate officers are not personally drawn into gift decision making.

In the second place, corporations pay more attention than foundations do to the direct and indirect benefit that any grant might return to them. If they can show that a particular grant will increase community goodwill, train students in specialties the company may need, or expand potential sales of the company's products in the future, this grant will be more acceptable to the board of directors and stockholders. Some companies achieve all three ends. For example, Apple has donated its computers to grade schools, high schools, and colleges to increase students' computer skills. Not only do the donations enhance the company's reputation as a "good citizen," involved in education; Apple also knows that people tend to buy what they are already familiar with, and that the students and their families will be more likely to purchase the same brand of computer they learned on.

In the third place, corporations can make more types of gifts than foundations can. An educational institution can approach a business firm for money, securities, goods, and services.

Effective corporate fund raising requires the institution's development office to know how to efficiently identify good corporate prospects. Of the thousands of business enterprises that might be approached, relatively few are appropriate to any specific institution. Furthermore, educational institutions may have the staff and other resources to cultivate only a few corporate givers. The best prospects for corporate fund raising have the following characteristics:

1. *Local corporations.* Corporations located in the same area as the school or college are excellent prospects. A university, for example, can base its appeal on the continuing education and other benefits to the corporation's employees, and a business school can point to well-prepared graduates employed by the corporation. Corporations find it hard to refuse support to worthwhile institutions in their area.

2. *Kindred activities.* Corporations located in a kindred field to the institution's are excellent prospects. The leading automobile manufacturers are interested in supporting mechanical engineering programs, and accounting firms support accounting education and related programs.

3. *Declared areas of support.* An institution should target corporations that have a declared interest in supporting its type of institution. Some corporations channel all or most of their contributions to education, with some favoring grants to small institutions, others to faculty research, and so on.

4. *Large givers.* Large corporations and those with generous giving levels are good prospects. Yet fund raisers must realize that these companies receive numerous requests and may favor those educational institutions in the local area or a kindred field. A recent survey of corporate giving found that corporations tend to keep giving to the same institutions, so those currently receiving aid may find it easier in the future than those who are not currently recipients. Regional offices of major corporations are often not in a position to make a donation without the approval of the home office.

5. *Personal relationships or contacts.* Educational institutions should review their personal contacts as a clue to corporations that they might solicit. A university's board of trustees consists of influential people who can open many doors for corporate solicitations. Corporations tend to respond to peer influence in their giving.

6. *Specific capability.* The fund raiser may identify a corporation as a prospect because it has a unique resource needed by the institution. Thus, a school might solicit an instrument company for a donation of science laboratory equipment.

The preceding criteria will help the institution identify a number of corporations that are worth approaching for contributions. Corporations in the institution's geographical area or field are worth cultivating on a continuous basis aside from specific grant requests, increasingly through "affiliates" programs. However, when the institution is seeking to fund a specific project, it needs to identify the best prospects and develop a marketing plan from scratch. We will illustrate the planning procedure in connection with the following example:

A well-known private university was seeking to raise $5 million to build a new engineering library. Its existing library was wholly inadequate and a handicap to attracting better students to the engineering school. The university was willing to name the new library after a major corporate donor that would supply at least 60 percent ($3 million) of the money being sought. This donor would be the "bell cow" that would attract additional corporate donors to supply the rest.

The first step called for the university to identify one or more major corporations to approach. The fund raisers recognized that major prospects would have two characteristics: They would be wealthy corporations, and they would have a high interest in this project. The fund raisers developed the matrix shown in Figure 17-2 and proceeded to classify corporations by their giving potential and their interest potential. In classifying corporations, they realized that oil companies fell in the top left cell. Oil companies have high profits ("giving potential") and a high interest in engineering schools ("interest potential"). They also want to give money to good causes to win public goodwill. The university decided that approaching an oil company would make good sense.

Which oil company? Here, the university applied additional criteria. An oil company located in the same geographical area had already given a major donation to this university for another project; it was ruled out. The university considered whether it had any good contacts with some of the other oil companies. It identified one oil corporation in the East in which several of its graduates held important management positions. In addition, a member of the university's board of trustees—a major-bank president—knew the chairman of the oil company. It was decided on the basis of this and other factors to approach this oil company for support.

The next step called for preparing a *prospect solicitation plan*. As a start,

FIGURE 17-2 Classifying prospective corporate donors by level of interest and giving potential

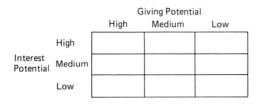

the university fund raisers researched the oil company's sales, profits, major officers, recent giving record, and other characteristics. This information was useful in deciding whom to approach at the corporation, how much to ask for, what benefits to offer, and so on. A decision was made to approach the corporation's chairman, ask for $3 million for the new engineering library, and offer to name the library after the corporation.

The final step called for *plan implementation*. The bank president arranged an appointment to visit the oil corporation's chairman, who was an old friend. He was accompanied by the the university's president and also the vice president for development. When they arrived, they met the chairman and the oil company's foundation director. They made their presentation, and the chairman said the proposal would be given careful consideration. A subsequent meeting was held on the university's campus, and ultimately the oil corporation granted the money to the university.

The oil company responded positively to this solicitation because the proposal stood high on its four major criteria:

1. The proposal had to be worthwhile from a societal point of view. In this case, an engineering library would contribute toward better-trained engineers in the United States.
2. The corporation had to feel that the soliciting institution was worthwhile and would handle the grant well. Here, the oil company had full confidence in the university.
3. The proposal should create some direct benefit, if possible, for the oil company. In this case, the oil company recognized a number of benefits: It would have an "in" on the best new graduates; it would memorialize its name on the campus; and it would get good publicity for supporting this private university.
4. The oil company foundation placed value on the personal relationships involved. The fact that an important bank president had taken the time to personally present the proposal to the oil company chairman was an important factor in the careful consideration of the proposal.

In general, corporations pay attention to these criteria in considering whether to "buy" a particular proposal, and therefore the "seller" (fund raiser) should weave them into its planning and presentation.

Government

Another major source of funds is government agencies at the federal, state, and local levels that are able to make grants to worthwhile causes. As an example, the federal government set up the National Endowment for the Humanities to support faculty research and other projects in the humanities. Other government agencies make grants to support university teaching and research. Many colleges appoint a director of government grants to concentrate on cultivating opportunities in this sector; large universities will have a grants office and staff. The director will monitor announcements of government grant opportunities that might have potential for his or her institution, as well as spend time in Washington and elsewhere getting to know officers at relevant agencies.

Government agencies normally require the most detailed paperwork in preparing proposals. On the other hand, the agencies are very willing to review proposals, placing the main weight on the proposal's probable contribution to the public interest. Certain topics become "hot," and the granting agencies look for the best proposals they can find on these topics. They pay less attention to agency benefit or to personal relations with the requesting institutions. Furthermore, some government agencies are mandated to ensure wide geographical dispersion of grants.

COORDINATING FUND-RAISING ACTIVITIES

We have described the most frequently used approaches for each major donor market. The development office must decide which donor segments should receive the most attention and then design a plan for each segment. The totality of fund-raising activities must be carefully scheduled and coordinated to ensure that they will reinforce each other and yield the desired results.

For most educational institutions, the fund-raising focus is on donations for current needs and for endowment. From time to time, an institution will undertake a capital campaign to raise a very large amount for specific building projects and other capital needs. Whether this is an *annual giving campaign* or a *capital campaign*, the principle is the same:

> A *campaign* is an organized and time-sequenced set of activities and events for raising a given sum of money within a particular time period.

Capital campaigns require the most careful planning. Here are some major considerations:

1. An educational institution should not run a capital campaign too often. After one university ended its five-year capital campaign, it would not launch another one for at least three to five years. This "spacing" is necessary if the capital campaigns are to retain their specialness in the minds of donors.

2. The institution has to make decisions on the capital campaign's goal and duration. The goal should be achievable, for there is nothing more embarrassing than failing to reach the goal. And the campaign should not last too long, because it will eventually lose its momentum.

3. The institution should try to add a matching-gift feature to the campaign, whereby some wealthy donors or foundations promise to match—say, dollar for dollar—the money raised. Early in the planning, the institution has to find and cultivate challenge grants.

4. The institution should prepare an attractive booklet showing the main items that the money will buy.

5. The campaign strategy calls for approaching various potential donor groups in a planned sequence. First, board members should be asked for large gifts to be in hand even before the campaign begins. Next, potential large donors should be approached. These steps will create the impression that the campaign is generating much support and enthusiasm, and others will want to get on the bandwagon.

Despite careful planning, prospecting, and other activities, some contributions come as a complete surprise. An example is Max Herman Stein's donation to Stanford, cited earlier. Many experienced fund raisers know of large donations from people who happened to visit the campus or see a press release about the school and who developed an interest in supporting the institution; and also of seemingly rather small donations that increased tremendously in value (see Exhibit 17-2). Such surprises add to the excitement

EXHIBIT 17-2 A donation that grew

> When a graduate of the University of Santa Clara's master of business administration program dropped by the school in 1976, he gave an unrestricted gift of 2,500 shares of a company he had started three years before.
>
> The gift that Glenn Klimek gave was stock in Dysan Corp., a company that he had helped found. The company was privately owned and the stock had no established market value.
>
> Santa Clara's money-handling people had the stock appraised, and a value of $12,000 was placed on the Klimek gift.
>
> By 1981, the stock had a value of $700,000, and, what pleases the people at Santa Clara, the stock is still carried as an unrestricted gift. . . .
>
> Santa Clara established an endowed chair in Klimek's name in its school of business. . . .
>
> Klimek returned to Santa Clara when the chair named after him was endowed. First to sit in the chair was Dr. Albert V. Bruno, a professor of marketing under whom Klimek studied. . . .
>
> Advice to business professors: Never forget about bread being cast upon the waters.

SOURCE: Donald K. White, "Santa Clara U. Struck It Rich," *San Francisco Chronicle*, June 30, 1981 © San Francisco Chronicle, 1981. Reprinted with permission.

of fund raising and remind fund raisers that each donor is important and that each impression the institution makes may be decisive.

EVALUATING FUND-RAISING EFFECTIVENESS

Each institution must make a continuous effort to improve its fund-raising effectiveness through evaluating its recent results, especially in the face of increasingly sophisticated competition and scarce funds. Fund-raising effectiveness must be evaluated by results, not merely by effort, as in Figure 17-3.

The institution can evaluate its fund-raising results on a macro and a micro level. We will consider each in turn.

FIGURE 17-3

SOURCE: Cathy Carlson, *The Chronicle of Higher Education*, September 21, 1983, p. 33. Copyright © 1983 by *The Chronicle of Higher Education*. Reprinted with permission.

Macroevaluation

Educational institutions use several methods to evaluate their overall fund-raising effectiveness. They are described below.

Percentage of Goal Reached. Institutions that set an annual goal start by reviewing how close they came to achieving the goal. Every institution wants to achieve or exceed its goal. This creates a temptation to set the goal low enough to ensure success. The development director may favor a low goal so that he or she will look good. The institution's president, however, may be tempted to push for a high goal to induce the development office to work harder.

Composition of Gifts. The institution should examine the composition of the money raised, looking at trends in the two major components:

$$\text{Gifts} = \text{Number of donors} \times \text{Average gift size}$$

Number of donors. Each institution hopes to increase the number of donors each year. The institution should pay attention to the number of donors in relation to the potential number of donors. For example, suppose that about 20 percent of Northwestern's alumni contribute each year. The development office should ask not only why 20 percent give, but also why 80 percent do not give. The development officer should interview a sample of alumni nongivers and identify the importance of such reasons as, "did not enjoy Northwestern as a student," "do not like the way Northwestern is evolving," "disagree with policies of the school in which I graduated," "couldn't care less," "was never asked," and so on. Each of these reasons suggests a possible plan of action.

Average gift size. A major objective of the fund-raising institution is to increase the size of the average gift. The development office should review the size distribution of gifts. Table 17–1 shows the size distribution of gifts to a major university. This table shows the importance of the major gift: The top nine donors contributed more dollars than are found in any other gift-size class. The table also shows that the gift-size class of $10,000–$25,000 does not have as many members as it should have. The development office should estimate the potential number of additional gifts that might be obtained in each size class against the current number to determine the size classes of gifts that deserve targeted effort in the next period.

Composition of the Donor Base. The institution will want to examine the number and size of gifts and the number of donors by categories or segments of the donor group. For example, it will want to track the percentage of donors and donations coming from alumni, and from other donor groups such as parents, current students, faculty, and trustees. Trends up or down may be signals

TABLE 17-1   Size distribution of gifts to a university

SIZE OF GIFT	DONORS	AMOUNT
$5,000,000 and above	9	$ 59,000,000
1,000,000–5,000,000	28	44,000,000
500,000–1,000,000	34	23,000,000
100,000–500,000	210	43,000,000
25,000–100,000	350	16,000,000
10,000–25,000	400	6,000,000
Less than $10,000		14,000,000
All bequests		20,000,000
	Total	$225,000,000

that the institution is doing a better or worse job of appealing to specific groups and that changes should be made. The institution will also track funds from foundations and corporations in the same way.

Market Share. For some institutions, their share or rank in fund raising among comparable institutions can indicate whether they are doing a competent job. For example, a private midwestern university compared its results to the results of five comparable universities and found it was trailing in the number of alumni givers and in the amount raised through government grants. The university took steps to give more attention to these two areas.

Expense/Contribution Ratio. The fund-raising institution is ultimately interested in its net revenue, not gross revenue. Donors want their contributions to be used for significant purposes and are more reluctant to give if they feel that an excessive share of contributed dollars goes for fund-raising expenses. An average-size college or university will spend about 10 percent of the amount raised on direct fund-raising expenses. There are some economies of scale in fund raising, so that a large institution may spend as little as 5 percent, whereas a small school may spend 15 percent or more.[8]

Microevaluation

The institution should also rate its individual staff members on their fund-raising effectiveness. This is not always done. One university vice president for development said he had a general idea of the funds brought in by each staff member, but not specific numbers. Many gifts were the result of several staff people working together—one identifying the prospect, another grooming him, and still another getting the check. Still, it would be worthwhile to evaluate each individual's performance as a basis for praise, additional training and supervision, or dismissal. As an example, one university rates staff members who work with foundations by using the following indicators (the numbers are illustrative):

Number of leads developed	30
Number of proposals written	20
Average value of proposal	$40,000
Number of proposals closed	10
Percentage of proposals closed	50%
Average value closed	$39,000
Average cost per proposal closed	$6,000
Cost per dollar raised	.20

SUMMARY

Fund raising is a major task for most educational institutions. Fund raising has evolved through several stages, from begging to an emphasis on short-term activities to, most recently, fund raising as development and part of the institution's institutional advancement efforts. Marketers assume that the act of giving is really an exchange process in which the donor invests in the institution in return for some largely intangible benefit.

Applying marketing to fund raising calls for laying the groundwork by developing a thorough strategic plan for the institution. Fund raising then becomes the means for attracting the financial resources to carry out the elements of the strategic plan.

Once the overall institutional strategy is established, the institution needs to establish its fund-raising goals to guide the fund-raising effort. Goals are set on either an incremental basis, need basis, or opportunity basis, or some combination of these.

The development office has to be organized to conduct the necessary marketing research and other tasks necessary to plan and implement fund-raising activities. Each major donor market should be segmented according to interest in the institution, ability to donate, and other relevant segmentation variables. The development staff should select the most promising donor segments and prepare plans for contacting and appealing to each. These activities need to be sequenced and coordinated for maximum results.

Finally, the development office needs to conduct regular evaluations of fund-raising results. Macroevaluation consists of analyzing the percentage of the goal reached, the composition of the gifts, the average gift size, the composition of the donor base, the market share, and the expense/contribution ratio. Micro-evaluation consists of evaluating the performance of each individual fund raiser.

NOTES

[1] These statistics come from *Giving USA—1982 Annual Report: A Compilation of Facts and Trends on American Philanthropy for the Year 1982* (New York: American Association of Fund-Raising Counsel, Inc., 1983).

[2] "Bequests Come In All Forms and Sizes—But Each Is Vital," *The Stanford Observer*, April 1981, p. 9.

[3] William G. Flanagan and Kevin McManus, "Some Dare Call It Charity," *Forbes* (Personal Affairs Section), Fall 1983, p. 242.

[4] Two useful articles on researching foundations are F. Roger Thaler, "What You Need to Know in Researching Foundations," in J. David Ross, ed., *Understanding and Increasing Foundation Support* (New Directions for Institutional Advancement No. 11, 1981), pp. 19–24; and Carol M. Kurzig, "The Foundation Center and Its Role in Research," in the same publication, pp. 25–40.

[5] Here are some useful sources of advice on writing grant proposals: Lois DeBakey and Selma DeBakey, "The Art of Persuasion; Logic and Language in Proposal Writing," *Grants Magazine*, Vol. 1, No. 1 (March 1978), 43–60; F. Lee Jacquette and Barbara J. Jacquette, *What Makes a Good Proposal* (New York: The Foundation Center, 1973); Robert A. Mayer, *What Will a Foundation Look for When You Submit a Grant Proposal?* (New York: The Foundation Center, 1972); and Suzanne Perry, "Getting a Foundation Grant Takes More Than a Good Idea, Program Officers Say," *The Chronicle of Higher Education*, October 20, 1982, p. 25.

[6] See W. Noel Johnson, "Using Total Institutional Resources in Foundation Solicitation," in Ross, *Understanding and Increasing Foundation Support*, pp. 59–67. Johnson explains how various groups beyond the administration and the development office can help in relationship marketing.

[7] *Giving USA—1982, op. cit.*

[8] This is the subject of an issue of *New Directions in Institutional Advancement* entitled, *Analyzing the Cost Effectiveness of Fund Raising*, Warren Heeman, ed., No. 3, 1979.

chapter 18

EVALUATING
MARKETING
PERFORMANCE

"As open-door community colleges of higher learning, the City Colleges of Chicago welcome adults of all ages who wish to work toward a college degree, prepare for a career by acquiring a marketable skill, increase potential for promotion or study for self-enrichment. . . . Each [college] reflects the need of its particular area, whether it be an educational program, social service, or cultural enrichment."
————From the *City Colleges of Chicago Catalog*

Truman College, opened in 1976, is one of eight community colleges making up the City Colleges of Chicago system. Truman's location in Uptown, north of Chicago's Loop, has profoundly shaped its mission and its student body. Uptown has historically been a magnet for new immigrant groups arriving in Chicago. As these immigrants become established, they move on to more affluent parts of the city. Uptown is currently characterized by arson, crime, unemployment, bums, and bag ladies; yet it is also a focal point for major urban-redevelopment efforts. Truman College was intended to be a resource for that change.

The college's students are diverse in age, ethnic background, and occupational goals. Ten percent are 19 years old or younger, 40 percent are over 35, and 30 percent are over 40. Ethnic groups and nationalities attending the college include blacks, Latinos, Native Americans, Koreans, Indonesians, Russians, Iranians, and Cubans. Some of the immigrants who attend Truman are well educated but simply lack English skills. Ninety percent of Truman's students combine work and school.

Truman's president has stated that the college should be an active catalyst for change and development in the community, "giving hope, aspiration, and renewal to the area." Some Truman faculty feel that the college should focus on educational programs that enable community members to improve themselves and move on, rather than emphasizing social-service programs. The local community, with over 100 community organizations, has generally looked favorably on the college, but Uptown's redevelopment threatens to displace the poor and could change Truman's student mix over time.

The college has many assets. The building is attractive, modern, and clean, and reflects an orientation to students in its design: The classrooms are on the outside walls with windows; staff offices are open and are located on the inside. The college has highly regarded programs in nursing and English as a second language, and unique programs specifically for immigrants from Russia, Southeast Asia, and Korea, among others. Truman has enjoyed increasing enrollment (about 5 percent per year) while other Chicago city colleges are losing students.

SOURCE: Based on Michelle Moeller Chandler and Leslie Ann Goldgehn, "Truman College: A Marketing Audit," unpublished paper, Northwestern University, 1980.

Truman College is reasonably successful in carrying out its mission now, but it will need to respond as its surrounding community inevitably changes. And even though adapted to many present needs, Truman may be overlooking some important programs and services that would strengthen the institution and enhance its contribution to the community.

How does an educational institution determine how well it is performing? Some schools and colleges rarely take a long look at their accomplishments and problems. They wait for major problems to overtake them before considering how to alter their course. Other educational institutions want to take steps to improve their performance, but the administration and faculty may be unsure how to proceed. The institution that seeks to be excellent, to be distinctive, and to provide a high level of satisfaction usually develops a strategy in line with its mission, resources, and potential. It must plan how best to match the resources it has to offer with the needs and wants of defined groups of potential students, donors, and others.

Evaluating marketing performance can take place at several levels in the institution. The type of evaluation will depend on the institution's commitment to marketing and on its stage in the implementation process. For example, in earlier chapters, we described methods for identifying marketing problems, and for analyzing marketing performance, including market-share analysis, analysis of competition, enrollment and fund-raising yields, performance-to-expense ratios, image analysis, attitude tracking, student-satisfaction measures, retention/attrition measurement, and other indicators of effectiveness.

From time to time, educational institutions should undertake a critical review of their overall marketing effectiveness. Each school and college should periodically reassess its performance in serving its desired markets. Two assessment tools are available—a *marketing-effectiveness rating review* and a *marketing audit*.

MARKETING-EFFECTIVENESS RATING REVIEW

Suppose a university president wants to know how well the institution is performing. He or she could review application and enrollment trends, fund-raising records, faculty teaching performance ratings, levels of grants and funded research, and other objective measures of performance. The president might assume that reasonably consistent performance in each area would indicate that the institution was on course, and that any declines signaled a problem.

In fact, institutional effectiveness is not necessarily revealed by current performance. Good results may be due to the college's having the right programs at the right time, rather than having a strategic plan for continuing to offer appropriate programs. Improvements in program offerings might attract better students and increase the effectiveness of the institution beyond current expectations. Another component of the institution may be encountering difficulties in spite of excellent marketing planning. It would be premature to change direction too soon.

The marketing effectiveness of an institution—or school or department— is reflected in the degree to which it exhibits five major attributes of a marketing orientation: *a consumer-oriented philosophy, an integrated marketing commitment, adequate marketing information, a strategic orientation*, and *effective implementation*. Each attribute can be measured. Table 18-1 presents a *marketing-effectiveness rating instrument* based on these five attributes. This form is tailored for the admissions office but can be adapted for use by the development office or by other functional areas of the institution. The instrument in Table 18-1 would be filled out by the director of admissions and others in the admissions office. The scores would then be summarized.

Few educational institutions achieve scores within the superior range of 26 to 30 points in each functional area. Most receive scores in the fair range, indicating that people in the institution see room for marketing improvement. The scores on each attribute indicate which elements of effective marketing action need the most attention. Each functional area can then establish a plan for correcting its major marketing weaknesses.

The marketing-effectiveness rating review process does not address the institution's quality, which is ultimately of great importance to any educational institution. The rating process reveals areas in which the institution can improve its marketing efforts, but the institution must undertake other analyses to assess the actual and potential quality of its faculty, students, and academic programs. Here, the institution may use reputational ratings of academic institutions and departments, site reviews (as by accreditation teams or experts brought in as consultant/reviewers), faculty publications and research grants received, teaching evaluations, graduate-school acceptances and honors received by graduates, and other measures of quality.

TABLE 18-1   Marketing-effectiveness rating instrument for admissions (*Check one answer for each question*)

CONSUMER-ORIENTED PHILOSOPHY

SCORE

A. Does the admissions officer participate in the overall college planning process?

- 0 ☐ The admissions officer does not participate in college planning. The officer is simply given recruitment goals set by the central administration.
- 1 ☐ The admissions officer is asked for certain data and suggestions relative to college needs but does not participate in the formal college planning process.
- 2 ☐ The admissions officer is a participant in the annual and long-range planning of the college's future.

B. What is the dominant philosophy of the admissions office?

- 0 ☐ Wait and see how many applications come in and go out and "beat the pavement" to fill the "sales gap."
- 1 ☐ Reach out everywhere and anywhere students can be found.
- 2 ☐ Identify major college sources, rate them on their potential student yield, and allocate time and choose strategies accordingly.

C. How aware and responsive is the admissions office to major environmental trends and developments?

- 0 ☐ The admissions office pays little attention to the changing environment.
- 1 ☐ The admissions office keeps informed but is slow to respond to new opportunities.
- 2 ☐ The admissions office is on top of changing trends and opportunities and is quick to respond.

INTEGRATED MARKETING COMMITMENT

SCORE

D. Does the admissions officer have sufficient influence or control over the resources that matter to effective recruitment?

- 0 ☐ No.
- 1 ☐ Somewhat.
- 2 ☐ Yes.

E. Is the admissions officer in close touch with the faculty and deans?

- 0 ☐ The admissions officer rarely meets faculty members to learn what they are doing.
- 1 ☐ The admissions officer occasionally attends faculty functions to sense possible opportunities for admission strategy.
- 2 ☐ The admissions officer cultivates close relations with the faculty or specific faculty members to sense possible admissions opportunities.

F. Does the admissions office make good use of volunteers?

- 0 ☐ Volunteers are expected to work hard for the college, and little motivation is provided.
- 1 ☐ Volunteers are thanked in the course of their work.
- 2 ☐ Volunteers are treated to special benefits and acknowledgment and helped to feel like a major force in the total effort.

TABLE 18-1 (continued)

ADEQUATE MARKETING INFORMATION

SCORE

G. Is the information system adequate and easy to use?

0 ☐ The information system is missing some important data and is not conveniently organized.

1 ☐ The information system contains most of the needed data and is conveniently organized.

2 ☐ The information system contains most of the needed data and is conveniently organized.

H. When were the latest studies conducted of the perceptions and attitudes of key college sources toward the institution?

0 ☐ Several years ago.

1 ☐ A few years ago.

2 ☐ Recently.

I. What effort is expended to measure and improve the cost-effectiveness of different recruitment approaches?

0 ☐ Little or no effort.

1 ☐ Some effort.

2 ☐ Substantial effort.

STRATEGIC ORIENTATION

SCORE

J. What is the extent of formal recruitment planning?

0 ☐ The admissions office does little or no formal recruitment planning.

1 ☐ The admissions office develops an annual recruitment plan.

2 ☐ The admissions office develops a detailed annual recruitment plan and a careful long-range development plan that is updated annually.

K. What is the quality of the current recruitment strategy?

0 ☐ The current strategy is not clear.

1 ☐ The current strategy is clear and represents a continuation of traditional strategy.

2 ☐ The current strategy is clear, innovative, data-based, and well reasoned.

L. What is the extent of contingency thinking and planning?

0 ☐ The admissions officer does little or no contingency thinking.

1 ☐ The admissions officer does some contingency thinking but little formal contingency planning.

2 ☐ The admissions officer formally identifies the most important contingencies and develops contingency plans.

TABLE 18-1 (continued)

EFFECTIVE IMPLEMENTATION

SCORE

M. How well are the recruitment strategies, policies, and techniques communicated and implemented up and down the line?

0 ☐ Poorly.
1 ☐ Fairly.
2 ☐ Successfully.

N. Does the admissions office have adequate resources, and does it use them effectively?

0 ☐ The resources are inadequate for the job to be done.
1 ☐ The resources are adequate but they are not employed optimally.
2 ☐ The resources are adequate and are employed efficiently.

O. What are the quality and adequacy of written communications going to the market?

0 ☐ The written communications are inadequate and poor in execution.
1 ☐ The written communications are adequate but uneven in execution.
2 ☐ The written communications are adequate and high in quality.

Total Score
The instrument is used in the following way. The appropriate answer is checked for each question. The scores are added—the total will be between 0 and 30. The following scale shows the level of marketing effectiveness: 0– 5 = None   16–20 = Good 6–10 = Poor   21–25 = Very good 11–15 = Fair   26–30 = Superior

THE MARKETING AUDIT

At some point, the college's president and trustees may conclude that developing an integrated institutional strategy requires a more thorough approach. The recommended approach for assessing overall marketing effectiveness is a *marketing audit*:[1]

> A marketing audit is a *comprehensive, systematic, independent,* and *periodic* examination of an institution's marketing environment, objectives, strategies, and activities with a view to determining problem areas and opportunities and recommending a plan of action to improve the institution's marketing performance.

Let us examine the marketing audit's four characteristics:

1. *Comprehensive.* The marketing audit covers all the major marketing-related issues facing the institution, not just a few trouble spots. It would be

called a functional audit if it covered only the admissions office, or student services, or some other component of the institution's contact with markets. Although functional audits are useful, they are sometimes misleading in locating the real source of the problem. For example, a decline in enrollment may be a symptom not of an inadequate admissions office, but of a weak curriculum or changing demographics. A comprehensive marketing audit is usually more effective in locating the real source(s) of an institution's marketing-related problems.

2. Systematic. The marketing audit involves an orderly sequence of diagnostic steps covering the institution's marketing environment, internal marketing organization, programs and services, and specific marketing activities. The diagnosis is followed by a corrective-action plan involving both short-term and long-term actions to improve the institution's effectiveness.

3. Independent. The marketing audit is normally conducted by an inside or outside party who has sufficient independence to obtain the confidence of the top administration and to exercise the needed objectivity.

4. Periodic. The marketing audit should be carried out periodically instead of only when there is a crisis. The results of an audit should be useful for an institution that is seemingly successful, as well as for one in deep trouble.

Some educators resist the term *audit* because it connotes an after-the-fact analysis of quantifiable data in a formalistic manner. Goldgehn reports that the term *marketing audit* aroused feelings of hostility and apprehension from administrators and faculty who "feared the marketing consultant would come to campus armed with a flashy Madison Avenue advertising campaign and all the charm of an IRS auditor."[2] For that reason, she retitled her marketing-audit instrument a "marketing opportunity analysis." Regardless of the term used, the marketing audit includes the same issues and tools.

A marketing audit is typically carried out by an outside evaluator, a consultant with expertise in marketing and marketing research who is knowledgeable about educational institutions and their environments. Such a consultant typically brings experience from working with a number of institutions and can work with the contracting institution's administration, faculty, and staff in laying out a marketing plan and guiding them in its implementation. The consultant becomes a trainer and guide. The institution should be prepared to listen to bad news as well as good from the consultant, and administrators and others should not try to keep the consultant away from sensitive areas.[3]

The Components of a Marketing Audit

A marketing audit consists of examining the major components of the institution's marketing situation. Our list of components is drawn from the marketing audit developed by Goldgehn.[4]

- *Historical and cultural analysis* includes current information, history of the institution, history of programs and services, the events leading to the initiation of the study, and the current institutional climate. This part of the audit places the current institutional environment in historical perspective.

- *Marketing environment analysis* is an assessment of the internal and external trends and significant groups that affect the institution. The following aspects of the institution's environment are analyzed: curricular programs, student services, publics, markets, students, distribution, competition, demographic trends, economic and political factors, social and cultural factors, and technology.
- *Marketing planning analysis* assesses how the institution's mission has been translated into planning, including a marketing plan. This phase includes an evaluation of the planning function and planning mechanisms of the institution.
- *Marketing strategy analysis* reviews the institution's strategies relating to program selection, positioning, market segmentation, and competition, and the extent to which the current strategy is appropriate in the light of the existing and anticipated environment and opportunities.
- *Marketing organization analysis* is an evaluation of the formal marketing structure of the institution, or, when no formal marketing structure exists, of the various functions that support marketing.
- *Marketing information analysis* evaluates the information and research capabilities and needs of the institution.
- *Pricing analysis* evaluates the monetary and budgetary needs of the institution, including an analysis of tuition, costs, fund-raising effectiveness, and the market response to tuition.
- *Administrative-department analysis* reviews the administrative departments that support the marketing effort of the institution, typically including admissions, financial aid, development, and institutional relations.
- *Curricular-program analysis* considers the institution's programs, degrees, majors, and courses in relation to student markets, publics, and societal trends. This analysis has implications for recruitment programs in the various program areas. Supporting resources, including the library and student services programs, can be reviewed in this phase.

The complexity of the marketing audit will vary with the size and complexity of the institution and its current situation. Many institutions conduct an audit for the first time when there are major problems or opportunities, and top administrators and trustees face important decisions. The relative emphasis given to each audit component may vary depending on the institution's circumstances.

Steps in the Audit Process

Carrying out a marketing audit involves several tasks that may be spread out over several weeks or months. The following five steps are typical of most marketing audits:

Preparation for the Audit. The marketing audit begins with a meeting between the auditor and the institution's president (and other top administrators, as determined by the president) to work out an agreement on the objectives, coverage, depth, data sources, and timing of the audit. A major objective of this meeting is to establish shared expectations about what the audit should accomplish, and to ensure that the audit is being conducted with the full support and involvement of the institution's top administration. Following the meeting, the auditor should provide a detailed plan covering who is to be interviewed, the themes to be covered, and other issues that will affect the scheduling and cost of the audit. Once the proposed plan and terms are accepted, the auditor can proceed to gather information.

Information Gathering. The most time-consuming step in the auditing process is the gathering of information. The cardinal rule in marketing auditing is: Don't rely solely on the institution's administrators for information and opinion. The auditor will interview faculty, staff, students, alumni, community members, and other people and groups who are knowledgeable about the institution and/or whose opinions about it can have an effect. The auditor constantly keeps in mind the aims of the audit, so that each interview or other data-collection step contributes information relevant to the analysis.

Analysis of Information. The auditor next faces the task of identifying themes in the information and making evaluative judgments about the institution's current status and potential. It is at the analysis step that the auditor's experience, independence, and objectivity are most essential. In the process of analyzing the available information, the auditor may decide to conduct additional interviews or seek out other information to fill in gaps.

Preparation of Findings and Recommendations. The auditor then prepares a written report presenting the major findings and recommendations of the audit.

Presentation of Findings and Recommendations. In addition to delivering the written report, the auditor may also be asked to present the audit findings and recommendations to the institution's president, other administrators, and the board of trustees. Such sessions give the participants an opportunity to clarify their understanding of the report and initiate the process of developing or revising the institution's marketing plans.

Kendall College is a private liberal arts college located in Evanston, Illinois.[5] It was founded as a two-year college in 1934 to provide a low-cost private education during the Depression, and by the 1970s, it had become a "college of last chance" for underachieving graduates of high-quality, highly competitive suburban high schools. The college offered remedial courses, counseling, tutoring, and a supportive environment, which helped many students to complete the A.A. degree and to transfer to respected four-year colleges.

In the early 1970s, Kendall College experienced declining enrollments, an unfocused curriculum, demoralized faculty, a poor college image, and depleted endowment. In the mid-1970s, a consultant carried out a feasibility study that led to the development of a four-year career-oriented curriculum with a strong liberal arts base. The first junior class entered in September 1976. By 1981, the college achieved a complete financial turnaround.

In the 1980s, Kendall and similar small private colleges face new challenges. In 1981, a marketing audit was conducted at Kendall. Here are some of the auditor's findings:

1. Most of Kendall's students are highly satisfied with their experience at the college. Two-thirds of the enrolled students would recommend Kendall to a friend or family member.
2. Kendall's image in Evanston, the nearby suburbs, and the Chicago metropolitan area is almost nonexistent. Located only two blocks from Northwestern University, the college has been eclipsed by its much larger neighbor.
3. Kendall's tuition is well below the average for similar private four-year colleges. This comparatively low tuition, together with financial aid and the ability to live at home, makes Kendall competitive with public institutions while offering the advantages of a small private college.
4. Kendall would like to attract more highly motivated students and become less dependent on attracting remedial students.
5. Kendall continues to appeal mainly to 18- to 21-year-old students who live nearby, but this traditional college-age group is shrinking.

From these and other findings, the auditor prepared a report with recommendations.

From Audit to Marketing Plan

The purpose of a marketing audit is to improve the institution's marketing effectiveness. The audit may reveal that some aspects of the institution's functioning could be improved. It may disclose a growing divergence between the institution's present activities and current or future trends. To realize the full benefits of a marketing audit, the institution's leaders must be willing to listen to bad news as well as good, and they must be willing and able to make recommended changes in the institution's functioning.

The recommendations of a marketing audit should direct the institution's subsequent marketing planning. The auditor often consults in the planning process, working with the administrators, faculty, and staff who actually develop the marketing plan and carry it out.

At this point, we have returned to the theme with which we began—the importance of sound strategic planning. This book has described the steps in the strategic planning process and how strategic planning is reflected in marketing activities. The marketing audit process is a checkpoint in the continuing cycle of planning and implementation that leads to improved institutional effectiveness.

SUMMARY

Strategic marketing planning and implementation depend upon periodic assessment of marketing performance. Two assessment tools are available. The marketing-effectiveness rating instrument profiles the institution's marketing effectiveness in terms of consumer-oriented philosophy, integrated marketing commitment, adequate marketing information, strategic orientation, and effective implementation. The marketing audit is a comprehensive, systematic, independent, and periodic examination of the institution's marketing environment, objectives, strategies, and activities. The purpose of a marketing audit is to determine marketing problem areas and to suggest corrective short-term and long-term action plans to improve the institution's overall marketing effectiveness.

NOTES

[1] Although marketing audits have been conducted in the for-profit sector for over 30 years, their use by educational institutions is relatively recent. For background on marketing audits, see Philip Kotler, William Gregor, and William Rodgers, "The Marketing Audit Comes of Age," *Sloan Management Review*, Winter 1977, pp. 25–43. The single work that presents a marketing audit for small, less-selective liberal arts colleges is Leslie A. Goldgehn, "A Marketing Opportunity Analysis: Application of a Strategic Marketing Audit to Higher Education," unpublished doctoral dissertation, Northwestern University, 1982.

[2] Goldgehn, "A Marketing Opportunity Analysis," p. 140.

[3] *Ibid.*, pp. 35–36.

[4] These components are based on Goldgehn, "A Marketing Opportunity Analysis," pp. 128–43. Specific audit questions for eight of the nine components appear in "A Marketing Opportunity Analysis," pp. 235–69.

[5] This case is summarized, with permission, from Goldgehn, "A Marketing Opportunity Analysis," pp. 77–85 and 313–45.

INDEX

Adaptive institution, 119
Advertising, 296–314
  budget determination, 300–301
  defined, 297
  donated, 301
  evaluation, 312–14
  expenditure-level testing, 314
  inquiry cost analysis, 314
  media selection, 306–11
  media testing, 314
  message decision, 301–6
  message execution, 305–6
  message selection, 302–3
  reach and frequency, 300
  readiness states, 298–300
  setting objectives for, 297–98
  target response, 298–300
  timing, 311–12
AIDA model, 280
Atmospherics, 270–71

Boston Consulting Group (BCG)
  portfolio approach, 135, 137
Brand image, 207

Branding, 225–26
Brand perception, 207
Breakeven analysis, 247–48
Budget. **See** Marketing expenditure level

Chain-ratio method, 163–65
Cognitive dissonance theory, 35
College and University Environment Scales (CUES), 116–17
Communications, 277–92
  effectiveness of, 291–92
  elements of, 278–79
  steps in planning, 279–81
Competition, 140–45
  analysis of, 140–45
  roles, 144–45
  types of, 141–42
Consumer:
  defined, 197
Consumer buying process, 197–216
  decision evaluation, 203–10
  decision execution, 210–11
  for individuals, 198–213

Consumer buying process, *(cont.)*
  for organizations, 213–16
  influences on, 204–5
  information gathering, 200–203
  information sources, 202–3
  need arousal, 198–200
  postdecision assessment, 211–13
  roles in, 203
  stages in, 198
Control, marketing, 84–85, 89–92
  annual plan, 89–91
  revenue-cost, 91–92
  strategic, 92
Copy testing, advertising, 312–13
Corporations, as donors, 213–16,
    367–70
Cost:
  effectiveness, 334–35, 374–76
  effort, 242
  psychic, 242
  time, 242
Cost-effectiveness, 334–35, 374–76
  of fund raising, 374–76
  of recruiting, 334–45
Cost recovery, 246
Critical success requirements, 120

Delphi method, 106–7
Demands, 20–21
Demand states, 52
Differential advantage, 121–22
Direct mail, 309–11, 362–63
  guidelines, 310–11
Director of marketing services, 33–
    34
  job description, 33
Distinctive competencies, 120–21,
    125
Distribution channels, 263–64,
    271–73
  alternative, 271–73
Distribution decisions, 260–74
  facilities design, 269–71
  location, 261–62, 268–69

need for new facilities, 266–69
objectives, 265–66
Donor markets, 360–71
  corporations, 367–70
  foundations, 364–67
  government, 370–71
  individual, 260–64

Environmental analysis, 75–76
Environmental forecasting, 104–8
  computer simulation, 107
  consensus methods, 106–7
  cross-impact matrix, 107
  Delphi method, 106–7
  trend extrapolation, 105–6
Environmental scanning, 99–104
Environmental threat, 75, 101–3
  defined, 101
  matrix, 102
  responses to, 103
Exchange, 21–23
  defined, 21
  flows, 22–23
Expectations-performance theory,
    34–35

Facilities, 266–71
  design of, 269–71
  locating new, 266–69
Feedback, 281
Focus group interviews, 58–59, 285
Foundations, 364–67
Fund raising, 353–76
  campaigns, 371–72
  coordination, 371–73
  development approach to, 354–
    55
  direct mail, 362–63
  effectiveness, evaluation of, 373–
    76
  goals and strategy, 356–58

groundwork for, 356
organizing for, 358–60
personal solicitation, 361–62
phonathons, 363–64
Fund-raising campaigns, 371–72
annual giving, 371
capital, 371–72

Goal formulation, 76–77, 126–28
steps in, 126–28

Image, 38–44
defined, 38
importance of, 37
measurement, 38–42
modification, 42–43
relation to behavior, 44
study, 122
theories of formation, 41–42
Importance weights, 207–9
Information sources, 202–3
credibility, 203, 281
Inquiry cost analysis, 314
Institutional advancement, 353
Institutional Goals Inventory (IGI),
127–28
Intermediaries, facilitating, 273–74

Macroenvironment, 97
adaptation to, 97–99
analysis, 108–11
forces, 97
Market:
available, 160
core, 186–87
defined, 149, 160
penetrated, 161
potential, 160

primary, 327
qualified available, 161
safety, 186–87
secondary, 327–28
served, 161
special test, 186–97
wish, 186–87
Market coverage strategy, 150–51,
189–93
Market demand measurement,
159–62
area market, 165–67
forecasting, 168–71
future, 168–71
market share, 167–68
market tests, 169–70
middleman estimates, 169
statistical demand analysis, 170–
71
time-series analysis, 170
total market, 163–65
Marketing:
benefits of, 12–13
characteristics of, 7–8
criticisms of, 13–14
defined, 7
Marketing audit, 52–53, 380, 384–
88
components of, 385–86
defined, 384
process, 386–88
Marketing control. See Control,
marketing
Marketing-effectiveness rating review, 380–84
Marketing environment, 23–28
Marketing expenditure level, 84,
300–301, 331–32, 375
Marketing information system, 41
analytical marketing system, 67–
68
defined, 41
intelligence system, 54–55
internal records system, 53–54
marketing research, 55–66
Marketing mix, 83, 153–54
defined, 153
Marketing mix strategy, 153–54

Marketing opportunity, 101–2,
  138–40
  defined, 101
  matrix, 102, 138–40
Marketing orientation, 10
  steps in creating, 30–34
Marketing plan, 79–85
  action program, 84–85
  budget, 84
  contents, 79
  executive summary, 80
  goals and objectives, 83
  marketing strategy, 83–84
  situation analysis, 80–82
Marketing problems, 50–53
  audit, 52–53
  demand states, 52
  identification of, 50–53
  problem inventory, 50–52
Marketing research, 55–66
  defined, 55
  experimental, 65–66
  exploratory, 57–59
  focus group interviews, 58–59
  formal, 59–65
  objectives, 56–57
  observational, 58
  problem definition, 56–57
  qualitative interviewing, 58–59
  sampling, 62–65
  survey research, 59–65
Marketing strategy, 83–84, 132–55
  defined, 132
Market potential, 163
Market segmentation, 150–52, 177–
  89
  age and life cycle, 180
  attitudes, 185
  behavioristic, 183–85
  benefits sought, 183
  demographic, 180–82
  geographical, 178, 180
  lifestyle, 182
  loyalty status, 184
  multivariable, 185–86
  organizational, 186–88
  personality, 182

  preference, 177
  psychographic, 182
  readiness stage, 184–85
  requirements for, 188–89
  selecting segments, 192–93
  sex, 180–82
  social class, 182
  usage rate, 183
  user status, 183
  Values and Lifestyles (VALS),
    185–86
Mass marketing, 150, 175
Media selection, 280–81
Message development, 280
Middlemen, 273
Mission, 77, 122–26
  characteristics, 125
  statement, 126
  ways to define, 123–25

Needs, 20–21, 199–200
  hierarchy of, 200
New-program development, 226–34
  concept development, 230–31
  idea generation, 229–30
  idea screening, 229–30
  introduction and management,
    233–34
  market definition, 227–29
  marketing strategy, 231–32
  market testing, 233
  opportunity identification, 227–
    30
  program design, 232
  steps in, 227–34

Objectives, 77, 127, 129
Opportunity identification, 75–76,
  138–40, 229–30
Organizational design, 78–79

Packaging, 225
Personal solicitation, 361–62
Phonathons, 363–64
Planning, marketing, 72–88
  computer-based models, 87
  contingency, 87
  long-range, 86
  process, 87–88
  rolling, 86
  systems, 85–88
Portfolio analysis, 133–37
  academic portfolio approach,
    133–34
  Boston Consulting Group ap-
    proach, 135, 137
Positioning, 145–49, 152–53
President:
  responsibilities of, 18–19, 30–32
Price, 241–57
  approaches to setting, 252–54
  barriers, 244
  consumer perceptions of, 242–
    44, 256
  effective, 243
  effects of changes in, 254–57
  elasticity of demand, 255–56
  examples of, 241–42
  relationship with quality, 243,
    256
Pricing objectives, 247–48
  breakeven, 247–48
  cost recovery, 246
  setting, 244–47
  surplus maximization, 245
  usage maximization, 245
Pricing strategy, 247–52
  competition-oriented, 251–52
  cost-oriented, 247–49
  demand-oriented, 250–51
Product, 221–38
  attributes, 206–210
  augmented, 226
  core, 223–24
  decisions, 221–26
  defined, 221
  development of new, 226–34
  life cycle, 234–38

services as, 222–23
  tangible, 224–26
Production orientation, 11–12
Product life cycle, 234–38
  patterns, 234–35
  stages, 234–38
Product/market opportunity matrix,
  138–40
Product orientation, 11
Program: **See also** Product
  new-program development, 226–
    34
Program elimination, 134–36, 237–
  38
  guidelines for, 134–36
Proposal preparation, 366–67
Public opinion surveys, **See** Survey
  research
Public relations process, 283–87
  cost-effective strategies for, 286
  evaluation, 286–87
  identification of publics, 283–84
  image and attitude goals, 285–86
  image and attitude measure-
    ment, 284–85
  role of president/principal in, 282
Public relations tools, 287–91
  audiovisual materials, 288
  events, 289–90
  institutional-identity media, 288
  news, 289
  personal contact, 291
  speeches, 290–91
  telephone information services,
    291
  written materials, 287–88
Public(s), 24–28
  defined, 24
  external, 27–28
  internal, 24–26
  relation to market, 28

Quality, 225
Questionnaires, 59–62

Reach and frequency, advertising, 300
Readiness states, 298–300
Recall tests, 313
Recognition tests, 313
Resource analysis, 76, 116–21
  institutional environment, 116–17
  institutional life cycle, 117–19
  potential for change, 119–120
  preparation, 120–122
Resources, 116, 125
  intangible, 116
  tangible, 116
Response, 279–280, 298–300
Responsive institution, 18–19, 28–30
  levels of, 28–30
Revenue function, 246–47

Samples, 62–65
  types of, 64
Satisfaction, 34–37
  balance with goals, 37
  cognitive dissonance theory, 35
  defined, 34
  expectations-performance theory, 34–35
  measurement of, 36–37
Satisfaction, measurement of, 337–43
  complaint systems, 36–37
  panels, 338
  surveys, 338–42
Segmentation. See Market segmentation
Selling orientation, 12
Semantic differential, 40–41
Services, 222–23. See also Product
Societal marketing orientation, 10–11
Source attributes, 281
Source credibility, 203, 281
Statistical demand analysis, 170–71
Strategic planning, 72–79

defined, 73
process, 73–79
Strategy formulation, 77–79, 132–54
  academic portfolio, 133–34
  BCG matrix, 135, 137
  competitive positioning, 145–49, 152–53
  defined, 132
Student recruitment, 319–35
Student-recruitment process, 322–35
  evaluation, 334–35
  goals and objectives, 325–26
  implementation, 333–34
  marketing expenditure level, 331–32
  marketing mix, 330–31
  marketing research, 326–29
  marketing strategy, 329–33
  problem identification, 322–25
  target-market selection, 330
Surplus maximization, 245
Survey research, 59–65, 285

Target audience selection, 279, 298
Target marketing, 150, 176, 189–91
Target markets, 83, 298, 330
Time-series analysis, 170
Trustees, 24–26

Usage maximization, 245
Utility function, 207

Volunteers, 26

Wants, 20–21, 200